Android™ Wireless Application Development

Android Wireless Application Development

Shane Conder
Lauren Darcey

✦✦ Addison-Wesley

Upper Saddle River, NJ • Boston • Indianapolis • San Francisco
New York • Toronto • Montreal • London • Munich • Paris • Madrid
Cape Town • Sydney • Tokyo • Singapore • Mexico City

The publisher offers excellent discounts on this book when ordered in quantity for bulk purchases or special sales, which may include electronic versions and/or custom covers and content particular to your business, training goals, marketing focus, and branding interests. For more information, please contact:

U.S. Corporate and Government Sales
(800) 382-3419
corpsales@pearsontechgroup.com

For sales outside the United States please contact:

International Sales
international@pearson.com

Visit us on the Web: informit.com/aw

Library of Congress Cataloging-in-Publication Data:

Conder, Shane, 1975-
    Android wireless application development / Shane Conder, Lauren Darcey.
        p. cm.
    Includes bibliographical references and index.
    ISBN 978-0-321-62709-4 (pbk. : alk. paper) 1. Mobile computing. 2. Android (Electronic resource) 3. Application software–Development. 4. Wireless communication systems. I. Darcey, Lauren, 1977- II. Title.
    QA76.59.C65 2009
    621.3845'6–dc22
                                                2009027111

ISBN-13: 978-0-321-62709-4
ISBN-10: 0-321-62709-1
Text printed in the United States on recycled paper at

RR Donnelley Crawfordsville, Indiana

Second Printing December 2009

Editor-in-Chief
Mark Taub

Acquisitions Editor
Trina MacDonald

Development Editor
Songlin Qiu

Managing Editor
Patrick Kanouse

Project Editor
Bethany Wall

Copy Editor
Apostrophe Editing Services

Indexer
Tim Wright

Proofreader
Jovana San Nicolas-Shirley

Technical Reviewers
Dan Galpin
Tony Hillerson
Ronan Schwarz

Publishing Coordinator
Olivia Basegio

Multimedia Developer
Dan Scherf

Designer
Gary Adair

Compositor
Bronkella Publishing, LLC

❖

*This book is dedicated to Bit, Nibble, Stack, Queue,
Heap, and Null.*

❖

Acknowledgments

This book would never have been written without the guidance and encouragement we received from a number of supportive individuals, including our editorial team, coworkers, friends, and family. We'd like to thank the Android developer community, Google, and the Open Handset Alliance for their vision and expertise. Throughout this project, our editorial team at Pearson Education (Addison-Wesley) always had the right mix of professionalism and encouragement. Thanks especially to Trina MacDonald, Olivia Basegio, and Songlin Qiu and our crack team of technical reviewers: Dan Galpin, Tony Hillerson, and Ronan Schwarz. We'd also like to thank Chris Haseman and Chris King for their early book input and Ray Rischpater for his longtime encouragement and advice on technical writing. Amy Badger must be commended for her wonderful illustrations and Hans Bodlaender for letting us use the nifty chess font he developed as a hobby project.

We'd also like to extend a special thanks to Professor Tracy Larrabee, who once taught a fateful class titled "Technical Writing for Computer Engineers" at the University of California, Santa Cruz. Tracy did her utmost to ensure that computer science and engineering students graduated with the ability to write understandable business correspondence and readable technical specifications. If we wrote anything coherent in this book, you should thank her. If we messed up, it's totally not her fault because we didn't let her review it first (Shane says, "out of fear"). Incidentally, this course was one of the first Shane and Lauren took together back in college and can be considered where they first "met."

Finally, we'd like to acknowledge and thank Jon Stewart and Stephen Colbert for continually reminding us of the dangers of shameless book promotion. Guys, this is your "Darcey/Conder bump"—milk it for all it's worth.

About the Authors

Shane Conder has extensive development experience and has focused his attention on mobile and embedded development for the past decade. He has designed and developed many commercial applications for BREW, J2ME, Palm, Windows Mobile, and Android. Shane has written extensively about the mobile industry and evaluated mobile development platforms on his tech blogs and is well known within the blogosphere. Shane received a B.S. degree in computer science from the University of California.

A self-admitted gadget freak, Shane always has the latest phone or laptop. He can often be found fiddling with the latest new technologies, such as Amazon Web Services, Android, iPhone, Google App Engine, and other shiny, new technologies that activate the creative part of his brain. He also enjoys traveling the world with his geeky wife, even if she did make him dive with 4-meter-long great white sharks, and he almost got eaten by a lion in Kenya. He admits that it was his fault they got attacked by monkeys in Japan and that perhaps he should have written his own bio. (Author's note: Wait, what?!)

Lauren Darcey is responsible for the technical leadership and direction of a small software company specializing in mobile technologies—Android being the most exciting and promising for the future. With almost two decades of experience in professional software production, Lauren is a recognized authority in enterprise architecture and the development of commercial-grade mobile applications. Lauren received a B.S. degree in computer science from the University of California, Santa Cruz.

Lauren spends her copious free time traveling the world with her geeky mobile-minded husband and is an avid nature photographer. Her work has been published in books and newspapers around the world. In South Africa, she dove with 4-meter-long great white sharks and got stuck between a herd of rampaging hippopotami and an irritated bull elephant. She's been attacked by monkeys in Japan, gotten stuck in a ravine with two hungry lions in Kenya, gotten thirsty in Egypt, narrowly avoided a coup d'état in Thailand, and walked part of the Great Wall of China, where she took the photograph that graces the cover of this book.

Introduction

Pioneered by the Open Handset Alliance and Google, Android is a hot, new, free, open source mobile platform making waves in the wireless world. This book provides comprehensive guidance for software development teams on designing, developing, testing, debugging, and distributing professional Android applications. If you're a veteran mobile developer, you can find tips and tricks to streamline the development process and take advantage of Android's unique features. If you're new to mobile development, this book provides everything you need to make a smooth transition from traditional software development to mobile development—specifically, its most promising new platform: Android.

Who Should Read This Book

This book includes tips for successful mobile development based on our years in the mobile industry and covers everything you need to run a successful Android project from concept to completion. We cover how the mobile software process differs from traditional software development, including tricks to save valuable time and pitfalls to avoid. Regardless of the size of your project, this book can work for you.

This book was written for three primary audiences:

- **Software developers** who want to learn to develop professional Android applications

    The bulk of this book is primarily targeted at software developers with Java experience but not necessarily mobile development experience. More seasoned developers of mobile applications can learn how to take advantage of Android and how it differs from the other technologies of the mobile development market today.

- **Quality assurance personnel** tasked with testing Android applications

    Whether they are black box or white box testing, quality assurance engineers can find this book invaluable. We devote several chapters to mobile QA concerns including topics such as developing solid test plans and defect tracking systems for mobile applications, how to manage handsets, and how to test applications thoroughly using all the Android tools available.

- **Project managers** planning and managing Android development teams

    Managers can use this book to help plan, hire, and execute Android projects from start to finish. We cover project risk management and how to keep Android projects running smoothly.

- **Other Audiences**

  This book is useful not only to a software developer, but also for the corporation looking at potential vertical market applications; the entrepreneur thinking about a cool phone application; and the hobbyists looking for some fun with their new phone. Businesses seeking to evaluate Android for their specific needs (including feasibility analysis) can also find the information provided valuable. Anyone with an Android handset and a good idea for a mobile application can put this book to use for fun and profit.

Key Questions Answered in this Book

This book answers the following questions:

1. What is Android?
2. How is Android different from other mobile technologies and how can developers take advantage of these differences?
3. How do developers use the Eclipse Development Environment for Java to develop and debug Android applications on the emulator and handsets?
4. How are Android applications structured?
5. How do developers design robust user interfaces for mobile—specifically for Android?
6. What capabilities does the Android SDK have and how can developers use them?
7. How does the mobile development process differ from traditional desktop development?
8. What development strategies work best for Android development?
9. What do managers, developers, and testers need to look for when planning, developing, and testing a mobile development application?
10. How do mobile teams design bulletproof Android applications for publication?
11. How do mobile teams package Android applications for deployment?
12. How do mobile teams make money from Android applications?

How This Book Is Structured

This book is divided into seven parts. The first five parts are primarily of interest to developers; Parts VI and VII provide lots of helpful information for project managers and quality assurance personnel as well as developers.

Here is an overview of the various parts in this book:

- Part I: An Overview of Android

  Part I provides an introduction to Android, explaining how it differs from other mobile platforms. You become familiar with the Android SDK and tools, install the development tools, and write and run your first Android application—on the emulator and on a handset.

- Part II: Android Application Design Essentials

  Part II introduces the design principles necessary to write Android applications. You learn how Android applications are structured and how to include resources like strings, graphics, and user interface components in your projects.

- Part III: Android User Interface Design Essentials

  Part III dives deeper into how user interfaces are designed in Android. You learn about the core user interface element in Android: the `view`. You'll also learn about the basic drawing and animation abilities provided in the Android SDK.

- Part IV: Using Common Android APIs

  Part IV is a series of chapters, each devoted to a deeper understanding of the most important APIs within the Android SDK, such as the data and storage APIs (including file and database usage as well as content providers), networking, telephony, Location-Based Services (LBS), multimedia and 3D graphics APIs, and the optional hardware APIs available.

- Part V: More Android Application Design Principles

  Part V covers more advanced Android application design principles such as notifications and services.

- Part VI: Deploying Your Android Application to the World

  Part VI covers the software development process for mobile, from start to finish, with tips and tricks for project management, software developers, and quality assurance personnel.

- Part VII: Appendixes

  Part VII includes several helpful quick-start guides for the Android development tools: the emulator, ADB and DDMS, and a SQLite tutorial.

Android Development Environment Used in This Book

The Android code in this book was written using the following development environments:

- Windows Vista SP1 and Mac OS X 10.5.6
- Eclipse Java IDE Version 3.4 (Ganymede)
- Eclipse JDT plug-in and Web Tools Platform (WTP)
- Sun Java SE Development Kit (JDK) 6 Update 10
- Android SDK Version 1.1 R1 and Version 1.5 R1

> **Note**
> Many of the examples have also been tested using the Android SDK on Fedora 8 and Windows XP installations.

Supplementary Materials Available

The source code that accompanies this book is provided on a CD at the end of this book and on the publisher Web site: www.informit.com/title/9780321627094.

Lauren Darcey and Shane Conder run a book blog at http://androidbook.blogspot.com, where you can find the latest news about the Android topics covered here.

Where to Find More Information

There is a vibrant, helpful Android developer community on the web. Here are a number of useful Web sites for Android developers and followers of the wireless industry:

- Android Developer Website—The Android SDK and developer reference site
  http://developer.android.com/
- Open Handset Alliance—Android manufacturers, operators, and developers
  www.openhandsetalliance.com/
- Android Market—Buy and sell Android applications
  www.android.com/market/
- anddev.org—An Android developer forum
  www.anddev.org
- Google Team Android Apps—Open source Android applications
  http://apps-for-android.googlecode.com/
- FierceDeveloper—A weekly newsletter for wireless developers
  www.fiercedeveloper.com/
- FierceWireless—A daily digest for the wireless industry
  www.fiercewireless.com/
- FierceMobileContent—A daily digest of mobile content and marketing
  www.fiercemobilecontent.com/
- Wireless Developer Network—Daily news on the wireless industry
  www.wirelessdevnet.com/
- Developer.com—A developer-oriented site with mobile articles
  www.developer.com/

Conventions Used in This Book

This book uses the following conventions:

- is used to signify to readers that the authors meant for the continued code to appear on the same line. No indenting should be done on the continued line.
- Code or programming terms are set in `monospace` text.

This book also presents information in the following sidebars:

Tip

Tips provide useful information or hints related to the current text.

Note

Notes provide additional information that might be interesting or relevant.

Caution

Cautions provide hints or tips about pitfalls that might be encountered and how to avoid them.

What's New in Android SDK 1.5

This special sidebar calls out the new and interesting features available in the latest version of the Android SDK.

Contacting the Authors

Both Lauren and Shane welcome your comments. If you have questions or feedback regarding this book, please visit our book blog at http://androidbook.blogspot.com or email us at androidwirelessdev@gmail.com.

An Overview of Android

## 1

Introducing Android

The mobile development community is at a tipping point. Mobile users demand more choice, more opportunities to customize their phones, and more functionality. Mobile operators want to provide value-added content to their subscribers in a manageable and lucrative way. Mobile developers want the freedom to develop the powerful mobile applications users demand with minimal roadblocks to success. Finally, handset manufacturers want a stable, secure, and affordable platform to power their devices. Upuntil now single mobile platform has adequately addressed the needs of all the parties.

Enter Android, which is a potential game-changer for the mobile development community. An innovative and open platform, Android is well positioned to address the growing needs of the mobile marketplace.

This chapter explains what Android is, how and why it was developed, and where the platform fits in to the established mobile marketplace.

A Brief History of Mobile Software Development

To understand what makes Android so compelling, we must examine how mobile development has evolved and how Android differs from competing platforms.

Way Back When

Remember way back when a phone was just a phone? When we relied on fixed land-lines? When we ran for the phone instead of pulling it out of our pocket? When we lost our friends at a crowded ballgame and waited around for hours hoping to reunite? When we forgot the grocery list (Figure 1.1) and had to find a payphone or drive back home again?

Those days are long gone. Today, commonplace problems like these are easily solved with a one-button speed dial or a simple text message like "WRU?" or "20?" or "Milk and?"

Figure 1.1   Mobile phones have become a crucial shopping accessory.

Our mobile phones keep us safe and connected. Nowadays, we roam around freely, relying on our phones not only to keep in touch with friends, family, and coworkers, but also to tell us where to go, what to do, and how to do it. Even the most domestic of events seem to revolve around my mobile phone.

Consider the following true, but slightly enhanced for effect, story:

Once upon a time, on a warm summer evening, I was happily minding my own business cooking dinner in my new house in rural New Hampshire when a bat swooped over my head, scaring me to death.

The first thing I did—while ducking—was pull out my cell and send a text message to my husband, who was across the country at the time: "There's a bat in the house!"

My husband did not immediately respond (a divorce-worthy incident, I thought at the time), so I called my Dad and asked him for suggestions on how to get rid of the bat.

He just laughed.

Annoyed, I snapped a picture of the bat with my phone and sent it to my husband and my blog, simultaneously guilt-tripping him and informing the world of my treacherous domestic wildlife encounter.

Finally, I Googled "get rid of a bat" and followed the helpful do-it-yourself instructions provided on the Web for people in my situation. I also learned that late August is when baby bats often leave the roost for the first time and learn to fly. Newly aware that I had a baby bat on my hands, I calmly got a broom and managed to herd the bat out of the house.

Problem solved—and I did it all with the help of my trusty cell phone, the old LG VX9800.

My point here? Mobile phones can solve just about *anything*—and we rely on them for *everything* these days.

You notice that I used half a dozen different mobile applications over the course of this story. Each application was developed by a different company and had a different user interface. Some were well designed; others not so much. I paid for some of the applications, and others came on my phone.

As a user, I found the experience functional, but not terribly inspiring. As a mobile developer, I wished for an opportunity to create a more seamless and powerful application that could handle all I'd done and more. I wanted to build a better bat trap, if you will.

Before Android, mobile developers faced many roadblocks when it came to writing applications. Building the better application, the unique application, the competing application, the hybrid application, and incorporating many common tasks such as messaging and calling in a familiar way were often unrealistic goals.

To understand why, let's take a brief look at the history of mobile software development.

"The Brick"

The Motorola DynaTAC 8000X was the first commercially available cell phone. First marketed in 1983, it was 13 x 1.75 x 3.5 inches in dimension, weighed about 2.5 pounds, and allowed you to talk for a little more than half an hour. It retailed for $3,995, plus hefty monthly service fees and per-minute charges.

We called it "The Brick," and the nickname stuck for many of those early mobile phones we alternatively loved and hated. About the size of a brick, with a battery power just long enough for half a conversation, these early mobile handsets were mostly seen in the hands of traveling business execs, security personnel, and the wealthy. First-generation mobile phones were just too expensive. The service charges alone would bankrupt the average person, especially when roaming.

Early mobile phones were not particularly full featured. (Although, even the Motorola DynaTAC, shown in Figure 1.2, had many of the buttons we've come to know well, such as the SEND, END, and CLR buttons.) These early phones did little more than make and receive calls and, if you were lucky, there was a simple contacts application that wasn't impossible to use.

These first-generation mobile phones were designed and developed by the handset manufacturers. Competition was fierce and trade secrets were closely guarded. Manufacturers didn't want to expose the internal workings of their handsets, so they usually developed the phone software in-house. As a developer, if you weren't part of this inner circle, you had no opportunity to write applications for the phones.

It was during this period that we saw the first "time-waster" games begin to appear. Nokia was famous for putting the 1970s video game *Snake* on some of its earliest monochrome phones. Other manufacturers followed, adding games like Pong, Tetris, and Tic-Tac-Toe.

Figure 1.2   The first commercially available mobile phone: the Motorola DynaTAC.

These early phones were flawed, but they did something important—they changed the way people thought about communication. As mobile phone prices dropped, batteries improved, and reception areas grew, more and more people began carrying these handy devices. Soon mobile phones were more than just a novelty.

Customers began pushing for more features and more games. But, there was a problem. The handset manufacturers didn't have the motivation or the resources to build every application users wanted. They needed some way to provide a portal for entertainment and information services without allowing direct access to the handset.

And what better way to provide these services than the Internet?

Wireless Application Protocol (WAP)

It turned out allowing direct phone access to the Internet didn't scale well for mobile.

By this time, professional Web sites were full color and chock full of text, images, and other sorts of media. These sites relied on JavaScript, Flash, and other technologies to enhance the user experience and were often designed with a target resolution of 800x600 pixels and higher.

When the first clamshell phone, the Motorola StarTAC, was released in 1996, it merely had a LCD 10-digit segmented display. (Later models would add a dot-matrix type display.) Meanwhile, Nokia released one of the first slider phones, the 8110—fondly referred to as "The Matrix Phone," as the phone was heavily used in films. The 8110 could display four lines of text with 13 characters per line. Figure 1.3 shows some of the common phone form factors.

Figure 1.3   Various mobile phone form factors: the candy bar, the slider, and the clamshell.

With their postage stamp-sized low-resolution screens and limited storage and processing power, these phones couldn't handle the data-intensive operations required by traditional Web browsers. The bandwidth requirements for data transmission were also costly to the user.

The Wireless Application Protocol (WAP) standard emerged to address these concerns. Simply put, WAP was a stripped-down version of HTTP, which is the backbone protocol of the Internet. Unlike traditional Web browsers, WAP browsers were designed to run within the memory and bandwidth constraints of the phone. Third-party WAP sites served up pages written in a markup language called Wireless Markup Language (WML). These pages were then displayed on the phone's WAP browser. Users navigated as they would on the Web, but the pages were much simpler in design.

The WAP solution was great for handset manufacturers. The pressure was off—they could write one WAP browser to ship with the handset and rely on developers to come up with the content users wanted.

The WAP solution was great for mobile operators. They could provide a custom WAP portal, directing their subscribers to the content they wanted to provide, and rake in the data charges associated with browsing, which were often high.

Developers and content providers didn't deliver. For the first time, developers had a chance to develop content for phone users, and some did so, with limited success.

Most of the early WAP sites were extensions of popular branded Web sites, such as CNN.com and ESPN.com, looking for new ways to extend their readership. Suddenly phone users accessed the news, stock market quotes, and sports scores on their phones.

Commercializing WAP applications was difficult, and there was no built-in billing mechanism. Some of the most popular commercial WAP applications that emerged during this time were simple wallpaper and ringtone catalogues, allowing users to personalize their phones for the first time. For example, the users browsed a WAP site and requested a specific item. They filled out a simple order form with their phone number and their handset model. It was up to the content provider to deliver an image or audio file compatible with the given phone. Payment and verification were handled through various premium-priced delivery mechanisms such as Short Message Service (SMS), Enhanced Messaging Service (EMS), Multimedia Messaging Service (MMS), and WAP Push.

WAP browsers, especially in the early days, were slow and frustrating. Typing long URLs with the numeric keypad was onerous. WAP pages were often difficult to navigate. Most WAP sites were written once for all phones and did not account for individual phone specifications. It didn't matter if the end-user's phone had a big color screen or a postage stamp-sized monochrome one; the developer couldn't tailor the user's experience. The result was a mediocre and not very compelling experience for everyone involved.

Content providers often didn't bother with a WAP site and instead just advertised SMS short codes on TV and in magazines. In this case, the user sent a premium SMS message with a request for a specific wallpaper or ringtone, and the content provider sent it back. Mobile operators generally liked these delivery mechanisms because they received a large portion of each messaging fee.

WAP fell short of commercial expectations. In some markets, such as Japan, it flourished, whereas in others, like the United States, it failed to take off. Handset screens were too small for surfing. Reading a sentence fragment at a time, and then waiting seconds for the next segment to download, ruined the user experience, especially because every second of downloading was often charged to the user. Critics began to call WAP "Wait and Pay."

Finally, the mobile operators who provided the WAP portal (the default home page loaded when you started your WAP browser) often restricted which WAP sites were accessible. The portal allowed the operator to restrict the number of sites users could browse and to funnel subscribers to the operator's preferred content providers and exclude competing sites. This kind of walled garden approach further discouraged third-party developers, who already faced difficulties in monetizing applications, from writing applications.

Proprietary Mobile Platforms

It came as no surprise when users wanted more—they will always want more.

Writing robust applications such as graphic-intensive video games with WAP was nearly impossible. The 18-year-old to 25-year-old sweet-spot demographic—the kids with the disposable income most likely to personalize their phones with wallpapers and ringtones—looked at their portable gaming systems and asked for a device that was both a phone and a gaming device or a phone and a music player. They argued that if devices such as Nintendo's Game Boy could provide hours of entertainment with only five buttons, why not just add phone capabilities? Others looked to their digital cameras, Palms, Blackberries, iPods, and even their laptops and asked the same question. The market seemed to be teetering on the edge of device convergence.

Memory was getting cheaper; batteries were getting better; and PDAs and other embedded devices were beginning to run compact versions of common operating systems such as Linux and Windows. The traditional desktop application developer was suddenly a player in the embedded device market, especially with Smartphone technologies such as Windows Mobile, which they found familiar.

Handset manufacturers realized that if they wanted to continue to sell traditional handsets, they needed to change their protectionist policies pertaining to handset design and expose their internal frameworks, at least, to some extent.

A variety of different proprietary platforms emerged—and developers are still actively creating applications for them. Some Smartphone devices ran Palm OS (now Garnet OS) and RIM Blackberry OS. Sun Microsystems took its popular Java platform and J2ME emerged (now known as Java Micro Edition [Java ME]). Chipset maker Qualcomm developed and licensed its Binary Runtime Environment for Wireless (BREW). Other platforms, such as Symbian OS, were developed by handset manufacturers such as Nokia, Sony Ericsson, Motorola, and Samsung. The Apple iPhone OS (OS X iPhone) joined the ranks in 2008. Figure 1.4 shows several different phones, all of which have different development platforms.

Figure 1.4   Phones from various mobile device platforms.

Many of these platforms have associated developer programs. These programs keep the developer communities small, vetted, and under contractual agreements on what they can and cannot do. These programs are often required and developers must pay for them.

Each platform has benefits and drawbacks. Of course, developers love to debate over which platform is "the best." (Hint: It's usually the platform we're currently developing for.)

The truth is no one platform has emerged victorious. Some platforms are best suited for commercializing games and making millions—if your company has brand backing. Other platforms are more open and suitable for the hobbyist or vertical market applications. No mobile platform is best suited for all possible applications. As a result, the mobile phone has become increasingly fragmented, with all platforms sharing part of the pie.

For manufacturers and mobile operators, handset product lines became complicated fast. Platform market penetration varies greatly by region and user demographic. Instead of choosing just one platform, manufacturers and operators have been forced to sell phones for all the different platforms to compete. We've even seen some handsets supporting multiple platforms. (For instance, Symbian phones often also support J2ME.)

The mobile developer community has become as fragmented as the market. It's nearly impossible to keep track of all the changes in the market. Developer specialty niches have formed. The platform development requirements vary greatly. Mobile software developers work with distinctly different programming environments, different tools, and different programming languages. Porting among the platforms is often costly and not straightforward. Keeping track of handset configurations and testing requirements, signing and certification programs, carrier relationships, and application marketplaces have become complex spin-off businesses of their own.

It's a nightmare for the ACME Company wanting a mobile application. Should they develop a J2ME application? BREW? iPhone? Windows Mobile? Everyone has a different kind of phone. ACME is forced to choose one or, worse, all of the above. Some platforms allow for free applications, whereas others do not. Vertical market application opportunities are limited and expensive.

As a result, many wonderful applications have not reached their desired users, and many other great ideas have not been developed at all.

The Open Handset Alliance

Enter search advertising giant Google. Now a household name, Google has shown an interest in spreading its brand and suite of tools to the wireless marketplace. The company's business model has been amazingly successful on the Internet, and technically speaking, wireless isn't that different.

Google Goes Wireless

The company's initial forays into mobile were beset with all the problems you would expect. The freedoms Internet users enjoyed were not shared by mobile phone subscribers. Internet users can choose from the wide variety of computer brands, operating systems, Internet service providers, and Web browser applications.

Nearly all Google services are free and ad driven. Many applications in the Google Labs suite would directly compete with the applications available on mobile phones. The applications range from simple calendars and calculators to navigation with Google Maps and the latest tailored news from News Alerts—not to mention corporate acquisitions like Blogger and YouTube.

When this approach didn't yield the intended results, Google decided to a different approach—to revamp the entire system upon which wireless application development was based, hoping to provide a more open environment for users and developers: the Internet model. The Internet model allowes users to choose between freeware, shareware, and paid software. This enables free market competition among services.

Forming of the Open Handset Alliance

With its user-centric, democratic design philosophies, Google has led a movement to turn the existing closely guarded wireless market into one where phone users can move between carriers easily and have unfettered access to applications and services. With its vast resources, Google has taken a broad approach, examining the wireless infrastructure from the FCC wireless spectrum policies to the handset manufacturers' requirements, application developer needs, and mobile operator desires.

Next, Google joined with other like-minded members in the wireless community and posed the following question: What would it take to build a better mobile phone?

The Open Handset Alliance (OHA) (Figure 1.5) was formed in November 2007 to answer that very question. The OHA is a business alliance comprised of many of the largest and most successful mobile companies on the planet. Its members include chip makers, handset manufacturers, software developers, and service providers. The entire mobile supply chain is well represented.

open handset alliance

Figure 1.5   The Open Handset Alliance.

Working together, OHA members began developing a nonproprietary open standard platform that would aim to alleviate the aforementioned problems hindering the mobile community. They called it the Android project.

Google's involvement in the Android project has been extensive. The company hosts the open source project and provides online documentation, tools, forums, and the

Software Development Kit (SDK). Google has also hosted a number of events at conferences and the Android Developer Challenge, a contest to encourage developers to write killer Android applications—for $10 million dollars in prizes.

Manufacturers: Designing the Android Handsets

More than half the members of the OHA are handset manufacturers, such as Samsung, Motorola, HTC, and LG, and semiconductor companies, such as Intel, Texas Instruments, NVIDIA, and Qualcomm. These companies are helping design the first generation of Android handsets.

The first shipping Android handset—the T-Mobile G1—was developed by handset manufacturer HTC with service provided by T-Mobile. It was released in October 2008. Many other Android handsets are slated for 2009 and early 2010.

Content Providers: Developing Android Applications

When users have Android handsets, they need those killer apps, right?

Google has led the pack, developing Android applications, many of which, like the email client and Web browser, are core features of the platform. OHA members, such as eBay, are also working on Android application integration with their online auctions.

The first Android Developer Challenge received 1,788 submissions—all newly developed Android games, productivity helpers, and a slew of Location-Based Services (LBS). We also saw humanitarian, social networking, and mash-up apps. Many of these applications have debuted with users through the Android Market—Google's software distribution mechanism for Android.

Mobile Operators: Delivering the Android Experience

After you have the phones, you have to get them out to the users. Mobile operators from Asia, North America, Europe, and Latin America have joined the OHA, ensuring a market for the Android movement. With almost half a billion subscribers, telephony giant China Mobile is a founding member of the alliance. Other operators have signed on as well.

Taking Advantage of All Android Has to Offer

Android's open platform has been embraced by much of the mobile development community—extending far beyond the members of the OHA.

As Android phones and applications become more readily available, many in the tech community anticipate other mobile operators and handset manufacturers will jump on the chance to sell Android phones to their subscribers, especially given the cost benefits compared to proprietary platforms. Already, North American operators, such as Verizon Wireless and AT&T, have shown an interest in Android, and T-Mobile already provides handsets.

If the open standard of the Android platform results in reduced operator costs in licensing and royalties, we could see a migration to open handsets from proprietary platforms such as BREW, Windows Mobile, and even the Apple iPhone. Android is well suited to fill this demand.

Android Platform Differences

Android is hailed as "the first complete, open, and free mobile platform."

- **Complete:** The designers took a comprehensive approach when they developed the Android platform. They began with a secure operating system and built a robust software framework on top that allows for rich application development opportunities.
- **Open:** The Android platform is provided through open source licensing. Developers have unprecedented access to the handset features when developing applications.
- **Free:** Android applications are free to develop. There are no licensing or royalty fees to develop on the platform. No required membership fees. No required testing fees. No required signing or certification fees. Android applications can be distributed and commercialized in a variety of ways.

Android: A Next Generation Platform

Although Android has many innovative features not available in existing mobile platforms, its designers also leveraged many tried-and-true approaches proven to work in the wireless world. It's true that many of these features appear in existing proprietary platforms, but Android combines them in a free and open fashion, while simultaneously addressing many of the flaws on these competing platforms.

The Android mascot is a little green robot, shown in Figure 1.6. You'll see this little guy (girl?) often used to depict Android-related materials.

Android is the first in a new generation of mobile platforms, giving its platform developers a distinct edge on the competition. Android's designers examined the benefits and drawbacks of existing platforms and then incorporate their most successful features. At the same time, Android's designers avoided the mistakes others suffered in the past.

Figure 1.6   The Android mascot.

Free and Open Source

Android is an open source platform. Neither developers nor handset manufacturers pay royalties or license fees to develop for the platform.

The underlying operating system of Android is licensed under GNU General Public License Version 2 (GPLv2), a strong "copyleft" license where any third-party improvements must continue to fall under the open source licensing agreement terms. The Android framework is distributed under the Apache Software License (ASL/Apache2), which allows for the distribution of both open and closed source derivations of the source code. Commercial developers (handset manufacturers especially) can choose to enhance the platform without having to provide their improvements to the open source community. Instead, developers can profit from enhancements such as handset-specific improvements and redistribute their work under whatever licensing they want.

Android application developers have the ability to distribute their applications under whatever licensing scheme they prefer. Developers can write open source freeware or traditional licensed applications for profit and everything in between.

Familiar and Inexpensive Development Tools

Unlike some proprietary platforms that require developer registration fees, vetting, and expensive compilers, there are no upfront costs to developing Android applications.

Freely Available Software Development Kit

The Android SDK and tools are freely available. Developers can download the Android SDK from the Android Web site after agreeing to the terms of the Android Software Development Kit License Agreement.

Familiar Language, Familiar Development Environments

Developers have several choices when it comes to integrated development environments (IDEs). Many developers choose the popular and freely available Eclipse IDE to design and develop Android applications. Eclipse is the most popular IDE for Android development and there is an Android plug-in available for facilitating Android development. Android applications can be developed on the following operating systems:

- Windows XP or Vista
- Mac OS X 10.4.8 or later (x86 only)
- Linux (tested on Linux Ubuntu 6.06 LTS, Dapper Drake)

Reasonable Learning Curve for Developers

Android applications are written in a well-respected programming language: Java.

The Android application framework includes traditional programming constructs, such as threads and processes and specially designed data structures to encapsulate objects commonly used in mobile applications. Developers can rely on familiar class libraries, such as `java.net` and `java.text`. Specialty libraries for tasks like graphics and database management are implemented using well-defined open standards like OpenGL Embedded Systems (OpenGL ES) or SQLite.

Enabling Development of Powerful Applications

In the past, handset manufacturers often established special relationships with trusted third-party software developers (OEM/ODM relationships). This elite group of software developers wrote native applications, such as messaging and Web browsers, which shipped on the handset as part of the phone's core feature set. To design these applications, the manufacturer would grant the developer privileged inside access and knowledge of a handset's internal software framework and firmware.

On the Android platform, there is no distinction between native and third-party applications, enabling healthy competition among application developers. All Android applications use the same libraries. Android applications have unprecedented access to the underlying hardware, allowing developers to write much more powerful applications. Applications can be extended or replaced altogether. For example, Android developers are now free to design email clients tailored to specific email servers such as Microsoft Exchange or Lotus Notes.

Rich, Secure Application Integration

If you recall the bat story I previously shared, you'll note that I accessed a wide variety of phone applications in the course of a few moments: text messaging, phone dialer, camera, email, picture messaging, and the browser. Each was a separate application running on the phone—some built-in and some purchased. Each had its own unique user interface. None were truly integrated.

Not so with Android. One of the Android platform's most compelling and innovative features is well-designed application integration. Android provides all the tools necessary to build a better "bat trap," if you will, by allowing developers to write applications that leverage core functionality such as Web browsing, mapping, contact management, and messaging seamlessly. Applications can also become content providers and share their data among each other in a secure fashion.

Platforms like Symbian have suffered from setbacks due to malware. Android's vigorous application security model helps protect the user and the system from malicious software.

No Costly Obstacles to Publication

Android applications have none of the costly and time-intensive testing and certification programs required by other platforms such as BREW and Symbian.

A "Free Market" for Applications

Android developers are free to choose any kind of revenue model they want. They can develop freeware, shareware, or trial-ware applications, ad-driven, and paid applications. Android was designed to fundamentally change the rules about what kind of wireless applications could be developed. In the past, developers faced many restrictions that had little to do with the application functionality or features:

- Store limitations on the number of competing applications of a given type
- Store limitations on pricing, revenue models, and royalties
- Operator unwillingness to provide applications for smaller demographics

With Android, developers can write and successfully publish any kind of application they want. Developers can tailor applications to small demographics, instead of just large-scale money-making ones often insisted upon by mobile operators. Vertical market applications can be deployed to specific, targeted users.

Because developers have a variety of application distribution mechanisms to choose from, they can pick the methods that work for them instead of being forced to play by others' rules. Android developers can distribute their applications to users in a variety of ways.

- Google developed the Android Market (Figure 1.7), a generic Android application store with a revenue-sharing model.
- Handango.com added Android applications to its existing catalogue using their billing models and revenue sharing model.
- Developers can come up with their own delivery and payment mechanisms.

Mobile operators are still free to develop their own application stores and enforce their own rules, but it will no longer be the only opportunity developers have to distribute their applications.

Figure 1.7   The Android market.

Android might be the next generation in mobile platforms, but the technology is still in its early stages. Early Android developers have had to deal with the typical roadblocks associated with a new platform: frequently revised SDKs, lack of good documentation, and market uncertainties. There are only a handful of Android handsets available to consumers at this time.

On the other hand, developers diving into Android development now benefit from the first-to-market competitive advantages we've seen on other platforms such as BREW and Symbian. Early developers who give feedback are more likely to have an impact on the long-term design of the Android platform and what features will come in the next version of the SDK. Finally, the Android forum community is lively and friendly. Incentive programs, such as the Android Developer Challenge, have encouraged many new developers to dig into the platform.

A New and Growing Platform

What's New in Android 1.5

The much-anticipated Android 1.5 SDK, released in late April 2009, provided a number of substantial improvements to both the underlying software libraries and the Android development tools and build environment. Also, the Android system received some much-needed UI "polish," both in terms of visual appeal and performance.

Although most of these upgrades and improvements were welcome and necessary, the new SDK version did cause some upheaval within the Android developer community. A number of published applications required retesting and resubmission to the Android Marketplace to conform to the new SDK requirements, which were quickly rolled out to all Android phones in the field as a firmware upgrade, rendering older applications obsolete.

The Android Platform

Android is an operating system and a software platform upon which applications are developed. A core set of applications for everyday tasks, such as Web browsing and email, are included on Android handsets.

As a product of the Open Handset Alliance's vision for a robust and open source development environment for wireless, Android is an emerging mobile development platform. The platform was designed for the sole purpose of encouraging a free and open market that all mobile applications phone users might want to have and software developers might want to develop.

Android's Underlying Architecture

The Android platform is designed to be more fault-tolerant than many of its predecessors. The handset runs a Linux operating system, upon which Android applications are executed in a secure fashion. Each Android application runs in its own virtual machine (Figure 1.8). Android applications are managed code; therefore, they are much less likely to cause the phone to crash, leading to fewer instances of device corruption (also called "bricking" the phone, or rendering it useless).

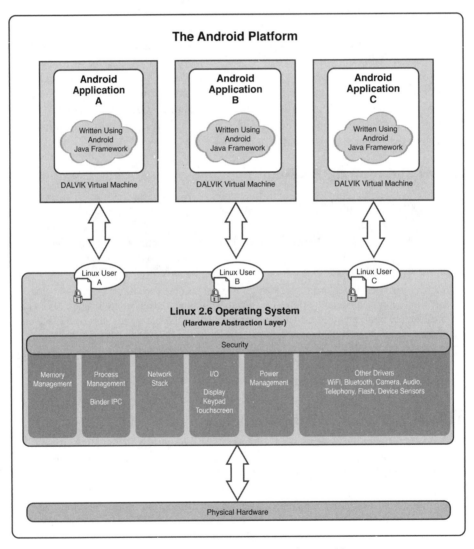

Figure 1.8   Diagram of the Android platform architecture.

The Linux Operating System

The Linux 2.6 kernel (Figure 1.9) handles core system services and acts as a hardware abstraction layer (HAL) between the physical hardware of the handset and the Android software stack.

Figure 1.9   Tux, the Linux kernel mascot.

What's New in Android 1.5

For Android 1.5, the Linux kernel received an upgrade from version 2.6.25 to 2.6.27. Although this type of change might not have an obvious effect for the typical Android developer, it is important to note that the kernel can and will be upgraded frequently. These seemingly minor incremental updates often include major security, performance, and functional features.

Kernel changes often have an impact on the security of the underlying device operating system and provide features and improvements for OEM-level Android device manufacturers. When stable, these features can be exposed to developers as part of an Android SDK upgrade, in the form of new APIs and performance enhancements to existing features.

The Android 1.5 version provides substantial feature enhancements, many of which tie back to features of the upgraded Linux kernel. Although the kernel memory footprint is larger, overall system performance has improved and a number of bugs have been fixed.

Some of the core functions the kernel handles include

- Enforcement of application permissions and security
- Low-level memory management
- Process management and threading
- The network stack
- Display, keypad input, camera, WiFi, Flash memory, audio, and binder (IPC) driver access

Android Application Runtime Environment

Each Android application runs in a separate process, with its own instance of the Dalvik virtual machine (VM). Based on the Java VM, the Dalvik design has been optimized for mobile devices. The Dalvik VM has a small memory footprint and multiple instances of the Dalvik VM can run concurrently on the handset.

Security and Permissions

The integrity of the Android platform is maintained through a variety of security measures.

Applications as Operating System Users

When an application is installed, the operating system creates a new user profile associated with the application. Each application runs as a different user, with its own private files on the file system, a user ID, and a secure operating environment.

The application executes in its own process with its own instance of the Dalvik VM and under its own user ID on the operating system.

Explicitly Defined Application Permissions

To access shared resources on the system, Android applications register for the specific privileges they require. Some of these privileges enable the application to use phone functionality to make calls, access the network, and control the camera and other hardware sensors. Applications also require permission to access shared data containing private and personal information such as user preferences, user's location, and contact information.

Applications might also enforce their own permissions by declaring them for other applications to use. The application can declare any number of different permission types, such as read-only or read-write permissions, for finer control over the application.

Limited Ad-Hoc Permissions

Applications that act as content providers might want to provide some on-the-fly permissions to other applications for specific information they want to share openly. This is done using ad-hoc granting and revoking of access to specific resources using Uniform Resource Identifiers (URIs).

URIs index specific data assets on the system, such as images and text. Here is an example of a URI that provides the phone numbers of all contacts:

```
content://contacts/phones
```

To understand how this permission process works, let's look at an example.

Let's say we've got an application that keeps track of the user's public and private birthday wish lists. If this application wanted to share its data with other applications, it could grant URI permissions for the public wish list, allowing another application permission to access this list without explicitly having to ask for it.

Application Signing for Trust Relationships

All Android applications packages are signed with a certificate, so users know that the application is authentic. The private key for the certificate is held by the developer. This helps establish a trust relationship between the developer and the user. It also allows the developer to control which applications can grant access to one another on the system. No certificate authority is necessary; self-signed certificates are acceptable.

Developing Android Applications

The Android SDK provides an extensive set of application programming interfaces (APIs) that is both modern and robust. Android handset core system services are exposed and accessible to all applications. When granted the appropriate permissions, Android applications can share data among one another and access shared resources on the system securely.

Android Programming Language Choices

Android applications are written in Java (Figure 1.10). For now, the Java language is the developer's only choice on the Android platform. There has been some speculation that other programming languages, such as C++, might be added in future versions of Android.

Figure 1.10   Duke, the Java mascot.

No Distinctions Made Between Native and Third-Party Applications

Unlike other mobile development platforms, there is no distinction between native applications and developer-created applications on the Android platform. Provided the application is granted the appropriate permissions, all applications have the same access to core libraries and the underlying hardware interfaces.

Android handsets ship with a set of native applications such as a Web browser and contact manager. Third-party applications might integrate with these core applications and even extend them to provide a rich user experience.

Commonly Used Packages

With Android, mobile developers no longer have to reinvent the wheel. Instead, developers use familiar class libraries exposed through Android's Java packages to perform common tasks such as graphics, database access, network access, secure communications, and utilities (such as XML parsing).

The Android packages include support for

- Common user interface widgets (Buttons, Spin Controls, Text Input)
- User interface layout
- Secure networking and Web browsing features (SSL, WebKit)
- Structured storage and relational databases (SQLite)
- Powerful 2D and 3D graphics (SGL and OpenGL ES 1.0)
- Audio and visual media formats (MPEG4, MP3, Still Images)
- Access to optional hardware such as Location-Based Services (LBS), WiFi, and Bluetooth

Android Application Framework

The Android application framework provides everything necessary to implement your average application. The Android application lifecycle involves the following key components:

- Activities are functions the application performs.
- Groups of views define the application's layout.
- Intents inform the system about an application's plans.
- Services allow for background processing without user interaction.
- Notifications alert the user when something interesting happens.

Android Applications can interact with the operating system and underlying hardware using a collection of managers. Each manager is responsible for keeping the state of some underlying system service. For example, there is a `LocationManager` that facilitates interaction with the location-based services available on the handset. The `ViewManager` and `WindowManager` manage user interface fundamentals.

Applications can interact with one another by using or acting as a `ContentProvider`. Built-in applications such as the Contact manager are content providers, allowing third-party applications to access contact data and use it in an infinite number of ways. The sky is the limit.

Summary

Mobile software development has evolved over time. Android has emerged as a new mobile development platform, building on past successes and avoiding past failures of other platforms. Android was designed to empower the developer to write innovative applications. The platform is open source, with no up-front fees, and developers enjoy many benefits over other competing platforms.

Now it's time to dive deeper and start writing Android code, so you can evaluate what Android can do for you. In the next chapter, we configure the Android development environment and take a brief walk through the Android SDK.

References and More Information

Android Development http://developer.android.com
Open Handset Alliance: http://www.openhandsetalliance.com

2

Your Android Development Environment

Android developers write and test applications on their computers and then deploy those applications onto the actual device hardware for further testing.

In this chapter, you will install and configure all the appropriate tools you need to start developing Android applications. We'll also explore the Android Software Development Kit (SDK) installation and all it has to offer.

Configuring Your Development Environment

To write Android applications, you must configure your programming environment for Java development. The Java Development Kit (JDK), the Eclipse development environment, and the Android SDK are available for download on the Web at no cost.

Supported Operating Systems

Android applications can be written on the following operating systems:

- Windows XP or Vista
- Mac OS X 10.4.8 or later (x86 only)
- Linux (tested on Linux Ubuntu 6.06 LTS, Dapper Drake)

Available Space

You need approximately 2GB of space to safely install all the tools you need to develop Android applications. This includes installing the JDK, the Eclipse development environment, the Android SDK, and the tools and plug-ins.

Installing the Java Development Kit

Android applications can be developed using the following versions of Sun's JDK:

- JDK 5
- JDK 6

The Java Runtime Environment (JRE) alone is not sufficient to develop Android applications. You can read the license agreement and download the latest version of the Java Standard Edition JDK at Sun's Web site http://java.sun.com/javase/downloads/index.jsp.

The Sun JDK has a friendly Installer Wizard and is very straightforward.

Notes on Windows Installations

The full Windows installation of the JDK6 needs approximately 600MB of available space.

Notes on Mac OS X Installations

On Mac OS X systems, the built-in JDK is sufficient. No further downloads are needed. For more information, see http://developer.apple.com/java/.

Notes on Linux OS Installations

If you already have the JDK installed, be sure that it is the JDK 5 or JDK 6. Some Linux platforms ship with J2SE v1.4, and this is not sufficient.

> **Caution**
>
> Although we've used JDK 6, Android was built using JDK 5, and thus not all features of JDK 6 are supported.

Installing the Eclipse Development Environment for Java

Most developers use the popular Eclipse Integrated Development Environment (IDE) for Android development. You can develop Android applications using Eclipse 3.3 (Europa) or Eclipse 3.4 (Ganymede, as shown in Figure 2.), as shown in Figure 2.1, both of which are available for Windows, Mac, and Linux operating systems.

If this is your first Eclipse project, you probably want to choose the Eclipse IDE for Java EE Developers. This version of the Eclipse IDE includes the Eclipse JDT plug-in and the optional Web Tools Platform (WTP). You can read the license agreement and download the Eclipse IDE for Java EE Developers at www.eclipse.org/downloads/.

> **Tip**
>
> The Eclipse project is member supported, so if you like the Eclipse environment for Android development, consider showing your support for this open source project by becoming a member of the Eclipse Foundation at www.eclipse.org/membership/.

Figure 2.1   Eclipse 3.4 (Ganymede) installer screen.

The Eclipse package comes as a compressed zip file. There is no installer. Unzip the package into the desired folder, and then follow the specific notes for your target operating system.

Notes on Windows Installations

The full Windows installation of the Eclipse environment needs approximately 400MB of available space. The Eclipse package comes as a compressed zip file (175MB).

After you install the files in the appropriate location, navigate to the Eclipse.exe executable and create a shortcut on your desktop. Edit the shortcut and modify the target field with any command line arguments you want.

Notes on Mac OS X Installations

If you install Eclipse on a Mac OS X system, you should make sure to review the README.html file included with the Eclipse package. The Readme file covers how to pass command-line arguments to Eclipse using the eclipse.ini file and how to run more than one instance of Eclipse so you can work with multiple project workspaces simultaneously.

Notes on Linux OS Installations

The Ubuntu package manager doesn't include the Eclipse 3.3 package, so you need to head over to the Eclipse Web site and download the appropriate package.

Other Development Environments

You can use other development environments, such as JetBrains IntelliJ IDEA, to develop Android applications, but only Eclipse is tightly integrated with the Android SDK. Your development environment must fully support JDK 5 or JDK 6. The Gnu Compiler for Java (gcj) is not compatible with the Android platform system requirements.

If you decide to use an IDE other than Eclipse, you can find more information about configuring your environment for Android development at the Android Web site http://developer.android.com/guide/developing/other-ide.html.

Installing the Android Software Development Kit

Next, you need to install the SDK to develop Android applications. The Android SDK includes the Android JAR file (Android application framework classes) and Android documentation, tools, and sample code.

There is no installer for the Android SDK, just unzip the compressed file into the desired folder. The compressed SDK files require approximately 100MB of hard drive space and uncompress to a size of approximately 250MB. You can download the Android SDK at http://developer.android.com/sdk/.

Notes on Windows Installations

To update your PATH variable to include the Android tools directory, right click Computer, and choose Properties. On Vista, you also need to click the Advanced System Settings. Continue by clicking on the Advanced tab of the System Properties and press the Environment Variables button. You should now see a window that looks like Figure 2.2.

Figure 2.2   The Windows environmental variables.

Under the System Variables section, edit the PATH variable and add the path to the tools directory (Figure 2.3).

Figure 2.3   Updating the Windows environmental variable PATH.

Notes on Mac OS X Installations

To update your PATH variable to include the Android tools directory, edit your .bash_profile file in your Home directory.

Notes on Linux OS Installations

To update your PATH variable to include the Android tools directory, edit your ~/.bash_profile, ~/.bashrc, or ~/.profile file.

Installing and Configuring the Android Plug-In for Eclipse (ADT)

The Android Plug-In for Eclipse (ADT) allows seamless integration with many of the Android development tools. If you use Eclipse, it's highly recommended that you install the plug-in because it can make your life much easier. The plug-in includes various wizards for creating and debugging Android projects.

To install the ADT, you must launch Eclipse and install a custom software update. Follow these steps to install the plug-in. When complete, your Available Software tab should look similar to Figure 2.4.

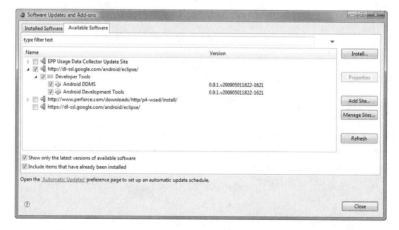

Figure 2.4   Adding a remote site to the Software Updates to access the Android Plug-In.

1. Launch Eclipse.
2. Select Help, Software Updates.
3. Select the Available Software tab.
4. Click the Add Site button.
5. Add a remote site: https://dl-ssl.google.com/android/eclipse/.

Note

If the site fails, try http://dl-ssl.google.com/android/eclipse/.

6. On the Available Software Updates tab, check the Android site you just added.
7. Press the Install button.
8. Follow the installation instructions (Figure 2.5) and install the Android Plug-In.

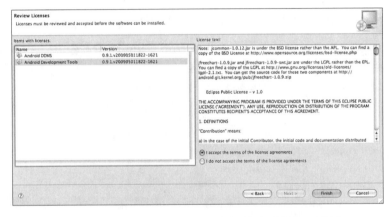

Figure 2.5   Installing the Android Plug-In for Eclipse (ADT).

9. Restart Eclipse after the software update completes.

After you install the Android SDK Eclipse Plug-In, you should update your Eclipse preferences to point at the Android SDK.

To do this, launch Eclipse and choose Window, Preferences (or Eclipse, Preferences on Mac OS X), as shown in Figure 2.6. Select the Android preferences and set the path to where you installed the Android SDK.

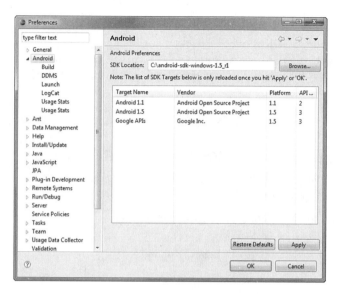

Figure 2.6   Setting the Eclipse Preferences for Android.

Troubleshooting the ADT Installation

Google has documented a number of operating system–specific issues with installation of the ADT plug-in at http://developer.android.com/sdk/1.5_r1/installing.html.

Upgrading the Android Software Development Kit

The Android SDK is currently in development, which means inevitably, you need to upgrade the version of the SDK on your machine. Changes to the Android SDK might include addition, update, and removal of features; package name changes; and updated tools.

With each new version of the SDK, Google provides the following useful documents:

- **An Overview of Changes:** A brief description of major changes to the SDK
- **An API Diff Report:** A complete list of specific changes to the SDK
- **Release Notes**: A list of known issues with the SDK

Upgrading the Android SDK typically involves installing the new SDK, updating path variables, and reconfiguring existing Android development tools. After you upgrade the development environment, you need to port your Android applications to the new SDK. You can find out more about upgrading the Android SDK at http://developer.android.com/sdk/ and follow the link to "Upgrading."

Problems with the Android Software Development Kit

Because the Android SDK is under active development, you might come across problems with the SDK. If you think you've found a problem, you can find a list of open issues and their status at the Android project Issue Tracker Web site. You can also submit new issues for review.

The Issue Tracker Web site is http://code.google.com/p/android/issues/list. For more information about logging defects, check out http://source.android.com/report-bugs.

Configuring Your Android Hardware for Debugging

Each Android phone model might have different debugging configurations. Your Android device must be enabled for debugging via a USB connection.

Configuring Your T-Mobile G1 for USB Debugging

From the Home screen of the T-Mobile G1, select Menu, Settings, Applications, Development. Enable the USB Debugging option.

> **Tip**
>
> The option to have the phone stay awake while charging, found in the development settings, is also useful for long sessions where the phone might often go to sleep while you are in the middle of looking at code you are debugging.

Configuring Your Operating System for Device Debugging

To install and debug Android applications on hardware such as the T-Mobile G1, you need to configure your operating system to access the phone via USB.

Notes on Windows Installations

You need to install the Android USB driver. The driver is available at http://dl.google.com/android/android_usb_windows.zip. Unzip the driver files. Connect your phone to your computer via the USB cable and select the driver.

> **Tip**
>
> As of this writing, the driver is not a signed driver, so you need to override the security settings of Windows by choosing to install the driver software even though it can't be verified.

Notes on Mac OS X Installations

On a supported Mac, all you need to do is plug in the USB cable to the Mac and the device. There is no additional configuration needed.

Notes on Linux OS Installations

Ubuntu Linux installations require a rules file using the following steps:

1. Login as root administrator.
2. Create a file: `/etc/udev/rules.d/50-android.rules`.

3a. For Gusty (7.10)/Hardy (8.04) Ubuntu Linux installations, the file should contain:
`SUBSYSTEM=="usb", SYSFS{idVendor}=="0bb4", MODE="0666".`

3b. For Dapper (6.06) Ubuntu Linux installations, the file should contain:
`SUBSYSTEM=="usb_device", SYSFS{idVendor}=="0bb4", MODE="0666".`

4. Now use the shell command: `chmod a+rx /etc/udev/rules.d/50-android.rules`.

The Development Environment Used in This Book

The rest of this book uses the following development environment configuration, unless otherwise noted:

- T-Mobile G1 (Android Phone Hardware)
- Windows Vista, Service Pack 1 (Operating System)
- Sun Java SE Development Kit (JDK) 6 Update 10
- Eclipse Java IDE Version 3.4 (Ganymede)
- Eclipse JDT Plug-In and Web Tools Platform (WTP)
- Android SDK Version 1.1 and SDK Version 1.5

Exploring the Android Software Development Kit

The Android SDK comes with five major components: the Android SDK License Agreement, the Android Documentation, Application Framework, Tools, and Sample Applications.

The Android SDK License Agreement

Before you can download the Android SDK, you must review and agree to the Android SDK License Agreement, as shown in Figure 2.7. This agreement is a contract between you (the developer) and Google (copyright holder of the Android SDK).

Figure 2.7   The Android SDK download site with the Android SDK
License Agreement.

Even if someone at your company has agreed to the Licensing Agreement on your behalf, it is important for you, the developer, to be aware of a few important points.

1. **Rights granted:** Google (as the copyright holder of Android) grants you a limited, worldwide, royalty-free, nonassignable, and nonexclusive license to use the SDK solely to develop applications for the Android platform. Google (and third-party contributors) are granting you license, but they still hold all copyrights and intellectual property rights to the material. Using the Android SDK does not grant you permission to use any Google brands, logos, or trade names. You will not remove any of the copyright notices therein. Third-party applications that your applications interact with (other Android apps) are subject to separate terms and fall outside this agreement.

2. **SDK usage:** You may only develop Android applications. You may not make derivative works from the SDK or distribute the SDK on any device or distribute part of the SDK with other software.

3. **SDK changes and backward compatibility:** Google may change the Android SDK at any time, without notice, without regard to backward compatibility.

Although Android API changes were a major issue with prerelease versions of the SDK, the 1.0 and 1.1 releases have been reasonably stable due to the fact that a strong revisioning system has been implemented to seamlessly integrate with the phone hardware in the field.

4. **Android application developer eights:** You retain all rights to any Android software you develop with the SDK, including intellectual property rights.

5. **Android application privacy requirements:** You agree that your applications will protect the privacy and legal rights of its users. If your application uses or accesses personal and private information about the user (usernames, passwords, and so on), then your application will provide an adequate privacy notice and keep that data stored securely.

6. **Android application malware requirements:** You are responsible for all applications you develop. You agree not to write disruptive applications or malware. You are solely responsible for all data transmitted through your application.

7. **Additional terms for specific Google APIs:** Use of the Android Maps API is subject to further Terms of Service (specifically use of the following packages: `com.google.android.maps` and `com.android.location.Geocoder`). You must agree to these additional terms before using those specific APIs and always include the Google Maps copyright notice provided. Use of Google Data APIs (Google Apps, Blogger, Google Calendar, Google Finance Portfolio Data, Picasa, YouTube, and so on) is limited to what access your application has been explicitly granted permission for by the user.

8. **Develop at your own risk:** Any harm that comes about from developing with the Android SDK is your own fault and not Google's.

The Android SDK Documentation

What's New in Android 1.5

The on-disk documentation was redesigned and greatly improved for Android 1.5. The documentation is now divided into three main sections: SDK provides installation and upgrade details, Dev Guide introduces Android and covers best practices and development tips from the Android team, and Reference provides a drill-down listing of the Android APIs with detailed coverage of specific classes and interfaces.

A copy of the Android documentation is provided in the Docs subfolder (as shown in Figure 2.8). The Android Developers Guide is provided in HTML format, and you can also access the latest help files online at http://developer.android.com/guide/index.html.

Figure 2.8   The Android SDK documentation.

The Android Application Framework

The Android application framework is provided in the `Android.jar` file. The Android SDK is made up of several important packages, as shown in Table 2.1.

Table 2.1   **Important Packages in the Android SDK**

Top-Level Package	Purpose
android.*	Android application fundamentals
com.google.android.maps	Google Map interface (requires additional terms of service and an apiKey)
dalvik.*	Dalvik Virtual Machine support for debugging and such
java.*	Core classes and familiar generic utilities for networking, security, math, and such
javax.*	Encryption support
junit.*	Unit testing support
org.apache.http.*	Hypertext Transfer Protocol (HTTP) protocol support
org.json	JavaScript Object Notation (JSON) support
org.w3c.dom	W3C Java bindings for the Document Object Model Core (XML and HTML)
org.xml.sax.*	Simple API for XML (SAX) support for XML
org.xmlpull.*	High-performance XML parsing

The Android Tools

The Android SDK provides many tools to design, develop, debug, and deploy your
Android applications. The Eclipse Plug-In incorporates many of these tools seamlessly
into your development environment.

Android Emulator

The Android emulator, shown in Figure 2.9, is the most important tool provided with
the Android SDK.

The emulator runs on your computer and behaves much as a mobile device would.
You can load Android applications into the emulator, test, and debug them.

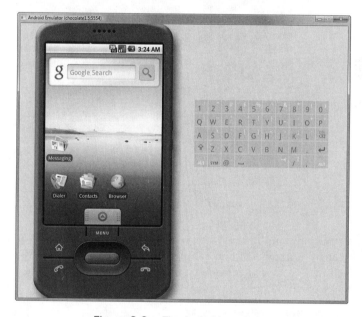

Figure 2.9   The Android emulator.

The emulator is a generic device and not tied to any one specific phone configuration.
The emulator supports various skins to mimic the look and feel of different devices.

As more Android phones are developed, we will likely see skins for the specific
phones. For now, there are four basic skins: the default HVGA-Portrait Mode (Figure
2.9), HVGA-Landscape Mode (Figure 2.10), QVGA-Landscape Mode (Figure 2.10), and
QVGA-Portrait Mode (Figure 2.10).

> **Tip**
>
> You should be aware that the Android emulator is a substitute for a real Android device,
> but an imperfect one. The emulator is a valuable tool for testing but cannot fully replace
> testing on the actual target device.

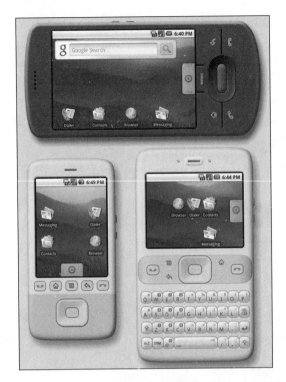

Figure 2.10   Various Android emulator skins available.

For more information about the emulator, see Appendix A, "The Android Emulator Quick-Start Guide." You can also find exhaustive information about the Android emulator in the Android SDK Documentation: http://developer.android.com/guide/developing/tools/emulator.html.

Dalvik Debug Monitor Service (DDMS)

The Dalvik Debug Monitor Service (DDMS) is integrated into Eclipse using the Android Development Tools Plug-In (Figure 2.11). This tool provides you with direct access to the device—whether it's the emulator virtual device or the physical device. You use DDMS to view and manage processes and threads running on the device, view heap data, attach to processes to debug, and a variety of other tasks.

For more information about the DDMS, see Appendix B, "The Android DDMS Quick-Start Guide." You can also find exhaustive details about DDMS in the Android SDK Documentation: http://developer.android.com/guide/developing/tools/ddms.html.

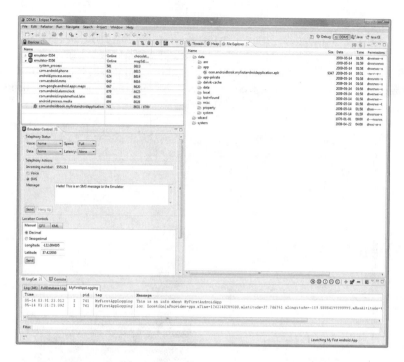

Figure 2.11   Using DDMS integrated into an Eclipse perspective.

Android Debug Bridge (ADB)

The Android Debug Bridge (ADB) is a client-server tool used to allow developers to
debug Android code on the emulator and the device using a standard Java IDE such as
Eclipse. The DDMS and the Android Development Plug-In for Eclipse both use the
ADB to facilitate interaction between the development environment and the device (or
emulator).

Developers can also use ADB to interact with the device file system, install Android
applications manually, and issue shell commands. For example, the `sqlite3` shell
commands allow you to access device database. The Application Exerciser Monkey
commands generate random input and system events to stress test your application. One
of the most important aspects of the ADB for the developer is its logging system
(`Logcat`).

For more information about the ADB, see Appendix C, "The Android Debug Bridge
Quick-Start Guide." For an exhaustive reference, see the Android SDK Documentation
at http://developer.android.com/guide/developing/tools/adb.html.

Android Hierarchy Viewer

The Android Hierarchy Viewer (Figure 2.12), a visual tool that illustrates layout component relationships, helps developers design and debug user interfaces. Developers can use this tool to inspect the `view` properties and develop pixel-perfect layouts. For more information about user interface design and the Hierarchy Viewer, see Chapter 7, "Designing Android User Interfaces with Layouts."

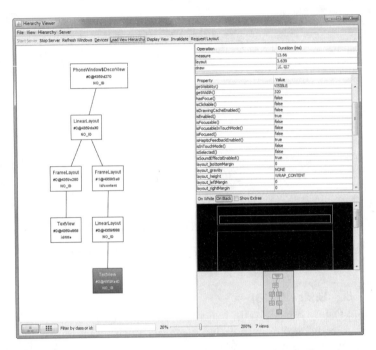

Figure 2.12   Screenshot of the Android Hierarchy Viewer in action.

Other Tools

Android SDK has many other tools. Some tools, such as the Android Asset Packaging Tool (`aapt`) are provided for application deployment purposes.

Other tools are special purpose utilities. For example, the Draw Nine-patch tool allows you to design stretchable PNG images. The mksdcard tool helps developers simulate SD cards in the emulator.

There are other tools, such as activitycreator, which are used by developers not leveraging the Eclipse Android plug-in to create stub files, `ant` build files, IntelliJ project files, and the like.

You can read about all the Android tools at http://developer.android.com/guide/developing/tools/index.html.

The Android Sample Applications

The Android SDK provides many samples and demo applications to help you learn the ropes of Android Development. Some of the demo applications are

- **Snake:** A simple game that demonstrates bitmap drawing and key events.
- **NotePad:** A simple list application that demonstrates database access.
- **LunarLander:** A simple game that demonstrates drawing and animation.
- **JetBoy (Android SDK 1.5 only):** A simple starship asteroid game that demonstrates using the SONiVOX JET interactive music engine. For more information, see the "SONiVOX JETCreator User Manual" provided within the SDK Developer Guide.
- **SoftKeyboard (Android SDK 1.5 only):** An example of a custom input method for a soft keyboard implementation.
- **ApiDemos:** A menu-driven utility that demonstrates a wide variety of Android APIs, from user interface widgets to application lifecycle components such as services, alarms, and notifications.

Summary

In this chapter, you installed everything you need to start writing Android applications, including the appropriate JDK, the Eclipse development environment, and the Android SDK.

You should now have a reasonable development environment configured to write Android applications. In the next chapter, you write your first Android application and familiarize yourself with running and debugging applications in the emulator and on the device.

References and More Information

Google's Android Developer Guide: http://developer.android.com/guide/index.html
Android SDK Download Site: http://developer.android.com/sdk/
Android SDK License Agreement: http://developer.android.com/sdk/terms.html
Google Data APIs: http://code.google.com/apis/gdata/

3

Writing Your First Android Application

You should now have a workable Android development environment on your computer. Hopefully, you also have some Android hardware as well. Now it's time for you to start writing some Android code.

In this chapter, you learn how to add and create Android projects in Eclipse. You ensure that your Android development environment is set up correctly. You also write and debug your first Android application in the software emulator and on the device—in this case, we show you with the T-Mobile G1.

Testing Your Development Environment

The best way to make sure you configured your development environment correctly is to take an existing Android application and run it.

First, you add one of the sample applications provided as part of the Android Software Development Kit (SDK) to the Eclipse environment and run it in the Android emulator. Then you write your first Android application and interact with it on the emulator and on hardware.

The Android SDK ships with several sample demo applications, including a simple game called Snake. To use the Snake application, you must create a new project in your Eclipse workspace, configure a launch configuration for that project, and run it.

Adding the Snake Application to a Project in Your Eclipse Workspace

The first thing you need to do is add the Snake project to your Eclipse workspace. To do this, follow these steps:

1. Choose File, New, Project.

2. Choose Android, Android Project wizard (see Figure 3.1).

> **Tip**
>
> After you use the Android Project wizard once, you can create subsequent projects using File, New, Android Project.

Figure 3.1   Creating a new Android project.

3. Change the Contents to Create project from existing source.

4. Browse to your Android samples directory.

5. Choose the Snake directory. All the project fields will be filled in for you from the Manifest file (see Figure 3.2).

6. Choose Finish. You now see the Snake project files in your workspace (see Figure 3.3).

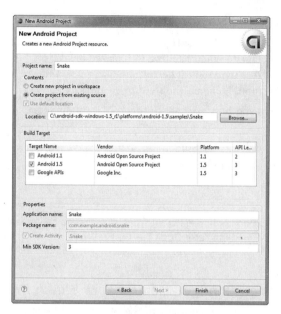

Figure 3.2   The Snake project details.

Figure 3.3   The Snake project files.

Creating an Android Virtual Device (AVD) for Your Snake Project

The next step is to create an Android Virtual Device (AVD) that describes what type of device you want to emulate when running the Snake application. For this example, we create a simple AVD that represents a default installation of Android 1.5, upon which we run the Snake application. Here are the steps to create a basic AVD:

1. From the command line, navigate to the `tools` subdirectory of the Android SDK directory.

2. On the command line, type `android create avd -n vanilla1.5 -t 2`.

3. Wait for the command to complete.

> **Tip**
>
> For more information on creating different types of AVDs you can create, check out Appendix A, "The Android Emulator Quick-Start Guide."

Creating a Launch Configuration for Your Snake Project

Next, you must create a launch configuration in Eclipse to configure under what circumstances the Snake application will launch. The launch configuration is where you configure the emulator options to use and the entry point for your application.

You can create Run Configurations and Debug Configurations separately, with different options. These configurations are created under the Run menu in Eclipse (Run, Run Configuration and Run, Debug Configuration).

Follow these steps to create a basic Run Configuration for the Snake application:

1. Choose Run, Run Configurations (or right-click the Project and Choose Run As).

2. Double-click on Android Application.

3. Name your Run Configuration `SnakeRunConfiguration` (see Figure 3.4).

4. Switch to the Target tab and choose the vanilla1.5 AVD created earlier from the preferred AVD listing, as shown in Figure 3.5.

You can set other options on the Target and Common tabs, but we have left the defaults for now.

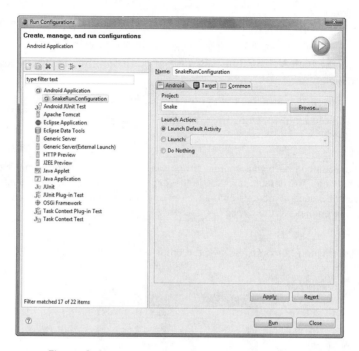

Figure 3.4   The Snake project launch configuration.

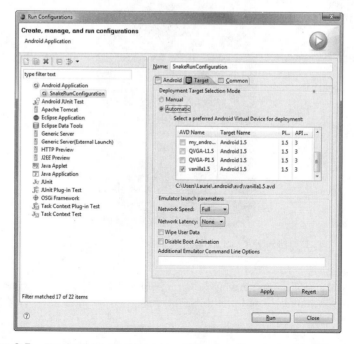

Figure 3.5   The Snake project launch configuration, Target tab with AVD selected.

Running the Snake Application in the Android Emulator

Now you can run the Snake application using the following steps:

1. Choose the Run As icon drop-down menu on the toolbar (the green circle with the triangle).

2. Pull the drop-down menu and choose the SnakeRunConfiguration you created.

3. The Android emulator starts up; this might take a moment.

Tip

Make sure you don't have your Android device plugged in to your development machine via USB at this time. The default selection in the Target tab of the Run Configuration for Device Target Selection mode is Automatic, so Snake might launch on your device instead of within the emulator if the device is attached.

4. Press the Menu button to unlock the emulator, as shown in Figure 3.6.

Figure 3.6   The Android emulator launching (locked).

5. The Snake application starts, as shown in Figure 3.7. You can interact with it through the emulator and play the game.

Figure 3.7   The Snake game.

Building Your First Android Application

Now it's time to write your first Android application. You start with a simple Hello World project and build upon it to illustrate some of the features of Android.

Creating and Configuring a New Android Project

You can create a new Android project in much the same way you did in the previous section when you added the Android application, Snake, to your Eclipse workspace.

The first thing you need to do is create a new project in your Eclipse workspace. Choose File, New, Android Project.

Your Project Name determines the Project icon in your Eclipse workspace and the project directory on the operating system. In this case, we named the project `MyFirstAndroidApp`.

We create a New Project, so we choose Create New Project in Workspace and put the project files in the default location on disk.

Select a Build Target. In this case, choose Android 1.5, which automatically sets the Minimum SDK Version to API Level 3.

Use standard package namespace conventions for Java, for example, `com.`
`mycompany.android.yourappname`. All code in this book falls under the
`com.androidbook.*` namespace, so for this project, an appropriate Package Name is
`com.androidbook.myfirstandroidapp`.

The Application Name is the friendly name of the application and the name shown
with the icon on the application launcher. In this case, the Application Name is My First
Android App, as shown in Figure 3.8.

Figure 3.8   Creating a new project: MyFirstAndroidApp.

Finally, choose Finish. Eclipse and the Android plug-in then create an empty project
for you.

Core Files and Directories of the Android Application

Every Android application has a set of core files that are created and are used to define
the functionality of the application (Table 3.1). The following files are created by default
with a new Android application.

Table 3.1   **Important Android Project Files and Directories**

Android File	General Description
AndroidManifest.xml	The **AndroidManifest.xml** file is a global application description file. It defines your application's capabilities and permissions and how it runs.
default.properties	The **default.properties** file is an automatically created project file. It defines your application's build target and other build system options, as required.
src Folder	Required folder where all source code for the application resides.
src/com.androidbook. myfirstandroidapp/ MyFirstAndroidApp.java	Core source file that defines the entry point of your Android application.
gen Folder	Required folder where autogenerated resource files for the application reside.
gen/com.androidbook. myfirstandroidapp/R.java	Application resource management source file generated for you and should not be edited.
res Folder	Required folder where all application resources are managed. Application resources include animations, drawable image assets, layout files, XML files, data resources like strings, and raw files.
res/drawable/icon.png	Application icon displayed on the launcher screen.
res/layout/main.xml	Single screen layout file.
res/values/strings.xml	Application string resources.

There are a number of other files saved on disk as part of the Eclipse project in the workspace. Discussing these Eclipse files is beyond the scope of this book.

Creating an AVD for Your Project

The next step is to create an AVD that describes what type of device you want to emulate when running the application. For this example, we create a more complex AVD that represents an installation of Android 1.5 with Google Maps support and a 1GB SD card. Follow these steps to create a basic AVD:

1. From the command line, navigate to the `tools` subdirectory of the Android SDK directory.
2. On the command line, type

```
android create avd -n mapSd1.5 -t 3 -c 1024M
```

3. Wait for the command to complete. It can take a few minutes.

> **Tip**
>
> Again, for more information on creating different types of AVDs and working with the Android emulator, check out Appendix A.

Creating a Launch Configuration for Your Project

Next, you must create a launch configuration in Eclipse to configure under what circumstances `MyFirstAndroidApp` launches. The launch configuration is where you configure what emulator options to use and the entry point for your application. You can create Run Configurations and Debug Configurations separately, with different options.

These configurations are created under the Run menu in Eclipse (Run, Run Configuration and Run, Debug Configuration). Follow these steps to create a basic Run Configuration for `MyFirstAndroidApp`:

1. Choose Run, Run Configurations.
2. Double-click on Android Application.
3. Name your Run Configuration `MyFirstAndroidAppRunConfig`.
4. Browse to the `MyFirstAndroidApp` project you created in your workspace.
5. Choose the second tab called Target. Set the Device Target Selection Mode to Manual.

> **Tip**
>
> If you leave the Device Target Selection mode on Automatic when you choose Run or Debug in Eclipse, your application will automatically be installed and run on the device if it's plugged in. Otherwise, it starts in the emulator with the specified AVD. By choosing Manual, you will always be prompted for whether (a) you want your application launched in an existing emulator, (b) you want your application launched in a new emulator instance and allowed to specify an AVD, or (c) you want your application launched on the device (if it's plugged in). If any emulator is already running, the device is then plugged in, and the mode is set to Automatic, you see this same prompt, too.

6. Click Apply, then click Close.
7. You now have a run configuration for your application.

Running Your Android Application in the Emulator

Now you can run `MyFirstAndroidApp` using the following steps:

1. Choose the Run As icon drop-down menu on the toolbar (the green circle with the triangle like a "play" button).
2. Pull the drop-down menu and choose the `MyFirstAndroidAppRunConfig` you created. (If you do not see it listed, choose the Run Configurations item and select

the appropriate configuration. It shows up on this drop-down list the next time you run the configuration.)

3. Because you chose the Manual Target Selection mode, you are now prompted for your emulator instance. Change the selection to start a new emulator instance, and check the box next to the AVD you created called mapSd1.5, as shown in Figure 3.9.

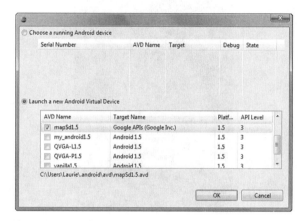

Figure 3.9   Choosing a Target Selection mode manually.

4. The Android emulator starts up. This might take a moment.

Tip

It can take a long time for the emulator to start up. You might want to leave it around while you work and reattach to it as needed. The tools in Eclipse handle reinstalling the application and relaunching the application, so you can more easily keep the emulator loaded all the time.

5. Press the Menu button to unlock the emulator.
6. MyFirstAndroidApp starts, as shown in Figure 3.10.
7. Click the Home button in the Emulator to end the application.
8. Pull the Drawer up (the gray circle with a triangle in it at the bottom of the emulator screen) to see installed applications. Your screen looks something like Figure 3.11.
9. Click on the My First Android Application icon to launch it again.

Figure 3.10   My First Android app running in the emulator.

Figure 3.11   My First Android App application icon shown in the Drawer.

Debugging Your Android Application in the Emulator

Before we go any further, you need to become familiar with debugging in the emulator. To illustrate some useful debugging tools, let's manufacture an error in `MyFirstAndroidApp.`

In your project, edit the file `MyFirstAndroidApp.java` and create a new method called `forceError()` in your class and make a call to this method in your `onCreate()` method. The `forceError()` method forces a new unhandled error in your application.

The `forceError()` method should look something like this:

```
public void forceError() {
    if(true) {
        throw new Error("Whoops");
    }
}
```

> **Tip**
>
> Eclipse has perspectives (each a set of specific panes) for coding and debugging. You can switch between perspectives by choosing the appropriate name in the top right corner of the Eclipse environment. The Java perspective arranges the appropriate panes for coding and navigating around the project. The Debug perspective allows you to set breakpoints, view `LogCat` information, and debug. The Dalvik Debug Monitor Service (DDMS) perspective allows you to monitor and manipulate emulator and device status.

It's probably helpful at this point to run the application and watch what happens. In the emulator, you see that `MyFirstAndroidApp` has stopped unexpectedly. You are prompted with a dialog allowing you to forcefully close the application, as shown in Figure 3.12.

Shut down the application and the emulator. Now it's time to debug.

This time, choose to Debug your application. To do this, click on the little bug drop-down list (or Run, Debug Configurations) and choose the Launch configuration you created for `MyFirstAndroidApp`. It takes a moment for the emulator to start up, and you need to click through some dialog boxes, such as the one shown in Figure 3.13, the first time your application attaches to the debugger.

In Eclipse, use the Debug perspective to set breakpoints, step through code, and watch the LogCat logging information about your application. This time, when the application fails, you can determine the cause using the debugger. In Eclipse, if you examine the LogCat logging pane, you see that your application was forced to exit due to an unhandled exception.

Figure 3.12   My First Android app crashing gracefully.

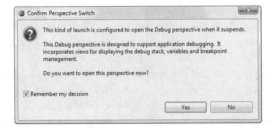

Figure 3.13   Switching debug perspectives for Android emulator
debugging.

Specifically, there's a red `AndroidRuntime` error: `java.lang.Error: Whoops`.

Back in the emulator, click the Force Close button. Now set a breakpoint on the
`forceError()` method by right-clicking on the left side of the line of code and choosing Toggle Breakpoint (or Ctrl+Shift+B).

> **Tip**
>
> In Eclipse, you can step through code using Step Into (F5), Step Over (F6), Step Return (F7), and Resume (F8).
>
> On Mac OS X, you might find that the F8 key is mapped globally. If you want to use the keyboard convenience command, you might want to change the keyboard mapping in Eclipse by choose Eclipse, Preferences, General, Keys and finding the entry for Resume and changing it to something else. Alternatively, you can change the Mac OS X global mapping by going to System Preferences, Keyboard & Mouse, Keyboard Shortcuts and then changing the mapping for F8 to something else.

In the emulator, restart your application and step through your code. You see `MyFirstAndroidApp` throw the exception and then the exception shows up in the Variable Browser pane of the Debug Perspective. Expanding the variables contents shows that it is the "Whoops" error.

This is a great time to crash your application repeatedly and get used to the controls. While you're at it, switch over to the DDMS perspective. You note the emulator has a list of processes running on the phone, such as `system_process` and `com.android.phone`. If you launch `MyFirstAndroidApp`, you see `com.androidbook.myfirstandroidapp` show up as a process on the emulator listing. Force the app to close because it crashes, and you note that it disappears from the process list. You can use DDMS to kill processes, inspect threads and the heap, and access the phone file system.

> **Tip**
>
> You can find out more about the Android Emulator in Appendix A.

Adding Logging Support to Your Android Application

Before you start diving into the various features of the Android SDK, you want to familiarize yourself with logging, a valuable resource for debugging and learning Android. Android logging features are in the `Log` class of the `android.util` package.

Some helpful methods in the `android.util.Log` class are shown in Table 3.2.

Table 3.2   **Important `android.util.Log` Methods**

Method	Purpose
Log.e()	Log errors
Log.w()	Log warnings
Log.i()	Log informational messages
Log.d()	Log Debug messages
Log.v()	Log Verbose messages

To add logging support to `MyFirstAndroidApp`, edit the file `MyFirstAndroidApp.java`. First, you must add the appropriate import statement for the `Log` class.

```
import android.util.Log;
```

> **Tip**
>
> To save time in Eclipse, you can use the imported classes in your code and add the imports needed by hovering over the imported class name and choosing the Add Imported Class option.
>
> You can also use the Organize imports command (Ctrl+Shift+O in Windows or command+shift+O on a Mac) to have Eclipse automatically organize your imports. This removes unused imports and adds new ones for packages used but not imported. If naming conflict arises, as it often does with the Log class, you can choose the package you intended to use.

Next, within the `MyFirstAndroidApp` class, declare a constant string that you use to tag all logging messages from this class. You can use the LogCat utility within Eclipse to filter your logging messages to this debug tag:

```
private static final String DEBUG_TAG= "MyFirstAppLogging";
```

Now, within the `onCreate()` method, you can log something informational:

```
Log.i(DEBUG_TAG, "Info about MyFirstAndroidApp");
```

> **Caution**
>
> While you're here, you want to comment out your previous `forceError()` call so that your application doesn't fail.

Now you're ready to run `MyFirstAndroidApp.` Save your work and debug it in the emulator. You notice that your logging messages appear in the LogCat listing, with the Tag field *MyFirstAppLogging*.

> **Tip**
>
> You might want to create a `LogCat` filter for only messages tagged with your debug tag. To do this, click the green plus sign button in the `LogCat` pane of Eclipse. Name your filter `Just MyFirstApp` and fill in the Log Tag with your tag *MyFirstAppLogging*. Now you have a second `LogCat` tab with only your logging information shown.

Adding Some Media Support to Your Application

Next, let's add some pizzazz to `MyFirstAndroidApp` by having the application play an MP3 music file. Android media player features are found in the `MediaPlayer` class of the `android.media` package.

You can create `MediaPlayer` objects from existing application resources or by specifying a target file using a Uniform Resource Identifier (URI). For simplicity, we begin by accessing an MP3 using the `Uri` class from the `android.net` package.

Some methods in the `android.media.MediaPlayer` and `android.net.Uri` classes are shown in Table 3.3.

Table 3.3   **Important MediaPlayer and URI Parsing Methods**

Method	Purpose
`MediaPlayer.create()`	Creates a new Media Player with a given target to play
`MediaPlayer.start()`	Starts media playback
`MediaPlayer.stop()`	Stops media playback
`MediaPlayer.release()`	Releases the resources of the Media Player object
`Uri.parse()`	Instantiates a Uri object from an appropriately formatted URI address

To add MP3 playback support to `MyFirstAndroidApp`, edit the file `MyFirstAndroidApp.java`. First, you must add the appropriate import statements for the `MediaPlayer` class.

```
import android.media.MediaPlayer;
import android.net.Uri;
```

Next, within the `MyFirstAndroidApp` class, declare a member variable for your `MediaPlayer` object.

```
private MediaPlayer mp;
```

Now, create a new method called `playMusicFromWeb()` in your class and make a call to this method in your `onCreate()` method. The `playMusicFromWeb()` method creates a valid `Uri` object, creates a `MediaPlayer` object and starts the MP3 playing. If the operation should fail for some reason, the method logs a custom error with your logging tag.

The `playMusicFromWeb()` method should look something like this:

```
public void playMusicFromWeb() {
    try {
        Uri file = Uri.parse(
Â"http://www.perlgurl.org/podcast/archives/podcasts/PerlgurlPromo.mp3");
        mp = MediaPlayer.create(this, file);
        mp.start();
    }
    catch (Exception e) {
        Log.e(DEBUG_TAG, "Player failed", e);
    }
}
```

And finally, you want to cleanly exit when the application shuts down. To do this, you need to override the `onStop()` method and stop the `MediaPlayer` object and release its resources.

> **Tip**
>
> In Eclipse, you can right-click within the class and choose Source (or Alt+Shift+S). Choose the option Override/Implement Methods and check the `onStop()` method.

The `onStop()` method should look something like this:

```
protected void onStop() {
    if (mp != null) {
        mp.stop();
        mp.release();
    }
    super.onStop();
}
```

Now, if you run `MyFirstAndroidApp` in the emulator (and you have an Internet connection to grab the data found at the URI location), your application plays the MP3. When you shut the application down, the `MediaPlayer` is stopped and released appropriately.

Adding Some Location-Based Services Support to Your Application

Your application knows how to say Hello, but it doesn't know where it's located. Now it's a good time to become familiar with some simple location-based calls to get the GPS coordinates.

Configuring the Location of the Emulator

The emulator does not have location sensors, so the first thing you need to do is seed your emulator with GPS coordinates. To do this, launch your emulator in debug mode with an AVD supporting the Google Maps add-ins and follow these steps:

In the Emulator:

1. Close MyFirstAndroidApp by pressing the Home button.
2. Choose Maps.
3. Click the Menu button.
4. Choose the My Location menu item. (It looks like a target.)

In Eclipse:

5. Click the DDMS perspective in the top right corner.
6. You see an Emulator Control pane on the left side of the screen. Scroll down to the Location Control.

7. Manually enter the longitude and latitude of your location. (Note they are in reverse order.)

8. Click Send.

Back in the emulator, you notice the Google Map now shows the location you seeded. Your screen should now display your location as Yosemite Valley, as shown in Figure 3.14.

Figure 3.14   Setting the location of the emulator to Yosemite Valley.

Your emulator now has a simulated location.

Tip

To find a specific set of coordinates, you can go to http://maps.google.com. Navigate to the location you want; center the map on the location by right-clicking the map. Choose link to map and copy the URL. Take a closer look at the URL and weed out the "ll" variable, which represents the latitude/longitude of the location. For example, the Yosemite Valley link has the value ll=37.746761, -119.588542, which stands for Latitude: 37.746761 and Longitude: -119.588542.

Finding the Last Known Location

To add location support to `MyFirstAndroidApp`, edit the file
`MyFirstAndroidApp.java`. First, you must add the appropriate import statements.

```
import android.location.Location;
import android.location.LocationManager;
```

Now, create a new method called `getLocation()` in your class and make a call to this
method in your `onCreate()` method. The `getLocation()` method gets the last known
location on the phone and logs it as an informational message. If the operation should
fail for some reason, the method logs an error.

The `getLocation()` method should look something like this:

```
public void getLocation() {
    try {
        LocationManager locMgr = (LocationManager)
            getSystemService(LOCATION_SERVICE);
        Location recentLoc = locMgr.
            getLastKnownLocation(LocationManager.GPS_PROVIDER);
        Log.i(DEBUG_TAG, "loc: " + recentLoc.toString());
    }
    catch (Exception e) {
        Log.e(DEBUG_TAG, "Location failed", e);
    }
}
```

Finally, your application requires special permissions to access location-based functionality. You must register this permission in your `AndroidManifest.xml` file. To add
location-based service permissions to your application, perform the following steps:

1. Double-click on the `AndroidManifest.xml` file.
2. Switch to the Permissions tab.
3. Click the Add button and choose Uses Permission.
4. In the right pane, select `android.permission.ACCESS_FINE_LOCATION`.
5. Save the file.

Now, if you run `MyFirstAndroidApp` in the emulator, your application logs the GPS
coordinates you provided to the emulator as an informational message, viewable in the
`LogCat` pane of Eclipse.

Debugging Your Application on the Hardware

You mastered running applications in the emulator. Now let's put the application on real
hardware, such as the T-Mobile G1. First, you must register your application as
Debuggable in your `AndroidManifest.xml` file. To do this, perform the following steps:

1. Double-click on the `AndroidManifest.xml` file.
2. Change to the Application tab.

3. Set the Debuggable Application Attribute to True.

4. Save the file.

You can also modify the `application` element of the `AndroidManifest.xml` file directly with the `android:debuggable` attribute, as shown here:

```
<application ... android:debuggable="true">
```

If you forget to set the `debuggable` attribute to `true`, the handset shows the dialog for waiting for the debugger to connect until you choose Force Close and update the manifest file. Debugging on the handset is like on the emulator, but with a couple of exceptions. You cannot use the emulator controls to do things such as send an SMS or configure the location to the device but you can perform real actions (true SMS, actual location data) instead.

> **Tip**
>
> If you feel especially energetic, you can continue with the Notepad Tutorial provided as part of the Android SDK documentation. You can find the Notepad exercises under the Android SDK documentation at Documentation, Getting Started, Notepad tutorial.

Summary

This chapter showed you how to create your first Android application. You started by testing your development environment using a sample application from the Android SDK, and then you created a new Android application from scratch using the Android Eclipse plug-in. You also learned how to make some quick modifications to the application, demonstrating some features you learn more about in future chapters.

In the next few chapters, you learn the finer points about defining your Android application using the application manifest file and how the application lifecycle works. You also learn how to organize your application resources, such as images and strings, for use within your application.

References and More Information

"Hello, Android" Tutorial: http://developer.android.com/guide/tutorials/hello-world.html

Notepad Tutorial: http://developer.android.com/guide/tutorials/notepad/index.html

Android Application Design Essentials

## 4

Understanding the Anatomy of an Android Application

Classical computer science classes often define a program in terms of functionality and data, and Android applications are no different. They perform tasks, display information to the screen, and act upon data from a variety of sources.

Developing Android applications for mobile devices with limited resources requires a thorough understanding of the application lifecycle. Android also uses its own terminology for these application building blocks—terms such as `Activity` and `View`. This chapter familiarizes you with the different components of Android applications and how to configure the important file every Android application must include, the Android Manifest file.

The Life Cycle of an Android Application

This section introduces you to the terminology used in Android application development and provides you with a more thorough understanding of how Android applications function and interact with one another.

Performing Application Tasks with Activities

An Android application is a collection of tasks, each of which is called an `Activity`. Each `Activity` within an application has a unique task or purpose.

The Android `Activity` class (`android.app.Activity`) is core to any Android application. Much of the time, you define and implement an `Activity` for each screen in your application. For example, a simple game application might have the following five Activities, as shown in Figure 4.1:

- **A Startup or Splash screen:** This `Activity` serves as the primary entry point to the application. It displays the application name and version information and transitions to the Main menu after a short interval.

- **A Main Menu screen:** This `Activity` acts as a switch to drive the user to the core Activities of the application. Here the users must choose what they want to do within the application.
- **A Game Play screen:** This `Activity` is where the core game play occurs.
- **A High Scores screen:** This `Activity` might display game scores or settings.
- **A Help/About screen:** This `Activity` might display the information the user might need to play the game.

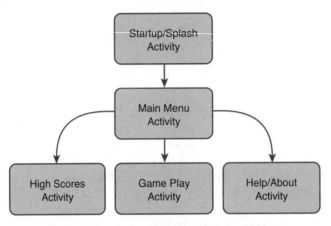

Figure 4.1   A simple game with five activities.

Transitioning Between Activities with Intents

As previously mentioned, Android applications can have multiple entry points. There is no `main()` function, such as you find in iPhone development. Instead, a specific `Activity` can be designated as the main `Activity` to launch by default within the `AndroidManifest.xml` file; we talk more about this file in the "Defining Your Application Using the Android Manifest File" section of this chapter.

Other Activities might be designated to launch under specific circumstances. For example, a music application might designate a generic `Activity` to launch by default from the Application menu, but also define specific alternative entry point Activities for accessing specific music playlists by playlist ID or artists by name.

Launching a New Activity by Class Name

You can start activities in several ways. The simplest method is to use the Application Context object to call the `startActivity()` method, which takes a single parameter, an `Intent`.

An `Intent` (`android.content.Intent`) is an asynchronous message mechanism used by the Android operating system to match task requests with the appropriate

`Activity` or `Service` (launching it, if necessary) and to dispatch broadcast `Intents` events to the system at large.

For now, though, we focus on `Intents` and how they are used with Activities. The following line of code calls the `startActivity()` method with an explicit `Intent`. This Intent requests the launch of the target `Activity` named `MyDrawActivity` by its class. This class is implemented elsewhere within the package.

```
startActivity(new Intent(getApplicationContext(),
➥MyDrawActivity.class));
```

This line of code might be sufficient for some applications, which simply transition from one `Activity` to the next. However, you can use the `Intent` mechanism in a much more robust manner. For example, you can use the `Intent` structure to pass data between Activities.

Creating Intents with Action and Data

You've seen the simplest case to use an `Intent` to launch a class by name. Intents need not specify the component or class they want to launch explicitly. Instead, you can create an Intent Filter and register it within the Android Manifest file. The Android operating system attempts to resolve the `Intent` requirements and launch the appropriate `Activity` based on the filter criteria.

The guts of the `Intent` object are composed of two main parts: the *action* to be performed and the *data* to be acted upon. You can also specify action/data pairs using `Intent Action` types and `Uri` objects. As you saw in the last chapter, a `Uri` object represents a string that gives the location and name of an object. Therefore, an `Intent` is basically saying "do this" (the action) to "that" (the `Uri` describing what resource to do the action to).

The most common action types are defined in the `Intent` class, including `ACTION_MAIN` (describes the main entry point of an `Activity`) and `ACTION_EDIT` (used in conjunction with a `Uri` to the data edited). You also find `Action` types that generate integration points with Activities in other applications, such as the Browser or Phone Dialer.

Launching an Activity Belonging to Another Application

Initially, your application might be starting only Activities defined within its own package. However, with the appropriate permissions, applications might also launch external Activities within other applications. For example, a Customer Relationship Management (CRM) application might launch the Contacts application to browse the Contact database, choose a specific contact, and return that Contact's unique identifier to the CRM application for use.

Here is an example of how to create a simple `Intent` with a predefined `Action` (`ACTION_DIAL`) to launch the Phone Dialer with a specific phone number to dial in the form of a simple `Uri` object.

```
Uri number = Uri.parse(tel:5555551212);
Intent dial = new Intent(Intent.ACTION_DIAL, number);
startActivity(dial);
```

A list of commonly used Google application Intents can be found at http://d.android.com/guide/appendix/g-app-intents.html. Also available is the developer managed Registry of Intents protocols at OpenIntents, found at www.openintents.org/en/intentstable, which has a growing list of intents available from third-party applications and those within the Android SDK.

Passing Additional Information Using Intents

You can also include additional data in an `Intent`. The `Extras` property of an `Intent` is stored in a `Bundle` object. The `Intent` class also has a number of helper methods for getting and setting name/value pairs for many common datatypes.

For example, the following `Intent` includes two extra pieces of information, a `string` value and a `boolean`:

```
Intent intent = new Intent(this, MyActivity.class);
intent.putExtra("SomeStringData","Foo");
intent.putExtra("SomeBooleanData",false);
```

> **Tip**
>
> The Android convention for the key name for "extra" data is to include a package prefix, for example, `com.androidbook.Multimedia.SomeStringData`.

Organizing Activities and Intents in Your Application Using Menus

As previously mentioned, your application likely has a number of screens, each with its own `Activity`. There is a close relationship between menus, Activities and Intents. You'll often see a menu used in two different ways with Activities and Intents.

- **Main Menu:** Acts as a switch in which each menu item launches a different `Activity` in your application. For instance, menu items for launching the Play Game `Activity`, the High Scores `Activity`, and the Help `Activity`.

- **Drill-Down:** Acts as a directory in which each menu item launches the same `Activity`, but each item passes in different data as part of the `Intent` (for example, a menu of all database records). Choosing a specific item might launch the Edit Record `Activity`, passing in that particular item's unique identifier.

Working with Services and Broadcast Receivers

Trying to wrap your head around Activities, Intents, Intent Filters, and the lot when you start with Android development can be daunting. We have tried to distill everything you need to know to start writing Android applications with multiple `Activity` classes, but we'd be remiss if we didn't mention that there's a lot more here, much of which is discussed throughout the book with practical examples.

Specifically, we haven't talked about how `Intent` objects figure into the creation of a `Service` or a `Broadcast`. However, we need to give you a "heads up" about this because we talk about these concepts later in this chapter when configuring the Android Manifest file for your application.

Working with Services

An Android `Service` is basically an `Activity` without a user interface. It can run as a background process or act much like a Web service does, processing requests from third parties. You can use Intents and Activities to launch Services using the `startService()`, `bindService()` methods. Any `Services` exposed by an Android application must be registered in the Android Manifest file.

> **Note**
>
> We talk a lot more about Services in Chapter 17, "Working with Services."

Working with Broadcasts

`Intent` objects serve yet another purpose. You can broadcast an `Intent` object (via a call to `broadcastIntent()`) to the Android system, and any application interested can receive that broadcast (called a `BroadcastReceiver`). Your application might do both send and listen actions for such `Intent` objects. These types in `Intent` objects are generally used to inform the greater system that something interesting has happened and use special `Intent Action` types.

For example, the `Intent Action ACTION_BATTERY_LOW` broadcasts a warning when the battery is low. If your application is a battery-hogging `Service` of some kind, you might want to listen for this `Broadcast` and shut down your `Service` until the battery power is sufficient. You can register to listen for battery/charge level changes by listening for the broadcast `Intent` object with the `Intent Action ACTION_BATTERY_CHANGED`. There are also broadcast `Intent` objects for other interesting system events, such as SD card state changes, applications being installed or removed, and the wallpaper being changed.

> **Note**
>
> We talk more about hardware and the battery in Chapter 15, "Using Android's Optional Hardware APIs," in which you see practical examples of the use of `BroadcastReceiver` objects.

The Lifecycle of an Android Activity

Android applications can be multiprocess, and the Android operating system allows multiple applications to run concurrently, provided memory and processing power is available. Applications can have background processes, and applications can be interrupted and paused when events such as phone calls occur. There can be only one active application visible to the user at a time—specifically, a single application `Activity` will be in the foreground at any given time.

The Android operating system keeps track of all `Activity` objects running by placing them on an `Activity` stack. When a new `Activity` starts, the `Activity` on the
top of the stack (current foreground `Activity`) pauses, and the new `Activity` pushes
onto the top of the stack. When that `Activity` finishes, that `Activity` is removed from
the activity stack, and the previous `Activity` in the stack resumes.

Android applications are responsible for managing their state and their memory,
resources, and data. They must pause and resume seamlessly. Understanding the different
states within the `Activity` lifecycle is the first step to designing and developing robust
Android applications.

Using `Activity` **Callbacks to Manage Application State and Resources**

Different important state changes within the `Activity` lifecycle are punctuated by a
series of important method callbacks. These callbacks are shown in Figure 4.2.

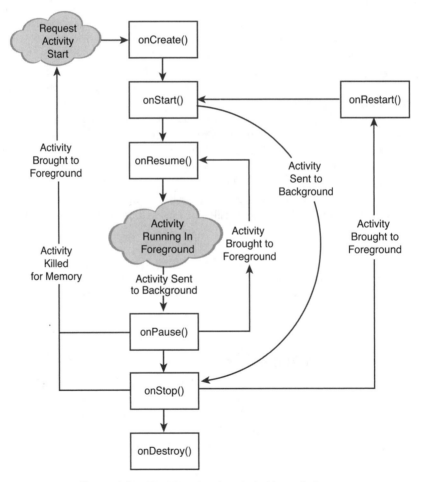

Figure 4.2   The lifecycle of an Android `Activity`.

Now let's describe some of the most important `Activity` callbacks, when they are called, and what they are used for.

Initializing Static Activity Data in `onCreate()`

When an `Activity` first starts, the `onCreate()` method is called. The `onCreate()` method has a single parameter, a `Bundle`, which will be null if this is a newly started `Activity`. If this `Activity` was killed for memory reasons and is now restarted, the `Bundle` contains the previous state information for this `Activity` so that it can reinitiate. It is appropriate to perform any setup, such as layout and data binding, in the `onCreate()` method. This includes calls to the `setContentView()` method.

Initializing and Retrieving Activity Data in `onResume()`

When the `Activity` reaches the top of the activity stack and becomes the foreground process, the `onResume()` method is called. Although the `Activity` might not be visible yet to the user, this is the most appropriate place to retrieve any instances to resources (exclusive or otherwise) that the `Activity` needs to run. Often, these resources are the most process-intensive, so we only keep these around while the `Activity` is in the foreground.

> **Tip**
>
> The `onResume()` method is the appropriate place to start audio, video, and animations.

Stopping, Saving and Releasing `Activity` Data in `onPause()`

When another `Activity` moves to the top of the activity stack, the current `Activity` is informed that it is being pushed down the activity stack by way of the `onPause()` method.

Here, the `Activity` should stop any audio, video, and animations it started in the `onResume()` method. This is also where you must deactivate resources such as database `Cursor` objects if you have opted to manage them manually as opposed to having them managed automatically.

> **Note**
>
> Android provides a number of helper utilities for managing queries and Cursor objects. We talk more about these methods in Chapter 9, "Using Android Data and Storage APIs."

The `onPause()` method can also be the last chance for the `Activity` to clean up and release any resources it does not need while in the background. You need to save any uncommitted data here, in case your application does not resume.

> **Tip**
>
> Android applications with data input do not need to follow the typical web form template (data fields plus Submit and Cancel button). Instead, data can be saved as the user inputs each field, thus simplifying the user interface and the `onPause()` method. A button should be provided for Cancel, but Save can be implicit.

The `Activity` can also save state information to `Activity`-specific preferences, or applicationwide preferences. We talk more about preferences in Chapter 9.

The `Activity` needs to perform anything in the `onPause()` method quickly. The new foreground `Activity` will not be started until the `onPause()` method returns.

> **Caution**
>
> Generally speaking, any resources and data retrieved in the `onResume()` method should be released in the `onPause()` method. If not, there is a chance that these resources can't be cleanly released if the process is terminated.

What's New in Android 1.5

Two new `Activity` callbacks were introduced in Android 1.5: `onUserInteraction()` and `onUserLeaveHint()`.

The `onUserInteraction()` callback occurs when a key, touch, or trackball event initiates while your `Activity` runs. Only the initial event causes this callback—you will not get a call for the key down, key pressed, or key up events, but only for the initial user interaction.

The `onUserLeaveHint()` callback occurs only immediately before the `onPause()` callback when your `Activity` is about to transition to the background as a result of user interaction (such as pressing the Back or Home keys). This callback does not occur if the `Activity` is paused due to some another `Activity` coming into the foreground.

Used together, you can see how these helpful new callbacks can manage status bar notifications, especially when the user wants to cancel the current operation.

Avoiding *Activity* Objects Being Killed

Under low-memory conditions, the Android operating system can kill the process for any `Activity` that has been paused, stopped, or destroyed. This essentially means that any `Activity` not in the foreground is subject to a possible shutdown.

If the `Activity` is killed after `onPause()`, the `onStop()` and `onDestroy()` methods might not be called. The more resources released by an `Activity` in the `onPause()` method, the less likely the `Activity` is to be killed while in the background.

The act of killing an `Activity` does not remove it from the activity stack. Instead, the `Activity` state is saved into a `Bundle` object, assuming the `Activity` implements and uses `onSaveInstanceState()` for custom data, though some `View` data is automatically saved. When the user returns to the `Activity` later, the `onCreate()` method is called again, this time with a valid `Bundle` object as the parameter.

> **Tip**
>
> So why does it matter if your application is killed when it is straightforward to resume?
> Well, it's primarily about responsiveness. The application designer must strike a delicate
> balance between maintaining data and the resources it needs to resume quickly, without
> degrading the CPU and system resources while paused in the background.

Saving *Activity* **State into a** *Bundle* **with** *onSaveInstanceState()*

If an `Activity` is vulnerable to being killed by the Android operating system due to low
memory, the `Activity` can save state information to a `Bundle` object using the
`onSaveInstanceState()` callback method. This call is not guaranteed under all circumstances, so use the `onPause()` method for essential data commits.

> **Tip**
>
> You might want to use the `onSaveInstanceState()` method to store nonessential infor-
> mation such as uncommitted form field data or any other state information that might
> make the user's experience with your application less cumbersome.

When this `Activity` is returned to later, this `Bundle` will be passed into the
`onCreate()` method, allowing the `Activity` to return to the exact state it was in when
the `Activity` paused. You can also read `Bundle` information after the `onStart()` callback method using the `onRestoreInstanceState()` callback.

Destroy Static `Activity` **Data in** `onDestroy()`

When an `Activity` is being destroyed, the `onDestroy()` method is called. The
`onDestroy()` method is called for one of two reasons: The `Activity` has completed its
lifecycle voluntarily, or the `Activity` is being killed by the Android operating system
because it needs the resources.

> **Tip**
>
> The `isFinishing()` method returns false if the `Activity` has been killed by the
> Android operating system. This method can also be helpful in the `onPause()` method.
> However, the `Activity` might still be killed in the `onStop()` method at a later time.

Managing `Activity` **Transitions**

In the course of the lifetime of an Android application, the user might transition
between a number of different `Activity` instances. At times, there might be multiple
`Activity` instances on the activity stack. Developers need to pay attention to the lifecycle of each `Activity` during these transitions.

Some `Activity` instances—such as the application splash/startup screen—are shown and then permanently discarded when the Main menu screen `Activity` takes over. The user cannot return to the splash screen `Activity` without relaunching the application.

Tip

In this case, use the `startActivity()` and appropriate `finish()` methods.

Other `Activity` transitions are temporary, such as a child `Activity` displaying a dialog box, and then returning to the original `Activity` (which was paused on the activity stack and now resumes). In this case, the parent `Activity` launches the child `Activity` and expects a result.

Tip

In this case, use the `startActivityForResult()` and `onActivityResult()` methods.

Defining Your Application Using the Android Manifest File

The `AndroidManifest.xml` file is a specially formatted XML file that must accompany each Android application. This file contains important information about the application's identity. Here you define the application's name and version information and what application components the application relies upon, what permissions the application requires to run, and other application configuration information.

Tip

If you use Eclipse with the Android Plug-In for Eclipse (ADT), the Android project Wizard creates the initial `AndroidManifest.xml` file for you.

The manifest resides at the top level of your Android project. Again, if you use the ADT, you can use the Android Manifest file editor (Figure 4.3).

You can also edit the XML directly by clicking on the far-right tab of the File Editor, as shown in Figure 4.4.

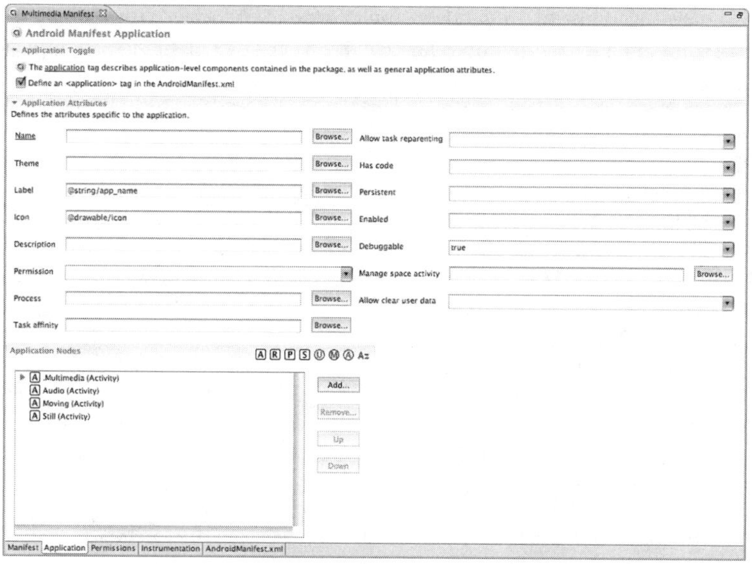

Figure 4.3   The Android Manifest file in the Eclipse File Editor.

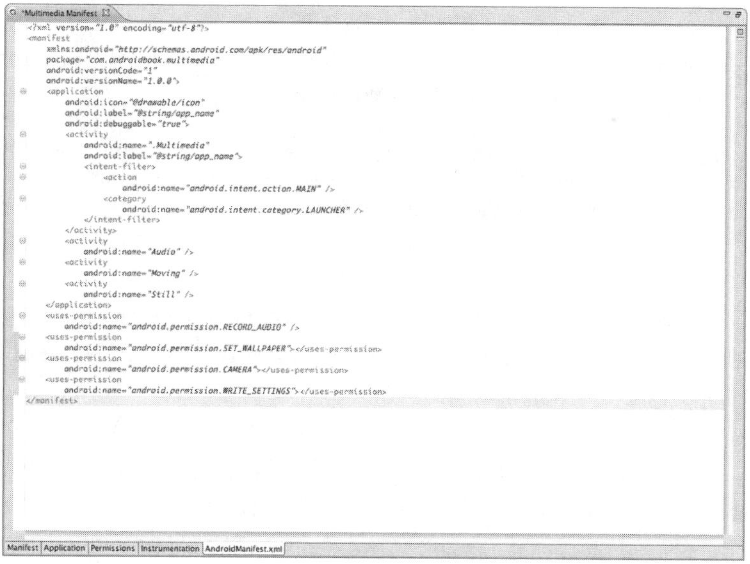

Figure 4.4   Editing the underlying XML of the Android Manifest file.

Most Android Manifest files include a single `<manifest>` tag with a single `<application>` tag. Here is a sample `AndroidManifest.xml` file for an application called Multimedia:

```xml
<?xml version="1.0" encoding="utf-8"?>
<manifest
    xmlns:android="http://schemas.android.com/apk/res/android"
    package="com.androidbook.multimedia"
    android:versionCode="1"
    android:versionName="1.0.0">
    <application
        android:icon="@drawable/icon"
        android:label="@string/app_name"
        android:debuggable="true">
        <activity
            android:name=".MainMenuActivity"
            android:label="@string/app_name">
            <intent-filter>
                <action android:name="android.intent.action.MAIN" />
                <category
                    android:name="android.intent.category.LAUNCHER"/>
            </intent-filter>
        </activity>
        <activity android:name="AudioActivity" />
        <activity android:name="MovingActivity" />
        <activity android:name="StillActivity" />
    </application>
    <uses-permission android:name="android.permission.RECORD_AUDIO" />
    <uses-permission android:name="android.permission.SET_WALLPAPER"/>
    <uses-permission android:name="android.permission.CAMERA"/>
    <uses-permission android:name="android.permission.WRITE_SETTINGS"/>
</manifest>
```

Now let's sum up what this file tells us about the Multimedia application:

- The application uses the package name `com.androidbook.multimedia`.
- The application version name is 1.0.0.
- The application version code is 1.
- The application name and label are stored in the resource string called `@string/app_name` within the `/res/values/strings.xml` resource file.
- The application icon is the graphic file called `icon` (could be a PNG, JPG or GIF) within the `/res/drawable` directory.
- The application has four Activities (`MainMenuActivity`, `AudioActivity`, `MovingActivity`, and `StillActivity`).
- The `MainMenuActivity` Activity is the primary entry point for the application.

- The application requires the following permissions to run: the ability to record audio, the ability to set the wallpaper on the device, the ability to access the built-in camera, and the ability to write settings.

Now let's talk about some of these important configurations in detail.

> **Caution**
>
> Although you can use an `@string` reference for some fields, such as the `android:versionName`, some publishing systems don't support this. For more information on publishing, see Chapter 20, "Selling Your Android Application."

Managing Your Application's Identity

Your application's Android Manifest file defines the application properties. The package name must be defined within the Android Manifest file within the `<manifest>` tag using the `package` attribute like such:

```
<manifest
    xmlns:android="http://schemas.android.com/apk/res/android"
    package="com.androidbook.multimedia"
    android:versionCode="1"
    android:versionName="1.0.0">
```

Versioning Your Application

Versioning your application appropriately is vital to maintaining your application in the field. Intelligent versioning can help reduce confusion and make product support and upgrades simpler. There are two different version attributes defined within the `<manifest>` tag: the version name and the version code.

The version name (`android:versionName`) is a user-friendly, developer-defined version attribute. This information is displayed to users when they manage applications on their device and when they download the application from marketplaces. Developers use this version information to keep track of their application versions in the field. We discuss appropriate application versioning for mobile applications in detail in Chapter 18, "The Mobile Software Development Process."

The Android operating system uses the version code (`android:versionCode`) that is a numeric attribute to manage application upgrades. We discuss the version code further in Chapter 20.

Providing Your Application with a Name and Application Icon

You can set the application icon (`android:icon`) and application friendly name (`android:label`) as attributes within the `<application>` tag of the Android Manifest file. In this example, we set them to assets defined within the application graphic and string resources:

```
<application android:icon="@drawable/icon"
    android:label="@string/app_name">
```

> **Tip**
>
> We see a lot of Android applications on the market using the default icon. Making a cus-
> tom icon for your Android application gives it pizzazz and differentiates your application
> from others. Making a custom icon is easy; simply create a 48x48 pixel PNG file, add it as
> a Drawable resource to your application, and set the android:icon property to your
> new icon.

You can also set optional attributes like the application description (android:
description).

Registering Activities and Other Application Components

Each Activity within the application must be defined within the Android Manifest file
with an <activity> tag. For example, the following XML excerpt defines an
Activity class called AudioActivity:

```
<activity android:name="AudioActivity" />
```

This Activity must be defined as a class within the com.androidbook.multimedia
package.

> **Caution**
>
> You must define the <activity> tag for an Activity or it will not launch. It is quite
> common for developers to implement an Activity and then try to troubleshoot why it
> isn't running properly, only to realize they forgot to register it in the Android Manifest file.
> Until they look through the LogCat output, the error merely looks like a typical crash, too,
> further confusing the developer.

Designating a Primary Entry Point Activity for Your Application Using an Intent Filter

An Activity can be designated as the primary entry point by configuring its Intent
Filter in the application's AndroidManifest.xml file with the MAIN action type and
the LAUNCHER category.

The following tag of XML configures the Activity called MainMenuActivity as
the primary launching point of the application:

```
<activity
    android:name=".MainMenuActivity"
    android:label="@string/app_name">
    <intent-filter>
        <action android:name="android.intent.action.MAIN" />
        <category android:name="android.intent.category.LAUNCHER"/>
    </intent-filter>
</activity>
```

Configuring Other `Intent` Filters

The Android operating system uses Intent filters to resolve implicit `Intents`. That is, `Intents` that do not specify the `Activity` or Component they want launched. Intent filters can be applied to `Activities`, `Services`, and `BroadcastReceivers`. The filter declares that this component is open to receiving any `Intent` sent to the Android operating system that matches its criteria.

Intent filters are defined using the `<intent-filter>` tag and must contain at least one `<action>` tag but can also contain other information, such as `<category>` and `<data>` blocks. Here we have a sample intent filter block, which might be found within an `<activity>` block:

```
<intent-filter>
    <action android:name="android.intent.action.VIEW" />
        <category android:name="android.intent.category.BROWSABLE" />
        <category android:name="android.intent.category.DEFAULT" />
        <data android:scheme="geoname"/>
</intent-filter>
```

This intent filter definition uses a predefined action called VIEW, the action for viewing particular content. It is also BROWSABLE and uses a scheme of "geoname" so that when a Uri starts with "geoname://", the activity with this intent filter launches. You can read more about this particular intent filter in Chapter 11, "Using Location-Based Services (LBS) APIs."

> **Tip**
>
> You can define custom actions unique to your application. If you do so, be sure to document these actions if you want them to be used by third parties.

A single `Activity` can serve multiple purposes. Instead of putting all intent filters under that single `Activity`, you can use aliases to group different intent filters and other metadata with the same underlying `Activity`. You achieve this by using the `<activity-alias>` tag.

Registering Services and BroadcastReceivers

Activities, Services, and BroadcastReceivers must be registered within the Android Manifest file. Services are also registered using the `<service>` tag, and BroadcastReceivers are registered using the `<receiver>` tag. Both Services and BroadcastReceivers use `Intent` filters.

> **Note**
>
> You learn more about Services in Chapter 17 and use BroadcastReceiver objects in later chapters of the book.

Registering Content Providers

If your application acts as a Content Provider, effectively exposing a shared data service for use by other applications, it must declare this capability within the Android Manifest file using the `<provider>` tag. Configuring a Content Provider involves determining what subsets of data are shared and what permissions are required to access them, if any.

> **Note**
> We will talk more about Content Providers in Chapter 9.

Working with Permissions

The Android operating system has been locked down so that applications have limited capability to adversely affect operations outside their process space. Instead, Android applications run within the bubble of their own virtual machine, with their own Linux user account (and related permissions).

Registering Permissions Your Application Requires

Android applications have no permissions by default. Instead, any permissions for shared resources or privileged access—whether its shared data, such as the Contacts database, or access to underlying hardware, such as the built-in camera—must be explicitly registered within the Android Manifest file. These permissions will be granted when the application is installed.

> **Tip**
> When users install the application, they are informed what permissions the application requires to run and must approve these permissions. Request only the permissions your application requires.

The following XML excerpt for the preceding Android Manifest file defines a permission using the `<uses-permission>` tag to gain access to the built-in camera.

```
<uses-permission android:name="android.permission.CAMERA" />
```

A complete list of the permissions can be found in the `android.Manifest.permission` class. Your application manifest should include only the permissions required to run. The user is informed what permissions each Android application requires at install time.

> **Tip**
> You might find that, in certain cases, permissions are not enforced (you can operate without the permission). In these cases, it would be prudent to request the permission anyway for two reasons. First, because the user will be informed that the application is performing those sensitive actions, and second, because the permission could be enforced in a later SDK version.

Registering Permissions Your Application Grants to Other Applications

Applications can also define their own permissions by using the `<permission>` tag. Permissions must be described and then applied to specific application components, such as Activities, using the `android:permission` attribute.

Tip

Use Java-style scoping for unique naming of application permissions (for example, `com.androidbook.MultiMedia.ViewMatureMaterial`).

Permissions can be enforced at several points:

- When starting an `Activity` or `Service`
- When accessing data provided by a Content Provider
- At the function call level
- When sending or receiving broadcasts by an `Intent`

Permissions can have three primary protection levels: `normal`, `dangerous`, and `signature`. The `normal` protection level is a good default for fine-grained permission enforcement within the application. The `dangerous` protection level is used for higher risk activities, which might adversely affect the device. Finally, the `signature` protection level permits any application signed with the same certificate to use that component for controlled application interoperability.

Note

You learn more about application signing in Chapter 20.

Permissions can be broken down into categories, called `permission groups`, which describe or warn why specific Activities require permission. For example, permissions might be applied for Activities that expose sensitive user data like location and personal information (`android.permission-group.LOCATION` and `android.permission-group.PERSONAL_INFO`), access underlying hardware (`android.permission-group.HARDWARE_CONTROLS`), or perform operations that might incur fees to the user (`android.permission-group.COST_MONEY`). A complete list of permission groups is available within the `Manifest.permission_group` class.

Enforcing Content Provider Permissions at the `Uri` Level

You can also enforce fine-grained permissions at the `Uri` level using the `<grant-uri-permissions>` tag.

Specifying Application Input Hardware and Software Requirements

Android 1.5 introduced a tag in the manifest file called `<uses-configuration>`. This tag identifies all hardware and software input configurations required by the application.

For example, if the application requires only touch screen input using a finger, the following `<uses-configuration>` tag would be included within the `<manifest>` tag:

```
<uses-configuration android:reqTouchScreen="finger" />
```

There are different configuration attributes for five-way navigation, the hardware keyboard and keyboard types; navigation devices such as the directional pad, trackball, and wheel; and touch screen settings. The configurations supported at this time are shown in Table 4.1.

Table 4.1 **Configuration Attributes Available with the** `<uses-configuration>` **Manifest Tag**

Attribute Name	Attribute Description	Attribute Values
`android:reqFiveWayNav`	Whether the application requires a five-way navigation control such as a directional pad, trackball, or navigation wheel.	`true`, `false`
`android:reqHardKeyboard`	Whether the application requires a hardware keyboard.	`true`, `false`
`android:reqKeyboardType`	What type of keyboard is required, if any. Note: These keyboards can be hardware keyboards or software keyboards.	"`undefined`" (default) "`nokeys`" No keyboard required. "`qwerty`" Standard QWERTY keyboard required. "`twelvekey`" Twelve-key keypad required.
`android:reqNavigation`	What type of navigation device is required, if any.	"`undefined`" (default) "`nonav`" No navigation control required. "`dpad`" Directional pad required. "`trackball`" Trackball required. "`wheel`" Navigation wheel required.
`android:reqTouchScreen`	What type of touch screen is required, if any.	"`undefined`" (default) "`notouch`" No touch screen required. "`stylus`" Stylus touch screen required. "`finger`" Finger touch screen required.

There is no "OR" support within a given attribute. If your application requires any hardware keyboard and touch screen input using a finger or a stylus, you need to include two separate <uses-configuration> tags in your manifest file, as follows:

```
<uses-configuration android:reqHardKeyboard="true"
    android:reqTouchScreen="finger" />
<uses-configuration android:reqHardKeyboard="true"
    android:reqTouchScreen="stylus" />
```

Tip

If an application requires some sort of directional navigation control but isn't picky about what kind, simply set the android:reqFiveWayNav attribute to true and do not include the android:reqNavigation attribute, which defaults to the value "undefined."

Working with Libraries and Android SDK Versions

You can specify the minimum Android SDK your application requires and register any secondary packages your application links to within the Android Manifest file.

Specifying the Minimum Android SDK Version

By default, Android applications are assumed to be compatible with all full versions of the Android SDK (1.0 and up, no beta versions).

If your application requires a different SDK version to run, you must specify this explicitly using the <uses-sdk> tag within the <manifest> tag block. The <uses-sdk> tag has a single attribute called android:minSdkVersion, which is an integer.

This value does not directly correspond to the SDK version. Instead, it is the revision of the API Level associated with that SDK set by the developers of the Android SDK. You need to check the SDK documentation to determine the API level value for each version.

For example, if your application requires APIs introduced in Android SDK 1.1, you would check that SDK's documentation and find that Android SDK 1.1 (Release 1) is defined as API Level 2. Therefore, add the following to your Android Manifest file within the <manifest> tag block:

```
<uses-sdk android:minSdkVersion="2" />
```

Whereas, if your application requires Android SDK 1.5 R1, your minimum SDK version would be 3, like this:

```
<uses-sdk android:minSdkVersion="3" />
```

It's that simple. You need to use the lowest SDK version possible because this information is checked at install time, and you want your application to be compatible with the largest pool of handsets available.

The `minSdkVersion` tag is now required to publish applications on the Android Market. We talk more about preparing your application for publication in Chapter 20.

Linking to Other Packages

By default, every application is linked to the standard Android packages (such as `android.app`) and is aware of its own package. However, if your application links to additional packages, they must be registered within the `<application>` tag of the Android Manifest file using the `<uses-library>` tag. For example:

```
<uses-library android:name="com.mylibrary.stuff" />
```

Defining Other Application Configuration Settings in the Manifest File

We have now covered the basics of the Android Manifest file, but there are many other settings configurable within the Android Manifest file using different tag blocks, not to mention attributes within each tag we already discussed.

Some other features you can configure within the Android Manifest file include

- Setting applicationwide themes as `<application>` tag attributes
- Configuring instrumentation settings using the `<instrumentation>` tag

For more detailed descriptions of each property and attribute available (and there are many), check the Android documentation.

Summary

We tried to strike a balance between providing a thorough reference without overwhelming you with details you won't need to know when developing the average Android application. Instead, we focused on the details you need to know to move forward developing Android applications and to understand every example provided within this book.

`Activity` and `View` classes are the core building blocks of any Android application. Each `Activity` performs a specific task within the application, often with a single user interface screen consisting of `View` widgets. Each `Activity` is responsible for managing its own resources and data through a series of lifecycle callbacks. The transition from one `Activity` to the next is achieved through the `Intent` mechanism. An `Intent` object acts as an asynchronous message that the Android operating system processes and responds to by launching the appropriate `Activity` or `Service`. You can also use `Intent` objects to broadcast systemwide events to any interested BroadcastReceivers listening.

Each Android application has a specially formatted XML file called `AndroidManifest.xml`. This file describes the application's name and version information, and what permissions it requires to run and what application components it contains. The Android Manifest file is used by the Android operating system to install and run the application.

## 5

Managing Application Resources

The well-written application accesses its resources programmatically instead of hard coding them into the source code. This is done for a variety of reasons. Storing application resources in a resource table is a more organized approach to development and makes the code more readable and maintainable. Externalizing resources such as strings make it easier to localize applications for different languages and geographic regions.

In this chapter, you learn how Android applications store and access important resources such as strings, graphics, and other data. You also learn how to organize Android resources within the project files for localization and different device configurations.

What Are Resources?

All applications are composed of two parts: functionality and resources. The functionality is the code that determines how your application behaves. This includes any algorithms that make the application run. Resources include text strings, images and icons, audio files, videos, and other assets used by the application.

Where and How Application Resources Are Stored

Android resource files are stored separately from the java class files in the Android project. Most common resource types are stored in XML. You can also store raw data files and graphics as resources.

The Resource Directory Hierarchy

Resources are organized in a strict directory hierarchy within the Android project. All resources must be stored under the /res project directory in specially named subdirectories that must be lowercase.

Different resource types are stored in different directories. The most common resource subdirectories generated by default when you create an Android project using the Eclipse plug-in are shown in Table 5.1.

Table 5.1   Default Android Resource Directories

Resource Subdirectory	Purpose
/res/drawable/	Graphics Resources
/res/layout/	User Interface Resources, Widgets
/res/values/	Simple Data like Strings, Color Values, and such

Using the Android Asset Packaging Tool

If you use the Eclipse with the Android Development Tools Plug-In (ADT), you find that adding resources to your project is simple. The plug-in detects new resources when you add them to your project resource directory /res and automatically uses an underlying Android Software Development Kit (SDK) tool called the Android Asset Packaging Tool (aapt) to compile your resources so that you can access them programmatically.

The aapt packages your application for installation on the emulator or the hardware, but it also compiles the appropriate application resources into an automatically generated source file called R.java, which you find in the /src directory of your project. Your application relies on the R.java file, as it exposes the resource table for your application.

If you use a different development environment, you need to use the aapt tool command-line interface to compile your resources and package your application binaries to deploy to the phone or emulator. You can find the aapt in the /tools directory of the Android SDK.

> Tip
>
> Build scripts can use the aapt for automation purposes and to create archives of assets and compile them efficiently for your application. The tool can be configured using command–line arguments to package only including assets for a specific device configuration or target language, for example. All resources for all targets are included by default.

Resource Value Types

Android applications rely on many different types of resources, such as text labels, image graphics, and color schemes, for user interface design.

These resources are stored in the /res directory of your Android project in a strict (but reasonably flexible) set of directories and files. All resources filenames must be lowercase and simple (letters, numbers, and underscores only).

The resource types supported by the Android SDK and how they are stored within the project are shown in Table 5.2.

Table 5.2   How Different Resource Types are Stored in Android Project Resource Directories

Resource Type of	Required Directory	Filename	Key XML Element, if applicable
Strings	/res/values/	**strings.xml (suggested)**	<string>
Arrays of Strings	/res/values/	**arrays.xml (suggested)**	<string-array>
Color Values	/res/values/	**colors.xml (suggested)**	<color>
Dimensions	/res/values/	**dimens.xml (suggested)**	<dimen>
Simple Drawables (Paintable)	/res/values/	**drawables.xml (suggested)**	<drawable>
Bitmap Graphics	/res/drawable/	Examples: **img.png, img.jpg, img.9.png, img.gif, red_oval.xml**	Supported graphics files or Drawable definition XML files like shapes.
Animation Sequences (Tweening)	/res/anim/	Examples: **fancy_anim1.xml, fancy_anim2.xml**	<set>, <alpha>, <scale>, <translate>, <rotate>
Menu Files	/res/menu/	Examples: **my_menu1.xml, more_options.xml**	<menu>
XML Files	/res/xml/	Examples: **some.xml, more.xml**	Defined by the developer.
Raw Files	/res/raw/	Examples: **some_audio.mp3, some_video.mp4, some_text.txt**	
Layout Files	/res/layout/	Examples: **start_screen.xml, main_screen.xml, help_screen.xml**	Varies. Must be a layout element.
Styles and Themes	/res/values/	**styles.xml, themes.xml** (Suggested)	<style>

Tip

Some resource files, such as animation files and graphics, are referenced by variables named from their filename, so name your files appropriately.

Storing Different Resource Value Types

The aapt traverses all properly formatted files in the /res directory hierarchy and generates the class file R.java in your source code directory /src to access all variables.

Later in this chapter, we cover how to store and use each different resource type in detail, but for now, you need to understand that different types of resources are stored in different ways.

Storing Simple Resource Types Like Strings

Simple resource value types like strings, colors, dimensions, and other primitives are stored under the /res/values project directory in XML files. Each resource file under the /res/values directory must begin with the following XML header:

```
<?xml version="1.0" encoding="utf-8"?>
```

Next comes the root node <resources> followed by the specific resource element types like <string> or <color>. Each resource is defined using a different element name.

Although the XML file names are arbitrary, the best practice is to store your resources in separate files to reflect their types, such as strings.xml, colors.xml, and so on. However, there's nothing stopping the developers from creating multiple resource files for a given type, such as two separate xml files called bright_colors.xml and muted_colors.xml, if they so choose.

Storing Graphics, Animations, Menus, and Files

In addition to simple resource types stored in the /res/values directory, you can also store animations, graphics, arbitrary XML files, and raw files as resources. These types of resources are not stored in the /res/values directory, but instead stored in specially named directories according to their type. For example, you can include graphics in the /res/drawable directory. Again, make sure you name these files appropriately because the resource name will be derived from the filename. For example, a file called flag.png in the /res/drawable directory will be given the name R.drawable. flag.

Resource Naming Conventions

Call us old school, but we still believe in naming primitive resources according to their types using Hungarian Notation or something like it. This helps avoid naming clashes and confusion in code and can make porting easier and less prone to error. We know Java has reflection, and you can always figure out what type an object is, but we find it useful to differentiate variables visually. For example, we can tell that strSoups is a string, whereas astrSoups is a string-array.

Accessing Resources Programmatically

Developers access specific application resources using the `R.java` class file and its sub-classes, which are automatically generated when you add resources to your project (if you use Eclipse). You can refer to any resource identifier in your project by name. For example, the following string resource named hello is accessed in the code as:

```
R.string.hello
```

This variable is not the actual data associated with the string named hello. Instead, you use this resource identifier to retrieve the resource of that type (which happens to be string).

For example, a simple way to retrieve the string text is to call:

```
String myString = getResources().getString(R.string.hello);
```

First, you retrieve the Resources instance for your application Context (`android.content.Context`) which is, in this case, `this` because the Activity class extends Context. Then you use the Resources instance to get the appropriate kind of resource you want. You find that the Resources class (`android.content.res.Resources`) has methods for every kind of resource.

Before we go any further, we find it can be helpful to dig in and create some resources, so let's create a simple example. Don't worry if you don't understand every aspect of the exercise. You can find out more about each different resource type later in this chapter.

An Example: Setting Simple Resource Values Using Eclipse

Developers can define the simpler resource types by editing resource XML files manually and using the aapt to compile them and generate the `R.java` file or by using the handy ADT Plug-Ins built in the resource editor.

To illustrate how to set resources using the Eclipse plug-in, let's create a new Android project called ResourceRoundup.

Tip

You can find the ResourceRoundup project on the CD provided at the end of this book or online at the book Web site.

After you create the new project, navigate to the `/res/values/strings.xml` file in Eclipse and double click on the file to edit it. Your `strings.xml` resource file opens in the right pane and should look something like Figure 5.1.

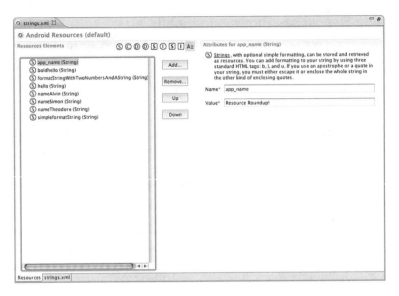

Figure 5.1   The string resource file in the Eclipse Resource Editor (Editor view).

There are two tabs at the bottom of this pane. The Resources tab provides a friendly method to insert primitive resource types such as strings, colors, and dimension resources easily. The `strings.xml` tab shows the raw XML resource file you are creating. Sometimes, editing the XML file manually is much faster, especially if you add a number of new resources.

Click the `strings.xml` tab, and your pane should look something like Figure 5.2.

Figure 5.2   The string resource file in the Eclipse Resource Editor (XML view).

Now add some resources using the Add button on the Resources tab. Specifically, create the following resources:

- A color resource named `prettyTextColor` with a value of #ff0000
- A dimension resource named `textPointSize` with a value of 14pt
- A drawable resource named `redDrawable` with a value of #F00

Now you have several resources of various types in your `strings.xml` resource file. If you switch back to the XML view, you see that the Eclipse resource editor has added the appropriate XML elements to your file, which now should look something like this:

```xml
<?xml version="1.0" encoding="utf-8"?>
<resources>
    <string name="app_name">Use Some Resources</string>
    <string
        name="hello">Hello World, UseSomeResources</string>
    <color name="prettyTextColor">#ff0000</color>
    <dimen name="textPointSize">14pt</dimen>
    <drawable name="redDrawable">#F00</drawable>
</resources>
```

Save the `strings.xml` resource file. The Eclipse plug-in automatically generates the `R.java` file in your project, with the appropriate resource IDs, which allow you to programmatically access your resources after they are compiled into the project. If you navigate to your `R.java` file, which is located under the `/src` directory in your package, it looks something like this:

```java
package com.androidbook.resourceroundup;
public final class R {
    public static final class attr {
    }
    public static final class color {
        public static final int prettyTextColor=0x7f050000;
    }
    public static final class dimen {
        public static final int textPointSize=0x7f060000;
    }
    public static final class drawable {
        public static final int icon=0x7f020000;
        public static final int redDrawable=0x7f020001;
    }
    public static final class layout {
        public static final int main=0x7f030000;
    }
    public static final class string {
        public static final int app_name=0x7f040000;
        public static final int hello=0x7f040001;
    }
}
```

Now you are free to use these resources in your code. If you navigate to your resourceroundup.java source file, you can add some lines to retrieve your resources and work with them, like this:

```
import android.graphics.drawable.ColorDrawable;
...
String myString = getResources().getString(R.string.hello);
int myColor =
    getResources().getColor(R.color.prettyTextColor);
float myDimen =
    getResources().getDimension(R.dimen.textPointSize);
ColorDrawable myDraw = (ColorDrawable)getResources().
    getDrawable(R.drawable.redDrawable);
```

Some resource types, such as string arrays, are more easily added to resource files by editing the XML by hand. For example, if we go back to the strings.xml file and choose the strings.xml tab, we can add a string array to our resource listing by adding the following XML element:

```
<?xml version="1.0" encoding="utf-8"?>
<resources>
    <string name="app_name">Use Some Resources</string>
    <string
        name="hello">Hello World, UseSomeResources</string>
    <color name="prettyTextColor">#ff0000</color>
    <dimen name="textPointSize">14pt</dimen>
    <drawable name="redDrawable">#F00</drawable>
    <string-array name="flavors">
        <item>Vanilla</item>
        <item>Chocolate</item>
        <item>Strawberry</item>
    </string-array>
</resources>
```

Save the strings.xml file, and now this string array named "flavors" is available in your source file R.java, so you can use it programmatically in resourcesroundup.java like this:

```
String[] aFlavors =
    getResources().getStringArray(R.array.flavors);
```

Now you have a general idea how to add simple resources using the Eclipse plug-in, but there are quite a few different types of data available to add as resources. Now let's have a look at how to add each different type of resource to your project.

Working with Resources

In this section, we look at the specific types of resources available for Android applications, how they are defined in the project files, and how you can access this resource data programmatically.

For each type of resource type, you learn what types of values can be stored and in what format. Some resource types (like Strings and Colors) are well supported with the Android Plug-in Resource Editor, whereas others (like Animation sequences) are more easily managed by editing the XML files directly.

Working with String Resources

String resources are among the simplest resource types available to the developer. String resources might show text labels on form views and for help text. The application name is also stored as a string resource, by default.

String resources are defined in XML under the /res/values project directory and compiled into the application package at build time. All strings with apostrophes or single straight quotes need to be escaped or wrapped in double straight quotes. Some examples of well-formatted string values are shown in Table 5.3.

Table 5.3   String Resource Formatting Examples

String Resource Value	Displays As
Hello, World	Hello, World
"User's Full Name:"	User's Full Name:
User\'s Full Name:	User's Full Name:
She said, \"Hi.\"	She said, "Hi."
She\'s busy but she did say, \"Hi.\"	She's busy but she did say, "Hi."

You can edit the strings.xml file directly by clicking on the file and choosing the strings.xml tab (as opposed to the Resources tab). You can edit the file directly, adding string resources. These resources will automatically be added to your R.java class file when you save.

String values are appropriately tagged with the <string> tag and represent a name-value pair. The name attribute is how you refer to the specific string programmatically, so name these resources wisely.

Here's an example of a simple string resource file /res/values/strings.xml:

```
<?xml version="1.0" encoding="utf-8"?>
<resources>
    <string name="app_name">Resource Viewer</string>
    <string name="test_string">Testing 1,2,3</string>
    <string name="test_string2">Testing 4,5,6</string>
</resources>
```

Bold, Italic, and Underlined Strings

You can also add three HTML-style attributes to string resources. These are bold, italic, and underlining. You specify the styling using the <b>, <i>, and <u> tags. For example:

```
<string
  name="txt"><b>Bold</b>,<i>Italic</i>,<u>Line</u></string>
```

Using `String` Resources as Format Strings

You can create format strings, but you need to escape all bold, italic, and underlining tags if you do so. For example, this text shows a score and the "win" or "lose" string:

```
<string
    name="winLose">Score: %1$d of %2$d! You %3$s.</string>
```

If you wanted to include bold, italic, or underlining in this format string, you need to escape the format tags. For example, if want to italicize the "win" or "lose" string at the end, your resource would look like this:

```
<string name="winLoseStyled">Score: %1$d of %2$d! You
➥&amp;lt;i&gt;%3$s&amp;lt;/i&gt;.</string>
```

Using String Resources Programmatically

As shown earlier in this chapter, accessing string resources in code is straightforward. There are two primary ways in which you can access this string resource.

The following code accesses your application's string resource named hello, returning only the string. All HTML-style attributes (bold, italic, and underlining) are stripped from the string.

```
String myStrHello =
    getResources().getString(R.string.hello);
```

You can also access the string and preserve the formatting by using this other method:

```
CharSequence myBoldStr =
    getResources().getText(R.string.boldhello);
```

To load a format string, you need to make sure any format variables are properly escaped. One way to do this is to use the `TextUtils.htmlEncode()` method:

```
import android.text.TextUtils;
...
String mySimpleWinString;
mySimpleWinString =
    getResources().getString(R.string.winLose);
String escapedWin = TextUtils.htmlEncode("Won");
String resultText =
    String.format(mySimpleWinString, 5, 5, escapedWin);
```

The resulting text in the `resultText` variable is

```
Score: 5 of 5! You Won.
```

Now if you have styling in this format string like the preceding `winLoseStyled` string resource, you need to take a few more steps to handle the escaped italic tags.

```
import android.text.Html;
import android.text.TextUtils;
...
String myStyledWinString;
myStyledWinString =
    getResources().getString(R.string. winLoseStyled);
String escapedWin = TextUtils.htmlEncode("Won");
String resultText =
    String.format(myStyledWinString, 5, 5, escapedWin);
CharSequence styledResults = Html.fromHtml(resultText);
```

The resulting text in the `styledResults` variable is

```
Score: 5 of 5! You <i>won</i>.
```

This variable, `styledResults`, can then be used in user interface widgets like `TextView` objects, where styled text is displayed correctly.

Working with `String` Arrays

You can specify lists of strings in resource files. This can be a good way to store menu options and drop-down list values. `String` arrays are defined in XML under the `/res/values` project directory and compiled into the application package at build time.

`String` arrays are appropriately tagged with the `<string-array>` tag and a number of `<item>` child tags, one for each string in the array. Here's an example of a simple array resource file `/res/values/arrays.xml`:

```xml
<?xml version="1.0" encoding="utf-8"?>
<resources>
    <string-array name="flavors">
        <item>Vanilla Bean</item>
        <item>Chocolate Fudge Brownie</item>
        <item>Strawberry Cheesecake</item>
        <item>Coffee, Coffee, Buzz Buzz Buzz</item>
        <item>Americone Dream</item>
    </string-array>
    <string-array name="soups">
        <item>Vegetable minestrone</item>
        <item>New England clam chowder</item>
        <item>Organic chicken noodle</item>
    </string-array>
</resources>
```

As shown earlier in this chapter, accessing string arrays resources is easy. The following code retrieves a string array named `flavors`:

```
String[] aFlavors =
    getResources().getStringArray(R.array.flavors);
```

Working with Colors

Android applications can store RGB color values, which can then be applied to other screen elements. You can use these values to set the color of text or other elements, like the screen background. Color resources are defined in XML under the `/res/values` project directory and compiled into the application package at build time.

RGB color values always start with the hash symbol (#). The alpha value can be given for transparency control. The following color formats are supported:

- #RGB (Example: #F00 is 12-bit color, red)
- #ARGB (Example: #8F00 is 12-bit color, red with alpha 50 percent)
- #RRGGBB (Example: #FF00FF is 24-bit color, magenta)
- #AARRGGBB (Example: #80FF00FF is 24-bit color, magenta with alpha 50 percent)

Color values are appropriately tagged with the `<color>` tag and represent a name-value pair. Here's an example of a simple color resource file: `/res/values/colors.xml`:

```
<?xml version="1.0" encoding="utf-8"?>
<resources>
    <color name="background_color">#006400</color>
    <color name="text_color">#FFE4C4</color>
</resources>
```

The example at the beginning of the chapter accessed a color resource. Color resources are simply integers. The following code retrieves a color resource called `prettyTextColor`:

```
int myResourceColor =
    getResources().getColor(R.color.prettyTextColor);
```

Working with Dimensions

Many user interface layout widgets such as text controls and buttons are drawn to specific dimensions. These dimensions can be stored as resources. Dimension values always end with a unit of measurement tag.

Dimension values are appropriately tagged with the`<dimen>` tag and represent a name-value pair. Dimension resources are defined in XML under the `/res/values` project directory and compiled into the application package at build time.

The dimension units supported are shown in Table 5.4.

Table 5.4   **Dimension Unit Measurements Supported**

Unit of Measurement	Description	Resource Tag Required	Example
Pixels	Actual screen pixels	px	20px
Inches	Physical measurement	in	1in
Millimeters	Physical measurement	mm	1mm
Points	Common font Measurement	pt	14pt
Density-Independent Pixels	Pixels relative to 160dpi screen	dp	1dp
Scale-Independent Pixels	Best for scalable font display	sp	14sp

Here's an example of a simple dimension resource file `/res/values/dimens.xml`:

```
<?xml version="1.0" encoding="utf-8"?>
<resources>
    <dimen name="FourteenPt">14pt</dimen>
    <dimen name="OneInch">1in</dimen>
    <dimen name="TenMillimeters">10mm</dimen>
    <dimen name="TenPixels">10px</dimen>
</resources>
```

Dimension resources are simply floating point values. The following code retrieves a dimension resource called `textPointSize`:

```
float myDimension =
    getResources().getDimension(R.dimen.textPointSize);
```

Working with Simple Drawables

You can specify simple colored rectangles by using the `drawable` resource type, which can then be applied to other screen elements. These `drawable` types are defined in specific paint colors, much like the `Color` resources are defined.

Simple paintable `drawable` resources are defined in XML under the `/res/values` project directory and compiled into the application package at build time. Paintable `drawable` resources use the `<drawable>` tag and represent a name-value pair. Here's an example of a simple `drawable` resource file `/res/values/drawables.xml`:

```
<?xml version="1.0" encoding="utf-8"?>
<resources>
    <drawable name="red_rect">#F00</drawable>
</resources>
```

Although it might seem a tad confusing, you can also create XML files that describe other `Drawable` subclasses, such as `ShapeDrawable`. `Drawable` XML definition files are stored in the `/res/drawable` directory within your project along with image files.

> **Caution**
>
> This is *not* the same as storing `<drawable>` resources, which are paintable `drawables`. `PaintableDrawable` resources are stored in the `/res/values` directory, as explained in the previous section.

Here's a simple `ShapeDrawable` described in the file `/res/drawable/red_oval.xml`:

```xml
<?xml version="1.0" encoding="utf-8"?>
<shape
    xmlns:android=
        "http://schemas.android.com/apk/res/android"
    android:shape="oval">
    <solid android:color="#f00"/>
</shape>
```

We talk more about graphics and drawing shapes in Chapter 8, "Drawing and Working with Animation in Android."

Drawable resources defined with `<drawable>` are simply rectangles of a given color, which is represented by the Drawable subclass `ColorDrawable`. The following code retrieves a `ColorDrawable` resource called `redDrawable`:

```java
import android.graphics.drawable.ColorDrawable;
...
ColorDrawable myDraw = (ColorDrawable)getResources().
    getDrawable(R.drawable.redDrawable);
```

Working with Images

Applications often include visual elements such as icons and graphics. Android supports several image formats that can be directly included as resources for your application. These image formats are shown in Table 5.5.

Table 5.5   **Image Formats Supported in Android**

Supported Image Format	Description	Required Extension
Portable Network Graphics (PNG)	Preferred Format (Lossless)	.png
Nine-Patch Stretchable Images	Preferred Format (Lossless)	.9.png
Joint Photographic Experts Group (JPG)	Acceptable Format (Lossy)	.jpg, .jpeg
Graphics Interchange Format	Discouraged Format	.gif

These image formats are all well supported by popular graphics editors such as Adobe Photoshop, GIMP, and Microsoft Paint. The Nine-Patch Stretchable Graphics can be created from PNG files using the `draw9patch` tool included with the Android SDK under the `/tools` directory.

> **Tip**
>
> All resources filenames must be lowercase and simple (letters, numbers, and underscores only). This rule applies to all files, including graphics.

Adding image resources to your project is easy. Simply drag the image asset into the `/res/drawable` directory, and it will automatically be included into the application package at build time.

Working with Nine-Patch Stretchable Graphics

Phone screens come in various dimensions. It can be handy to use stretchable graphics to allow a single graphic that can scale appropriately for different screen sizes and orientations or different lengths of text. This can save you or your designer a lot of time in creating graphics for many different screen sizes.

Android supports Nine-Patch Stretchable Graphics for this purpose. Nine-Patch graphics are simply PNG graphics that have patches, or areas of the image, defined to scale appropriately, instead of scaling the entire image as one unit. Often the center segment is transparent.

In Figure 5.3, you can see how the image (shown as the square) is divided into nine patches.

Nine-Patch Stretchable Graphics can be created from PNG files using the `draw9patch` tool included with the `Tools` directory of the Android SDK. The interface for the `draw9patch` tool (see Figure 5.4) is straightforward. In the left pane, you can define the Nine-Patch guides to your graphic to define how it will scale when stretched. In the right pane, you can preview how your graphic will behave when scaled with the patches you defined.

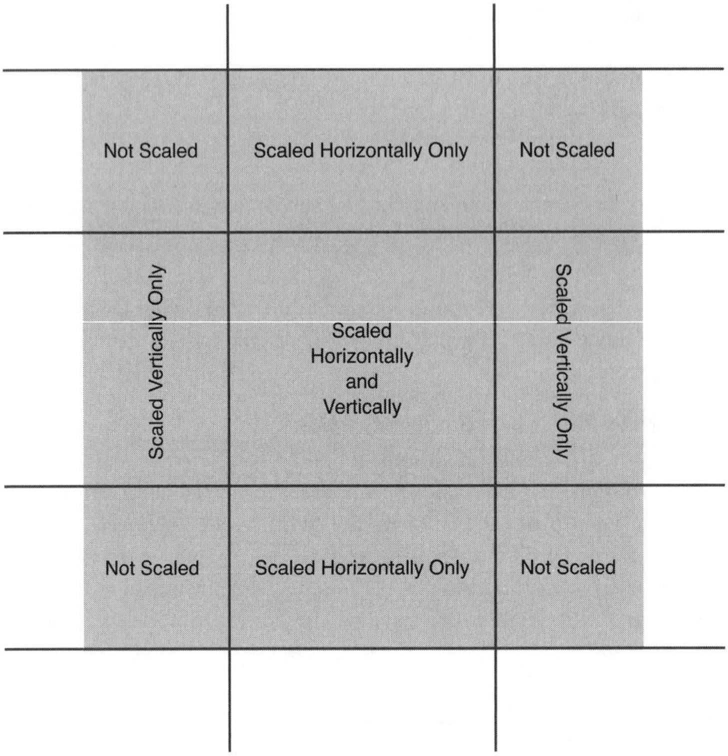

Not Scaled	Scaled Horizontally Only	Not Scaled
Scaled Vertically Only	Scaled Horizontally and Vertically	Scaled Vertically Only
Not Scaled	Scaled Horizontally Only	Not Scaled

Figure 5.3   How a Nine-Patch Graphic of a Square is Scaled.

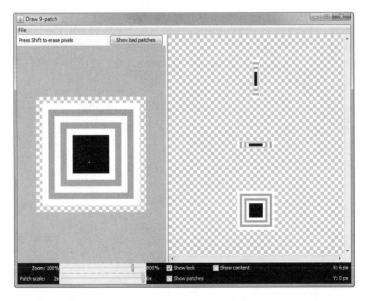

Figure 5.4   A simple PNG file before Nine-Patch processing.

To create a Nine–Patch graphic from a PNG file using the `draw9patch` tool, perform the following steps:

1. Launch `draw9patch.bat` in your Android SDK `tools` directory.
2. Drag a PNG file into the left pane (or use File, Open Nine–Patch)
3. Click the Show Patches check box at the bottom of the left pane.
4. Set your Patch Scale appropriately (higher to see more marked results).
5. Click along the right edge of your graphic to set a horizontal patch guide.
6. Click along the top edge of your graphic to set a vertical patch guide.
7. View the results in the right pane; move patch guides until the graphic stretches as desired, as shown in Figure 5.5 and Figure 5.6).
8. To delete a patch guide, press shift and click on the guide pixel (black).
9. Save your graphic with the extension `.9.png` (for example, `little_black_box.9.png`).

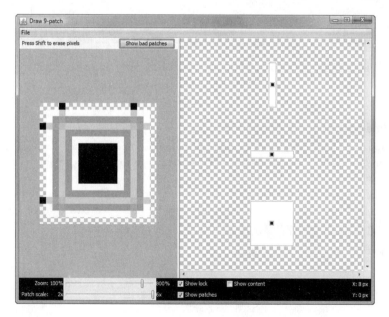

Figure 5.5   A Nine-Patch PNG file after Nine-Patch Processing with some patch guides defined.

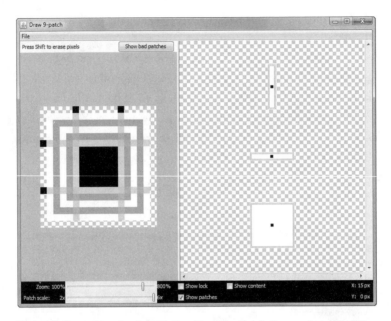

Figure 5.6   A Nine-Patch PNG file after Nine-Patch Processing with different patch guides defined.

Using Image Resources Programmatically

Images resources are simply another kind of `Drawable` called a `BitmapDrawable`. Most of the time, you need only the resource ID of the image to set as an attribute on a user interface widget.

For example, if I dropped the graphics file `flag.png` into the `/res/drawable` directory and added an `ImageView` widget to my main layout, we could set the image to be displayed programmatically in the layout this way:

```
import android.widget.ImageView;
…
ImageView flagImageView =
    (ImageView)findViewById(R.id.ImageView01);
flagImageView.setImageResource(R.drawable.flag);
```

If you want to access the `BitmapDrawable` object directly, you simply request that resource directly as follows:

```
import android.graphics.drawable.BitmapDrawable;
…
BitmapDrawable bitmapFlag = (BitmapDrawable)
    getResources().getDrawable(R.drawable.flag);
int iBitmapHeightInPixels =
```

```
      bitmapFlag.getIntrinsicHeight();
int iBitmapWidthInPixels = bitmapFlag.getIntrinsicWidth();
```

And finally, if you work with Nine-Patch graphics, the call to getDrawable() returns a NinePatchDrawable instead of a BitmapDrawable object.

```
import android.graphics.drawable.NinePatchDrawable;
...
NinePatchDrawable stretchy = (NinePatchDrawable)
    getResources().getDrawable(R.drawable.pyramid);
int iStretchyHeightInPixels =
    stretchy.getIntrinsicHeight();
int iStretchyWidthInPixels = stretchy.getIntrinsicWidth();
```

Working with Animation

Android supports animation and *tweening*. Some animation features include scaling, fading, and rotation. These actions can be applied simultaneously or sequentially and might use different interpolators.

Animation sequences are not tied to a specific graphic file, so you can write one sequence and then use it for a variety of different graphics. For example, you can make moon, star, and diamond graphics all pulse using a single scaling sequence or spin using a rotate sequence.

Graphic animation sequences can be stored as specially formatted XML files in the /res/anim directory and are compiled into the application binary at build time.

Here's an example of a simple animation resource file /res/anim/spin.xml that defines a simple rotate operation, rotating the target graphic counterclockwise four times in place, taking 10 seconds to complete:

```
<?xml version="1.0" encoding="utf-8" ?>
<set xmlns:android
    ="http://schemas.android.com/apk/res/android"
    android:shareInterpolator="false">
    <set>
        <rotate
            android:fromDegrees="0"
            android:toDegrees="-1440"
            android:pivotX="50%"
            android:pivotY="50%"
            android:duration="10000" />
    </set>
</set>
```

The Android SDK provides some helper utilities for loading and using animation resources. These utilities are found in the android.view.animation.AnimationUtils class.

If we go back to the example of a `BitmapDrawable` earlier, we can now add some animation simply by adding the following code to load the animation resource file `spin.xml` and set the animation in motion.

```
import android.view.animation.Animation;
import android.view.animation.AnimationUtils;
import android.widget.ImageView;
...
ImageView flagImageView =
    (ImageView)findViewById(R.id.ImageView01);
flagImageView.setImageResource(R.drawable.flag);
...
Animation an =
    AnimationUtils.loadAnimation(this, R.anim.spin);
flagImageView.startAnimation(an);
```

Now you have your graphic spinning. Notice that we loaded the animation using the base class object `Animation`. You can also extract specific animation types using the sub-classes that match: `RotateAnimation`, `ScaleAnimation`, `TranslateAnimation`, and `AlphaAnimation`.

You learn more about graphics and animation in Chapter 8.

Working with Menus

You can also include menu resources in your project files. Like animation resources, menu resources are not tied to a specific widget or control but can be reused in any menu control.

Each menu resource (which is a set of individual menu items) is stored as a specially formatted XML files in the `/res/menu` directory and are compiled into the application package at build time.

Here's an example of a simple menu resource file `/res/menu/speed.xml` that defines a short menu with four items in a specific order:

```
<menu xmlns:android
    ="http://schemas.android.com/apk/res/android">
    <item
        android:id="@+id/start"
        android:title="Start!"
        android:orderInCategory="1"></item>
    <item
        android:id="@+id/stop"
        android:title="Stop!"
        android:orderInCategory="4"></item>
    <item
        android:id="@+id/accel"
        android:title="Vroom! Accelerate!"
        android:orderInCategory="2"></item>
```

```
    <item
        android:id="@+id/decel"
        android:title="Decelerate!"
        android:orderInCategory="3"></item>
</menu>
```

You can create menus using the Eclipse plug-in, which can access the various configuration attributes for each menu item. In the previous case, we set the title (label) of each menu item and the order in which the items display. Now, you can use string resources for those titles, instead of typing the strings in. For example:

```
<menu xmlns:android=
    "http://schemas.android.com/apk/res/android">
    <item
        android:id="@+id/start"
        android:title="@string/start"
        android:orderInCategory="1"></item>
    <item
        android:id="@+id/decel"
        android:title="@string/stop
        android:orderInCategory="2"></item>
</menu>
```

To access the preceding menu resource called /res/menu/speed.xml, simply override the method onCreateOptionsMenu() in your application:

```
public boolean onCreateOptionsMenu(Menu menu) {
    getMenuInflater().inflate(R.menu.speed, menu);
    return true;
}
```

That's it. Now if you run your application and press the menu button, you see the menu. You learn a lot more about menus and menu event handling in Chapter 6, "Exploring User Interface Screen Elements."

Working with XML Files

You can include arbitrary XML resource files to your project. These XML files should be stored in the /res/xml directory and are compiled into the application package at build time.

The Android SDK has a variety of packages and classes available for XML manipulation. You learn more about XML handling in Chapter 9, "Using Android Data and Storage APIs," and Chapter 10, "Using Android Networking APIs." For now, we create an XML resource file and access it through code.

First, put a simple XML file in /res/xml directory. In this case, the file my_pets.xml with the following contents can be created:

```xml
<?xml version="1.0" encoding="utf-8"?>
<pets>
    <pet name="Bit" type="Bunny" />
    <pet name="Nibble" type="Bunny" />
    <pet name="Stack" type="Bunny" />
    <pet name="Queue" type="Bunny" />
    <pet name="Heap" type="Bunny" />
    <pet name="Null" type="Bunny" />
    <pet name="Nigiri" type="Fish" />
    <pet name="Sashimi II" type="Fish" />
    <pet name="Kiwi" type="Lovebird" />
</pets>
```

Now you can access this XML file as a resource programmatically in the following manner:

```java
XmlResourceParser myPets =
    getResources().getXml(R.xml.my_pets);
```

Finally, to prove this is XML, here's one way you might churn through the XML and extract the information:

```java
import org.xmlpull.v1.XmlPullParserException;
import android.content.res.XmlResourceParser;
...
int eventType = -1;
while (eventType != XmlResourceParser.END_DOCUMENT) {
    if(eventType == XmlResourceParser.START_DOCUMENT) {
        Log.d(DEBUG_TAG, "Document Start");
    } else if(eventType == XmlResourceParser.START_TAG) {

        String strName = myPets.getName();
        if(strName.equals("pet")) {
            Log.d(DEBUG_TAG, "Found a PET");
            Log.d(DEBUG_TAG,
                "Name: "+myPets.
                    getAttributeValue(null, "name"));
            Log.d(DEBUG_TAG,
                "Species: "+myPets.
                    getAttributeValue(null, "type"));
        }
    }
    eventType = myPets.next();
}
Log.d(DEBUG_TAG, "Document End");
```

Working with Raw Files

Your application can also include raw files as part of its resources. Raw files your application might use include audio files, video files, and other file formats not supported by the Android Resource packaging tool appt.

All raw resource files are included in the /res/raw directory and are added to your package without further processing.

Caution

All resources filenames must be lowercase and simple (letters, numbers, and underscores only). This also applies to raw file filenames even though the tools don't process these files, other than to put them in your application package.

The resource filename must be unique to the directory and should be descriptive because the filename (without the extension) becomes the name by which the resource is accessed.

You can access raw file resources and any resource from the /res/drawable directory (bitmap graphics files, anything not using the <resource> XML definition method). Here's one way to open a file called the_help.txt:

```
import java.io.InputStream;
...
InputStream iFile =
    getResources().openRawResource(R.raw.the_help);
```

References to Resources

You can reference resources instead of duplicating them. For example, your application might want to reference a single string resource in multiple string arrays.

The most common use of resource references is in layout XML files, where layouts can reference any number of resources to specify attributes for layout colors, dimensions, strings, and graphics. Another common use is within style and theme resources.

Resources are referenced using the following format:

```
@[optional_package_name:]resource_type/variable_name
```

Recall previously when we had a string-array of soup names. If we wanted to localize the soup listing, a better way to create the array would be to create individual string resources for each soup name and then store the references to those string resources in the string-array (instead of the text).

To do this, we would define the string resources in the /res/strings.xml file like this:

```
<?xml version="1.0" encoding="utf-8"?>
<resources>
    <string name="app_name">Application Name</string>
```

```
        <string name="chicken_soup"
            >Organic Chicken Noodle</string>
        <string name="minestrone_soup"
            >Veggie Minestrone</string>
        <string name="chowder_soup"
            >New England Lobster Chowder</string>
</resources>
```

And then we could define a localizable string-array that references the above string resources by name in the /res/arrays.xml file like this:

```
<?xml version="1.0" encoding="utf-8"?>
<resources>
    <string-array name="soups">
        <item>@string/minestrone_soup</item>
        <item>@string/chowder_soup</item>
        <item>@string/chicken_soup</item>
    </string-array>
</resources>
```

> **Tip**
>
> Save the strings.xml file first so that the string resources (which are picked up by the appt and included in the R.java class) are defined prior to trying to save the arrays.xml file, which references those particular string resources. Otherwise, you might get the following error:
>
> Error: No resource found that matches the given name.

You can also use references to make aliases to other resources. For example, you can alias the system resource for the OK string to an application resource name by including the following in your strings.xml resource file:

```
<?xml version="1.0" encoding="utf-8"?>
<resources>
    <string id="app_ok">@android:string/ok</string>
</resources>
```

You learn more about all the different system resources available later in this chapter.

Working with Layouts

Much as web designers use HTML, user interface designers can use XML to define Android application screen elements and layout.

Layout resource files are included in the /res/layout/ directory and are compiled into the application package at build time. Layout files might include many user interface controls and define the layout for an entire screen or describe custom controls used in other layouts.

Here's a simple example of a layout file (/res/layout/main.xml) that sets the screen's background color and displays some text in the middle of the screen (see Figure 5.7). You can find this layout file in the Resource Viewer Android project provided on the CD and on the book Web site.

Figure 5.7   How the Main.xml layout file displays in the emulator.

The main.xml layout file references a number of other resources, including colors, strings, and dimension values, all of which were defined in the strings.xml, colors.xml, and dimens.xml resource files. The color resource for the screen background color and resources for a TextView control's color, string, and text size follows:

```
<?xml version="1.0" encoding="utf-8"?>
<LinearLayout xmlns:android=
    "http://schemas.android.com/apk/res/android"
    android:orientation="vertical"
    android:layout_width="fill_parent"
    android:layout_height="fill_parent"
    android:background="@color/background_color">
    <TextView
```

```
        android:id="@+id/TextView01"
        android:layout_width="fill_parent"
        android:layout_height="fill_parent"
        android:text="@string/test_string"
        android:textColor="@color/text_color"
        android:gravity="center"
        android:textSize="@dimen/FortyPt"></TextView>
</LinearLayout>
```

The preceding layout describes all the visual elements on a screen. In this example, a `LinearLayout` control is used as a container for other user interface widgets—here, a single `TextView` that displays a line of text.

You can also encapsulate specific layout features in their own layout files and then include those common widgets in other layout files using the `<include>` tag. For example, you can use the following `<include>` tag that would include another layout file called `/res/layout/mygreenrect.xml` in `main.xml`:

```
<include layout="@layout/mygreenrect"/>
```

Designing Layouts in Eclipse

Layouts can be designed and previewed in Eclipse. If you click on the project file `/res/layout/main.xml`, which is provided with any new Android project, you see a Layout tab, which shows you the preview of the layout, and a main.xml tab, which shows you the raw XML of the layout file.

As with most user interface designers, the Android plug-in works well for your basic layout needs, allows you to create user interface controls such as `TextView` and `Button` widgets easily, and allows setting their properties in the Properties pane.

> **Tip**
>
> Moving the Properties pane to the far right of the workspace in the Eclipse Java perspective makes it easier to browse and set properties when designing layouts.

Now is a great time to get to know the layout resource designer. Create a new Android project called ParisView. The ParisView project is also available on the CD and book Web site. Navigate to the `/res/layout/main.xml` layout file and double-click it to open it in the resource editor. It's quite simple by default, only a black (empty) rectangle and string of text.

Below in the Resource pane of the Eclipse perspective, you notice an Outline tab. This outline is the XML hierarchy of this layout file. By default, you see a `LinearLayout`. If you expand it, you see it contains one `TextView` widget.

Click on the `TextView` widget. You'll see that the Properties pane of the Eclipse perspective now has all the properties available for that object. If you scroll down to the property called `Text`, you'll see that it's set to a string resource variable `@string/hello`.

Tip

You can also select specific layout widgets by clicking on them in the layout designer. The currently selected widget will be highlighted in red. We prefer to use the Outline view, so we can be sure we are clicking on what we expect.

You can use the layout designer to set and preview layout widget properties. For example, you can modify the `TextView` property called `Text Size` by typing 18pt (a dimension, you recognize). You see the results of your change to the property immediately in the preview area, as shown in Figure 5.8.

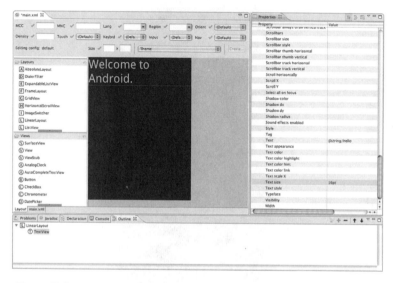

Figure 5.8   Designing a layout file using Eclipse (CHANGING the TextView Text Size).

Take a moment to switch to the `main.xml` tab. You notice that the properties you set are now in the XML. If you save and run your project in the emulator now, you see similar results to what you see in the designer preview.

Now go back to the Outline pane. You see a green plus and a red minus button. You can use these buttons to add and remove widgets to your layout file. For example, select the `LinearLayout` from the Outline view, and click the green button to add a control within that container object.

Choose the `ImageView` object. Now you have a new widget in your layout. You can't actually see it yet because it is not yet fully defined.

Drag two PNG graphics files (or JPG) into your `/res/drawable` project directory, naming them `flag.png` and `background.png`. Now, browse the properties of your

ImageView widget, and set the Src property by clicking on the resource browser button labeled […].You can browse all the Drawable resources in your project and select the flag resource you just added.You can also set this property manually by typing @drawable/flag.

Now, you see that the graphic shows up in your preview.While we're at it, select the LinearLayout object and set its Background property to the background Drawable you added.

If you save the layout file and run the application in the emulator (see Figure 5.9) or on the phone, you see results much like you did in the resource designer preview pane.

Figure 5.9   A layout with a LinearLayout, TextView, and
ImageView, shown in the Android emulator.

Using Layout Resources Programmatically

Layouts, whether they are Button or ImageView widgets, are all derived from the View class. Here's how you would retrieve a TextView object named TextView01:

```
TextView txt = (TextView)findViewById(R.id.TextView01);
```

You can also access the underlying XML of a layout resource much as you would any XML file.The following code retrieves the main.xml layout file for XML parsing:

```
XmlResourceParser myMainXml =
    getResources().getLayout(R.layout.main);
```

Developers can also define custom layouts with unique attributes. We talk much more about layout files and designing Android user interfaces in Chapter 7, "Designing Android User Interfaces with Layouts."

Working with Styles

Android user interface designers can group layout element attributes together in styles. Layout widgets are all derived from the `View` base class, which has many useful attributes. Individual widgets, such as `Checkbox`, `Button`, and `TextView`, have specialized attributes associated with their behavior.

Styles are tagged with the `<style>` tag and should be stored in the `/res/values/` directory. Style resources are defined in XML and compiled into the application binary at build time.

> **Tip**
>
> Styles cannot be previewed using the Android Eclipse Plug-In but are shown in the Emulator correctly.

Here's an example of a simple style resource file `/res/values/styles.xml` containing two styles, one for mandatory form fields and one for optional form fields on `TextView` and `EditText` objects:

```
<?xml version="1.0" encoding="utf-8"?>
<resources>
    <style name="mandatory_text_field_style">
        <item name="android:textColor">#000000</item>
        <item name="android:textSize">14pt</item>
        <item name="android:textStyle">bold</item>
    </style>
    <style name="optional_text_field_style">
        <item name="android:textColor">#0F0F0F</item>
        <item name="android:textSize">12pt</item>
        <item name="android:textStyle">italic</item>
    </style>
</resources>
```

Many useful style attributes are colors and dimensions. It would be more appropriate to use references to resources. Here's the `styles.xml` file again; this time the color and text size fields are available in the other resource files `colors.xml` and `dimens.xml`:

```
<?xml version="1.0" encoding="utf-8"?>
<resources>
    <style name="mandatory_text_field_style">
        <item name="android:textColor"
            >@color/mand_text_color</item>
        <item name="android:textSize"
            >@dimen/important_text</item>
        <item name="android:textStyle">bold</item>
```

```
        </style>
        <style name="optional_text_field_style">
            <item name="android:textColor"
                >@color/opt_text_color</item>
            <item name="android:textSize"
                >@dimen/unimportant_text</item>
            <item name="android:textStyle">italic</item>
        </style>
    </resources>
```

Now, if you can create a new layout with a couple of `TextView` and `EditText` text widgets, you can set each widget's style attribute by referencing it as such:

```
style="@style/name_of_style"
```

Here we have a form layout called `/res/layout/form.xml` that does that:

```
<?xml version="1.0" encoding="utf-8"?>
<LinearLayout
    xmlns:android=
        "http://schemas.android.com/apk/res/android"
    android:orientation="vertical"
    android:layout_width="fill_parent"
    android:layout_height="fill_parent"
    android:background="@color/background_color">
    <TextView
        android:id="@+id/TextView01"
        style="@style/mandatory_text_field_style"
        android:layout_height="wrap_content"
        android:text="@string/mand_label"
        android:layout_width="wrap_content" />
    <EditText
        android:id="@+id/EditText01"
        style="@style/mandatory_text_field_style"
        android:layout_height="wrap_content"
        android:text="@string/mand_default"
        android:layout_width="fill_parent"
        android:singleLine="true" />
    <TextView
        android:id="@+id/TextView02"
        style="@style/optional_text_field_style"
        android:layout_width="wrap_content"
        android:layout_height="wrap_content"
        android:text="@string/opt_label" />
    <EditText
        android:id="@+id/EditText02"
        style="@style/optional_text_field_style"
        android:layout_height="wrap_content"
        android:text="@string/opt_default"
        android:singleLine="true"
```

```
            android:layout_width="fill_parent" />
    <TextView
            android:id="@+id/TextView03"
            style="@style/optional_text_field_style"
            android:layout_width="wrap_content"
            android:layout_height="wrap_content"
            android:text="@string/opt_label" />
    <EditText
            android:id="@+id/EditText03"
            style="@style/optional_text_field_style"
            android:layout_height="wrap_content"
            android:text="@string/opt_default"
            android:singleLine="true"
            android:layout_width="fill_parent" />
</LinearLayout>
```

The resulting layout has three fields, each made up of one TextView for the label and
one EditText where the user can input text. The mandatory style is applied to the
mandatory label and text entry. The other two fields use the optional style. The resulting
layout would look something like Figure 5.10.

Figure 5.10   A layout using two styles, one for mandatory fields and
another for optional fields.

We talk much more about styles in Chapter 7.

Using Style Resources Programmatically

Styles are applied to specific layout widgets like `TextView` and `Button` objects. Usually, you want to supply the style resource `id` when you call the widget's constructor. For example, the style named `myAppIsStyling` would be referred to as `R.style.myAppIsStyling`.

Working with Themes

Themes are much like styles, but instead of being applied to one layout element at a time, they are applied to all elements of a given activity (which, generally speaking, means one screen).

Themes are defined in exactly the same way as styles. Themes use the `<style>` tag and should be stored in the `/res/values` directory. The only difference is that instead of applying that named style to a layout element, you define it as the `Theme` attribute of an activity in the `AndroidManifest.xml` file.

We talk much more about themes in Chapter 7.

Referencing System Resources

You can access system resources in addition to your own resources. The `android` package contains all kinds of resources, which you can browse by looking in the `android.R` subclasses. Here you find system resources for

- Animation sequences for fading in and out
- Arrays of email/phone types (home, work, and such)
- Standard system colors
- Dimensions for application thumbnails and icons
- Many commonly used `drawable` and layout types
- Error strings and standard button text
- System styles and themes

You can reference system resources the same way you use your own; set the package name to `android`. For example, to set the background to the system color for darker gray, you set the appropriate background color attribute to `@android:color/darker_gray`. You can access system resources much like you access your application's resources. Instead of using your application resources, use the Android package's resources under the `android.R` class.

If we go back to our animation example, we could have used a system animation instead of defining our own. Here is the same animation example again, except it uses a system animation to fade in:

```
import android.view.animation.Animation;
import android.view.animation.AnimationUtils;
import android.widget.ImageView;
...
ImageView flagImageView =
    (ImageView)findViewById(R.id.ImageView01);
flagImageView.setImageResource(R.drawable.flag);
...
Animation an = AnimationUtils.
    loadAnimation(this, android.R.anim.fade_in);
flagImageView.startAnimation(an);
```

Note

The default Android resources are all provided as part of the Android SDK installation under the `/tools/lib/res/default` directory. Here you can examine all the drawable resources, full XML layout files, and everything else found in the `android.R.*` package.

Managing Multiple Application Configurations

Resources can be further organized to be tailored to the specific language and regional settings of the device and screen state and input methods. Perhaps two of the most common cases developers need to be aware of are for internationalization and localization purposes and to design a single application that can run smoothly on different phone screens and screen orientations.

Warning

In Android 1.1, only English (with no specific regions) was supported, but many more languages and locales were added as part of the Android 1.5 system image. Some languages, such as English, French, and German are supported with regional differences (American versus British English) whereas others, such as Spanish, do not have regional support at the time of this writing but will hopefully be added soon.

The locale support provided in Android 1.5, broken down into languages and specific regions (where applicable), is shown in Table 5.6.

Table 5.6   **Languages and Regions Supported in Android 1.5**

Language	Region
Chinese	PRC (zh_CN)
	Taiwan (zh_TW)
Czech	Czech (cs_CZ), no specific regions
Dutch	Netherlands (nl_NL)
	Belgium (nl_BE)

Table 5.6   **Continued**

Language	Region
English	US (en_US)
	Britain (en_GB)
	Canada (en_CA)
	Australia (en_AU)
	New Zealand (en_NZ)
	Singapore (en_SG)
French	France (fr_FR)
	Belgium (fr_BE)
	Canada (fr_CA)
	Switzerland (fr_CH)
German	Germany (de_DE)
	Austria (de_AT)
	Switzerland (de_CH)
	Liechtenstein (de_LI)
Italian	Italy (it_IT)
	Switzerland (it_CH)
Japanese	Japanese (ja_JP), no specific regions
Korean	Korean (ko_KR), no specific regions
Polish	Polish (pl_PL), no specific regions
Russian	Russian (ru_RU), no specific regions
Spanish	Spanish (es_ES), no specific regions

To change the locale setting on the emulator or the device (requires at least Android 1.5), you need to perform the following steps:

1. Navigate to the Home screen.
2. Press the Menu button.
3. Choose the Settings option.
4. Scroll down and choose the Locale & Text settings.
5. Choose the Set Locale option.
6. Select the locale you want to change the system to, for example, French (France).

Tip

You might want to memorize changing this setting because you need to navigate back to this screen in the foreign language to change it back.

After you change the locale setting on the Android system, all applications will use the most specific resources available for that locale. For example, if your application provides French language strings, the Android application framework will use those strings automatically as part of the application. If no specific localization resources are available, the default are used.

> **Tip**
>
> We included a simple example project called "MultiNational" on the CD to illustrate how you can organize application resources to provide functionality based upon device configurations. This project includes some support for English and French, including specific regional support for Great Britain. It also includes a fallback for any language or region not explicitly supported.

Specifying Resources for Localization and Device Configurations

To organize application resources by these criteria, developers must create specific directory names so that the Android system can choose the most appropriate resources at runtime.

You can apply these directory name qualifiers to the resource subdirectories such as `/res/values/` and `/res/drawable/`. Qualifiers are tacked on to the existing subdirectory name in a strict order, shown in descending order in Table 5.7. You must use a dash when combining multiple qualifiers. Qualifiers are always lowercase, and directories can only contain one qualifier of each type.

Table 5.7   Resource Directory Qualifiers Supported in Android

Directory Qualifier Type	Values Allowed	Comment

Language
Must be first qualifier (if multiple):
for example, `/res/values-en/`
	`en, fr, es,`
	`zh, ja, ko,`
	`de, fi`
		ISO 639-1 two letter language codes
		(Examples are English, French, Spanish, Chinese, Japanese, Korean, German, Finnish, but you can specify any.)

Region
Follows Language (if applicable):
for example, `/res/values`
`-en-rUS/`
	`rUS, rGB,`
	`rFR, rES,`
	`rMX, rCN,`
	`rJP, rKR,`
	`rDE, rFI`
		ISO 3166-1-alpha-2 region code in UPPERCASE preceded by a lowercase r.
		(Examples are United States, Great Britain, France, Spain, Mexico, China, Japanese, South Korea, Germany, Finland, but you can specify any.)

Table 5.7　**Continued**

Directory Qualifier Type	Values Allowed	Comment
Screen Orientation Follows Region (if applicable): for example, `/res/drawable-port/`	`port, land, square`	Portrait mode, Landscape mode, square screens.
Screen Pixel Density Follows Orientation (if applicable): for example, `/res/drawable-port-92dpi/`	`92dpi, 108dpi`	Depends on the devices available.
Touchscreen Type Follows Screen Pixel Density (if applicable): for example, `/res/values-port-notouch/`	`notouch, stylus, finger`	No touch screen, stylus only, finger touch screen.
Keyboard Mode Follows Touchscreen Type (if applicable): for example, `/res/drawable-keyshidden/`	`keysexposed, keyshidden`	Keyboard available, keyboard not available to user.
Primary Text Input Method Follows Keyboard Mode (if applicable): for example, `/res/values-port-notouch-12key/`	`nokeys, qwerty, 12key`	No keys (touch screen input only), a full qwerty keyboard, only a numeric keypad.
Primary Nontouchscreen Navigation Method Follows Text Input Method (if applicable): for example, `/res/values-notouch-wheel/`	`nonav, dpad, trackball, wheel`	Four-key directional pad, trackball (such as on the T-Mobile G1), scroll wheel.
Screen Dimensions Always the last qualifier of the directory: for example, `/res/drawables-en-port-640x480/`	`320x240, 640x480`	Largest dimension must be specified first.

Tip

No custom qualifiers are allowed. You, for example, are not allowed to name a directory `/res/values-en-rUS-port-finger-320x240-custom`.

Good examples of directories:

```
/res/values-en-rUS-port-finger
/res/drawables-en-rUS-land-640x480
/res/values-en-qwerty
```

Bad examples of directories:

```
/res/values-en-rUS-rGB
/res/values-en-rUS-port-FINGER-320x240
/res/values-en-rUS-port-finger-320x240-custom
/res/drawables-rUS-en
```

The first bad example will not work because you can have only one qualifier of a given type, and this one violates that rule by including both rUS and rGB. The second bad example violates the rule that qualifiers (with the exception of the Region) are always lowercase. The third bad example includes a custom attribute defined by the developer, but these are not currently supported. The last bad example violates the order in which the qualifiers must be placed: Language first, then Region, and so on.

Using Appropriate Configuration Resources Programmatically

There is currently no way to request resources of a specific configuration programmatically. For example, the developer cannot programmatically request the French or English version of the string resource. Instead, the Android system determines the resource at runtime, and developers refer only to the general resource variable name.

To make all this work, the developer must name individual resources by the same unique names in these directories. For example, in a "Hello, World" example, you might have two files called /res/values-en/strings.xml and /res/values-fr/strings.xml. In each file, you would define the same string with the same id.

The /res/values-en/strings.xml file would look like this:

```
<?xml version="1.0" encoding="utf-8"?>
<resources>
    <string name="app_name">Resource Viewer</string>
    <string name="hello">Hello in English!</string>
</resources>
```

The /res/values-fr/strings.xml file would look like this:

```
<?xml version="1.0" encoding="utf-8"?>
<resources>
    <string name="app_name">Resource Viewer</string>
    <string name="hello">Bonjour en Français!</string>
</resources>
```

A shared layout file in the /res/layout/ directory that displays the string refers to the string by the variable name @string/hello, without regard to which language or directory the string resource is in. The Android device knows how to choose the appropriate version based on the operating system language setting. A layout showing the text string would look like this:

```
<?xml version="1.0" encoding="utf-8"?>
<LinearLayout
```

```
    xmlns:android=
        "http://schemas.android.com/apk/res/android"
    android:orientation="vertical"
    android:layout_width="fill_parent"
    android:layout_height="fill_parent">
    <TextView
        android:layout_width="fill_parent"
        android:text="@string/hello"
        android:textSize="24pt"
        android:layout_height="fill_parent"
        android:gravity="center" />
</LinearLayout>
```

The string would be accessed programmatically like this:

```
String str = getString(R.string.hello);
```

Again, I've included a simple example project called "MultiNational" on the CD to illustrate how you can organize application resources to provide functionality based upon device configurations. This project doesn't have a line of code. Instead, all its functionality is handled by the careful organization of String, Drawable, and Layout resources.

The "MultiNational" application does two things: It displays a background image and a string. The text displayed changes based on the device language (three settings: English, French, or Anything Else). The background image displayed changes based on the language and the screen orientation (Portrait or Landscape). Also, to illustrate that the Android system will take the most specific resources available for a given locale, we included British English strings to illustrate how the graphics would match at the /res/drawables-en/ whereas the strings are pulled from /res/values-en-rGB.

As of Android 1.5, the internationalization support in Android is almost fully functional. You can test your application in the emulator and on the device. The Portrait and Landscape screen orientation support works in the Eclipse Layout Resource Designer on the emulator (you can change between Portrait and Landscape mode on-the-fly in the emulator by pressing the 7 key on the numeric keypad) and on the T-Mobile G1. Figure 5.11 shows the "MultiNational" application running in the emulator in the default English language.

You can then navigate to the Locale settings and change to French, English (United Kingdom), and any other locale setting to see how different resources are loaded. You can also get some idea of whether your resources are set up properly within the Eclipse Layout Resource Designer (see Figure 5.12). Here, you can change the settings to see what your layout would look like using different device configurations. This allows developers to get a head start on internationalization at the layout design stage, even before the application is ready for testing.

Figure 5.11   The MultiNational Application in Landscape and Portrait
modes in the emulator (English).

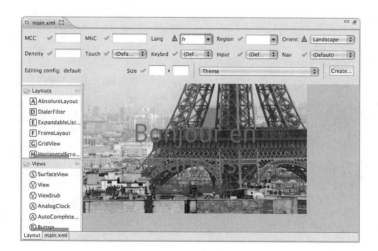

Figure 5.12   The MultiNational application in Landscape modes in the
Layout Designer (French).

Organizing Application Resources Efficiently

Choose your directory naming scheme carefully. Consider having a default configuration, which you don't set specifically, to provide a catch-all for assets, so they are always defined, regardless of the hardware configuration. Then add specific tailored resources, which overlay your defaults.

For example, if your T-Mobile G1 application generally requires the keyboard, you might design your application user interface in Landscape mode and store those assets in the default directories (for example, /res/drawable/). However, you might include some nondefault portrait mode resources for your application in more specific subset directory (/res/drawable-port).

Another method might be to keep your default language (for example, English) in the /res/values/strings.xml file, but as you add languages, create the appropriate string files for those languages. This means that your application will run on any nonspecified platform in English but also in target platforms you have specifically made string resources for in the local language, such as French or Korean.

Notice in the "MultiNational" project that we included a set of resources without language settings (the Earth backgrounds and the "Yo!" string, as shown in Figure 5.13). These are generic. These resources are used if the language setting is *not* set to English (en) or French (fr). Ideally, your application would also support square screen orientations but because we don't have a phone yet that has this screen type, we left it out of the example.

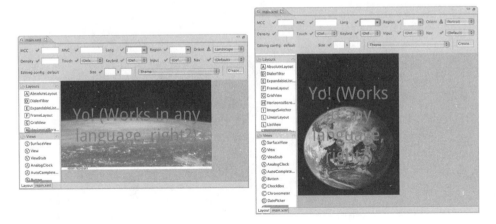

Figure 5.13   The MultiNational application in Landscape and Portrait mode in the Layout Designer with language set to anything other than English or French.

> **Tip**
>
> A number of new utility classes and methods were introduced in Android 1.5 for string and date manipulation, and region–specific phone number formatting.

Summary

Android applications rely on various types of resources, including strings, string arrays, colors, dimensions, drawable objects, graphics, animation sequences, layouts, styles, and themes. Resources can also be raw files. Many of these resources are defined with XML and organized into specially named project directories.

Resources are compiled and accessed using the `R.java` class file, which is automatically generated when the application resources are compiled. Developers access application and system resources programmatically using this special class.

In the next few chapters, you learn more about user interface design, creating layouts programmatically and using XML layout files, and more about all the user interface widgets available as part of the Android SDK. In Chapter 6, we dive further into the user interface components available in the Android SDK, specifically the various interactive widgets that can be used within these layouts—controls such as `Button`, `Spinner`, and `DatePicker` objects. Chapter 7 covers how to lay widgets out on the screen in various ways to organize user interface displays.

References and More Information

ISO 639-1 Languages: www.loc.gov/standards/iso639-2/php/code_list.php
ISO 3166-1-alpha-2 Regions: www.iso.org/iso/country_codes/iso_3166_code_lists/

III

Android User Interface Design Essentials

6

Exploring User Interface Screen Elements

Most Android applications inevitably need some form of user interface. In this chapter, we discuss the user interface elements available within the Android Software Development Kit (SDK). Some of these elements display information to the user whereas others gather information from the user.

You learn how to use a variety of different components and widgets to build a screen and how your application can listen for various actions performed by the user. Finally, you learn how to style widgets and apply themes to entire screens.

Introducing Android Views, Widgets, and Layouts

Before we go any further, we need to define a few terms. This gives you a better understanding of certain capabilities provided by the Android SDK before they are fully introduced. First, let's talk about the `View` and what it is to the Android SDK.

Introducing the Android View

The Android SDK has a Java packaged named `android.view`. This package contains a number of interfaces and classes related to drawing on the screen. However, when we refer to the `View` object, we actually refer to only one of the classes within this package, the `android.view.View` class.

The `View` class is the basic user interface building block within Android. It represents a rectangular portion of the screen. The `View` class serves as the base class for nearly all the widgets and layouts within the Android SDK.

Introducing the Android Widget

The Android SDK contains a Java package named `android.widget`. When we refer to widgets, we are typically referring to a class within this package. Widgets include almost anything within the Android SDK that you might want to draw, including `ImageView`,

`FrameLayout`, `EditText`, and `Button` objects. As mentioned previously, all widgets are typically derived from the `View` class.

This chapter is primarily about widgets that display and collect data from the user. We cover many of these basic widgets in detail.

> **Note**
>
> There is also another term, AppWidget, which was introduced in Android SDK 1.5. An AppWidget (`android.appwidget`) is an application extension, such as a desktop plug-in, which can be placed on the Android Home screen. We discuss AppWidgets in more depth in Chapter 7, "Designing Android User Interfaces with Layouts."

Introducing the Android Layout

One type of widget found within the `android.widget` package is the layout. An Android layout widget is still a `View` object, but it doesn't actually draw anything on the screen. Instead, it is a parent container for other widgets (children). Layout widgets determine how and where on the screen they draw child widgets following particular rules. For instance, the `LinearLayout` `View` draws its child widgets in a single horizontal row or a single vertical column. `AbsoluteLayout` widgets allow exact coordinates to be set for each child widget.

By necessity, we use some of the layout `View` objects within this chapter to illustrate how to use the widgets previously mentioned. However, we won't go into the details of the various layout types until the next chapter.

In Chapter 7 we organize various widgets within layouts and other containers. These special `View` widgets, which are derived from the `android.view.ViewGroup` class, are useful only when you understand the various simple widgets these containers can hold.

Displaying Text to Users with `TextView`

One of the most basic user interface elements, or widgets, in the Android SDK is the `TextView` widget. It is used, quite simply, to draw text on the screen. The `TextView` widget is primarily used to display fixed text strings or labels.

Frequently, the `TextView` widget is used by or is derived from other screen elements. As with most of the user interface elements, it is derived from `View` and is within the `android.widget` package. Because it is a `View`, all the standard attributes such as width, height, padding, and visibility can be applied to the object. However, as a text displaying control, many other `TextView` specific attributes can be applied to control widget behavior and how the text is viewed in a variety of situations.

First, though, let's see how to put some quick text up on the screen. The XML layout file tag used to display text on the screen is `<"TextView">`. You can set the `android:text` property of the `TextView` to be either a raw text string in the layout file or a reference to a string resource.

Here are examples of both methods to set the `android:text` attribute of a `TextView`. The first sets the text attribute to a raw string, the second to a string resource defined in the `strings.xml` resource file.

```
<TextView
    android:id="@+id/TextView01"
    android:layout_width="wrap_content"
    android:layout_height="wrap_content"
    android:text="Some sample text here" />
<TextView
    android:id="@+id/TextView01"
    android:layout_width="wrap_content"
    android:layout_height="wrap_content"
    android:text="@string/sample_text" />
```

To display this `TextView` on the screen, all your `Activity` needs to do is call the `setContentView()` method with the layout resource identifier in which you defined the preceding XML shown. You can change the text displayed programmatically by calling the `setText()` method on the `TextView` object. Retrieving the text is done with the `getText()` method.

Now let's talk about some of the more common attributes of `TextView` objects.

Configuring Layout and Sizing

Although you learn more about general layout in the Chapter 7, the `TextView` object has some special attributes that control how the text is drawn and flows. You can, for instance, set the `TextView` to be a single line high and a fixed width. If, however, you put a long string of text that can't fit, the text truncates abruptly. However, there are some attributes that control this.

> **Tip**
>
> When looking through the attributes available to `TextView` objects, you should be aware that the Android SDK actually has the full editable text input implementation as part of `TextView`. This means a lot of the attributes apply only to input fields, which are used primarily by the subclass `EditText` object. For example, the `autoText` attribute, which helps the user by fixing common spelling mistakes, is most appropriately set on editable text fields (`EditText`). There is no need to use this attribute normally when displaying only text.

The width of a `TextView` can be controlled in terms of the `ems` measurement rather than in pixels. An `em` is a term used in typography that is defined in terms of the point size of a particular font. (For example, the measure of an `em` in a 12-point font is 12 points.) This measurement allows better control over how much text is viewed, regardless of the font size. Through the `ems` attribute, you can set the width of the `TextView`. Additionally, you can use the `maxEms` and `minEms` attributes to set the maximum width and minimum width, respectively, of the `TextView` in terms of `ems`.

The height of a `TextView` can be set in terms of lines of text rather than pixels. Again, this is useful for controlling how much text can be viewed regardless of the font size. The lines attribute sets the number of lines that the `TextView` can display. You can also use `maxLines` and `minLines` to control the maximum height and minimum height, respectively, that the `Textview` displays.

Here is an example that combines these two types of sizing attributes. This `TextView` will be two lines of text high and 12 `ems` of text wide. The layout width and height are specified to the size of the `TextView` and are required attributes in the XML schema:

```
<TextView
    android:id="@+id/TextView04"
    android:layout_width="wrap_content"
    android:layout_height="wrap_content"
    android:lines="2"
    android:ems="12"
    android:text="@string/autolink_test" />
```

Instead of having the text only truncate at the end, as happens in the preceding example, we can enable the `ellipsize` attribute to replace the last couple of characters with an ellipsis (…) so the user knows that not all text is displayed.

Creating Contextual Links in Text

If your text contains references to email addresses, web pages, phone numbers, or even addresses, you might want to consider using the attribute `autoLink` (see Figure 6.1). The `autoLink` attribute has four values that can be used in combination with each other. When enabled, these `autoLink` attribute values create standard web-style links to the application that can act on that data type. For instance, setting the attribute to `web` automatically finds and links any URLs to web pages.

Your text can contain the following values for the `autoLink` attribute:

- `web`: Enables linking of URLs to web pages
- `email`: Enables linking of email addresses to the mail client with the recipient filled
- `phone`: Enables linking of phone numbers to the dialer application with the phone number filled out, ready to be dialed
- `map`: Enables linking of addresses to the map application to show the location

Figure 6.1   Three TextViews: Simple, AutoLink All (not clickable),
AutoLink All (clickable).

Turning on the `autoLink` feature relies on the detection of the various types within the Android SDK. In some cases, the linking might not be correct or might be misleading. Here is an example that links email and web pages, which are the most reliable in our opinion:

```
<TextView
    android:id="@+id/TextView02"
    android:layout_width="wrap_content"
    android:layout_height="wrap_content"
    android:text="@string/autolink_test"
    android:autoLink="web|email" />
```

There are two helper values for this attribute, as well. You can set it to `none` to make sure no type of data is linked. You can also set it to `all` to have all known types linked, as demonstrated in Figure 6.2. The default for a `TextView` is not to link any types. If you want the user to see these various data types highlighted but you don't want them to click on them, you can set the attribute `linksClickable` to `false`.

Figure 6.2   Clickable AutoLinks: URL launches browser, phone number
launches dialer, street address launches Google Maps.

Getting Text From Users with `EditText` and `Spinner`

The Android SDK provides a convenient widget called `EditText` to handle text input
from a user. The `EditText` class is derived from `TextView`. In fact, most of its functionality is contained within `TextView` but enabled when created as an `EditText`. The
`EditText` object has a number of useful features enabled by default, many shown in
Figure 6.3.

First, though, let's see how to define an `EditText` widget in an XML layout file:

```
<EditText
    android:id="@+id/EditText01"
    android:layout_height="wrap_content"
    android:hint="type here"
    android:lines="4"
    android:layout_width="fill_parent" />
```

This layout code shows a basic `EditText` element. There are a couple of interesting
things to note. First, the `hint` attribute puts some text in the edit box that will go away
when the user starts entering text. Essentially, this gives a hint to the user as to what
should go there. Next is the `lines` attribute, which defines how many lines tall the
input box will be. If this is not set, the entry field grows as the user enters text. However,
setting a size allows the user to scroll within a fixed sized to edit the text. This also
applies to the width of the entry.

Figure 6.3   Various styles of EditText widgets and Spinner and Button
Widgets.

By default, the user can perform a long press to bring up a context menu. This allows
the user some basic copy, cut, and paste operations (shown in Figure 6.4). You do not
need to provide any additional code for this useful behavior to benefit your users. You
can also highlight a portion of the text from code, too. A call to `setSelection()` does
this, and a call to `selectAll()` highlights the entire text entry field.

What's New in Android 1.5

One of the most exciting features introduced in Android 1.5 is the Text Input Method
Framework. This framework includes powerful predictive text support, downloadable Input
Method Editors (IMEs), and a Speech Recognition Framework (`android.speech`, handled
via the `android.speech.RecognizerIntent` intent). When used in conjunction with
the software keyboard, this functionality greatly enhanced the input method functionality of
the Android view hierarchy.

Although the `TextView` widget handles much of this seamlessly, developers might also
want to design custom text editors. This can be done by implementing the
`InputConnection (android.view.inputmethod.InputConnection)` interface in
association with your custom view.

Many new and useful text input and text utility methods have also been introduced in the
latest version of the Android SDK. For example, the developer can now listen for a number
of important `TextView` user events corresponding to input method changes. There are
also a number of new text classes and utility methods in the `android.text` package.

Figure 6.4   Long press on EditText widgets typically launches a Context
menu for Select, Cut and Paste.

The `EditText` object is essentially an editable `TextView`. This means that text can be
read from it in the same way as you did with `TextView`: by using the `getText()`
method. You can also set initial text to draw in the text entry area using the `getText()`
method. This is useful when a user edits a form that already has data. Finally, you can set
the `editable` attribute to `false`, so the user cannot edit the text in the field but can
still copy text out of it using a long press.

Helping the User with Auto Completion

In addition to providing a basic text editor with the `EditText` widget, the Android
SDK also provides a way to help the user out with entering commonly entered data into
forms. This functionality is provided through the auto-complete feature.

There are two forms of auto-complete. One is the more standard style of filling in the
entire text entry based on what the user types. If the user begins typing a string that
matches a word in a developer-provided list, the word can be finished for the user, if

they choose. This is done through the `AutoCompleteTextView` widget (Figure 6.5). The second method allows the user to enter a list of items, each of which has auto-complete functionality (also see Figure 6.5). These items must be separated in some way by providing a `Tokenizer` to the `MultiAutoCompleteTextView` object that handles this method. A common `Tokenizer` implementation is provided for comma-separated lists and is used by specifying the `MultiAutoCompleteTextView.CommaTokenizer` object. This can be helpful for lists of specifying common tags and the like.

Figure 6.5   Using AutoCompleteTextView (left) and
MultiAutoCompleteTextView (right).

Both of the auto-complete text editors use an adapter to get the list of text that they use to provide completions to the user. This example shows how to provide an `EditText` for the user that can help them type some of the basic colors from an array in the code:

```
final String[] COLORS = {
    "red", "green", "orange", "blue", "purple",
    "black", "yellow", "cyan", "magenta" };
```

```
ArrayAdapter<String> adapter =
    new ArrayAdapter<String>(this,
        android.R.layout.simple_dropdown_item_1line,
        COLORS);
AutoCompleteTextView text =
    (AutoCompleteTextView) findViewById(R.id.AutoCompleteTextView01);
text.setAdapter(adapter);
```

In this example, when the user starts typing in the field, if they start with one of the letters in the COLORS array, a drop-down list shows them all the available completions. Note that this does not limit what the users can enter. They are still free to enter any text that they choose (like puce). The adapter controls the look of the drop-down list. In this case, we use a built-in layout made for such things. Here is the layout resource definition for this AutoCompleteTextView widget:

```
<AutoCompleteTextView
    android:id="@+id/AutoCompleteTextView01"
    android:layout_width="fill_parent"
    android:layout_height="wrap_content"
    android:completionHint="Pick a color or type your own"
    android:completionThreshold="1" />
```

There are a couple more things to notice here. First, you can choose when the completion drop-down list shows by filling in a value for the completionThreshold attribute. In this case, we set it to a single character, so it will show immediately if there is a match. The default value is two characters of typing before it displays auto-completion options. Second, you can set some text in the completionHint attribute. This shows at the bottom of the drop-down list to help users out. Finally, the drop-down list for completions will be sized to the TextView. This means that it should be wide enough to show the completions and the text for the completionHint attribute.

The MultiAutoCompleteTextView is essentially the same as the regular auto-complete, except that you must assign a Tokenizer to it so that the control knows where each auto-completion should begin. The following is an example that uses the same adapter as the previous example but includes a Tokenizer for a list of user color responses, each separated by a comma:

```
MultiAutoCompleteTextView mtext =
    (MultiAutoCompleteTextView) findViewById(R.id.MultiAutoCompleteTextView01);
mtext.setAdapter(adapter);
mtext.setTokenizer(new MultiAutoCompleteTextView.CommaTokenizer());
```

As you can see, the only change actually is setting the Tokenizer. Here we used the built-in comma Tokenizer provided by the Android SDK. In this case, whenever a user chooses a color from the list, the name of the color is completed, and a comma is automatically added so that the user can immediately start typing in the next color. As before, this does not limit what the user can enter. If the user were to enter "maroon" and place a comma after that, the auto-completion starts again as they type another color regardless of the fact that it didn't help the user type in the color maroon. You can create your own `Tokenizer` by implementing the `MultiAutoCompleteTextView.Tokenizer` interface. You can do this if you'd prefer entries separated by a semicolon or some other more complex separators.

Constraining User Input with Input Filters

There are often times when you don't want the user to type just anything. Validating input after the user has entered something is one way to do this. However, a better way to avoid wasting the user's time is to filter the input. The `EditText` widget provides a way to set an `InputFilter` that does only this.

The Android SDK provides some `InputFilter` objects for use. There are `InputFilter` objects that enforce such rules as allowing only uppercase text and limiting the length of the text entered. You can create custom filters by implementing the `InputFilter` interface, which contains the single method called `filter()`. Here is an example of an `EditText` widget with two built-in filters that might be appropriate for a two-letter state abbreviation:

```
final EditText text_filtered =
    (EditText) findViewById(R.id.input_filtered);
text_filtered.setFilters(new InputFilter[] {
    new InputFilter.AllCaps(),
    new InputFilter.LengthFilter(2)
});
```

As you see, the `setFilters()` method call takes an array of `InputFilter` objects. This is useful for combining multiple filters, as shown. In this case, we're converting all input to uppercase. Additionally, we're setting the maximum length to two-characters long. As you can see in Figure 6.6, the `EditText` widget looks the same as any other, but if you try to type lowercase, it will be converted to uppercase, and the string is limited to two characters. This does not mean that all possible inputs will be valid, but it does help the user out so that they don't need to worry about making the input too long or bother with the case of the input. This also helps your application by guaranteeing that any text from this input will be a length of two. It does not constrain the input to only letters, though.

Figure 6.6   Filtering `EditText` to two capitalized characters.

Constraining User Input with Drop-Down Lists Using `Spinner` Widgets

Sometimes you want to limit the choices available for users to type. For instance, if users are going to enter the name of a state, we might as well limit them to only the valid states because this is a known set. Although you could do this by letting them type something and then blocking invalid entries, you can also provide similar functionality with a `Spinner` control. Like the auto-complete method, the possible choices for a spinner can come from an `Adapter`. You can also set the available choices in the layout definition by using the entries attribute with an array resource (specifically a string-array that is referenced as something like `@array/state-list`). The Spinner control isn't actually an `EditText` although it is frequently used in a similar fashion. Here is an example of the XML layout definition for a `Spinner` control for choosing a color:

```
<Spinner
    android:id="@+id/Spinner01"
    android:layout_width="wrap_content"
    android:layout_height="wrap_content"
```

```
android:entries="@array/colors"
android:prompt="@string/spin_prompt" />
```

This places a `spinner` control on the screen (Figure 6.7). When the user selects it, a pop-up shows the prompt text followed by a list of all the possible choices. This list allows only a single item to be selected at a time, and when one is selected the pop-up will go away.

Figure 6.7   Filtering Choices with a `spinner` control.

There are a couple of things to notice here. First, the `entries` attribute is set to the values that shows by assigning it to an array resource, referred to here as `@array/colors`.

Tip

See Chapter 5, "Managing Application Resources," for how to create an array resource.

Second, the `prompt` attribute is defined to a string resource. Unlike some other string attributes, this one is required to be a string resource. The prompt displays when the pop-up comes up and can be used to tell the user what kinds of values they are selecting from.

Because the `Spinner` control is not a `TextView`, but a list of `TextView` objects, you can't directly request the selected text from it directly. Instead, you have to retrieve the selected `View` and extract the text directly:

```
final Spinner spin = (Spinner) findViewById(R.id.Spinner01);
TextView text_sel = (TextView)spin. getSelectedView();
String selected_text = text_sel.getText();
```

As it turns out, you can request the currently selected `View` object, which happens to be a `TextView` in this case. This allows us to retrieve the text and use it directly. Alternatively, we could have called the `getSelectedItem()` or `getSelectedItemId()` methods to deal with other forms of selection.

Using Buttons, Check Boxes, and Radio Groups

Another common user interface element is the button. In this section, you learn about different kinds of buttons provided by the Android SDK. These include the basic `Button`, `ToggleButton`, `CheckBox`, and `RadioButton`. You can find examples of each button type in Figure 6.8.

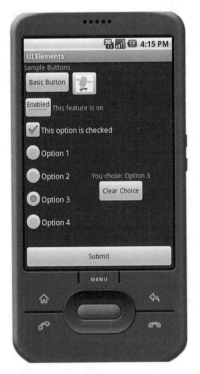

Figure 6.8   Various types of button widgets.

A basic `Button` is often used to perform some sort of action, such as submitting a form or confirming a selection. They can contain a text or image label.

A `CheckBox` is a button with two states—checked or unchecked. `CheckBox` widgets are often used to turn a feature on or off or to pick multiple items from a list.

A `ToggleButton` is similar to a `CheckBox`, but is used to visually show the state. The default behavior of a toggle is like that of a power on/off button.

A `RadioButton` provides selection of an item. Grouping `RadioButton` widgets together in a container called a `RadioGroup` enables the developer to enforce that only one `RadioButton` is selected at a time.

Using Basic Buttons

The `android.widget.Button` class provides a basic button implementation in the Android SDK. Within the XML layout resources, buttons are specified using the `Button` element. The primary attribute for a basic button is the text field. This is the label that appears on the middle of the button's face. You'll often use basic `Button` widgets for buttons with text such as "Ok," "Cancel," or "Submit."

> **Tip**
>
> You can find many common application string values in the Android system resource strings, exposed in `android.R.string`. There are strings for common button text like "yes," "no," "ok," "cancel," "copy." For more information on system resources, see Chapter 5.

The following XML layout resource file shows a typical `Button` widget definition.

```
<Button
    android:id="@+id/basic_button"
    android:layout_width="wrap_content"
    android:layout_height="wrap_content"
    android:text="Basic Button" />
```

A button won't do anything, other than animate, without some code to handle the click event. Here is an example of some code that handles a click for a basic button and displays a `Toast` message on the screen:

```
setContentView(R.layout.buttons);
final Button basic_button = (Button) findViewById(R.id.basic_button);
basic_button.setOnClickListener(new View.OnClickListener() {
    public void onClick(View v) {
        Toast.makeText(Buttons.this,
            "Button clicked", Toast.LENGTH_SHORT).show();
    }
});
```

To handle the click event for when a button is pressed, we first get a reference to the `Button` by its resource identifier. Next, the `setOnClickListener()` method is called. It requires a valid instance of the class `View.OnClickListener`. A simple way to provide this is to define the instance right in the method call. This requires implementing the `onClick()` method. Within the `onClick()` method, you are free to carry out whatever actions you need. Here, we simply display a message to the users telling them that the button was, in fact, clicked.

A button with its primary label as an image is an `ImageButton`. An `ImageButton` is, for most purposes, almost exactly like a basic button. Click actions are handled in the same way. The primary difference is that you can set its `src` attribute to be an image. Here is an example of an `ImageButton` definition in an XML layout resource file:

```
<ImageButton
    android:layout_width="wrap_content"
    android:layout_height="wrap_content"
    android:id="@+id/image_button"
    android:src="@drawable/droid" />
```

In this case, a small `drawable` resource is reference. You can see what this "Android" button looks like in Figure 6.8.

Using Check Boxes and Toggle Buttons

The check box button is often used in lists of items where multiple items can be selected. The Android check box contains a text attribute that appears to the side of the check box. This is used in a similar way to the label of a basic button. In fact, it's basically a `TextView` next to the button.

Here's an XML layout resource definition for a `CheckBox` widget:

```
<CheckBox
    android:id="@+id/checkbox"
    android:layout_width="wrap_content"
    android:layout_height="wrap_content"
    android:text="Check me?" />
```

You can see how this `CheckBox` is displayed in Figure 6.8.

The following example shows how to check for the state of the button programmatically and change the text label to reflect the change:

```
final CheckBox check_button = (CheckBox) findViewById(R.id.checkbox);
check_button.setOnClickListener(new View.OnClickListener() {
    public void onClick (View v) {
        TextView tv = (TextView)findViewById(R.id.checkbox);
            tv.setText(check_button.isChecked() ?
                "This option is checked" :
                "This option is not checked");
    }
});
```

This is similar to the basic button. A check box automatically shows the check as enabled or disabled. This allows us to deal with behavior in our application rather than worrying about how the button should behave. The layout shows that the text starts out one way but after the user pressed the button in changes to one of two different things depending on the checked state. As the code shows, the CheckBox is also a TextView.

A Toggle Button is similar to a check box in behavior but is usually used to show or alter the on or off state of something. Like the CheckBox, it has a state (checked or not). Also like the check box, the act of changing what displays on the button is handled for us. Unlike the CheckBox, it does not show text next to it. Instead, it has two text fields. The first attribute is textOn, which is the text that is shown on the button when its checked state is on. The second attribute is textOff, which is the text that is shown on the button when its checked state is off. The default text for these is "ON" and "OFF," respectively.

The following layout code shows a definition for a toggle button that shows "Enabled" or "Disabled" based on the state of the button:

```
<ToggleButton
    android:id="@+id/toggle_button"
    android:layout_width="wrap_content"
    android:layout_height="wrap_content"
    android:text="Toggle"
    android:textOff="Disabled"
    android:textOn="Enabled" />
```

This type of button will not actually display the value for the text attribute, even though it's a valid attribute to set. Here, the only purpose it serves is to demonstrate that it doesn't display. You can see what this ToggleButton looks like in Figure 6.8.

Using RadioGroups and RadioButtons

Radio buttons are often used when a user should be allowed to only select one item from a small group of items. For instance, a question asking for gender can give three options: male, female, and unspecified. Only one of these options should be checked at a time. The RadioButton objects are similar to CheckBox objects. They have a text label next to them, set via the text attribute, and they have a state (checked or unchecked). However, RadioButton objects can be grouped inside a RadioGroup that handles enforcing their combined states so that only one RadioButton can be checked at a time. If the user selects a RadioButton that is already checked, it does not become unchecked. However, you can provide the user with an action to clear the state of the entire RadioGroup so that none of the buttons are checked.

Here we have an XML layout resource with a `RadioGroup` containing four `RadioButton` objects (shown in Figure 6.8). The `RadioButton` objects have text labels, "Option 1," and so on. The XML layout resource definition is shown here:

```
<RadioGroup
    android:id="@+id/RadioGroup01"
    android:layout_width="wrap_content"
    android:layout_height="wrap_content">
    <RadioButton
        android:id="@+id/RadioButton01"
        android:layout_width="wrap_content"
        android:layout_height="wrap_content"
        android:text="Option 1"></RadioButton>
    <RadioButton
        android:id="@+id/RadioButton02"
        android:layout_width="wrap_content"
        android:layout_height="wrap_content"
        android:text="Option 2"></RadioButton>
    <RadioButton
        android:id="@+id/RadioButton03"
        android:layout_width="wrap_content"
        android:layout_height="wrap_content"
        android:text="Option 3"></RadioButton>
    <RadioButton
        android:id="@+id/RadioButton04"
        android:layout_width="wrap_content"
        android:layout_height="wrap_content"
        android:text="Option 4"></RadioButton>
</RadioGroup>
```

Handling actions on these `RadioButton` objects is handled through the `RadioGroup` object. The following example shows registering for clicks on the `RadioButton` objects within the `RadioGroup`:

```
final RadioGroup group = (RadioGroup)findViewById(R.id.RadioGroup01);
final TextView tv = (TextView)
    findViewById(R.id.TextView01);

group.setOnCheckedChangeListener(new
    RadioGroup.OnCheckedChangeListener() {
        public void onCheckedChanged(
            RadioGroup group, int checkedId) {
            if (checkedId != -1) {
                RadioButton rb = (RadioButton)
                    findViewById(checkedId);
                if (rb != null) {
                    tv.setText("You chose: " + rb.getText());
```

```
        }
    } else {
        tv.setText("Choose 1");
    }
  }
});
```

As this layout example demonstrates, there is not anything special that you need to do to make the `RadioGroup` and internal `RadioButton` objects work properly. The preceding code illustrates how to register to receive a notification whenever the `RadioButton` selection changes.

The code demonstrates that the notification contains the resource identifier for the specific `RadioButton` that was chosen, as assigned in the layout file. To do something interesting with this, you need to provide a mapping between this resource identifier (or the text label) to the corresponding functionality in your code. In the example, we query for the button that was selected, get its text, and assign its text to another `TextView` widget that we have on the screen.

As mentioned, the entire `RadioGroup` can be cleared so that none of the `RadioButton` objects are selected. The following example demonstrates how to do this in response to a button click outside of the `RadioGroup`:

```
final Button clear_choice = (Button) findViewById(R.id.Button01);
clear_choice.setOnClickListener(new View.OnClickListener() {
    public void onClick(View v) {
        RadioGroup group = (RadioGroup)
            findViewById(R.id.RadioGroup01);
        if (group != null) {
            group.clearCheck();
        }
    }
}
```

The action of calling the `clearCheck()` method triggers a call to the `onCheckedChangedListener()` callback method. This is why we have to make sure that the resource identifier we received is valid. Right after a call to the `clearCheck()` method, it will not be a valid identifier but instead will be set to the value –1 to indicate that no `RadioButton` is currently checked.

Figure 6.8 shows what all these buttons look like on a single screen. The code for this is provided on the CD provided with the book and the book Web site.

Getting Dates and Times from Users

The Android SDK provides a couple of widgets for getting date and time input from the user. The first is the `DatePicker` widget (shown in Figure 6.9). It can be used to get a month, day, and year from the user.

Figure 6.9   Date and time widgets.

The basic XML layout resource definition for a `DatePicker` follows:

```
<DatePicker
    android:id="@+id/DatePicker01"
    android:layout_width="wrap_content"
    android:layout_height="wrap_content" />
```

As you can see from this example, there aren't any attributes specific to the `DatePicker` widget. Like many of the other widgets, your code can register to receive a method call when the date changes. You do this by implementing the `onDateChanged()` method. However, this isn't done the usual way.

```
final DatePicker date = (DatePicker)findViewById(R.id.DatePicker01);
date.init(date.getYear(), date.getMonth(), date.getDayOfMonth(),
    new DatePicker.OnDateChangedListener() {
        public void onDateChanged(DatePicker view, int year,
            int monthOfYear, int dayOfMonth) {
                Date dt = new Date(year-1900,
                    monthOfYear, dayOfMonth, time.getCurrentHour(),
```

```
                time.getCurrentMinute());
            text.setText(dt.toString());
        }
    });
```

The preceding code sets the `DatePicker.OnDateChangedListener` by a call to the `DatePicker.init()` method. A `DatePicker` widget is initialized with the current date. A `TextView` is set with the date value that the user entered into the `DatePicker` widget. The value of 1900 is subtracted from the year parameter to make it compatible with the `java.util.Date` class.

A `TimePicker` widget (also shown in Figure 6.9) is similar to the `DatePicker` widget. It also doesn't have any unique attributes, either. However, to register for a method call when the values change, you call the more traditional method of `TimePicker.setOnTimeChangedListener()`.

```
time.setOnTimeChangedListener(new TimePicker.OnTimeChangedListener() {
    public void onTimeChanged(TimePicker view,
        int hourOfDay, int minute) {
            Date dt = new Date(date.getYear()-1900, date.getMonth(),
                date.getDayOfMonth(), hourOfDay, minute);
            text.setText(dt.toString());
    }
});
```

As in the previous example, this code also sets a `TextView` to a string displaying the time value that the user entered. Used together, the user can set a full date and time.

Indicating Information to Users

The Android SDK provides a number of widgets that can be used to visually show some form of information to the user. These indicator widgets include progress bars, clocks, and other similar controls.

Indicating Progress with `ProgressBar`

Applications commonly perform actions that can take a while. A good practice during this time is to show the user some sort of progress indicator, informing the user that the application is off "doing something." Applications can also show how far a user is through some operation, such as a playing a song or watching a video. The Android SDK provides several types of progress bars.

The standard one is a circular indicator that only animates. It does not show how complete an action is. It can, however, show that something is taking place. This is useful when an action is indeterminate in length. There are three sizes of this type of progress indicator (Figure 6.10).

Figure 6.10   Various types of progress and rating indicators.

The second type is a horizontal progress bar that can show the completeness of an action. (For example, you can see how much of a file is downloading.) This horizontal progress bar can also have a secondary progress indicator on it. This can be used, for instance, to show the completion of a downloading media file while that file plays.

This is an XML layout resource definition for a basic indeterminate progress bar:

```
<ProgressBar
    android:id="@+id/progress_bar"
    android:layout_width="wrap_content"
    android:layout_height="wrap_content" />
```

The default style is for a medium-size circular progress indicator; not a "bar" at all. The other two styles for indeterminate progress bar are progressBarStyleLarge and progressBarStyleSmall. This style animates automatically. The next sample shows the layout definition for a horizontal progress indicator:

```
<ProgressBar
    android:id="@+id/progress_bar"
    style="?android:attr/progressBarStyleHorizontal"
    android:layout_width="fill_parent"
```

```
android:layout_height="wrap_content"
android:max="100" />
```

We have also set the attribute for `max` in this sample to 100. This can help mimic a percentage progress bar. That is, setting the progress to 75 shows the indicator at 75 percent complete.

We can set the indicator progress status programmatically as follows:

```
mProgress = (ProgressBar) findViewById(R.id.progress_bar);
mProgress.setProgress(75);
```

You can also put these progress bars in your application's title bar (as shown in Figure 6.10). This can save screen real estate. This can also make it easy to turn on and off an indeterminate progress indicator without changing the look of the screen. Indeterminate progress indicators are commonly used to display progress on pages where items need to be loaded before the page can finish drawing. This is often employed on web browser screens. The following code demonstrates how to place this type of indeterminate progress indicator on your `Activity` screen:

```
requestWindowFeature(Window.FEATURE_INDETERMINATE_PROGRESS);
requestWindowFeature(Window.FEATURE_PROGRESS);
setContentView(R.layout.indicators);
setProgressBarIndeterminateVisibility(true);
setProgressBarVisibility(true);
setProgress(5000);
```

To use the indeterminate indicator on your `Activity` objects title bar, you need to request the feature `Window.FEATURE_INDETERMINATE_PROGRESS`, as previously shown. This shows a small circular indicator in the right side of the title bar. For a horizontal progress bar style that shows behind the title you need to enable the `Window.FEATURE_PROGRESS`. These features must be enabled before your application calls the `setContentView()` method, as shown in the preceding example.

You need to know about a couple of important default behaviors. First, the indicators are visible by default. Calling the visibility methods shown in the preceding example can set their visibility on or off. Second, the horizontal progress bar defaults to a maximum progress value of 10,000. In the preceding example, we set it to 5,000, which is equivalent to 50 percent. When the value reaches the maximum value, the indicators fade away so that they aren't visible. This happens for both indicators.

Indicating and Adjusting Progress with SeekBar

You have seen how to display progress to the user. What if, however, you want to allow the user some ability to move the indicator, for example, to set the current cursor position in a playing media file or to tweak a volume setting? This can be accomplished by using the `SeekBar` widget provided by the Android SDK. It's like the regular horizontal

progress bar, but includes a thumb, or selector, which can be dragged by the user. A
default thumb selector is provided, but any drawable item can be used as a thumb. In
Figure 6.10, we replace the default thumb with a little Android graphic.

Here we have an example of an XML layout resource definition for a simple
SeekBar:

```
<SeekBar
    android:id="@+id/seekbar1"
    android:layout_height="wrap_content"
    android:layout_width="240px"
    android:max="500" />
```

With this sample SeekBar, the user can drag the thumb to any value between 0 and
500. Although this is shown visually, it might be useful to show the user what exact
value they are selecting. To do this, you can provide an implementation of the
onProgressChanged() method, as shown here:

```
SeekBar seek = (SeekBar) findViewById(R.id.seekbar1);
seek.setOnSeekBarChangeListener(
    new SeekBar.OnSeekBarChangeListener() {
        public void onProgressChanged(
            SeekBar seekBar, int progress,boolean fromTouch) {
            ((TextView)findViewById(R.id.seek_text))
                .setText("Value: "+progress);
            seekBar.setSecondaryProgress(
                (progress+seekBar.getMax())/2);
        }
});
```

There are two interesting things to notice in this example. The first is that the
fromTouch parameter tells the code if the change came from the user input or if,
instead, it came from a programmatic change like we demonstrated with the regular
ProgressBar widgets. The second interesting thing is that the SeekBar still allows a
secondary progress value to be set. In this example, we set the secondary indicator to be
halfway between the user's selected value and the maximum value of the progress bar.
You might use this feature to show the progress of a video and the buffer stream.

Indicating and Adjusting Ratings with RatingBar

Although the SeekBar is useful for allowing a user to set a value, such as the volume,
the RatingBar has a more specific purpose: showing ratings or getting a rating from a
user. By default, this progress bar uses the star paradigm with five stars by default. A user
can drag across this horizontal to set a rating. A program can set the value, as well.
However, the secondary indicator cannot be used because it is used internally by this
particular control.

Here's an example of an XML layout resource definition for a `RatingBar` with four stars:

```
<RatingBar
    android:id="@+id/ratebar1"
    android:layout_width="wrap_content"
    android:layout_height="wrap_content"
    android:numStars="4"
    android:stepSize="0.25" />
```

This layout definition for a `RatingBar` demonstrates setting both the number of stars and the increment between each rating value. Here, users can choose any rating value between 0 and 4.0, but only in steps of 0.25. For instance, they can set a value of 2.25. This is visualized to the users, by default, with the stars partially filled. Figure 6.10 illustrates how the `RatingBar` behaves.

Although the value is indicated to the user visually, you might still want to show a numeric representation of this value to the user. This can be done by implementing the `onRatingChanged()` method of the `RatingBar.OnRatingBarChangeListener` class.

```
RatingBar rate = (RatingBar) findViewById(R.id.ratebar1);
rate.setOnRatingBarChangeListener(new
    RatingBar.OnRatingBarChangeListener() {
        public void onRatingChanged(RatingBar ratingBar,
            float rating, boolean fromTouch) {
                ((TextView)findViewById(R.id.rating_text))
                    .setText("Rating: "+ rating);
    }
});
```

The preceding example shows how to register the listener. When the user selects a rating using the control, a `TextView` is set to the numeric rating the user entered. One interesting thing to note is that, unlike the `SeekBar`, the implementation of the `onRatingChange()` method is called after the change is complete, usually when the user lifts a finger. That is, while the user is dragging across the stars to make a rating, this method isn't called. It is called when the user stops pressing the control.

Indicating the Passage of Time with the `Chronometer`

Sometimes you want to show time passing instead of incremental progress. In this case, you can use the `Chronometer` widget as a timer (Figure 6.11). This might be useful if it's the user that is taking time doing some task or in a game where some action needs to be timed. The `Chronometer` widget can be formatted with text, as shown in this XML layout resource definition:

```
<Chronometer
    android:id="@+id/Chronometer01"
    android:layout_width="wrap_content"
    android:layout_height="wrap_content"
    android:format="Timer: %s" />
```

Figure 6.11   Chronometer, DigitalClock and AnalogClock widgets with
title bar progress.

The `Chronometer` object's `format` attribute can be used to put text around the time
that displays. A `Chronometer` won't show the passage of time until its `start()` method
is called. To stop it, simply call its `stop()` method. Finally, you can change when the
timer is counting from. That is, you can set it to count from a particular time in the past
instead of from whenever it's started. You call the `setBase()` method to do this.

> **Tip**
>
> Experimentally, we have found the base value of 0 to be whenever the phone was last
> restarted.

In this next example code, the timer is retrieved from the `View` by its resource identifier.
We then check its base value and set it to 0. Finally, we start the timer counting up
from there.

```
final Chronometer timer =
    (Chronometer)findViewById(R.id.Chronometer01);
long base = timer.getBase();
Log.d(ViewsMenu.debugTag, "base = "+ base);
```

```
timer.setBase(0);
timer.start();
```

> **Tip**
>
> You can listen for changes to the `Chronometer` by implementing the
> `Chronometer.OnChronometerTickListener` interface.

Indicating the Current Time with the `AnalogClock` and `DigitalClock`

Displaying the time in an application is often not necessary because Android devices have a status bar to display the current time. However, there are two clock widgets available to display this information, if your application needs them.

First is the `DigitalClock` widget (Figure 6.11). This widget is a compact text display of the current time in standard numeric format based on the users' settings. It is a `TextView`, so anything you can do with a `TextView` you can do with this widget, except change its text. You can change the color and style of the text, for example.

By default, the `DigitalClock` widget shows the seconds and automatically updates as each second ticks by. Here is an example of an XML layout resource definition for a `DigitalClock` widget:

```
<DigitalClock
    android:id="@+id/DigitalClock01"
    android:layout_width="wrap_content"
    android:layout_height="wrap_content" />
```

The second clock widget is the `AnalogClock` (Figure 6.11). This is a dial-based clock that is a basic clock face with two hands, one for the minute and one for the hour. It also updates automatically as each minute passes. The image drawn for the clock scales appropriately with the size of its `View`.

Here is an example of an XML layout resource definition for an `AnalogClock` widget:

```
<AnalogClock
    android:id="@+id/AnalogClock01"
    android:layout_width="wrap_content"
    android:layout_height="wrap_content" />
```

The `AnalogClock` widget's clock face is simple. However you can set its minute and hour hands, and the clock face can be set to specific `drawable` resources, if you wanted to jazz it up. Neither of these clock widgets accept a different time or a static time to display. They can show only the current time in the current time zone of the device, so they are not particularly useful.

Providing Users with Options and Context Menus

You need to be aware of two special application menus for use within your Android applications: the options menu and the context menu.

Enabling the Options Menu

The Android SDK provides a method for users to bring up a menu by pressing the menu key from within the application (Figure 6.12). You can use options menus within your application to bring up help, to navigate, to provide additional controls, or to configure options. The `OptionsMenu` control can contain icons, submenus, and keyboard shortcuts.

Figure 6.12   An options menu.

For an options menu to show when the user presses the `Menu` button on their device, you need to override the implementation of `onCreateOptionsMenu()` in your `Activity`. Here is a sample implementation that gives the user three menu items to choose from:

```
public boolean onCreateOptionsMenu( android.view.Menu menu) {
    super.onCreateOptionsMenu(menu);

    menu.add("Forms")
        .setIcon(android.R.drawable.ic_menu_edit)
        .setIntent(new Intent(this, Forms.class));
    menu.add("Indicators")
        .setIntent(new Intent(this, Indicators.class))
        .setIcon(android.R.drawable.ic_menu_info_details);
    menu.add("Containers")
        .setIcon(android.R.drawable.ic_menu_view)
        .setIntent(new Intent(this, Containers.class));
    return true;
}
```

For each of the items that are added, we also set a built-in icon resource and assign an Intent to each item. The item title is given with a regular text string, for clarity. A resource identifier can be used, as well. For this example, there is no other handling or code needed. When one of these menu items is selected, the Activity described by the Intent starts.

This type of options menu can be useful for navigating to important parts of an application such as the help page, from anywhere within your application. Another great use for an options menu is to allow configuration options for a given screen. These options can be configured in the form of checkable menu items. The initial menu that appears when the user presses the menu button does not support checkable menu items. Instead, these menu items must be placed on a SubMenu control, which is a type of Menu that can be configured within a menu. SubMenu objects support checkable items but do not support icons or other SubMenu items. Building on the preceding example, the following is code for programmatically adding a SubMenu control to the previous Menu:

```
SubMenu style_choice = menu.addSubMenu("Style")
    .setIcon(android.R.drawable.ic_menu_preferences);
style_choice.add(style_group, light_id, 1, "Light")
    .setChecked(isLight);
style_choice.add(style_group, dark_id, 2, "Dark")
    .setChecked(!isLight);
style_choice.setGroupCheckable(style_group, true, true);
```

This code would be inserted before the return statement in the implementation of the onCreateOptionsMenu()method. It adds a single menu item with an icon to the previous menu, called "Style." When the "Style" option is clicked, a pop-up menu with the two items of the SubMenu control is displayed. These items are grouped together and the checkable icon, by default, looks like the radio button icon. The checked state is assigned during creation time.

To handle the event when a menu option item is selected, we also implement the onOptionsItemSelected() method, as shown here:

```
public boolean onOptionsItemSelected(MenuItem item) {
    if (item.getItemId() == light_id) {
        item.setChecked(true);
        isLight = true;
        return true;
    } else if (item.getItemId() == dark_id) {
        item.setChecked(true);
        isLight = false;
        return true;
    }

    return super.onOptionsItemSelected(item);
}
```

This method must call the super class's onOptionsItemSelected() method for basic behavior to work. The actual MenuItem object is passed in, and we can use that to retrieve the identifier that we previously assigned to see which one was selected and perform an appropriate action. Here, we switch the values and return. By default, a Menu control will go away when any item is selected, including checkable items. This means it's useful for quick settings but not as useful for extensive settings where the user might want to change more than one item at a time.

As you add more menu items to your options menu, you might notice that a "More" item automatically appears. This happens whenever six or more items are visible. If the user selects this, the full menu appears. The full, expanded menu doesn't show menu icons and although checkable items are possible, they should not be done here. Additionally, the full title of an item doesn't show. The initial menu, also known as the icon menu, shows only a portion of the title for each item. You can assign each item a condensedTitle attribute, which shows instead of a truncated version of the regular title. For example, instead of the title Instant Message, you can set the condensedTitle attribute to "IM."

Enabling the ContextMenu

The ContextMenu is a subtype of Menu that you can configure to display when a long-press is performed on a View. As the name implies, the ContextMenu provides for contextual menus to display to the user for performing additional actions on selected items.

ContextMenu objects are slightly more complex than OptionsMenu objects. You need to implement the onCreateContextMenu() method of your Activity for one to display. However, before that is called, you must call the registerForContextMenu() method and pass in the View you want to have a context menu for. This means each View on your screen can have a different context menu, which is appropriate as the menus are designed to be highly contextual.

Here we have an example of a `Chronometer` timer, which responds to a long-click with a context menu:

```
registerForContextMenu(timer);
```

After the call to the `registerForContextMenu()` method has been executed, the user can then long-click on the `View` to open the context menu. Each time this happens, your `Activity` gets a call to the `onCreateContextMenu()` method, and your code creates the menu each time the user performs the long click.

The following is an example of a context menu for the `Chronometer` widget, as previously used:

```
public void onCreateContextMenu(
    ContextMenu menu, View v, ContextMenuInfo menuInfo) {
    super.onCreateContextMenu(menu, v, menuInfo);

    if (v.getId() == R.id.Chronometer01) {
        getMenuInflater().inflate(R.menu.timer_context, menu);
        menu.setHeaderIcon(android.R.drawable.ic_media_play)
            .setHeaderTitle("Timer controls");
    }
}
```

Recall that any `View` widget can register to trigger a call to the `onCreateContextMenu()` method when a long-press is performed by the user. That means we have to check which `View` widget it was that the user tried to get a context menu for. Next, we inflate the appropriate menu from a menu resource that we defined with XML. Because we can't define header information in the menu resource file, we set a stock Android SDK resource to it and add a title. Here is the menu resource that is inflated:

```
<menu
    xmlns:android="http://schemas.android.com/apk/res/android">
    <item
        android:id="@+id/start_timer"
        android:title="Start" />
    <item
        android:id="@+id/stop_timer"
        android:title="Stop" />
    <item
        android:id="@+id/reset_timer"
        android:title="reset" />
</menu>
```

This defines three menu items. If this weren't a context menu, we could have assigned icons. However, context menus do not support icons, submenus, or shortcuts. For more information on setting `Menu` resources in XML, see Chapter 5.

Now we need to handle the `ContextMenu` clicks by implementing the `onContextItemSelected()` method in our `Activity`. Here's an example:

```
public boolean onContextItemSelected(MenuItem item) {
    super.onContextItemSelected(item);

    Chronometer timer = (Chronometer)findViewById(R.id.Chronometer01);
    switch (item.getItemId()) {
        case R.id.stop_timer:
            timer.stop();
            break;
        case R.id.start_timer:
            timer.start();
            break;
        case R.id.reset_timer:
            timer.setBase(SystemClock.elapsedRealtime());
            break;
    }
    return true;
}
```

Because we have only one context menu in this example, we find the `Chronometer` view for use in this method. This method is called regardless of which context menu the selected item is on, though, so you should take care to have unique resource identifiers or keep track of which menu is shown. This can be accomplished because the context menu is created each time it's shown.

Handling User Events

You've seen how to do basic event handling in some of the previous widget examples. For instance, you know how to handle when a user clicks on a button. There are a number of other events generated by various actions the user might take. This section briefly introduces you to some of these events.

First, though, we need to talk about the input states within Android.

Listening for Touch Mode Changes

The Android screen can be in one of two states. The state determines how the focus on `View` widgets is handled. When touch mode is on, typically only objects such as `EditText` get focus when selected. Other objects, because they can be selected directly by the user tapping on the screen, won't take focus but instead trigger their action, if any. When not in touch mode, however, the user can change focus between even more object types. These include buttons and other views that would normally need only a click to trigger their action. In this case, the user would use the arrow keys, trackball, or wheel to navigate between items and select them with the Enter or select keys.

Knowing what mode the screen is in is useful if you want to handle certain events. If, for instance, your application relies on the focus or lack of focus on a particular widget, your application might need to know if the phone is in touch mode because the focus behavior is likely different.

Your application can register to find out when the touch mode changes by using the addOnTouchModeChangeListener() method within android.view. ViewTreeObserver class. Your application needs to implement the ViewTreeObserver. OnTouchModeChangeListener class to listen for these events. Here is a sample implementation:

```
View all = findViewById(R.id.events_screen);
ViewTreeObserver vto = all.getViewTreeObserver();
vto.addOnTouchModeChangeListener(
    new ViewTreeObserver.OnTouchModeChangeListener() {
        public void onTouchModeChanged(
            boolean isInTouchMode) {
            events.setText("Touch mode: " + isInTouchMode);
        }
});
```

In this example, the top level View in the layout is retrieved. A ViewTreeObserver listens to a View and all its child View objects. Using the top level View of the layout means the ViewTreeObserver listens to events within the entire layout. An implementation of the onTouchModeChanged() method provides the ViewTreeObserver with a method to call when the touch mode changes. It merely passes in which mode the View is now in.

In this example, the mode is written to a TextView named events. We use this same TextView in further event handling examples to visually show on the screen which events our application has been told about. The ViewTreeObserver can enable applications to listen to a few other events on an entire screen.

By running this sample code, we can demonstrate the touch mode changing to true immediately when the user taps on the touch screen. Conversely, when the user chooses to use any other input method, the application reports that touch mode is false immediately after the input event, such as a key being pressed or the trackball or scroll wheel moving.

Listening for Events on the Entire Screen

You saw in the last section how your application can watch for changes to the touch mode state for the screen using the ViewTreeObserver class. The ViewTreeObserver also provides three other events that can be watched for on a full screen or an entire View and all of its children. These are

- PreDraw: Get notified before the View and its children are drawn
- GlobalLayout: Get notified when the layout of the View and its children might change, including visibility changes
- GlobalFocusChange: Get notified when the focus within the View and its children changes

Your application might want to perform some actions before the screen is drawn. You can do this by calling the method `addOnPreDrawListener()` with an implementation of the `ViewTreeObserver.OnPreDrawListener` class interface.

Similarly, your application can find out when the layout or visibility of a `View` has changed. This might be useful if your application is dynamically changing the display contents of a view and you want to check to see if a `View` still fits on the screen. Your application needs to provide an implementation of the `ViewTreeObserver.OnGlobalLayoutListener` class interface to the `addGlobalLayoutListener()` method of the `ViewTreeObserver` object.

Finally, your application can register to find out when the focus changes between a `View` widget and any of its child `View` widgets. Your application might want to do this to monitor how a user moves about on the screen. When in touch mode, though, there might be fewer focus changes than when the touch mode is not set. In this case, your application needs to provide an implementation of the `ViewTreeObserver.OnGlobalFocusChangeListener` class interface to the `addGlobalFocusChangeListener()` method. Here is a sample implementation of this:

```
vto.addOnGlobalFocusChangeListener(new
    ViewTreeObserver.OnGlobalFocusChangeListener() {
        public void onGlobalFocusChanged(
            View oldFocus, View newFocus) {
                if (oldFocus != null && newFocus != null) {
                    events.setText("Focus \nfrom: " +
                        oldFocus.toString() + " \nto: " +
                        newFocus.toString());
                }
            }
        }
    });
```

In this example, the same `ViewTreeObserver`, `vto`, and `TextView` events are used as in the previous example. This shows that both the currently focused `View` and the previously focused `View` pass to the listener. From here, your application can perform needed actions.

If your application merely wants to check values after the user has modified a particular `View`, though, you might need to only register to listen for focus changes of that particular `View`. This is discussed later in this chapter.

Listening for Long Clicks

In a previous section discussing the `ContextMenu` control, you learned that you can add a context menu to a `View` that is activated when the user performs a long-click on that view. A long-click is typically when users press on the touch screen and hold their finger there until an action is performed. However, a long-press event can also be triggered if the users navigate there with a nontouched, via a keyboard or trackball, method and then hold the Enter or Select key for a while. This action is also often called a press-and-hold action.

Although the context menu is a great typical use case for the long-click event, you can listen for the long-click event and perform any action you want. However, this is the same event that triggers the context menu. If you've already added a context menu to a View, you might not want to listen for the long-click event as other actions or side effects might confuse the user or even prevent the context menu from showing. As always with good user interface design, try to be consistent for usability sake.

Tip

Usually a long-click is an alternative action to a standard-click. If a left-click on a computer is the standard click, a long-click can be compared to a right-click.

Your application can listen to the long-click event on any View. The following example demonstrates how to listen for a long-click event on a Button widget.

```
Button long_press = (Button)findViewById(R.id.long_press);
long_press.setOnLongClickListener(new View.OnLongClickListener() {
    public boolean onLongClick(View v) {
        events.setText("Long click: " + v.toString());
        return true;
    }
});
```

First, the Button object is requested by providing its identifier. Then the setOnLongClickListener() method is called with our implementation of the View.OnLongClickListener class interface. The View that the user long-clicked on is passed in to onLongClick() event handler. Here again we use the same TextView as before to display text saying that a long-click occurred.

Listening for Gestures

In addition to listening for click events, the Android SDK also provides a way to detect gestures that the user performs on the touch screen. Unlike some other events, your application can't request for events on certain gestures. Instead, your application needs to provide data to the android.view.GestureDetector class.

To provide the data the GestureDetector class needs, you need to provide an implementation of the onTouchEvent() method within your Activity class. The onTouchEvent() method is provided with a MotionEvent object. This contains the data your GestureDetector needs. Simply call your GestureDetector object's onTouchEvent() method with this data. The following is an example implementation of this:

```
private GestureDetector mGestures = null;

public boolean onTouchEvent(MotionEvent event) {
```

```
    if (mGestures != null) {
        return mGestures.onTouchEvent(event);
    } else {
        return super.onTouchEvent(event);
    }
}
```

In addition, you need to instantiate your `GestureDetector` object. The event listener is assigned through the constructor for the `GestureDetector` class.

There are two interfaces that you can implement to listen for these events. The first is `GestureDetector.OnGestureListener`, which requires implementing all methods. The second is `GestureDetector.SimpleOnGestureListener`, which provides an implementation for all methods, returning **false** to them so that you can override only those that you actually want to listen to. The following is a list of the possible methods you can implement and the action they represent:

- `onDown:` Called when the user first presses on the touch screen.
- `onShowPress:` Called after users first presses the touch screen but before they lift up or move around on the screen; used to visually or audibly indicate that the press has been detected.
- `onSingleTapUp:` Called when the user lifts up (using the up `MotionEvent`) from the touch screen as part of a single-tap event.
- `onSingleTapConfirmed:` Called when a single-tap event occurs.
- `onDoubleTap:` Called when a double-tap event occurs.
- `onDoubleTapEvent:` Called when an event within a double-tap gesture occurs, including any down, move, and up `MotionEvent`.
- `onLongPress:` Similar to `onSingleTapUp`, but called if the users hold their finger down long enough to not be a standard click but also don't move their finger.
- `onScroll:` Called after users press and then move their finger in a steady motion and lift up.
- `onFling:` Called after the users press and then move their finger in an accelerating motion before lifting it. This is commonly called a flick gesture and usually results in some motion continuing after the users lift their finger.

The following is a sample implementation that shows listening for `onScroll` and `onFling`:

```
mGestures = new GestureDetector(
    new GestureDetector.SimpleOnGestureListener() {
    public boolean onFling(MotionEvent e1, MotionEvent e2,
        float velocityX, float velocityY) {
            events.setText("Fling! \nx= " +
                velocityX + "px/s\ny=" + velocityY + "px/s");
```

```
                return superonFling(e1, e2, velocityX, velocityY);
        }

        public boolean onScroll(
            MotionEvent e1, MotionEvent e2,
            float distanceX, float distanceY) {
            events.setText("Scroll! \nX = " +
                distanceX + "\nY = " +distanceY);
                    return super.onScroll(e1, e2, distanceX, distanceY);
        }
    });
```

We provide an implementation of the `GestureDetector.SimpleOnGestureListener` class because we will not be listening for all of the possible events, only `onFling` and `onScroll` events. First, we implement the `onFling()` method so that we can get fling, or flick, events. The first `MotionEvent` is where the users initially press. The second `MotionEvent` is where their finger was before they released to generate the flick. The velocities are the final values before they flicked. These can be used by your application to programmatically scroll or animate some displayed object beyond when the users presses on the screen. This is commonly done to scroll quickly by the users with multiple flicks.

Next, we provide an implementation for the `onScroll()` method. This is called frequently while Android detects `scroll` events while the users have their finger on the screen. This is different from the `fling` event in that it is called frequently rather than once. After a bunch of `onScroll` events, an `onFling` event can be called, too. Each `onScroll()` call contains the original `MotionEvent` in which the users initially click and the `MotionEvent` in which the users' finger is currently. The distance is from the last call to `onScroll()` and not the difference between the two. An object that moved along with the distances provided should track with the users' finger.

What your application does with the gestures is, of course, up to you. However, using gestures can greatly increase the intuitiveness and fluidity of your application. A good implementation feels natural to the user; a bad implementation can increase user frustration, so tread with care.

Listening for Focus Changes

We already discussed focus changes for listening for them on an entire screen. All `View` objects, though, can also trigger a call to listeners when their particular focus state changes. This is done by providing an implementation of the `View.OnFocusChange Listener` class to the `setOnFocusChangeListener()` method. The following is an example of how to listen for focus change events with an `EditText` widget:

```
TextView focus = (TextView)findViewById(R.id.text_focus_change);
```

```
focus.setOnFocusChangeListener(new View.OnFocusChangeListener() {
    public void onFocusChange(View v, boolean hasFocus) {
        if (hasFocus) {
            if (mSaveText != null) {
                ((TextView)v).setText(mSaveText);
            }
        } else {
            mSaveText = ((TextView)v).getText().toString();
            ((TextView)v).setText("");
        }
    }
}
```

In this implementation, we also use a private member variable of type `String` for
`mSaveText`. After retrieving the `EditText` view as a `TextView`, we do one of two
things. If the users move focus away from it, we store off the text they entered in
`mSaveText` and set the text to empty. If the users moves to it, though, we restore this
text. This has the amusing effect of hiding the text they entered when they are not
entering it. This can be useful on a form where multiple, lengthy text entries are needed
but you want to provide the users with an easy way to see which one they edit. It is also
useful for demonstrating a purpose for the focus listeners on a text entry. Other uses
might include validating text they enter after they navigate away or prefilling the text
entry the first time they navigate to it with something else they have entered.

Listening for Screen Orientation Changes

The Android devices on the market today have landscape and portrait modes and can
seamlessly transition between these orientations. To listen for orientation transitions
between modes, use the `OrientationEventListener` (`android.view.Orientation
EventListener`) to receive `SensorManager` events when the device orientation
changes.

> **Caution**
>
> Versions of the Android SDK prior to 1.5 R1 included a class called
> `OrientationListener`, which was used by many to handle screen orientation transi-
> tions. This class is now depreciated and should not be used. Additionally, in Android SDK
> 1.5, the screen will automatically adjust to the new orientation. This happens in a manner
> similar to a physical event that might have triggered the orientation change, such as the
> keyboard being slid open on the T-Mobile G1 handset. Developers should be aware that
> such SDK changes might break application behavior if it already monitored a similar event
> to the event monitored by the system.

> **Tip**
>
> For those unfamiliar with how orientation sensors work, the Novoda blog provides a helpful
> Orientation Sensor Cheat Sheet: www.novoda.com/blog/?p=77.

Working with Styles

A style is a group of common `View` attribute values. The style can then be applied to individual `View` widgets. Styles can include such settings as the font to draw with or the color of text. The specific attributes depend on the `View` drawn. In essence, though, each style attribute can change the look and feel of the particular object drawn.

In the previous examples of this chapter, you have seen how XML layout resource files can contain many references to attributes that control the look of `TextView` objects. You can use a style to define your application's standard `TextView` attributes once and then reference to the style either in an XML layout file or programmatically from within Java. For example, in Figure 6.13, we use one style to indicate mandatory form fields and another to indicate optional fields.

Figure 6.13   Using styles to indicate mandatory and optional text fields
in a form.

As we talked about in Chapter 5, styles are typically defined within the resource file `res/values/styles.xml`. The XML file consists of a `resources` tag with any number of `style` tags, which contain an `item` tag for each attribute and its value that will be applied with the style.

The following is an example with two different styles:

```xml
<?xml version="1.0" encoding="utf-8"?>
<resources>
    <style name="padded_small">
        <item name="android:padding">2px</item>
        <item name="android:textSize">8px</item>
    </style>
    <style name="padded_large">
        <item name="android:padding">4px</item>
        <item name="android:textSize">16px</item>
    </style>
</resources>
```

When applied, this style sets the padding to two pixels and the `textSize` to 8 pixels. The following is an example of how it is applied to a `TextView` from within a layout resource file:

```xml
<TextView
    style="@style/padded_small"
    android:layout_width="fill_parent"
    android:layout_height="wrap_content"
    android:text="Small Padded" />
```

Styles support inheritance; therefore, styles can also reference another style as a parent. This way, they pick up the attributes of the parent style. The following is an example of how this might be used:

```xml
<style name="red_padded">
    <item name="android:textColor">#F00</item>
    <item name="android:padding">3px</item>
</style>

<style name="padded_normal" parent="red_padded">
    <item name="android:textSize">12px</item>
</style>

<style name="padded_italics" parent="red_padded">
    <item name="android:textSize">14px</item>
    <item name="android:textStyle">italic</item>
</style>
```

Here you find two common attributes in a single style and a reference to them from the other two styles that have different attributes. Any style can be referenced as a parent style; however, only one style can be set as the style attribute of a `View`. Applying the `padded_italics` style that is already defined makes the text 14 pixels in size, italic, red, and padded. The following is an example of applying this style:

```
<TextView
    style="@style/padded_italics"
    android:layout_width="fill_parent"
    android:layout_height="wrap_content"
    android:text="Italic w/parent color" />
```

As you can see from this example, applying a style with a parent is no different than applying a regular style. In fact, a regular style can be used for applying to `Views` and used as a parent in a different style.

```
<style name="padded_xlarge">
    <item name="android:padding">10px</item>
    <item name="android:textSize">100px</item>
</style>
<style name="green_glow" parent="padded_xlarge">
    <item name="android:shadowColor">#0F0</item>
    <item name="android:shadowDx">0</item>
    <item name="android:shadowDy">0</item>
    <item name="android:shadowRadius">10</item>
</style>
```

Here the `padded_xlarge` style is set as the parent for the `green_glow` style. All six attributes will then be applied to any view that this style is set to.

Working with Themes

A theme is a collection of one or more styles (as defined in the resources) but instead of applying the style to a specific widget, the style is applied to all `View` objects within a specified `Activity`. Applying a theme to a set of `View` objects all at once simplifies making the user interface look consistent and can be a great way to define color schemes and other common widget attribute settings.

An Android theme is essentially a style that is applied to an entire screen. You can specify the theme programmatically by calling the `Activity` method `setTheme()` with the style resource identifier. Each attribute of the style will be applied to each `View` within that `Activity`, as applicable. Styles and attributes defined in the layout files explicitly override those in the theme.

For instance, consider the following style:

```
<style name="right">
    <item name="android:gravity">right</item>
</style>
```

This can be applied as a theme to the whole screen. This would cause any view displayed within that `Activity` to have its gravity attribute to be right-justified. Applying this theme is as simple as making the method call to the `setTheme()` method from within the `Activity`, as shown here.

```
setTheme(R.style.right);
```

You can also apply themes to specific `Activity` instances by specifying them as an attribute within the `<activity>` element in the `AndroidManifest.xml` file as follows:

```
<activity android:name=".myactivityname"
    android:label="@string/app_name"
    android:theme="@style/myAppIsStyling">
```

Unlike applying a style in an XML layout file, multiple themes can be applied to a screen. This allows for flexibility in defining style attributes in advance while applying different configurations of them based on what might be displayed on the screen. This is demonstrated in the follow code:

```
setTheme(R.style.right);
setTheme(R.style.green_glow);
setContentView(R.layout.style_samples);
```

In this example, both the `right` style and the `green_glow` style are applied as a theme to the entire screen. You can see the results of green glow and right-aligned gravity, applied to a variety of `TextView` widgets on a screen, as shown in Figure 6.14. Finally, we set the layout to the `Activity`. This must be done after setting the themes. That is, all themes must be applied before calling the method `setContentView()` or the `inflate()` method so that their attributes can take effect.

A combination of well-designed and thought-out themes and styles can make the look of your application consistent and easy to maintain. Android comes with a number of built-in themes that can be a good starting point. These include such themes as `Theme_Black`, `Theme_Light`, and `Theme_NoTitleBar_Fullscreen`. They are all variations on the system theme, `Theme`, which built-in apps use.

Figure 6.14   Packaging styles for glowing text, padding, and alignment
into a theme.

Summary

The Android SDK provides many useful user interface components, which developers
can use to create compelling and easy-to-use applications. This chapter introduced you
to many of the most useful widgets, discussed how each behaves, how to style them, and
how to handle events from the user.

    You learned how widgets can be combined to create user entry forms. Important
widgets for forms include `EditText`, `Button`, `RadioButton`, `CheckBox`, and `Spinner`.
You also learned about widgets that can indicate progress or the passage of time to users.

    In addition to drawing widgets on the screen, you learned how to detect user actions
such as clicks and focus changes and how to handle these events. Finally, you learned
how to style individual widgets and how to apply themes to entire screens (or more
specifically, a single `Activity`) so that your application will be styled consistently and
thoroughly.

We talked about many common user interface widgets in this chapter; however, there are many others. In Chapter 8, "Drawing and Working with Animation in Android," and Chapter 12, "Using Android Multimedia APIs," we use graphics widgets such as `ImageView` and `VideoView` to display drawable graphics and videos.

In the next chapter, you learn how to use various layout and container widgets to organize a variety of widgets on the screen easily and accurately. Additionally, you learn how to bind data to widgets to quickly display information to the user from various data sources.

7

Designing Android User Interfaces with Layouts

In this chapter, we discuss how to design user interfaces for Android applications. Here we focus on the various layout widgets you can use to organize screen elements in different ways. These layout objects include `LinearLayout`, `TableLayout`, `FrameLayout`, and `RelativeLayout`. We also cover some of the more complex `View` objects we call container views. These are `View` objects that can contain other `View` objects and widgets. Finally, we talk about extending application functionality beyond the typical boundaries using `AppWidgets`.

Creating User Interfaces in Android

Application user interfaces can be simple or complex, involving many different screens or only a few. Layouts and user interface widgets can be defined as application resources or created programmatically at runtime.

Creating Layouts Using XML Resources

As discussed in previous chapters, Android provides a simple way to create layout files in XML as resources provided in the `/res/layout` project directory. This is the most common and convenient way to build Android user interfaces and is especially useful for defining static screen elements and widget properties that are known in advance, and to set default attributes that can be modified at runtime programmatically.

> **Caution**
>
> If you use Eclipse layout resource designer to design user interfaces for your Android development, it can be helpful to preview the layouts created. This is useful for catching obvious issues, but the preview can't replicate the exact look and feel of the view the end user sees on the device or phone. For this, you must test your application on the emulator and most important on your target devices.

Almost any `ViewGroup` or `View` (or `View` subclass) attribute can be configured using the XML layout resource files. This method greatly simplifies the user interface design process, moving much of the static creation and layout of user interface widgets, and basic definition of widget attributes, to the XML, instead of littering the code. Developers reserve the ability to alter these layouts programmatically as necessary, but they can set all the defaults in the XML template.

You'll recognize the following as a simple layout file with a `LinearLayout` and a single `TextView` widget. This is the default layout file provided with any new Android project in Eclipse, referred to as `/res/layout/main.xml`:

```xml
<?xml version="1.0" encoding="utf-8"?>
<LinearLayout xmlns:android=
    "http://schemas.android.com/apk/res/android"
    android:orientation="vertical"
    android:layout_width="fill_parent"
    android:layout_height="fill_parent"
    >
<TextView
    android:layout_width="fill_parent"
    android:layout_height="wrap_content"
    android:text="@string/hello"
    />
</LinearLayout>
```

This block of XML shows a basic layout with a single `TextView`. The first line, which you might recognize from most XML files, is required. Because it's common across all the files, we do not show it in any other examples.

Next, we have the `LinearLayout` element. `LinearLayout` is a `ViewGroup` that shows each child `View` either in a single column or in a single row. When applied to a full screen, it merely means that each child `View` will be drawn under the previous `View` if the orientation is set to vertical or to the right of the previous `View` if orientation is set to horizontal.

Finally, there is a single child `View`, in this case a `TextView`. A `TextView` is a widget, which is also a `View`. A `TextView` draws text on the screen. In this case, it draws the text defined in the "`@string/hello`" string resource.

Creating only an XML file, though, won't actually draw anything on the screen. A particular layout is usually associated with a particular `Activity`. In your default Android project, there is only one Activity, which sets the `main.xml` layout by default. To associate the `main.xml` layout with the activity, use the method call `setContentView()` with the identifier of the `main.xml` layout. The ID of the layout matches the XML filename without the extension. In this case, the preceding example came from `main.xml`, so the identifier of this layout is simply `main`.

```java
setContentView(R.layout.main);
```

Creating Layouts Programmatically

You can also create user interface components at runtime programmatically, but for organization, this is best left for the odd case rather than the norm. The main reason is because the creating of layouts programmatically is onerous and difficult to maintain, whereas the XML resource method is visual and more organized.

The following example shows how to programmatically have an `Activity` instantiate a `LinearLayout` view and place two `TextView` objects within it. No resources whatsoever are used; actions are done at runtime instead.

```
public void onCreate(Bundle savedInstanceState) {
    super.onCreate(savedInstanceState);

    TextView text1 = new TextView(this);
    text1.setText("Hi there!");

    TextView text2 = new TextView(this);
    text2.setText("I'm second. I need to wrap.");
    text2.setTextSize((float) 60);

    LinearLayout ll = new LinearLayout(this);
    ll.setOrientation(LinearLayout.VERTICAL);
    ll.addView(text1);
    ll.addView(text2);

    setContentView(ll);
}
```

The `onCreate()` method is called when the `Activity` is created. The first thing this method does is some normal `Activity` housekeeping by calling the constructor for the base class.

Next, two `TextView` widgets are instantiated. The `Text` property of each `TextView` is set using the `setText()` method. All `TextView` attributes, such as `TextSize`, are set by making method calls on the `TextView` object. These actions perform the same function that you have in the past by setting the properties `Text` and `TextSize` using the Eclipse layout resource designer, except these properties are set at runtime instead of defined in the layout files compiled into your application package.

Tip

The XML property name is usually similar to the method calls for getting and setting that same widget property programmatically. For instance, `android:visibility` maps to the method `setVisibility()` and `getVisibility()`. In the preceding example `TextView`, the methods for getting and setting the `TextSize` property are `getTextSize()` and `setTextSize()`.

To display the `TextView` objects appropriately, we need to encapsulate them within a container of some sort (a layout). In this case, we use a `LinearLayout` with the orientation set to `VERTICAL` so that the second `TextView` begins beneath the first, each aligned to the left of the screen. The two `TextView` widgets are added to the `LinearLayout` in the order we want them to display.

Finally, we call the `setContentView()` method, part of your `Activity` class, to draw the `LinearLayout` and its contents on the screen.

As you can see, the code can rapidly grow in size as more `View` widgets are added and more attributes for each `View` are needed. Here is that same layout, now in an XML layout file called `/res/layout/main.xml`:

```xml
<?xml version="1.0" encoding="utf-8"?>
<LinearLayout xmlns:android=
    "http://schemas.android.com/apk/res/android"
    android:orientation="vertical"
    android:layout_width="fill_parent"
    android:layout_height="fill_parent"
    >
<TextView
    android:id="@+id/TextView1"
    android:layout_width="fill_parent"
    android:layout_height="wrap_content"
    android:text="Hi There!"
    />
<TextView
    android:id="@+id/TextView2"
    android:layout_width="fill_parent"
    android:layout_height="wrap_content"
    android:textSize="60px"
    android:text="I'm second. I need to wrap."
    />
</LinearLayout>
```

You might notice that this isn't a literal translation of the code example from the previous section, although the output will be identical, as shown in Figure 7.1.

First, in the XML layout files, `layout_width` and `layout_height` are required attributes. Next, you see that each `TextView` object has a unique `id` property assigned so that it can be accessed programmatically at runtime. Finally, the `textSize` property needs to have its units defined. The XML attribute takes a `dimension` type (as described in Chapter 5, "Managing Application Resources") instead of a float.

The end result differs only slightly from the programmatic method. However, it's far easier to read and maintain. Only one line of code is needed now to display this layout view. Again, that's

```
setContentView(R.layout.main);
```

Figure 7.1   Two different methods to create a screen have the same
result.

Organizing Your User Interface with ViewGroups

We talked in the previous chapter about how the class `View` is the building block for
user interfaces in Android. All user interface widgets, such as `Button`, `Spinner` and
`EditText`, are derived from the `View` class.

Now we talk about a special kind of `View` called a `ViewGroup`. The classes derived
from `ViewGroup` allow developers to display `View` objects (including all the user interface widgets you learned about in the previous chapter) on the screen in an organized
fashion.

Understanding the Relationship Between `View` and `ViewGroup`

Like other `View` objects, including the widgets talked about in the previous chapter,
`ViewGroup` objects control a rectangle of screen space. What makes `ViewGroup` different
from your typical widget is that `ViewGroup` objects contain other `View` objects. A `View`

that contains other `View` objects is called a parent view. The `View` objects the parent `View` contains are called child views, or children.

`View` child objects are added to a `ViewGroup` programmatically using the method `addView()`. In XML, child objects are added to a `ViewGroup` by defining the child `View` widget as a child node in the XML (within the parent XML element, as we've seen various times using the `LinearLayout ViewGroup`).

`ViewGroup` subclasses are broken down into two categories:

- Layout classes
- View container widgets

The Android SDK also provides the Hierarchy Viewer tool to help visualize the layouts you design, as discussed later in this chapter.

Using ViewGroups for Layout

The direct subclasses of `ViewGroup` are the classes ending with the word "Layout," for example, `LinearLayout`, `RelativeLayout`, and `FrameLayout`. Each of these layout classes are used to position groups of `View` objects (widgets) on the screen in different ways. For example, we've been using the `LinearLayout` to arrange various `TextView` and `EditText` widgets on the screen in a single vertical column. We could have used an `AbsoluteLayout` to specify the exact x/y coordinate locations of each widget on the screen instead, but this is not easily portable across many screen resolutions. Users do not generally interact with the `Layout` objects directly. Instead, they interact with the `View` objects they contain.

Using ViewGroups as `View` Containers

The second category of `ViewGroup` subclasses is the indirect subclasses. These special `View` objects act as `View` containers like `Layout` objects do, but they also provide some kind of functionality that allows users to interact with them like normal widgets. Unfortunately, these classes are not known by any handy names, instead they are named for the kind of functionality they provide.

Some classes that fall into this category include `Gallery`, `GridView`, `ImageSwitcher`, `ScrollView`, `TabHost`, and `ListView`. It can be helpful to consider these objects as different kinds of `View` browsers. A `ListView` displays each `View` as a list item, and the user can browse between the individual `View` objects using vertical scrolling capability. A `Gallery` is a horizontal scrolling list of `View` objects with a center "current" item; the user can browse the View objects in the `Gallery` by scrolling left and right. A `TabHost` is a more complex `View` container, where each Tab can contain a `View`, and the user chooses the tab by name to see the `View` contents.

Using the Hierarchy Viewer Tool

In addition to the Eclipse layout resource designer provided with the Android plug-in, the Android Software Development Kit (SDK) provides a user interface tool called the Hierarchy Viewer. The Hierarchy Viewer can be found in the Android SDK subdirectory called `/tools`.

The Hierarchy Viewer is a visual tool that allows you to inspect your Android application's `View` objects and their parent-child relationships. You can drill down on specific `View` objects and inspect individual `View` properties at runtime. You can even save screenshots of the current application state on the emulator or the device, although this feature is somewhat unreliable.

To launch the Hierarchy Viewer with your application in the emulator:

1. Launch your Android application in the emulator.
2. Navigate to the Android SDK `/tools` directory and launch the Hierarchy Viewer.
3. Choose your emulator instance from the Device listing.
4. Select the application you want to view from the windows available. For example, to load an application from this book, choose one like `com.androidbook.parisview`.
5. Click Load View Hierarchy button on the menu bar.

By default, the Hierarchy Viewer loads the Layout View of your application. This includes the parent-child view relationships shown as a Tree View. In addition, a property pane shows the various properties for each View node in the tree when they are selected. A wire-frame model of the `View` objects on the screen is shown and a red box highlights the currently selected view, which correlates to the same location on the screen.

> **Tip**
>
> You'll have better luck navigating your application `View` objects with the Hierarchy Viewer tool if you set your `View` object id properties to friendly names you can remember instead of the auto-generated sequential id tags provided by default.

Figure 7.2 shows the Hierarchy Viewer loaded with the ParisView project from Chapter 5, which was a one-screen application with a single `LinearLayout` with a `TextView` and an `ImageView` child widget within it. The bulk of the application is shown in the right subtree, starting with `LinearLayout` with the identifier `ParisViewLayout`. The other subtree is the Application title bar. A simple double-click on each child node opens that `View` object individually in its own window.

Each `View` can be separately displayed in its own window by selecting the appropriate `View` in the tree and choosing the Display View button on the menu bar. In Figure 7.2, you can also see that Display View is enabled on each of the child nodes: the `ImageView` with the flag, the `TextView` with the text, as well as the `LinearLayout` parent node (which includes its children), and lastly the application title bar.

You can use the Pixel Perfect view to closely inspect your application using a loupe (Figure 7.3). You can also load PNG mockup files to overlay your user interface and adjust your application's look. You can access the Pixel Perfect view by clicking the button with the Nine pixels on it at the bottom left of the Hierarchy Viewer. Click the button with the three boxes depicting the Layout view to return.

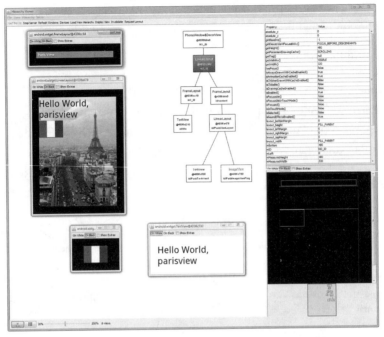

Figure 7.2   The ParisView Application, shown in the Hierarchy Viewer tool (Layout View).

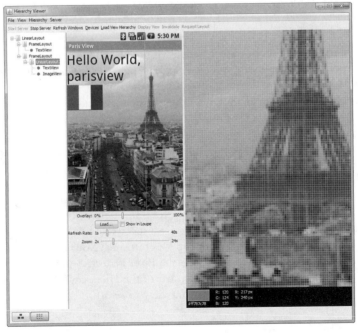

Figure 7.3   The ParisView Application, shown in the Hierarchy Viewer tool (Pixel Perfect View).

> **Caution**
>
> The Hierarchy Viewer is a useful tool, but it is also somewhat buggy (as you'll find if you pay any attention to the command window when using it in Windows). To get the Pixel Perfect view to work, we had to click and drag my mouse back and forth across the Normal View (the middle black box) repeatedly until the loupe target crosshairs started working and the application screen loaded. Hopefully, this tool will be improved in future versions of Android. For now, we are of the opinion that a tool that works sometimes is better than a tool that doesn't work at all.

The Hierarchy Viewer tool is invaluable for debugging drawing issues related to `View` widgets. If you wonder why something isn't drawing or if a `View` is even available, try launching the Hierarchy Viewer and checking that problem `View` objects' properties.

You can use the Hierarchy Viewer tool to interact and debug your application user interface. Specifically, developers can use the Invalidate and Request Layout buttons on the menu bar that correspond to `View.Invalidate()` and `View.requestLayout()` functions of the UI thread. These functions initiate `View` objects and draw or redraw them as necessary upon events.

Finally, you can also use the Hierarchy Viewer to deconstruct how other applications (especially sample applications) have handled their layout and displays. This can be helpful if you'd like to re-create a similar layout to another application, especially if it uses stock `View` types. However, you can also run across `View` types not provided in the SDK, and you need to implement those custom classes for yourself. For instance, choosing the Launcher window shows us that it uses views such as `CellLayout`—a view that isn't exposed in the SDK.

Using Built-In Layout Classes

We talked a lot about the `LinearLayout` layout, but there are several other types of layouts. Each layout has a different method and order in which it displays child `View` widgets on the screen. Layouts are derived from `android.view.ViewGroup`.

The types of layouts built-in to the Android SDK framework include

- `AbsoluteLayout`
- `FrameLayout`
- `LinearLayout`
- `RelativeLayout`
- `TableLayout`

All layouts, regardless of their type, have layout attributes. Layout attributes apply to any child `View` within that layout. Layout attributes can be set at runtime programmatically, but ideally they are set in the XML layout files using the following syntax:

```
android:layout_attribute_name="value"
```

There are several layout attributes that all `ViewGroup` objects share. These include size attributes and margin attributes. You can find basic layout attributes in the `ViewGroup.LayoutParams` class. The margin attributes allow each child `View` within a layout to have padding on each side. Find these attributes in the `ViewGroup.Margin` `LayoutParams` classes. There are also a number of `ViewGroup` attributes for handling child `View` drawing bounds and animation settings.

Some of the important attributes shared by all `ViewGroup` subtypes are shown in Table 7.1.

Table 7.1   **Important `ViewGroup` Attributes**

Attribute Name	Applies To	Description	Value
android:layout_ height	Parent view Child view	Height of the viewRequired attribute for child views in layouts	Dimension values or fill_parent wrap_content
android:layout_ width	Parent view Child view	Width of the viewRequired attribute for child views in layouts	Dimension values or fill_parent wrap_content
android:layout_ margin	Child view	Extra space on all sides of the view	Dimension values
android:layout_ marginTop	Child view	Extra space above the view	Dimension values
android:layout_ marginBottom	Child view	Extra space below the view	Dimension values
android:layout_ marginRight	Child view	Extra space on right side of the view	Dimension values
android:layout_ marginLeft	Child view	Extra space on left side of the view	Dimension values

Here's an XML layout resource example of a `LinearLayout` set to the size of the screen, containing one `TextView` that is set to its full height and the width of the `LinearLayout` (and therefore the screen).

```
<LinearLayout xmlns:android=
    "http://schemas.android.com/apk/res/android"
    android:layout_width="fill_parent"
    android:layout_height="fill_parent">
    <TextView
        android:id="@+id/TextView01"
        android:layout_height="fill_parent"
        android:layout_width="fill_parent" />
</LinearLayout>
```

Here is an example of a `Button` object with some margins set via XML used in a layout resource file.

```
<Button
    android:id="@+id/Button01"
    android:layout_width="wrap_content"
    android:layout_height="wrap_content"
    android:text="Press Me"
    android:layout_marginRight="20px"
    android:layout_marginTop="60px" />
```

Remember that layout elements can cover any rectangular space on the screen; it doesn't need to be the entire screen. Because layouts are `View` objects, layouts can be nested within each other. This allows for great flexibility when developers need to organize screen elements.

A layout such as an `AbsoluteLayout` might control only a small part of the screen, but that part of the screen will be defined in a pixel-perfect manner. It is also common to start with a `FrameLayout` or `LinearLayout` (as you've seen in many of the previous chapter examples) as the parent layout for the entire screen and then organize individual screen elements inside the parent layout using whichever layout type is most appropriate.

Now let's talk about each of the common layout types individually and how they differ from one another.

Tip

You can see an example of each layout in the Android project called SimpleLayout, which is available on the CD or at the book Web site.

Using `AbsoluteLayout`

An `AbsoluteLayout` view uses specific x/y coordinates of the child view for laying out each item to an exact location. This might be useful in cases where pixel-perfect layout is required. However, it's less flexible in that a pixel-specific layout will not adapt well to other device configurations with different screen sizes. It can be helpful when you want to control a specific area of a screen at the pixel level and then include this layout within another larger, more flexible layout on the screen.

Caution

The `AbsoluteLayout` view class was deprecated in Android 1.5 R1. However, we have chosen to continue to include it in our list of layouts because developers might use this type of layout to port applications from other mobile platforms to Android or other specific purposes. For now, you might still use this class; however, it could disappear at some point in the future. Under most circumstances, other popular layout types such as `FrameLayout` and `RelativeLayout` will suffice in place of `AbsoluteLayout`, so we encourage you to seek other solutions whenever possible.

Figure 7.4 shows an example screenshot with widgets not aligned in any particular way; their coordinates were specifically given.

Figure 7.4   An example of **AbsoluteLayout** usage.

You can find the layout attributes available for `AbsoluteLayout` child `View` objects in `android.widget.AbsoluteLayout.LayoutParams` class. Some of the important attributes specific to `AbsoluteLayout` child `View` objects are shown in Table 7.2.

Table 7.2   **Important `AbsoluteLayout` Attributes**

Attribute Name	Applies To	Description	Value
android:layout_x	Child view	X-axis coordinate for top-left corner of view within layout	Dimension values; for example, 100px
android:layout_y	Child view	Y-axis coordinate for top-left corner of view within layout	Dimension values; for example, 100px

Here's an example of an XML layout resource with an `AbsoluteLayout` and two child `View` objects, an `AnalogClock` and a `DigitalClock`:

```
<AbsoluteLayout xmlns:android=
    "http://schemas.android.com/apk/res/android"
    android:id="@+id/AbsoluteLayout01"
    android:layout_height="fill_parent"
```

```
        android:layout_width="fill_parent">
    <AnalogClock
        android:id="@+id/AnalogClock01"
        android:layout_width="wrap_content"
        android:layout_height="wrap_content"
        android:layout_x="0px"
        android:layout_y="0px" />
    <DigitalClock
        android:id="@+id/DigitalClock01"
        android:layout_width="wrap_content"
        android:layout_height="wrap_content"
        android:layout_x="190px"
        android:layout_y="100px" />
</AbsoluteLayout>
```

Using `FrameLayout`

A `FrameLayout` view is designed to display a stack of child `View` items. Multiple views can be added to this layout, but each `View` is drawn from the top-left corner of the layout. This can be used to show multiple images within the same region, as shown in Figure 7.5, and the layout is sized to the largest child `View` in the stack.

Figure 7.5   An example of `FrameLayout` usage.

You can find the layout attributes available for `FrameLayout` child `View` objects in `android.widget.FrameLayout.LayoutParams`. Some of the important attributes specific to `FrameLayout` views are shown in Table 7.3.

Table 7.3   Important **FrameLayout View** Attributes

Attribute Name	Applies To	Description	Value
android:foreground	Parent view	Drawable to draw over the content.	Drawable resources.
android:foregroundGravity	Parent view	Gravity of foreground drawable.	One or more constants separated by "|." The constants are top, bottom, left, right, center_vertical, fill_vertical, center_horizontal, fill_horizontal, center and fill.
android:measureAllChildren	Parent view	Restrict size of layout to all children or the children set to VISIBLE (and not the ones set to INVISIBLE).	True or false.
android:layout_gravity	Child view	A gravity constant that describes how to place the child View within the parent.	One or more constants separated by "|." The constants are top, bottom, left, right, center_vertical, fill_vertical, center_horizontal, fill_horizontal, center and fill.

Here's an example of an XML layout resource with a `FrameLayout` and two child `View` objects, both `ImageView` objects. The green rectangle is drawn first and the red oval is drawn on top of it. The green rectangle is larger, so it defines the bounds of the `FrameLayout`:

```
<FrameLayout xmlns:android=
    "http://schemas.android.com/apk/res/android"
    android:id="@+id/FrameLayout01"
    android:layout_width="wrap_content"
    android:layout_height="wrap_content"
    android:layout_gravity="center">
    <ImageView
        android:id="@+id/ImageView01"
        android:layout_width="wrap_content"
        android:layout_height="wrap_content"
        android:src="@drawable/green_rect"
        android:minHeight="200px"
        android:minWidth="200px" />
    <ImageView
        android:id="@+id/ImageView02"
        android:layout_width="wrap_content"
        android:layout_height="wrap_content"
        android:src="@drawable/red_oval"
        android:minHeight="100px"
        android:minWidth="100px"
        android:layout_gravity="center" />
</FrameLayout>
```

Using `LinearLayout`

A `LinearLayout` view organizes its child `View` objects in a single row, shown in Figure 7.6, or column, depending on whether its orientation attribute is set to horizontal or vertical. This is a very handy layout method for creating forms.

You can find the layout attributes available for `LinearLayout` child `View` objects in `android.widget.LinearLayout.LayoutParams`. Some of the important attributes specific to `LinearLayout` views are shown in Table 7.4.

Table 7.4   **Important `LinearLayout` View Attributes**

Attribute Name	Applies To	Description	Value
android:orientation	Parent view	Layout is a single row or a single column.	Horizontal or vertical.
android:gravity	Parent view	Gravity of child views within layout.	One or more constants separated by "|." The constants are top, bottom, left, right, center_vertical, fill_vertical, center_horizontal, fill_horizontal, center and fill.

Table 7.4   **Continued**

Attribute Name	Applies To	Description	Value
android:layout_gravity	Child view	Gravity of specific child view.	One or more constants separated by "|." The constants are top, bottom, left, right, center_vertical, fill_vertical, center_horizontal, fill_horizontal, center and fill.

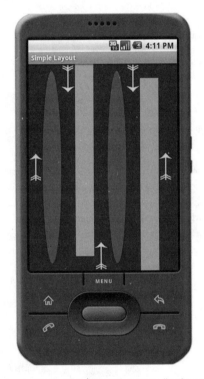

Figure 7.6   An example of LinearLayout (horizontal orientation).

There are many examples of LinearLayout usage in Chapter 5.

Using RelativeLayout

The RelativeLayout view allows you to specify where the child view widgets are in relation to each other. For instance, you can set a child View to be positioned "above" or "below" or "to the left of" or "to the right of" another View, referred to by its unique identifier. You can also align child View objects relative to one another or the parent layout edges. Combining RelativeLayout attributes can simplify creating interesting user interfaces without resorting to multiple layout groups to achieve a desired effect. Figure 7.7 shows how each of the button widgets is relative to each other.

Figure 7.7   An example of RelativeLayout usage.

You can find the layout attributes available for RelativeLayout child View objects in android.widget.RelativeLayout.LayoutParams. Some of the important attributes specific to RelativeLayout views are shown in Table 7.5.

Table 7.5   **Important `RelativeLayout` View Attributes**

Attribute Name	Applies To	Description	Value
android:gravity	Parent view	Gravity of child views within layout	One or more constants separated by "|." The constants are `top`, `bottom`, `left`, `right`, `center_vertical`, `fill_vertical`, `center_horizontal`, `fill_horizontal`, `center` and `fill`.
android:layout_centerInParent	Child view	Centers the view horizontally and vertically within the parent	True or false
android:layout_centerHorizontal	Child view	Centers the view horizontally within the parent	True or false
android:layout_centerVertical	Child view	Centers the view vertically within the parent	True or false
android:layout_alignParentTop	Child view	Aligns the view to the of top edge the parent	True or false
android:layout_alignParentBottom	Child view	Aligns the view to the of bottom edge the parent	True or false
android:layout_alignParentLeft	Child view	Aligns the view to the of left edge of the parent	True or false
android:layout_alignParentRight	Child view	Aligns the view to the of right edge of the parent	True or false
android:layout_alignRight	Child view	Aligns the view tothe of right edgeof the specified view (ID)	A View ID; for example, @id/ButtonCenter

Table 7.5   **Continued**

Attribute Name	Applies To	Description	Value
android:layout_alignLeft	Child view	Aligns the view to the of left edge of the specified view (ID)	A View ID; for example, @id/ButtonCenter
android:layout_alignTop	Child view	Aligns the view to the of top edge of the specified view (ID)	A View ID; for example, @id/ButtonCenter
android:layout_alignBottom	Child view	Aligns the view to the of bottom edge of the specified view (ID)	A View ID; for example, @id/ButtonCenter
android:layout_above	Child view	Positions bottom edge of this view above specified view (ID)	A View ID; for example, @id/ButtonCenter
android:layout_below	Child view	Positions top edge of this view below specified view (ID)	A View ID; for example, @id/ButtonCenter
android:layout_toLeftOf	Child view	Positions right edge of this view to the left of specified view (ID)	A View ID; for example, @id/ButtonCenter
android:layout_toRightOf	Child view	Positions left edge of this view to the right of specified view (ID)	A View ID; for example, @id/ButtonCenter

Here's an example of an XML layout resource with a RelativeLayout and two child View objects, a Button object aligned relative to its parent, and an ImageView aligned and positioned relative to the Button (and the parent):

```
<?xml version="1.0" encoding="utf-8"?>
<RelativeLayout xmlns:android=
```

```
        "http://schemas.android.com/apk/res/android"
        android:id="@+id/RelativeLayout01"
        android:layout_height="fill_parent"
        android:layout_width="fill_parent">
    <Button
        android:id="@+id/ButtonCenter"
        android:text="Center"
        android:layout_width="wrap_content"
        android:layout_height="wrap_content"
        android:layout_centerVertical="true"
        android:layout_centerInParent="true" />
    <ImageView
        android:id="@+id/ImageView01"
        android:layout_width="wrap_content"
        android:layout_height="wrap_content"
        android:layout_above="@id/ButtonCenter"
        android:layout_centerHorizontal="true"
        android:src="@drawable/arrow" />
</RelativeLayout>
```

Using `TableLayout`

A `TableLayout` view organizes children into rows, as shown in Figure 7.8. Individual
`View` objects are added within each row of the table using a `TableRow` layout `View`
(which is basically a horizontally oriented `LinearLayout`) for each row of the table.
Each column of the `TableRow` can contain one `View` (or layout with child `View`
objects). `View` items added to a `TableRow` are placed in columns in the order they are
added. You can specify the column number (zero-based) to skip columns as necessary
(bottom row shown in Figure 7.8 demonstrates this); otherwise the `View` will be put in
the next column to the right. Columns scale to the size of the largest `View` of that column. You can also include normal `View` objects instead of `TableRow` elements, if you
want the `View` to take up an entire row.

   You can find the layout attributes available for `TableLayout` child `View` objects in
`android.widget.TableLayout.LayoutParams`. You can find all the layout attributes
available for `TableRow` child `View` objects in `android.widget.TableRow.Layout
Params`. Some of the important attributes specific to `TableLayout View` objects are
shown in Table 7.6.

Table 7.6   Important **TableLayout** and **TableRow** View Attributes

Attribute Name	Applies To	Description	Value
android:collapseColumns	TableLayout	A comma-delimited list of column indices to collapse (0-based).	String or String Resource; for example, 0,1,3,5,7.
android:shrinkColumns	TableLayout	A comma-delimited list of column indices to shrink (0-based).	String or String Resource; for example, 0,1,3,5,7. "*" for all columns.
android:stretchColumns	TableLayout	A comma-delimited list of column indices to stretch (0-based).	String or String Resource; for example, 0,1,3,5,7. "*" for all columns.
android:layout_column	TableRow Child view	Index of column this view should be in (0-based).	Integer or Integer Resource; for example, 1.
android:layout_span	TableRow Child view	The number of columns this view should span across.	Integer or integer resource greater than or equal to 1; for example, 3.

Figure 7.8   An example of **TableLayout** usage.

Here's an example of an XML layout resource with a `TableLayout` with two rows (two `TableRow` child objects). The `TableLayout` is set to stretch the columns to the size of the screen width. The first `TableRow` has three columns; each cell has a `Button` object. The second `TableRow` puts only one `Button` view into the second column explicitly:

```
<TableLayout xmlns:android=
    "http://schemas.android.com/apk/res/android"
    android:id="@+id/TableLayout01"
    android:layout_width="fill_parent"
    android:layout_height="fill_parent"
    android:stretchColumns="*">
    <TableRow
        android:id="@+id/TableRow01">
        <Button
            android:id="@+id/ButtonLeft"
            android:text="Left Door" />
        <Button
            android:id="@+id/ButtonMiddle"
            android:text="Middle Door" />
        <Button
            android:id="@+id/ButtonRight"
            android:text="Right Door" />
    </TableRow>
    <TableRow
        android:id="@+id/TableRow02">
        <Button
            android:id="@+id/ButtonBack"
            android:text="Go Back"
            android:layout_column="1" />
    </TableRow>
</TableLayout>
```

Using Multiple Layouts on a Screen

Combining different layout methods on a single screen can create complex layouts. Remember that because a layout contains `View` objects and is, itself, a `View`, it can contain other layouts. Figure 7.9 demonstrates a combination of layout views used in conjunction to create a more complex and interesting screen.

Figure 7.9   An example of multiple layouts used together.

Using Built-In View Container Classes

Layouts are not the only View objects that can contain other View objects and widgets. Although layout views are useful for positioning other View objects on the screen, they aren't interactive. Now let's talk about the other kind of ViewGroup: the containers. These View objects often encapsulate other, simpler View types and allow the user some interactive ability to browse the child View objects in a standard fashion.

The types of ViewGroup containers built-in to the Android SDK framework include

- Lists, grids, and galleries with AdapterView
- Switchers with ViewFlipper, ImageSwitcher, TextSwitcher
- Tabs with TabHost and TabWidget
- Dialogs
- Scrolling with ScrollView and HorizontalScrollView
- Hiding and showing content with the SlidingDrawer

Using Data Driven `View` Containers with `AdapterViews`

Some of the `View` container widgets are designed for displaying repetitive `View` objects in a particular way. Examples of this type of `View` container widget include `ListView`, `GridView`, and `GalleryView`.

- **`ListView`:** Contains a vertically scrolling, horizontally filled list of `View` objects, each of which typically contains a row of data; the user can choose an item to perform some action upon.

- **`GridView`:** Contains a grid of `View` objects, with a specific number of columns; this container is often used with image icons; the user can choose an item to perform some action upon.

- **`GalleryView`:** Contains a horizontally scrolling list of `View` objects, also often used with image icons; the user can select an item to perform some action upon.

These containers are all types of `AdapterView` widgets. An `AdapterView` widget contains a set of child `View` widgets to display data from some data source. An `Adapter` generates these child `View` widgets from a data source. As this is an important part of all these container widgets, we talk about the `Adapter` objects first.

In this section, you learn how to bind data to `View` objects using `Adapter` objects. In the Android SDK, an `Adapter` reads data from some data source and provides a `View` object based on some rules, depending on the type of `Adapter` used. This `View` is be used to populate the `child View` objects of a particular `AdapterView`.

The most common Adapter classes are the `CursorAdapter` and the `ArrayAdapter`. The `CursorAdapter` gathers data from a `Cursor` whereas the `ArrayAdapter` gathers data from an array. A `CursorAdapter` is a good choice to use when using data from a database. The `ArrayAdapter` is a good choice to use when there is only a single column of data or when the data comes from a resource array.

There are some common elements to know about `Adapter` objects. When creating an `Adapter`, you provide a layout identifier. This layout is the template for filling in each row of data. The template you create contains identifiers for particular widgets that the `Adapter` assigns data to. A simple layout can contain as little as a single `TextView` widget. When making an `Adapter`, refer to both the layout resource and the identifier of the `TextView` widget. The Android SDK provides some common layout resources for use in your application.

Using the `ArrayAdapter`

An `ArrayAdapter` binds each element of the array to a single `View` within the layout resource. Here is an example of creating an `ArrayAdapter`:

```
private String[] items = {
    "Item 1", "Item 2", "Item 3" };
ArrayAdapter adapt =
    new ArrayAdapter<String>
        (this, R.layout.textview, items);
```

In this example, we have a `String` array called items. This is the array used by the `ArrayAdapter` as the source data. We also use a layout resource, which is the `View` that will be repeated for each item in the array. This is defined as follows:

```
<TextView xmlns:android=
    "http://schemas.android.com/apk/res/android"
    android:layout_width="fill_parent"
    android:layout_height="wrap_content"
    android:textSize="20px" />
```

This layout resource contains only a single `TextView`. However, a more complex layout can be used with the constructors that also take the resource identifier of a `TextView` within the layout. Each child `View` within the `AdapterView` that uses this `Adapter` gets one `TextView` instance with one of the strings from the `String` array.

If you have an array resource defined, you can also directly set the entries attribute for an `AdapterView` to the resource identifier of the array to automatically provide the `ArrayAdapter`.

Using the `CursorAdapter`

A `CursorAdapter` binds one or more columns of data to one or more `View` objects within the layout resource provided. This is best shown with an example. The following example demonstrates creating a `CursorAdapter` by querying the Contacts content provider. The `CursorAdapter` requires the use of a `Cursor`.

Note

For more information about the Android `Cursor` object, see Chapter 9, "Using Android Data and Storage APIs."

```
Cursor names = managedQuery(
    Contacts.Phones.CONTENT_URI, null, null, null, null);
startManagingCursor(names);
ListAdapter adapter = new SimpleCursorAdapter(
    this, R.layout.two_text,
    names, new String[] {
        Contacts.Phones.NAME,
        Contacts.Phones.NUMBER
    }, new int[] {
        R.id.scratch_text1,
        R.id.scratch_text2
    });
```

In this example, we present a couple of new concepts. First, you need to know that the `Cursor` must contain a field named `_id`. In this case, we know that the Contacts content provider does have this field. This field will be used later when you handle the user selecting a particular item.

We make a call to `managedQuery()` to get the `Cursor`. Then, we instantiate a `SimpleCursorAdapter` as a `ListAdapter`. Our layout, `R.layout.two_text`, has two `TextView` objects in it, which are used in the last parameter. `SimpleCursorAdapter` allows us to match up columns in the database with particular widgets in our layout. For each row returned from the query, we will get one instance of the layout within our `AdapterView`.

Binding Data to the `AdapterView`

Now that you have an `Adapter` object, you can apply this to one of the `AdapterView` widgets. Any of them will work. Although the `Gallery` technically takes a `SpinnerAdapter`, the instantiation of `SimpleCursorAdapter` also returns a `SpinnerAdapter`. Here is an example of this with a `ListView`, continuing on from the previous sample code:

```
((ListView)findViewById(R.id.list)).setAdapter(adapter);
```

The call to the `setAdapter()` method of the `AdapterView`, a `ListView` in this case, should come after your call to `setContentView()`. This is all that is required to bind data to your `AdapterView`. Figure 7.10 shows the same data in a `ListView`, `Gallery`, and `GridView`.

Figure 7.10   `ListView`, `Gallery`, and `GridView`: same data, same
list item, different layout views.

Handling Selection Events

`AdapterView` widgets are often used to present data to the user that they will be select-ing from. All three of the discussed widgets, `ListView`, `GridView`, and `Gallery`, allow your application to monitor for click events in the same way. You need to call `setOnItemClickListener()` on your `AdapterView` and pass in an implementation of the `AdapterView.OnItemClickListener` class. Here is an example implementation of this class:

```
av.setOnItemClickListener(
    new AdapterView.OnItemClickListener() {
    public void onItemClick(
        AdapterView<?> parent, View view,
        int position, long id) {
        Toast.makeText(Scratch.this, "Clicked _id="+id,
            Toast.LENGTH_SHORT).show();
    }
});
```

In the preceding example, `av` is our `AdapterView`. The implementation of the `onItemClick()` method is where all the interesting work happens. The parent parame-ter is the `AdapterView` where the item was clicked. This is useful if your screen has more than one `AdapterView` on it. The `View` parameter is the specific `View` within the item that was clicked. The position is the zero-based position within the list of items that the user selected. Finally, the `id` parameter is the value of the `_id` column for the partic-ular item that was selected. This is useful for querying for further information about that particular row of data that the item represents.

Your application can also listen for long-click events on particular items. Additionally, selected items can be listened for. Although the parameters are the same, your application receives a call as the highlighted item changes. This can be in response to the user scroll-ing with the arrow keys and not selecting an item for action.

Using the `ListActivity`

The `ListView` widget is commonly used for full-screen menus or lists of items to select from. As such, you might consider using `ListActivity` as the base class for such screens. Using the `ListActivity` can simplify these types of screens.

First, to handle item events, you now need to provide an implementation in your `ListActivity`. For instance, the equivalent of `onListItemClickListener` is to imple-ment the `onListItemClick()` method within your `ListActivity`.

Second, to assign an `Adapter`, a call to the `setListAdapter()` method is needed. This is done after the call to the `setContentView()` method. However, this hints at some of the limitations of using `ListActivity`.

To use `ListActivity`, the layout that is set with the `setContentView()` method must contain a `ListView` with the identifier set to `android:list`; this cannot be changed. Second, you can also have a `View` with an identifier set to `android:empty` to have a `View` display when no data is returned from the `Adapter`. Finally, this works only with `ListView` widgets, so it has limited use. However, when it does work for your application, it can save on some coding.

> **Tip**
>
> You can create `ListView` headers and footers using `ListView.FixedViewInfo` with the `ListView` methods `addHeaderView()` and `addFooterView()`.

Organizing Views with `TabActivity` and `TabHost`

The Android SDK has a flexible way to provide a tab interface to the user. A screen layout with tabs consists of a `TabActivity` and a `TabHost`. The `TabHost` consists of `TabSpecs`, a nested class of `TabHost`, which contains the tab information including the tab title and the contents of the tab. The contents of the tab can either be a predefined `View`, an `Activity` launched through an `Intent` object, or the `View` can be created with a factory provided by an implementation of `TabContentFactory`.

Tabs aren't as complex as they might sound at first. Each tab is effectively a container for a `View`. That `View` can come from any `View` that is ready to be shown, such as an XML layout file. Alternatively, that `View` can come from launching an `Activity`. The following example demonstrates each of these methods using `View` objects and `Activity` objects created in the previous examples of this chapter:

```
public class TabLayout
    extends TabActivity
    implements android.widget.TabHost.TabContentFactory {
    protected void onCreate(Bundle savedInstanceState) {
        super.onCreate(savedInstanceState);
        TabHost tabHost = getTabHost();
        LayoutInflater.from(this).inflate(
            R.layout.example_layout,
            tabHost.getTabContentView(), true);
        tabHost.addTab(tabHost.newTabSpec("tab1")
            .setIndicator("Grid").setContent(
                new Intent(this, GridLayout.class)));
        tabHost.addTab(tabHost.newTabSpec("tab2")
            .setIndicator("List").setContent(
                new Intent(this, List.class)));
        tabHost.addTab(tabHost.newTabSpec("tab3")
            .setIndicator("Basic").setContent(
                R.id.two_texts));
        tabHost.addTab(tabHost.newTabSpec("tab4")
            .setIndicator("Factory").setContent(
                this));
    }
```

```
public View createTabContent(String tag) {
    if (tag.compareTo("tab4") == 0) {
        TextView tv = new TextView(this);
        Date now = new Date();
        tv.setText("I'm from a factory. Created: "
            + now.toString());
        tv.setTextSize((float) 24);
        return (tv);
    } else {
        return null;
    }
}}}
```

This example creates a tabbed layout view with four tabs on it, as shown in Figure 7.11. The first tab is from the recent GridView sample. The second tab is from the ListView sample before that. The third tab is the basic layout with two TextView objects, fully defined in an XML layout file as previously demonstrated. Finally, the fourth tab is created with a factory.

Figure 7.11   Four tabs displayed.

The first action is to get the `TabHost` instance. This is the object that allows us to add `Intent` objects and `View` identifiers for drawing the screen. A `TabActivity` provides a method to retrieve the current `TabHost` object.

The next action is only loosely related to tab views. The `LayoutInflater` is used to turn the XML definition of a `View` into the actual `View` objects. This would normally happen when calling `setContentView()`, but we're not doing that. The use of the `LayoutInflater` is required for referencing the `View` objects by identifier, as is done for the third tab.

Finally, the code adds each of the four tabs to the `TabHost` in the order that they will be presented. This is accomplished by multiple calls to the `addTab()` method of `TabHost`. The first two calls are essentially the same. Each one creates a new `Intent` with the name of an `Activity` that launches within the tab. These are the same `Activity` classes used previously for full-screen display. If the `Activity` isn't designed for full screen use, this should work seamlessly.

Next, on the third tab, a layout `View` is added using its identifier. In the preceding call to the `LayoutInflater`, the layout file also contains an identifier matching the one used here at the top level of a `LinearLayout` definition. This is the same one used previously to show a basic `LinearLayout` example. Again, there was no need to change anything in this view for it to display correctly in a tab.

Next, a tab referencing the content as the `TabActivity` class is added. This is possible because the class itself also implements `TabHost.TabContentFactory`, which requires implementing the `createTabContent()` method. The view will be created the first time the user selects the tab, so no other information is needed here. The tag that creates this tab must be kept track of, though, as that's how the tabs are identified to the `TabHost`.

Finally, the method `createTabContent()` is implemented for use with the fourth tab. The first task here is to check the tag to see if it's the one kept track of for the fourth tab. When that is confirmed, an instance of the `TextView` object is created and a text string assigned to it, which contains the current time. The size of the text is set to 24 pixels. The time stamp used in this string can be used to demonstrate when the view is created and that it's not re-created by simple changing tabs.

The flexibility of tabs that Android provides is great for adding navigation to an application that has a bunch of views already defined. Few changes, if any, need to be made to existing `View` and `Activity` objects for them to work within the context of a `TabHost`.

Exploring Other View Containers

Many other display widgets and objects are available in Android for laying out and designing screens. Some of these are listed here.

- **Switchers:** A `ViewSwitcher` widget contains only two child `View` objects and only one of those is shown at a time. It switches between the two, animating as it does so. Primarily, the `ImageSwitcher`, shown in Figure 7.12, and `TextSwitcher` objects are used. Each one provides a way to set a new child `View`, either a `Drawable` resource or a text string, and then animates from what is displayed to the new contents. Chapter 8, "Drawing and Working with Animation in Android," discusses more about animation.

Figure 7.12   ImageSwitcher while in the middle of switching between two Drawable resources.

- **Dialogs:** A Dialog is not actually a View widget. Instead, it's like the Activity, but as a pop-up window. A dialog contains a layout in the same way as a full screen and exposes many of the same events, along with some new ones. Other forms of Dialog objects simplify their creation for specific tasks. Figure 7.13 shows an AlertDialog, asking the user to continue.

- **Scrolling:** Although any View widget contains attributes for scrollbars, one of the easiest ways to provide vertical scrolling for a View is with the ScrollView widget. In Android 1.5 R1, a horizontal scrolling mechanism was introduced called HorizontalScrollView. Use either scrolling container as a wrapper, around another View to make scrollbars appear. Additionally, the layout might change, especially sizes of children objects, because the scrolling relaxes the size constraints. Notice, in Figure 7.14, how the background image shows less on the right, but with the scrollbars the user can move around the image.

Figure 7.13   An **AlertDialog** prompting the user to continue.

Figure 7.14   The left screen has no scrollbar, while the right screen has
a scrollbar, visually indicating that the user can move around the image.

- **SlidingDrawer:** Another `View` container introduced for developers in Android 1.5 R1 is the `SlidingDrawer`. This mechanism includes two parts: a handle and a container view. The user drags the handle open and the internal contents are shown; then the user can drag the handle shut and the content disappears. The `SlidingDrawer` can be used horizontally or vertically and is always used from within a layout representing the larger screen. This makes the `SlidingDrawer` especially useful for application configurations such as game controls. Users can pull the drawer out, pausing the game, change some features, and then close the `SlidingDrawer` to resume their game. Figure 7.15 shows how the typical `SlidingDrawer` looks when pulled open. An example is included in the code on disk.

Figure 7.15   `SlidingDrawer` sliding open to show contents.

Using AppWidgets to Expose Application Views

Introduced officially in Android 1.5 R1, the AppWidget (or widget) provides a new level of application integration with the Android operating system previously not available to mobile developers. AppWidgets act like desktop plug-ins, which are tied back to some underlying Android application and are simply small `View` objects that have been exposed for use outside the typical boundaries of the application. AppWidgets are typically hosted in container objects such as the HOME screen, which serves as the Android device desktop.

So how might your application use AppWidgets? Well, in any number of ways:

- A travel application might include a simple AppWidget with the current flight security level.

- A picture gallery application might have a simple Picture of the Day AppWidget.

- A To-do application might include a simple AppWidget describing the number of high-priority outstanding items for the day, or the time of the user's next appointment in the calendar.

Figure 7.16 shows a variety of AppWidgets on the Android Home screen.

Figure 7.16   AppWidgets on the Home screen.

Applications that publish widgets are called AppWidget providers (much like applications can be content providers). A component that can contain AppWidgets is called an AppWidget host.

Becoming an AppWidget Provider

Many applications would benefit from becoming AppWidget providers. Although AppWidgets are small in screen size and functionality, they allow the user to benefit from some special functionality from your application without even launching it. They also serve to keep users *using* your application, by reminding them that they installed it.

Creating an AppWidget for your application involves the following steps:

1. Declare a `BroadcastReceiver` in your Android Manifest file, with an `Intent` filter for the `AppWidgetManager.ACTION_APPWIDGET_UPDATE` `Intent` and a `<meta-data>` tag supplying the XML resource file that describes your AppWidget `View`.

2. Create a specially formatted XML resource file for your AppWidget `View` using the `<appwidget-provider>` tag and attributes.

3. Implement the `AppWidgetProvider` class to handle widget `Intent` broadcasts, updates, and so on.

> **Tip**
>
> For a complete example of an AppWidget, see the ApiDemos sample application provided with the Android SDK.

Becoming an AppWidget Host

Although somewhat less common, applications might also become AppWidget hosts. AppWidget hosts (`android.appwidget.AppWidgetHost`) are simply containers that can embed and display AppWidgets. The implementation details of how such containers display different AppWidgets is left up to the developer. However, all AppWidget hosts begin by interacting with the AppWidget service, which serves up the AppWidgets available on the system. For more information on becoming an AppWidget host, see the Android SDK documentation.

Summary

The Android SDK provides a number of powerful methods for designing usable and great-looking screens. This chapter introduced you to many of these. You first learned about many of the Android layout widgets that can control the placement of your widgets on the screen. In many cases, these allow you have a single screen design that works on most screen sizes and aspect ratios.

You then learned about other objects that contain views and how to group or place them on the screen in a particular way. These included such display paradigms as the tab, typically used in a similar way that physical folder tabs are used, in addition to a variety of different widgets for placing data on the screen in a readable and browsable way.

Finally, you also learned how to extend your application by creating simple AppWidgets, which can be hosted by Android system views such as the Home screen.

You now have all the tools you need to develop applications with usable and exciting user interfaces. As you continue your learning with Android, you might want to look through the SDK for other widgets that can be useful to you.

8

Drawing and Working with Animation in Android

This chapter talks about the drawing and animation features built into Android, including creating custom `View` classes and working with `Canvas` and `Paint` to draw shapes, text, and animations to the screen. Then later, in Chapter 14, "Using Android 3D Graphics with OpenGL ES," we dive further into using the OpenGL ES library for 2D and 3D rendering.

Drawing on the Screen

We talked about layouts and the various `View` widgets available, but now we work at a slightly lower level and talk about drawing on the screen. With Android, we can draw images such as PNG and JPG graphics, text, or primitive shapes to the screen. We can paint them with various colors, styles, and gradients. We can modify them using standard image transforms. We can even animate drawables to give the illusion of motion.

> **Tip**
> We work with graphics in many of the sample applications available on the CD at the end of this book and on the book Web site. The code that follows is part of the "Drawing" sample application.

Working with Canvases and Paints

To draw to the screen, you need a valid `Canvas`. Typically we get a `Canvas` by extending the `View` class for our own purposes and implementing the `onDraw()` method.

For example, here's a simple `View` subclass called `ViewWithRedDot`. We override the `onDraw()` method to dictate what the `View` looks like, in this case it draws a red circle on a black background.

```
private static class ViewWithRedDot extends View {
    public ViewWithRedDot(Context context) {
```

```
        super(context);
    }

    @Override
    protected void onDraw(Canvas canvas) {
        canvas.drawColor(Color.BLACK);
        Paint circlePaint = new Paint();
        circlePaint.setColor(Color.RED);
        canvas.drawCircle(canvas.getWidth()/2,
            canvas.getHeight()/2,
            canvas.getWidth()/3, circlePaint);
    }
}
```

We can then use this `View` like any other layout. For example, we might override the `onCreate()` method in our `Activity` with the following:

```
setContentView(new ViewWithRedDot(this));
```

The resulting screen would look something like Figure 8.1.

Figure 8.1   The `ViewWithRedDot` view draws a red circle on a black
canvas background.

Understanding the Canvas

The `Canvas` (`android.graphics.Canvas`) holds the draw calls, in order, for a rectangle of space. There are methods available for drawing images, text, shapes, and support for clipping regions.

The dimensions of the `Canvas` are bound by the container view. You can retrieve the size of the `Canvas` using the `getHeight()` and `getWidth()` methods.

Understanding the Paint

In Android, `Paint` (`android.graphics.Paint`) stores far more than a color. The `Paint` class encapsulates the style and complex color and rendering information, which can be applied to a drawable like a graphic, or shape, or piece of text in a given `Typeface`.

Working with Paint Color

You can set the color of the `Paint` using the `setColor()` method. Standard colors are predefined within the `android.graphics.Color` class. For example, the following code sets the paint color to red:

```
Paint redPaint = new Paint();
redPaint.setColor(Color.RED);
```

Working with Paint Antialiasing

Antialiasing makes many graphics—whether they are shapes or Typefaces—look smoother on the screen. This property is set within the `Paint` of an object.

For example, the following code instantiates a `Paint` object with antialiasing enabled:

```
Paint aliasedPaint = new Paint(Paint.ANTI_ALIAS_FLAG);
```

Working with Paint Styles

`Paint` style controls how an object is filled with color. For example, the following code instantiates a `Paint` object and sets the Style to `STROKE`, which signifies that the object should be painted as a line drawing and not filled (the default):

```
Paint linePaint = new Paint();
linePaint.setStyle(Paint.Style.STROKE);
```

Working with Paint Gradients

You can create a gradient of colors using one of the gradient subclasses. The different gradient classes (Figure 8.2), including `LinearGradient`, `RadialGradient`, and `SweepGradient`, are available under the superclass `android.graphics.Shader`.

All gradients need at least two colors—a start color and an end color—but might contain any number of colors in an array. The different types of gradients are differentiated by the direction in which the gradient "flows." Gradients can be set to mirror and repeat as necessary.

You can set the `Paint` gradient using the `setShader()` method.

Figure 8.2   An example of a LinearGradient (top), a
RadialGradient (right), and a SweepGradient (bottom).

Working with Linear Gradients

A linear gradient is one that changes colors along a single straight line. The top-left circle
in Figure 8.2 is a linear gradient between black and red, which is mirrored.

This can be achieved by creating a LinearGradient and setting the Paint method
setShader() before drawing on a Canvas, as follows:

```
import android.graphics.Canvas;
import android.graphics.Color;
import android.graphics.LinearGradient;
import android.graphics.Paint;
import android.graphics.Shader;
...
Paint circlePaint = new Paint(Paint.ANTI_ALIAS_FLAG);
LinearGradient linGrad = new LinearGradient(0, 0, 25, 25,
    Color.RED, Color.BLACK,
    Shader.TileMode.MIRROR);
circlePaint.setShader(linGrad);
canvas.drawCircle(100, 100, 100, circlePaint);
```

Working with Radial Gradients

A radial gradient is one that changes colors starting at a single point and radiating outward in a circle. The smaller circle on the right in Figure 8.2 is a radial gradient between green and black.

This can be achieved by creating a `RadialGradient` and setting the `Paint` method `setShader()` before drawing on a `Canvas`, as follows:

```
import android.graphics.Canvas;
import android.graphics.Color;
import android.graphics.RadialGradient;
import android.graphics.Paint;
import android.graphics.Shader;
...
Paint circlePaint = new Paint(Paint.ANTI_ALIAS_FLAG);
RadialGradient radGrad = new RadialGradient(250,
    175, 50, Color.GREEN, Color.BLACK,
    Shader.TileMode.MIRROR);
circlePaint.setShader(radGrad);
canvas.drawCircle(250, 175, 50, circlePaint);
```

Working with Sweep Gradients

A sweep gradient is one that changes colors using slices of a pie. This type of gradient is often used for a color *chooser*. The large circle at the bottom of Figure 8.2 is a sweep gradient between red, yellow, green, blue, and magenta.

This can be achieved by creating a `SweepGradient` and setting the `Paint` method `setShader()` before drawing on a `Canvas`, as follows:

```
import android.graphics.Canvas;
import android.graphics.Color;
import android.graphics.SweepGradient;
import android.graphics.Paint;
import android.graphics.Shader;
...
Paint circlePaint = new Paint(Paint.ANTI_ALIAS_FLAG);
SweepGradient sweepGrad = new
    SweepGradient(canvas.getWidth()-175,
    canvas.getHeight()-175,
    new int[] { Color.RED, Color.YELLOW, Color.GREEN,
    Color.BLUE, Color.MAGENTA }, null);

circlePaint.setShader(sweepGrad);
canvas.drawCircle(canvas.getWidth()-175,
    canvas.getHeight()-175, 100,
    circlePaint);
```

Working with Paint Utilities for Drawing Text

The `Paint` class includes a number of utilities and features for rendering text to the screen in different typefaces and styles. Now is a great time to start drawing some text to the screen.

Working with Text

Android provides several default font typefaces and styles. Applications can also use custom fonts by including font files as application assets and loading them using the `AssetManager`, much as one would use resources.

> **Tip**
>
> The Typeface code that follows is part of the Drawing sample application available on the CD at the end of this book and on the book Web site.

Using Default Fonts and Typefaces

By default, Android uses the Sans Serif typeface, but Monospace and Serif typefaces are also available. The following code excerpt draws some antialiased text in the default typeface (Sans Serif) to a `Canvas`:

```
import android.graphics.Canvas;
import android.graphics.Color;
import android.graphics.Paint;
import android.graphics.Typeface;
...
Paint mPaint = new Paint(Paint.ANTI_ALIAS_FLAG);
Typeface mType;

mPaint.setTextSize(16);
mPaint.setTypeface(null);

canvas.drawText("Default Typeface", 20, 20, mPaint);
```

You can instead load a different typeface, such as Monotype:

```
Typeface mType = Typeface.create(Typeface.MONOSPACE,
    Typeface.NORMAL);
```

Perhaps you would prefer *italic* text, in which case you can simply set the style of the typeface and the font family:

```
Typeface mType = Typeface.create(Typeface.SERIF,
    Typeface.ITALIC);
```

Caution

Not all Typeface styles are supported by all Typeface families. Bold Sans Serif works, but Italics are not implemented. You need to check to make sure the style desired exists on the device.

You can set certain properties of a typeface such as antialiasing, underlining, and strike-through using the `setFlags()` method of the `Paint` object.

```
mPaint.setFlags(Paint.UNDERLINE_TEXT_FLAG);
```

Figure 8.3 shows some of the `Typeface` families and styles available by default on Android.

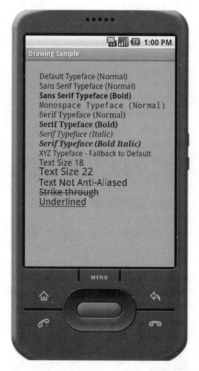

Figure 8.3   Some typefaces and typeface styles available on Android.

Using Custom Typefaces

You can easily use custom typefaces with your application by including the font file as an application asset and loading it on demand. Fonts might be used for a custom look-and-feel, for implementing language symbols that are not supported natively, or for custom symbols.

For example, we might want to use a handy chess font to implement a simple, scalable chess game. A chess font includes every symbol needed to implement a chessboard, including the board and the pieces. Hans Bodlaender has kindly provided a free chess font called *Chess Utrecht*. Using the *Chess Utrecht* font, the letter Q draws a black queen on a white square, whereas a q draws a white queen on a white square, and so on. This nifty font is available on the Web site www.chessvariants.com/d.font/utrecht.html as chess1.ttf.

To use a custom font such as *Chess Utrecht,* simply download the font from the Web site and copy the chess1.ttf file from your hard drive to the project directory /assets/fonts/ chess1.ttf.

Now you can load the Typeface programmatically much as you would any resource:

```
import android.graphics.Typeface;
import android.graphics.Color;
import android.graphics.Paint;
...
Paint    mPaint = new Paint(Paint.ANTI_ALIAS_FLAG);
Typeface mType =
    Typeface.createFromAsset(getContext().getAssets(),
    "fonts/chess1.ttf");
```

You can then use the *Chess Utrecht* typeface to "draw" a chessboard (see Figure 8.4) using the appropriate character sequences.

Figure 8.4   Using the *Chess Utrecht* font to draw a chessboard.

Measuring Text Screen Requirements

You can measure how large text with a given `Paint` will be and how big of a rectangle you need to encompass it all using the using the `measureText()` and `getTextBounds()` methods.

Working with Bitmaps

You can find lots of goodies for working with graphics such as bitmaps (including `NinePatch`) in the `android.graphics` package. The core class for bitmaps is `android.graphics.Bitmap`.

Drawing Bitmap Graphics on a Canvas

You can draw bitmaps onto a valid `Canvas`, such as within the `onDraw()` method of a `View`, using one of the `drawBitmap()` methods. For example, the following code loads a `Bitmap` resource and draws it on a canvas:

```
import android.graphics.Bitmap;
import android.graphics.BitmapFactory;
...
Bitmap pic = BitmapFactory.decodeResource(getResources(),
    R.drawable.bluejay);
canvas.drawBitmap(pic, 0, 0, null);
```

Scaling Bitmap Graphics

Perhaps you want to scale your graphic to a smaller size. In this case, you can use the `createScaledBitmap()` method (Figure 8.5), like this:

```
Bitmap sm = Bitmap.createScaledBitmap(pic, 50, 75, false);
```

You can preserve the aspect ratio of the `Bitmap` by checking the `getWidth()` and `getHeight()` methods and scaling appropriately.

Transforming Bitmaps Using Matrixes

You can use the helpful `Matrix` class to perform transformations on a `Bitmap` graphic. Use the `Matrix` class to perform tasks such as mirroring and rotating graphics, among other actions.

The following code uses the `createBitmap()` method to generate a new `Bitmap` that is a mirror of an existing `Bitmap` called `pic`:

```
import android.graphics.Bitmap;
import android.graphics.Matrix;
...
Matrix mirrorMatrix = new Matrix();
mirrorMatrix.preScale(-1, 1);

Bitmap mirrorPic = Bitmap.createBitmap(pic, 0, 0,
    pic.getWidth(), pic.getHeight(), mirrorMatrix, false);
```

Figure 8.5   A single source bitmap: Scaled, Tilted, Mirrored using
Android Bitmap classes.

You can perform a 30-degree rotation in addition to mirroring by using this `Matrix`
instead:

```
Matrix mirrorAndTilt30 = new Matrix();
mirrorAndTilt30.preRotate(30);
mirrorAndTilt30.preScale(-1, 1);
```

You can see the results of different combinations of tilt and mirror `Matrix` transforms in
Figure 8.5. When you're no longer using a `Bitmap`, you can free its memory using the
`recycle()` method:

```
pic.recycle();
```

There are a variety of other `Bitmap` effects and utilities available as part of the Android
SDK, but they are numerous and beyond the scope of this book. See the
`android.graphics` package for more details.

Working with Shapes

You can define and draw primitive shapes such as rectangles and ovals using the `ShapeDrawable` class in conjunction with a variety of specialized `Shape` classes. You can define `Paintable` drawables as XML resource files, but more often, especially with more complex shapes, this is done programmatically.

> **Tip**
>
> You can find example code of how to draw different shapes in the ShapeShifter sample project provided on the CD and on the book Web site.

Defining Shape Drawables as XML Resources

In Chapter 5, "Managing Application Resources," we showed you how to define primitive shapes such as rectangles using specially formatted XML files within the `/res/drawable/` resource directory.

For example, the following resource file called **/res/drawable/green_rect.xml** describes a simple, green rectangle shape drawable:

```
<?xml version="1.0" encoding="utf-8"?>
<shape xmlns:android=
➥"http://schemas.android.com/apk/res/android"
➥android:shape="rectangle">
    <solid android:color="#0f0"/>
</shape>
```

You can then load the shape resource and set it as the `Drawable` as follows:

```
ImageView iView = (ImageView)findViewById(R.id.ImageView1);
iView.setImageResource(R.drawable.green_rect);
```

You should note that many `Paint` properties can be set via XML as part of the `Shape` definition. For example, the following `Oval` shape is defined with a linear gradient (red to white) and stroke style information:

```
<?xml version="1.0" encoding="utf-8"?>
<shape xmlns:android
➥="http://schemas.android.com/apk/res/android"
➥android:shape="oval">
    <solid android:color="#f00"/>
    <gradient android:startColor="#f00"
        android:endColor="#fff"
        android:angle="180"/>
    <stroke android:width="3dp" android:color="#00f"
        android:dashWidth="5dp" android:dashGap="3dp"/>
</shape>
```

Defining Shape Drawables Programmatically

You can also define these `ShapeDrawable` instances programmatically. The different shapes of are available as classes within the `android.graphics.drawable.shapes` package. For example, the aforementioned green rectangle could be defined programmatically as follows:

```
import android.graphics.drawable.ShapeDrawable;
import android.graphics.drawable.shapes.RectShape;
...
ShapeDrawable rect = new ShapeDrawable(new RectShape());
rect.getPaint().setColor(Color.GREEN);
```

You can then set the `Drawable` for the `ImageView` directly:

```
ImageView iView = (ImageView)findViewById(R.id.ImageView1);
iView.setImageDrawable(rect);
```

The resulting green rectangle is shown in Figure 8.6.

Figure 8.6   A green rectangle.

Drawing Different Shapes

Some of the different shapes available within the
`android.graphics.drawable.shapes` package include

- Rectangles (and squares)
- Rectangles with rounded corners
- Ovals (and circles)
- Arcs and lines
- Other shapes defined as Paths

These shapes can be created and used as `Drawable` resources directly within `ImageView`
views, or you can find corresponding methods for creating these primitive shapes within
a `Canvas`.

Drawing Rectangles and Squares

Drawing rectangles and squares (rectangles with equal height/width values) is simply a
matter of creating a `ShapeDrawable` from a `RectShape` object. The `RectShape` object
has no dimensions but is bound by the container object, in this case the
`ShapeDrawable`. You can set some basic properties of the `ShapeDrawable`, such as the
Paint color and the default size.

For example, here we create a magenta-colored rectangle that is 100-pixels long and
2-pixels wide, which looks like a straight, horizontal line. We then set shape as the drawable for an `ImageView` so the shape can be displayed:

```
import android.graphics.drawable.ShapeDrawable;
import android.graphics.drawable.shapes.RectShape;
...
ShapeDrawable rect = new ShapeDrawable(new RectShape());
rect.setIntrinsicHeight(2);
rect.setIntrinsicWidth(100);
rect.getPaint().setColor(Color.MAGENTA);

ImageView iView = (ImageView)findViewById(R.id.ImageView1);
iView.setImageDrawable(rect);
```

Drawing Rectangles with Rounded Corners

You can create rectangles with rounded corners, which can be nice for making custom
buttons. Simply create a `ShapeDrawable` from a `RoundRectShape` object. The
`RoundRectShape` requires an array of eight float values, which signify the radii of the
rounded corners. For example, the following creates a simple cyan-colored, rounded-
corner rectangle:

```
import android.graphics.drawable.ShapeDrawable;
import android.graphics.drawable.shapes.RoundRectShape;
...
```

```
ShapeDrawable rndrect = new ShapeDrawable(new RoundRectShape( new float[] { 5, 5,
➥5, 5, 5, 5, 5, 5 },
    null, null));
rndrect.setIntrinsicHeight(50);
rndrect.setIntrinsicWidth(100);
rndrect.getPaint().setColor(Color.CYAN);
ImageView iView = (ImageView)findViewById(R.id.ImageView1);
iView.setImageDrawable(rndrect);
```

The resulting round rectangle is shown in Figure 8.7.

Figure 8.7   A cyan rectangle with rounded corners.

You can also specify an inner-rounded rectangle within the outer rectangle, if you so choose. The following creates an inner rectangle with rounded edges within the outer white rectangle with rounded edges:

```
import android.graphics.drawable.ShapeDrawable;
import android.graphics.drawable.shapes.RoundRectShape;
...
```

```
float[] outerRadii = new float[]{ 6, 6, 6, 6, 6, 6, 6, 6 };
RectF insetRectangle = new RectF(8, 8, 8, 8);
float[] innerRadii = new float[]{ 6, 6, 6, 6, 6, 6, 6, 6 };

ShapeDrawable rndrect = new ShapeDrawable(
    new RoundRectShape(
        outerRadii,insetRectangle , innerRadii));

rndrect.setIntrinsicHeight(50);
rndrect.setIntrinsicWidth(100);
rndrect.getPaint().setColor(Color.WHITE);
ImageView iView = (ImageView)findViewById(R.id.ImageView1);
iView.setImageDrawable(rndrect);
```

The resulting round rectangle with an inset rectangle is shown in Figure 8.8.

Figure 8.8   A white rectangle with rounded corners, with an inset rounded rectangle.

Drawing Ovals and Circles

You can create ovals and circles (ovals with equal height/width values) by creating a
`ShapeDrawable` using an `OvalShape` object. The `OvalShape` object has no dimensions
but is bound by the container object, in this case the `ShapeDrawable`. You can set some
basic properties of the `ShapeDrawable`, such as the Paint color and the default size. For
example, here we create a red oval that is 40-pixels high and 100-pixels wide, which
looks like a Frisbee:

```
import android.graphics.drawable.ShapeDrawable;
import android.graphics.drawable.shapes.OvalShape;
...
ShapeDrawable oval = new ShapeDrawable(new OvalShape());
oval.setIntrinsicHeight(40);
oval.setIntrinsicWidth(100);
oval.getPaint().setColor(Color.RED);
ImageView iView = (ImageView)findViewById(R.id.ImageView1);
iView.setImageDrawable(oval);
```

The resulting red oval is shown in Figure 8.9.

Figure 8.9   A red oval.

Drawing Arcs

You can draw arcs, which look like pie charts or Pac-Man, depending on the sweep angle you specify. You can create arcs by creating a `ShapeDrawable` by using an `ArcShape` object. The `ArcShape` object requires two parameters: a `startAngle` and a `sweepAngle`. The `startAngle` begins at 3 o'clock. Positive `sweepAngle` values sweep clockwise, negative values counterclockwise. You can create a circle by using the values 0 and 360.

The following code creates an arc that looks like a magenta Pac-Man:

```
import android.graphics.drawable.ShapeDrawable;
import android.graphics.drawable.shapes.ArcShape;
...
ShapeDrawable pacMan =
    new ShapeDrawable(new ArcShape(0, 345));
pacMan.setIntrinsicHeight(100);
pacMan.setIntrinsicWidth(100);
pacMan.getPaint().setColor(Color.MAGENTA);
ImageView iView = (ImageView)findViewById(R.id.ImageView1);
iView.setImageDrawable(pacMan);
```

The resulting arc is shown in Figure 8.10.

Figure 8.10   A magenta arc of 345 degrees (resembling Pac-Man).

Drawing Paths

You can specify any shape you want by breaking it down into a series of points along a path. The `android.graphics.Path` class encapsulates a series of lines and curves that make up some larger shape.

For example, the following `Path` defines a rough five-point star shape:

```
import android.graphics.Path;
...
Path p = new Path();
p.moveTo(50, 0);
p.lineTo(25,100);
p.lineTo(100,50);
p.lineTo(0,50);
p.lineTo(75,100);
p.lineTo(50,0);
```

You can then encapsulate this star `Path` in a `PathShape`, create a `ShapeDrawable`, and paint it yellow.

```
import android.graphics.drawable.ShapeDrawable;
import android.graphics.drawable.shapes.PathShape;
...
ShapeDrawable star =
    new ShapeDrawable(new PathShape(p, 100, 100));
star.setIntrinsicHeight(100);
star.setIntrinsicWidth(100);
star.getPaint().setColor(Color.YELLOW);
```

By default, this generates a star shape filled with the `Paint` color yellow (Figure 8.11).

Or, you can set the `Paint` style to `Stroke` for a line drawing of a star.

```
star.getPaint().setStyle(Paint.Style.STROKE);
```

The resulting star would look something like Figure 8.12.

> **Tip**
>
> The graphics support available within the Android SDK could be the subject of an entire book. There are many different drawing mechanisms and methods available within the Android SDK. When you have familiarized yourself with the basics, we highly recommend checking out the APIDemos sample application provided with the Android Software Development Kit (SDK), paying special attention to `com.example.android.apis.graphics` package (whose samples can be found under the APIDemos menu item called Graphics). For a simple game design, check out the Lunar Lander sample application as well.

Figure 8.11   A yellow star.

Figure 8.12   A yellow star using the stroke style of Paint.

Working with Animation

The Android platform supports three types of graphics animation:

- Animated GIF images
- Frame-by-frame animation
- Tweened animation

Animated GIFs store the animation frames within the image, and you simply include these GIFs like any other graphic drawable resource. For frame-by-frame animation, the developer must provide all graphics frames of the animation. However, with tweened animation, only a single graphic is needed, upon which transforms can be programmatically applied.

> **Tip**
>
> You can find examples of both of these animation methods in the ShapeShifter sample project provided on the CD and on the book Web site.

Working with Frame-by-Frame Animation

You can think of frame-by-frame animation as a digital flipbook in which a series of similar images display on the screen in a sequence, each subtly different from the last. When you display these images quickly, they give the illusion of movement. This technique is called frame-by-frame animation and is often used on the Web in the form of animated GIF images.

Frame-by-frame animation is best used for complicated graphics transformations that are not easily implemented programmatically.

For example, we can create the illusion of a genie juggling gifts using a sequence of three images, as shown in Figure 8.13.

Figure 8.13   Three frames for an animation of a genie juggling.

In each frame, the genie remains fixed, but the gifts are repositioned slightly. The smoothness of the animation is controlled by providing an adequate number of frames and choosing the appropriate speed on which to swap them.

The following code demonstrates how to load three `Bitmap` resources (our three genie frames) and create an `AnimationDrawable`. We then set the `AnimationDrawable` as the background resource of an `ImageView` and start the animation.

```
ImageView img = (ImageView)findViewById(R.id.ImageView1);

BitmapDrawable frame1 = (BitmapDrawable)getResources().
    getDrawable(R.drawable.f1);
BitmapDrawable frame2 = (BitmapDrawable)getResources().
    getDrawable(R.drawable.f2);
BitmapDrawable frame3 = (BitmapDrawable)getResources().
    getDrawable(R.drawable.f3);

int reasonableDuration = 250;
AnimationDrawable mAnimation = new AnimationDrawable();

mAnimation.addFrame(frame1, reasonableDuration);
mAnimation.addFrame(frame2, reasonableDuration);
mAnimation.addFrame(frame3, reasonableDuration);

img.setBackgroundDrawable(mAnimation);
```

To name the animation loop continuously, we can call the `setOneShot()` method:

```
mAnimation.setOneShot(false);
```

And to begin the animation, we call the `start()` method:

```
mAnimation.start();
```

We can end our animation at any time using the `stop()` method:

```
mAnimation.stop();
```

Although we used an `ImageView` background in this example, you can use a variety of different `View` widgets for animations. For example, you can instead use the `ImageSwitcher` view and change the displayed `Drawable` resource using a timer. This sort of operation is best done on a separate thread. The resulting animation might look something like Figure 8.14—you just have to imagine it moving.

Figure 8.14   The genie animation in the Android emulator.

Working with Tweened Animations

With tweened animation, you can provide a single `Drawable` resource—it is a `Bitmap` graphic (Figure 8.15, left), a `ShapeDrawable`, a `TextView` (Figure 8.15, right), or any other type of `View` object—and the intermediate frames of the animation are rendered by the system. Android provides tweening support for several common image transformations, including alpha, rotate, scale, and translate animations. You can apply tweened animation transformations to any `View`, whether it is an `ImageView` with a `Bitmap` or shape `Drawable`, or a layout like a `TableLayout`.

Defining Tweening Transformations

You can define tweening transformations as XML resource files or programmatically. All tweened animations share some common properties, including when to start, how long to animate, and whether to return to the starting state upon completion.

Figure 8.15   Rotating a green rectangle shape `drawable` (left) and a
`TableLayout` (right).

Defining Tweened Animations as XML Resources

In Chapter 5 we showed you how to store animation sequences as specially formatted
XML files within the `/res/anim/` resource directory. For example, the following
resource file called `/res/anim/spin.xml` describes a simple five-second rotation:

```
<?xml version="1.0" encoding="utf-8" ?>
<set xmlns:android
    = "http://schemas.android.com/apk/res/android"
    android:shareInterpolator="false">
    <rotate
        android:fromDegrees="0"
        android:toDegrees="360"
        android:pivotX="50%"
        android:pivotY="50%"
        android:duration="5000" />
</set>
```

Defining Tweened Animations Programmatically

You can also define these animations programmatically. The different types of transformations are available as classes within the `android.view.animation` package. For example, the aforementioned rotation animation can be defined as follows:

```
import android.view.animation.RotateAnimation;
...
RotateAnimation rotate = new RotateAnimation(
    0, 360, RotateAnimation.RELATIVE_TO_SELF, 0.5f,
    RotateAnimation.RELATIVE_TO_SELF, 0.5f);

rotate.setDuration(5000);
```

Defining Simultaneous and Sequential Tweened Animations

Animation transformations can happen simultaneously or sequentially by setting the `startOffset` and `duration` properties, which control when and for how long an animation takes to complete. Animations can be combined into the `<set>` tag (programmatically, using `AnimationSet`) to share properties.

For example, the following animation resource file **/res/anim/grow.xml** includes a set of two scale animations: First, we take 2.5 seconds to double in size, and then at 2.5 seconds, we start a second animation to shrink back to our starting size.

```xml
<?xml version="1.0" encoding="utf-8" ?>
<set xmlns:android=
    http://schemas.android.com/apk/res/android
    android:shareInterpolator="false">
    <scale
        android:pivotX="50%"
        android:pivotY="50%"
        android:fromXScale="1.0"
        android:fromYScale="1.0"
        android:toXScale="2.0"
        android:toYScale="2.0" />
    <scale
        android:startOffset="2500"
        android:duration="2500"
        android:pivotX="50%"
        android:pivotY="50%"
        android:fromXScale="1.0"
        android:fromYScale="1.0"
        android:toXScale="0.5"
        android:toYScale="0.5" />
</set>
```

Loading Animations

Loading animations is made simple by using the `AnimationUtils` helper class. The following code loads an animation XML resource file called **/res/anim/grow.xml** and applies it to an `ImageView` whose source resource is a green rectangle shape `drawable`:

```
import android.view.animation.Animation;
import android.view.animation.AnimationUtils;
...
ImageView iView = (ImageView)findViewById(R.id.ImageView1);
iView.setImageResource(R.drawable.green_rect);
Animation an =
    AnimationUtils.loadAnimation(this, R.anim.grow);
iView.startAnimation(an);
```

We can listen for `Animation` events, including the animation start, end, and repeat events, by implementing an `AnimationListener` class, such as the `MyListener` class shown here:

```
class MyListener implements Animation.AnimationListener {

    public void onAnimationEnd(Animation animation) {
        // Do at end of animation
    }

    public void onAnimationRepeat(Animation animation) {
        // Do each time the animation loops
    }

    public void onAnimationStart(Animation animation) {
        // Do at start of animation
    }
}
```

You can then register your `AnimationListener` as follows:

```
an.setAnimationListener(new MyListener());
```

Exploring the Four Different Tweening Transformations

Now let's look at each of the four types of tweening transformations individually. These types are

- Transparency changes (Alpha)
- Rotations (Rotate)
- Scaling (Scale)
- Movement (Translate)

Working with Alpha Transparency Transformations

Transparency is controlled using Alpha transformations. Alpha transformations can be used to fade objects in and out of view, or to layer them on the screen.

Alpha values range from 0.0 (fully transparent or invisible) to 1.0 (fully opaque or visible). Alpha animations involve a starting transparency (`fromAlpha`) and an ending transparency (`toAlpha`).

The following XML resource file excerpt defines a transparency-change animation, taking five seconds to fade in from fully transparent to fully opaque:

```
<alpha
    android:fromAlpha="0.0"
    android:toAlpha="1.0"
    android:duration="5000">
</alpha>
```

Programmatically, you can create this same animation using the `AlphaAnimation` class within the `android.view.animation` package.

Working with Rotating Transformations

Rotation operations can be used to spin objects clockwise or counterclockwise around a pivot point within the object's boundaries.

Rotations are defined in terms of degrees. For example, you might want to rotate an object completely once in a clockwise direction. To do this, you would set the `fromDegrees` property to 0 and the `toDegrees` property to 360. To rotate the object counterclockwise instead, you would set the `toDegrees` property to –360.

By default, the object pivots around the (0,0) coordinate, or the top-left corner of the object. This is great for rotations such as those of a clock's hands, but much of the time, you want to pivot from the center of the object; this is easily done by setting the pivot point, which can be a fixed coordinate or a percentage.

The following XML resource file excerpt defines a rotation animation, taking 5 seconds to rotate one full-time clockwise, pivoting from the center of the object:

```
<rotate
    android:fromDegrees="0"
    android:toDegrees="360"
    android:pivotX="50%"
    android:pivotY="50%"
    android:duration="5000" />
```

Programmatically, you can create this same animation using the `RotateAnimation` class within the `android.view.animation` package.

Working with Scaling Transformations

You can use scaling operations to stretch objects vertically and horizontally. Scaling operations are defined as relative scales. Think of the scale value of 1.0 as 100 percent, or full-size. To scale to half size or 50 percent, set the target scale value of 0.5.

You can scale horizontally and vertically on different scales or on the same scale (to preserve aspect ratio). You need to set four values for proper scaling: starting scale (`fromXScale`, `fromYScale`) and target scale (`toXScale`, `toYScale`). Again, you can use a pivot point to stretch your object from a specific (x,y) coordinate such as the center or another coordinate.

The following XML resource file excerpt defines a scaling animation, taking five seconds to double an object's size, pivoting from the center of the object:

```
<scale
    android:pivotX="50%"
    android:pivotY="50%"
    android:fromXScale="1.0"
    android:fromYScale="1.0"
    android:toXScale="2.0"
    android:toYScale="2.0"
    android:duration="5000" />
```

Programmatically, you can create this same animation using the `ScaleAnimation` class within the `android.view.animation` package.

Working with Moving Transformations

You can move objects around using translate operations. Translate operations move an object from one position on the (x,y) coordinate to another coordinate.

To perform a translate operation, you must specify the change, or delta, in the object's coordinates. You can set four values for translations: starting position (`fromXDelta`, `fromYDelta`) and relative target location (`toXDelta`, `toYDelta`).

The following XML resource file excerpt defines a translate animation, taking 5 seconds to move an object up (negative) by 100 on the y-axis. We also set the `fillAfter` property to be true, so the object doesn't "jump" back to its starting position when the animation finishes:

```
<translate android:toYDelta="-100"
    android:fillAfter="true"
    android:duration="2500" />
```

Programmatically, you can create this same animation using the `TranslateAnimation` class within the `android.view.animation` package.

Summary

The Android SDK comes with the `android.graphics` package, which includes powerful classes for drawing graphics and text to the screen in a variety of different ways. Some features of the graphics library include `Bitmap` graphics utilities, `Typeface` and font style support, `Paint` colors and styles, different types of gradients, and a variety of primitive and not-so-primitive shapes that can be drawn to the screen and even animated using tweening and frame-by-frame animation mechanisms.

IV

Using Common
Android APIs

9

Using Android Data and Storage APIs

Applications are about functionality and data. In this chapter, we explore the various ways you can store, manage, and share application data with Android. Applications can store and manage data in different ways.

Applications can use a combination of application preferences, the file system, and built-in SQLite database support to store information locally. Applications can access data within other applications on the Android system through content provider interfaces and expose internal application data to other applications by becoming a content provider.

The methods you choose depend on your application requirements. In this chapter, you learn how to use each of these features to store and interact with data.

Working with Application Preferences

Many applications need a lightweight data storage mechanism called shared preferences for storing application state, simple user information, configuration options, and other such information.

Android provides a simple preferences system for storing primitive application data at the `Activity` level and preferences shared across all of an application's activities. You cannot share preferences outside of the package. Preferences are stored as groups of key/value pairs. The following data types are supported as preference settings:

- Boolean values
- Float values
- Integer values
- Long values
- String values

Preference functionality can be found in the `SharedPreferences` interface of the `android.content` package. To add preferences support to your application, you must take the following steps:

1. Retrieve an instance of a `SharedPreferences` object.
2. Create a `SharedPreferences.Editor` to modify preference content.
3. Make changes to the preferences using the Editor.
4. Commit your changes.

Creating Private and Shared Preferences

Individual activities can have their own private preferences. These preferences are for the specific `Activity` only and are not shared with other activities within the application. The activity gets only one group of private preferences.

The following code retrieves the activity's private preferences:

```
import android.content.SharedPreferences;
...
SharedPreferences settingsActivity =getPreferences(MODE_PRIVATE);
```

Creating shared preferences is similar. The only two differences are that we must name our preference set and use a different call to get the preference instance:

```
import android.content.SharedPreferences;
...
SharedPreferences settings =
    getSharedPreferences("MyCustomSharedPreferences", 0);
```

Shared preferences can be accessed from any activity in the application by their name. There is no limit to the number of different shared preferences you can create. You can have some shared preferences called `UserNetworkPreferences` and another called `AppDisplayPreferences`. How you organize shared preferences is up to the developer, however, you want to declare your preference name as a variable (in a base class or header) so that you can reuse the name across multiple activities. For example:

```
public static final String PREFERENCE_FILENAME = "AppPrefs";
```

Searching and Reading Preferences

Reading preferences is straightforward. Simply retrieve the `SharedPreferences` instance you want to read. You can check for a preference by name, retrieve strongly typed preferences, and register to listen for changes to the preferences. Some helpful methods in the `SharedPreferences` interface are shown in Table 9.1.

Table 9.1   **Important** `android.content.SharedPreferences` **Methods**

Method	Purpose
`SharedPreferences.contains()`	Sees if a specific preference exists by name
`SharedPreferences.edit()`	Retrieves the editor to change these preferences
`SharedPreferences.getAll()`	Retrieves a Map of all preference key/value pairs
`SharedPreferences.getBoolean()`	Retrieves a specific Boolean-type preference by name
`SharedPreferences.getFloat()`	Retrieves a specific Float-type preference by name
`SharedPreferences.getInt()`	Retrieves a specific Integer-type preference by name
`SharedPreferences.getLong()`	Retrieves a specific Long-type preference by name
`SharedPreferences.getString()`	Retrieves a specific String-type preference by name

Adding, Updating, and Deleting Preferences

To change preferences, you need to open the preference `Editor`, make your changes, and commit them. Some helpful methods in the `SharedPreferences.Editor` interface are shown in Table 9.2.

Table 9.2   **Important** `android.content.SharedPreferences.Editor` **Methods**

Method	Purpose
`SharedPreferences.Editor.clear()`	Removes all preferences. This operation happens first, regardless of when it is called within an editing session. Then all other changes are made and committed.
`SharedPreferences.Editor.remove()`	Removes a specific preference by name. This operation happens first, regardless of when it is called within an editing session. Then all other changes are made and committed.
`SharedPreferences.Editor.putBoolean()`	Sets a specific Boolean-type preference by name
`SharedPreferences.Editor.putFloat()`	Sets a specific Float-type preference by name.

Table 9.2   **Continued**

Method	Purpose
SharedPreferences.Editor.putInt()	Sets a specific Integer-type preference by name.
SharedPreferences.Editor.putLong()	Sets a specific Long-type preference by name.
SharedPreferences.Editor.putString()	Sets a specific String-type preference by name.
SharedPreferences.Editor.commit()	Commits all changes from this editing session.

The following block of code retrieves the activity's private preferences, opens the preference editor, adds a long preference called SomeLong, and saves the change:

```
import android.content.SharedPreferences;
…
SharedPreferences settingsActivity = getPreferences(MODE_PRIVATE);
SharedPreferences.Editor prefEditor = settingsActivity.edit();
prefEditor.putLong("SomeLong", java.lang.Long.MIN_VALUE);
prefEditor.commit();
```

Tip

You can find the "SimplePrefs" project on the CD provided at the end of this book or online at the book Web site. This sample application illustrates how to create and use private preferences at the activity level and shared preferences at the application level.

Finding Preferences Data on the Android File System

Internally, application preferences are stored as XML files. You can access the preferences file using DDMS using the File Explorer. You find these files on the Android file system in the following directory:

/data/data/<package name>/shared_prefs/<preferences filename>.xml:

The preferences filename will be the Activity's class name for private preferences or the name you gave for the shared preferences. Here is an example of the file contents of a simple preference file with a preference in each data type:

```
<?xml version="1.0" encoding="utf-8" standalone="yes" ?>
<map>
    <string name="String_Pref">Test String</string>
    <int name="Int_Pref" value="-2147483648" />
    <float name="Float_Pref" value="-Infinity" />
    <long name="Long_Pref" value="9223372036854775807" />
    <boolean name="Boolean_Pref" value="false" />
</map>
```

Understanding the application preferences file format can be helpful for testing purposes. You can use Dalvik Debug Monitor Service (DDMS) to copy the preferences files to and from the device.

Note

For more information about using DDMS and the File Explorer, please see Appendix B, "The Android DDMS Quick-Start Guide."

Working with Files and Directories

Remember from Chapter 1, "Introducing Android," that each Android application is its own user on the underlying Linux operating system. It has its own private application directory and files. Within the Android SDK, you can also find a variety of standard java file utility classes (like `java.io`) for handling different types of files, such as text files, binary files, and XML files.

In Chapter 5, "Managing Application Resources," you also learned that Android applications can also include static raw and XML files as resources. Although retrieving the file is done slightly differently when accessing resources, the file can be read like any other file.

Android application files are stored in a standard directory hierarchy on the Android file system. You can browse an application's directory structure using the DDMS File Explorer.

Tip

There are two file-oriented sample projects on the CD provided at the end of this book and online at the book Web site. The "SimpleFiles" project is a barebones example of how to access the application directory structure and shows simple file-based operations. This project has no user interface. The "FileStreamOfConsciousness" project is a multithreaded application that interacts with the user, allowing them to write data to a file.

Exploring with the Android Application Directories

Android application data is stored on the Android file system in the following top-level directory:

`/data/data/<package name>/`

Several default subdirectories are created for storing databases, preferences, and files as necessary. You can also create other custom directories as needed. File operators all begin by interacting with the application `Context` object. Table 9.3 lists some important methods available for application file management. You can use all the standard `java.io` package utilities to work with `FileStream` objects and such.

Table 9.3   **Important** `android.content.Context` **File and Directory Management Methods**

Method	Purpose
`Context.openFileInput()`	Opens an application file for reading. These files are located in the `/files` subdirectory.
`Context.openFileOutput()`	Creates or opens an application file for writing. These files are located in the `/files` subdirectory.
`Context.deleteFile()`	Deletes an application file by name. These files must be located in the `/files` subdirectory.
`Context.fileList()`	Gets a list of all files in the `/files` subdirectory.
`Context.getFilesDir()`	Retrieves the application `/files` subdirectory object.
`Context.getCacheDir()`	Retrieves the application `/cache` subdirectory object.
`Context.getDir()`	Creates or retrieves an application subdirectory by name.

Creating and Writing to Files to the Default Application Directory

Android applications that require only the occasional file rely upon the helpful method called `openFileOutput()`. Use this method to create files in the default location under the application data directory:

/data/data/<package name>/files/

For example, the following code snippet creates and opens a file called **Filename.txt**. We write a sinÏgle line of text to the file and then close the file.

```
import java.io.FileOutputStream;
...
FileOutputStream fos;
String strFileContents = "Some text to write to the file.";
fos = openFileOutput("Filename.txt", MODE_PRIVATE);
fos.write(strFileContents.getBytes());
fos.close();
```

We can append data to the file by opening it with the mode set to MODE_APPEND:

```
import java.io.FileOutputStream;
...
FileOutputStream fos;
String strFileContents = "More text to write to the file.";
fos = openFileOutput("Filename.txt", MODE_APPEND);
fos.write(strFileContents.getBytes());
fos.close();
```

The file we created has the following path on the Android file system:

/data/data/<package name>/files/Filename.txt

Reading from Files in the Default Application Directory

Again we have a shortcut for reading files stored in the default **/files** subdirectory. The following code snippet opens a file called **Filename.txt** for read operations.

```
import java.io.FileInputStream;
…
String strFileName = "Filename.txt";
FileInputStream fis = openFileInput(strFileName);
```

Reading Raw Files Byte-by-Byte

File reading and writing operations are done using standard Java methods. Check out the subclasses of java.io.InputStream for reading bytes from different types of primitive file types. For example, DataInputStream is useful for reading one line at a time.

Here's a simple example of how to read a text file, line by line, and store it in a StringBuffer:

```
FileInputStream fis = openFileInput(filename);
StringBuffer sBuffer = new StringBuffer();
DataInputStream dataIO = new DataInputStream(fis);
String strLine = null;

while ((strLine = dataIO.readLine()) != null) {
    sBuffer.append(strLine + "\n");
}

dataIO.close();
fis.close();
```

> **Tip**
>
> The "SimpleFiles" project provided on the CD at the end of this book and online at the book Web site gives a variety of examples of how to read data from files.

Reading XML Files

The Android SDK includes several utilities for working with XML files, including SAX, an XML Pull Parser, and limited DOM, Level 2 Core support. The packages helpful for XML parsing on the Android platform are listed in Table 9.4.

Table 9.4   **Important XML Utility Packages**

Package	Description
android.sax.*	Framework to write standard SAX handlers
android.util.Xml.*	XML Utilities including the XMLPullParser
org.xml.sax.*	Core SAX functionality.
	Project: www.saxproject.org/
javax.xml.*	SAX and limited DOM, Level 2 Core support
org.w3c.dom	Interfaces for DOM, Level 2 Core
org.xmlpull.*	XmlPullParser and XMLSerializer interfaces.
	Project www.xmlpull.org/

Tip

The "ResourceRoundup" project for Chapter 5 provided on the CD at the end of this book and online at the book Web site gives an example of parsing a static XML file included as an application resource using the XmlPullParser called XmlResourceParser.

Working with Other Directories and Files on the Android File System

Using Context.openFileOutput() and Context.openFileInput() are great if you have a few files and you want them stored in the **/files** subdirectory, but if you have more sophisticated file management needs, you need to set up your own directory structure. To do this, you must interact with the Android file system using the standard java.io.File class methods.

The following code gets a File object for the **/files** application subdirectory and retrieves a list of all filenames in that directory:

```
import java.io.File;
...
File pathForAppFiles = getFilesDir();
String[] fileList = pathForAppFiles.list();
```

Here is a more generic method to create a file on the file system. This method works anywhere on the Android file system you have permission to access, not the **/files** directory:

```
import java.io.File;
import java.io.FileOutputStream;
...
File fileDir = getFilesDir();
String strNewFileName = "myFile.dat";
String strFileContents = "Some data for our file";
```

```
File newFile = new File(fileDir, strNewFileName);
newFile.createNewFile();

FileOutputStream fo =
    new FileOutputStream(newFile.getAbsolutePath());
fo.write(strFileContents.getBytes());
fo.close();
```

You can use `File` objects to manage files within a desired directory and create subdirectories. For example, you might want to store "track" files within "album" directories. Or perhaps you want to create a file in a directory other than the default.

Let's say you want to cache some data to speed up your application's performance and how often it accesses the network. In this instance, you might want to create a cache file. There is also a special application directory for storing cache files. These files are stored in the following location on the Android file system:

/data/data/<package name>/cache/

The following code gets a `File` object for the **/cache** application subdirectory, creates a new file in that specific directory, writes some data to the file, closes the file, and then deletes it:

```
File pathCacheDir = getCacheDir();
String strCacheFileName = "myCacheFile.cache";
String strFileContents = "Some data for our file";

File newCacheFile = new File(pathCacheDir, strCacheFileName);
newCacheFile.createNewFile();

FileOutputStream foCache =
    new FileOutputStream(newCacheFile.getAbsolutePath());
foCache.write(strFileContents.getBytes());
foCache.close();

newCacheFile.delete();
```

Storing Structured Data Using SQLite Databases

When your application requires a more robust data storage mechanism, you'll be happy to hear that the Android file system includes support for application-specific relational databases using SQLite. SQLite databases are lightweight and file-based, making them ideally suited for embedded devices.

These databases and the data within them are private to the application. To share application data with other applications, you must expose the data you want to share by making your application a content provider (discussed later in this chapter).

The Android SDK includes a number of useful SQLite database management classes. Many of these classes are found in the `android.database.sqlite` package. Here you can find utility classes for managing database creation and versioning, database management, and query builder helper classes to help you format proper SQL statements and queries. There are also specialized `Cursor` objects for iterating query results. You can also find all the specialized exceptions associated with SQLite.

Here we focus on creating databases within our Android applications. For that, we use the built-in SQLite support to programmatically create and use a SQLite database to store application information. However, if your application works with a different sort of database, you can also find more generic database classes (within the `android.database` package) to help you work with data from other providers.

In addition to programmatically creating and using SQLite databases, developers can also interact directly with their application's database using the `sqlite3` command-line tool accessible through the ADB shell interface. This can be an extremely helpful debugging tool for developers and quality assurance personnel, who might want to manage the database state (and content) for testing purposes.

> **Tip**
>
> For more information about designing SQLite databases and interacting with them via the command line tool, please see Appendix D, "The SQLite Quick-Start Guide." This appendix is divided into two parts: the first half is an overview of the most commonly used features of the `sqlite3` command-line interface and the limitations of SQLite compared to other flavors of SQL; the second half of the appendix includes a fully functional tutorial in which you build a SQLite database from the ground up and then use it. If you are new to SQL (or SQLite) or a bit rusty on your syntax, this tutorial is for you.

Creating a SQLite Database

Creating a SQLite database for your Android application can be done in several ways. To illustrate how to create and use a simple SQLite database, let's create an Android project called FullDatabase.

> **Tip**
>
> You can find the FullDatabase project on the CD provided at the end of this book or online at the book Web site. This project contains a single class that creates a SQLite database, populates it with several tables worth of data, queries and manipulates the data in various ways, and then deletes the database.

Creating a SQLite Database Instance Using the Application Context

The simplest way to create a new `SQLiteDatabase` instance for your application is to use the `openOrCreateDatabase()` method of your application `Context`, like this:

```
import android.database.sqlite.SQLiteDatabase;

...

SQLiteDatabase mDatabase;
```

```
mDatabase = openOrCreateDatabase(
    "my_sqlite_database.db",
    SQLiteDatabase.CREATE_IF_NECESSARY,
    null);
```

Finding the Application's Database File on the Device File System

Android applications store their databases (SQLite or otherwise) under in a special application directory:

/data/data/<application package name>/databases/<databasename>

So, in this case, the path to the database would be

/data/data/com.androidbook.FullDatabase/databases/my_sqlite_database.db

You can access your database using the `sqlite3` command-line interface using this path.

Configuring the SQLite Database Properties

Now that you have a valid `SQLiteDatabase` instance, it's time to configure it. Some important database configuration options include version, locale, and the thread-safe locking feature.

```
import java.util.Locale;
…
mDatabase.setLocale(Locale.getDefault());
mDatabase.setLockingEnabled(true);
mDatabase.setVersion(1);
```

Creating Tables and Other SQLite Schema Objects

Creating tables and other SQLite schema objects is as simple as forming proper SQLite statements and executing them. The following is a valid `CREATE TABLE` SQL statement. This statement creates a table called `tbl_authors`. The table has three fields: a unique `id` number, which auto-increments with each record and acts as our primary key, and `firstname` and `lastname` text fields.

```
CREATE TABLE tbl_authors (
id INTEGER PRIMARY KEY AUTOINCREMENT,
firstname TEXT,
lastname TEXT);
```

This `CREATE TABLE` SQL statement can be encapsulated in a static final String variable (called `CREATE_AUTHOR_TABLE`) and then executed on our database using the `execSQL()` method:

```
mDatabase.execSQL(CREATE_AUTHOR_TABLE);
```

The `execSQL()` method works for nonqueries. You can use it to execute any valid SQLite SQL statement. For example, you can use it to create, update, and delete tables, views, triggers, and other common SQL objects. In our application, we add another table called `tbl_books`. The schema for `tbl_books` looks like this:

```
CREATE TABLE tbl_books (
id INTEGER PRIMARY KEY AUTOINCREMENT,
title TEXT,
dateadded DATE,
authorid INTEGER NOT NULL CONSTRAINT authorid REFERENCES tbl_authors(id) ON DELETE
CASCADE);
```

Unfortunately, SQLite does not enforce foreign key constraints. Instead, we must enforce them ourselves using custom SQL triggers. So we create triggers, such as this one that enforces that books have valid authors:

```
private static final String CREATE_TRIGGER_ADD =
"CREATE TRIGGER fk_insert_book BEFORE INSERT ON tbl_books
FOR EACH ROW
BEGIN
SELECT RAISE(ROLLBACK, 'insert on table \"tbl_books\" violates foreign key con-
straint \"fk_authorid\"') WHERE  (SELECT id FROM tbl_authors WHERE id =
NEW.authorid) IS NULL;
END;";
```

We can then create the trigger simply by executing the `CREATE TRIGGER` SQL statement:

```
mDatabase.execSQL(CREATE_TRIGGER_ADD);
```

We need to add several more triggers to help enforce our link between the author and book tables, one for updating `tbl_books` and one for deleting records from `tbl_authors`.

Creating, Updating, and Deleting Database Records

Now that we have a database set up, we need to create some data. The `SQLiteDatabase` class includes three convenience methods to do that. They are, as you might expect: `insert()`, `update()`, and `delete()`.

Inserting Records

We use the `insert()` method to add new data to our tables. We use the `ContentValues` object to pair the column names to the column values for the record we want to insert. For example, here we insert a record into `tbl_authors` for J.K Rowling.

```
import android.content.ContentValues;
...
ContentValues values = new ContentValues();
values.put("firstname", "J.K.");
values.put("lastname", "Rowling");
long newAuthorID = mDatabase.insert("tbl_authors", null, values);
```

The `insert()` method returns the `id` of the newly created record. We use this author `id` to create book records for this author.

> **Tip**
>
> There is also another helpful method called `insertOrThrow()`, which does the same thing as the `insert()` method but throws a `SQLException` on failure, which can be helpful, especially if your inserts are not working and you'd really like to know why.

You might want to create simple classes (that is, class `Author` and class `Book`) to encapsulate your application record data when it is used programmatically. Notice that we did this in the FullDatabase sample project.

Updating Records

You can modify records in the database using the `update()` method. The `update()` method takes four arguments:

- The table to update records
- A `ContentValues` object with the modified fields to update
- An optional WHERE clause, in which ? identifies a WHERE clause argument
- An array of WHERE clause arguments, each of which will be substituted in place of the ?s from the second parameter.

Passing `null` to the WHERE clause modifies all records within the table. This can be useful for making sweeping changes to your database.

Most of the time, we want to modify individual records by their unique identifier. The following function takes two parameters: an updated book title and a `bookId`. We find the record in the table called `tbl_books` corresponding with the `id` and update that book's title. Again, we use the `ContentValues` object to bind our column names to our data values:

```
public void updateBookTitle(Integer bookId, String newtitle) {
    ContentValues values = new ContentValues();
    values.put("title", newtitle);
    mDatabase.update("tbl_books",
        values, "id=?", new String[] { bookId.toString() });
}
```

Because we are not updating the other fields, we do not need to include them in the `ContentValues` object. We include only the title field because it is the only field we change.

Deleting Records

You can remove records from the database using the `remove()` method. The `remove()` method takes three arguments:

- The table to delete the record from
- An optional WHERE clause, in which ? identifies a WHERE clause argument
- An array of WHERE clause arguments, each of which will be substituted in place of the ?s from the second parameter.

Passing `null` to the WHERE clause deletes all records within the table. For example, this function call deletes all records within the table called `tbl_authors`:

```
mDatabase.delete("tbl_authors", null, null);
```

Most of the time, though, we want to delete individual records by their unique identifier. The following function takes a parameter `bookId` and deletes the record corresponding to that unique `id` (primary key) within the table called `tbl_books`.

```
public void deleteBook(Integer bookId) {
    mDatabase.delete("tbl_books", "id=?",
        new String[] { bookId.toString() });
}
```

You need not use the primary key (`id`) to delete records. The WHERE clause is entirely up to you. For instance, the following function deletes all book records in the table `tbl_books` for a given author by the author's unique `id`.

```
public void deleteBooksByAuthor(Integer authorID) {
    int numBooksDeleted = mDatabase.delete("tbl_books", "authorid=?",
        new String[] { authorID.toString() });
}
```

Working with Transactions

Often you have multiple database operations you want to happen all together or not at all. You can use SQL Transactions to group operations together; if any of the operations fails, you can handle the error and either recover or rollback all operations. If the operations all succeed, you can then commit them. Here we have the basic structure for a transaction:

```
mDatabase.beginTransaction();
try {
    // Insert some records, updated others, delete a few
    // Do whatever you need to do as a unit, then commit it

    mDatabase.setTransactionSuccessful();
} catch (Exception e) {
    // Transaction failed. Failed! Do something here.
```

```
    // It's up to you.
} finally {
    mDatabase.endTransaction();
}
```

Now let's look at the transaction in a bit more detail. A transaction always begins with a call to `beginTransaction()` method and a `try/catch` block. If your operations are successful, you can commit your changes with a call to the `setTransactionSuccessful()` method. If you do not call this method, all your operations will be rolled back and not committed. Finally, you end your transaction by calling `endTransaction()`. It's as simple as that.

In some cases, you might recover from an exception and continue with the transaction. For example, if you have an exception for a read-only database, you can open the database and retry your operations.

Finally, note that transactions can be nested, while the outer transaction either committing or rolling back all inner transactions.

Querying SQLite Databases

Databases are great for storing data in any number of ways, but retrieving the data you want is what makes databases powerful. This is partly a matter of designing an appropriate database schema, and partly achieved by crafting SQL queries, most of which are SELECT statements.

Android provides many ways in which you can query your application database. You can run raw SQL query statements (strings), use a number of different SQL statement builder utility classes to generate proper query statements from the ground up, and bind specific user interface widgets such as container views to your backend database directly.

Working with Cursors

When results are returned from a SQL query, they are often accessed using a `Cursor` found in the `android.database.Cursor` class. `Cursor` objects are rather like file pointers; they allow random access to query results.

You can think of query results as a table, in which each row corresponds to a returned record. The `Cursor` object includes helpful methods for determining how many results were returned by the query and the column names (fields) for each returned record. The columns in the query results are defined by the query, not necessarily by the database columns. These might include calculated columns, column aliases, and composite columns.

`Cursor` objects are generally kept around for a time. If you do something simple (such as get a count of records or when you know you retrieved only a single simple record), you can execute your query and quickly extract what you need; don't forget to close the `Cursor` when you're done, as shown here:

```
// SIMPLE QUERY: select * from tbl_books
Cursor c = mDatabase.query("tbl_books",null,null,null,null,null,null);
// Do something quick with the Cursor here...
c.close();
```

Managing Cursors as Part of the Application Lifecycle

When a `Cursor` returns multiple records, or you do something more intensive, you need to consider running this operation on a thread separate from the UI thread. You also need to manage your `Cursor`.

`Cursor` objects must be managed as part of the application lifecycle. When the application pauses or shuts down, the `Cursor` must be deactivated with a call to the `deactivate()` method, and when the application restarts, the `Cursor` should refresh its data using the `requery()` method. When the `Cursor` is no longer needed, a call to `close()` must be made to release its resources.

As the developer, you can handle this by implementing `Cursor` management calls within the various lifecycle callbacks such as `onPause()`, `onResume()`, and `onDestroy()`.

If you're lazy, like us, and you don't want to bother handling these lifecycle events, you can hand off the responsibility of managing `Cursor` objects to the parent `Activity` by using the `Activity` method called `startManagingCursor()`. The `Activity` will handle the rest, deactivating and reactivating the `Cursor` as necessary and destroying the `Cursor` when the `Activity` is destroyed. You can always begin manually managing the `Cursor` object again later by simply calling `stopManagingCursor()`.

Here we perform the same simple query and then hand over `Cursor` management to the parent `Activity`:

```
// SIMPLE QUERY: select * from tbl_books
Cursor c = mDatabase.query("tbl_books",null,null,null,null,null,null);
startManagingCursor(c);
```

Note that, generally, the managed `Cursor` is a member variable of the class, scope-wise.

Iterating Rows of Query Results and Extracting Specific Data

You can use the `Cursor` to iterate those results, one row at a time using various navigation methods such as `moveToFirst()`, `moveToNext()`, and `isAfterLast()`.

On a specific row, you can use the `Cursor` to extract the data for a given column in the query results. Because SQLite is not strongly typed, you can always pull fields out as Strings using the `getString()` method, but you can also use the type-appropriate extraction utility function to enforce type safety in your application.

For example, the following method takes a valid `Cursor` object, prints the number of returned results, and then prints some column information (name and number of columns). Next, it iterates through the query results, printing each record.

```
public void logCursorInfo(Cursor c) {
    Log.i(DEBUG_TAG, "*** Cursor Begin *** " + " Results:" +
        c.getCount() + " Columns: " + c.getColumnCount());

    // Print column names
    String rowHeaders = "|| ";
    for (int i = 0; i < c.getColumnCount(); i++) {
```

```
        rowHeaders = rowHeaders.concat(c.getColumnName(i) + " || ");
    }

    Log.i(DEBUG_TAG, "COLUMNS " + rowHeaders);

    // Print records
    c.moveToFirst();
    while (c.isAfterLast() == false) {

        String rowResults = "|| ";
        for (int i = 0; i < c.getColumnCount(); i++) {
            rowResults = rowResults.concat(c.getString(i) + " || ");
        }

        Log.i(DEBUG_TAG,
            "Row " + c.getPosition() + ": " + rowResults);

        c.moveToNext();
    }
    Log.i(DEBUG_TAG, "*** Cursor End ***");
}
```

The output to the `LogCat` for this function might look something like Figure 9.1.

Figure 9.1   Sample log output for the `logCursorInfo()` method.

Executing Simple Queries

Your first stop for database queries should be the `query()` methods available in the `SQLiteDatabase` class. This method queries the database and returns any results as in a `Cursor` object.

The `query()` method we mainly use takes the following parameters:

- [`String`]: The name of the table to compile the query against
- [`String Array`]: List of specific column names to return (use `null` for all)
- [`String`] The WHERE clause: (use `null` for all; might include selection args as ?'s)

- [String Array]: Any selection argument values to substitute in for the ?'s above
- [String] GROUP BY clause: (null for no grouping)
- [String] HAVING clause: (null unless GROUP BY clause requires one)
- [String] ORDER BY clause: (if null, default ordering used)
- [String] LIMIT clause: (if null, no limit)

Previously in the chapter, we called the query() method with only one parameter set the table name.

```
Cursor c = mDatabase.query("tbl_books",null,null,null,null,null,null);
```

This is equivalent to the SQL query:

```
SELECT * FROM tbl_books;
```

> **Tip**
>
> The individual parameters for the clauses (WHERE, GROUP BY, HAVING, ORDER BY, LIMIT) are all Strings, but you do not need to include the keyword, such as WHERE. Instead, you include the part of the clause after the keyword.

So let's add a WHERE clause to our query, so we can retrieve one record at a time.

```
Cursor c = mDatabase.query("tbl_books", null,
    "id=?", new String[]{"9"}, null, null, null);
```

This is equivalent to the SQL query:

```
SELECT * tbl_books WHERE id=9;
```

Selecting all results might be fine for tiny databases, but it is not terribly efficient. You should always tailor your SQL queries to return only the results you require with no extraneous information included. Use the powerful language of SQL to do the heavy lifting for you whenever possible, instead of programmatically processing results yourself. For example, if you need only the titles of each book in the book table, you might use the following call to the query() method:

```
String asColumnsToReturn[] = { "title", "id" };
String strSortOrder = "title ASC";
Cursor c = mDatabase.query("tbl_books", asColumnsToReturn,
    null, null, null, null, strSortOrder);
```

This is equivalent to the SQL query:

```
SELECT title, id FROM tbl_books ORDER BY title ASC;
```

Executing More Complex Queries like Joins Using SQLiteQueryBuilder

As your queries get more complex and involve multiple tables, you want to leverage the SQLiteQueryBuilder convenience class, which can build complex queries programmatically.

When more than one table is involved, you need to make sure you refer to columns within a table by their fully qualified names. For example, the title column within the tbl_books table would be `tbl_books.title`. Here we use a `SQLiteQueryBuilder` to build and execute a simple INNER JOIN between two tables to get a list of books with their authors:

```
import android.database.sqlite.SQLiteQueryBuilder;
...
SQLiteQueryBuilder queryBuilder = new SQLiteQueryBuilder();

queryBuilder.setTables("tbl_books, tbl_authors");
queryBuilder.appendWhere("tbl_books.authorid=tbl_authors.id");

String asColumnsToReturn[] = {
    "tbl_books.title",
    "tbl_books.id",
    "tbl_authors.firstname",
    "tbl_authors.lastname",
    "tbl_books.authorid" };
String strSortOrder = "title ASC";

Cursor c = queryBuilder.query(mDatabase, asColumnsToReturn,
    null, null, null, null,strSortOrder);
```

First, we instantiate a new `SQLiteQueryBuilder` object. Then we can set the tables involved as part of our JOIN and the WHERE clause that determines how the JOIN occurs. Then, we call the `query()` method of the `SQLiteQueryBuilder` that is similar to the `query()` method we have been using, except we supply the `SQLiteDatabase` instance instead of the table name. The above query built by the `SQLiteQueryBuilder` is equivalent to the SQL query:

```
SELECT tbl_books.title,
tbl_books.id,
tbl_authors.firstname,
tbl_authors.lastname,
tbl_books.authorid
FROM tbl_books
INNER JOIN tbl_authors on tbl_books.authorid=tbl_authors.id
ORDER BY title ASC;
```

Executing Raw Queries Without Bothering with Builders and Column-Mapping

All these helpful Android query utilities can sometimes make building and performing a nonstandard or complex query too verbose. In this case, you might want to consider the `rawQuery()` method. The `rawQuery()` method simply takes a SQL statement `String` (with optional selection arguments if you include ?s) and returns a `Cursor` of results. If you know your SQL and you don't want to bother learning the ins and outs of all the different SQL query building utilities, this is the method for you.

For example, let's say we have a UNION query. These types of queries are feasible with the `QueryBuilder`, but their implementation is cumbersome when you start using column aliases and the like.

Let's say we want to execute the following SQL UNION query, which returns a list of all book titles and authors whose name contains the substring ow (that is *Hallows, Rowling*), as in the following:

```
SELECT title AS Name,
'tbl_books' AS OriginalTable
FROM tbl_books
WHERE Name LIKE '%ow%'
UNION
SELECT (firstname||' '|| lastname) AS Name,
'tbl_authors' AS OriginalTable
FROM tbl_authors
WHERE Name LIKE '%ow%'
ORDER BY Name ASC;
```

We can easily execute this by making a string that looks much like the original query and executing the `rawQuery()` method.

```
String sqlUnionExample = "SELECT title AS Name, 'tbl_books' AS
    OriginalTable from tbl_books WHERE Name LIKE ? UNION SELECT
    (firstname||' '|| lastname) AS Name, 'tbl_authors' AS OriginalTable
    from tbl_authors WHERE Name LIKE ? ORDER BY Name ASC;";

Cursor c = mDatabase.rawQuery(sqlUnionExample,
    new String[]{ "%ow%", "%ow%"});
```

We make the substrings (ow) into selection arguments, so we can use this same code to look for other substrings searches).

Closing and Deleting a SQLite Database

Although you should always close a database when you are not using it, you might on occasion also want to modify and delete tables and delete your database.

Deleting Tables and Other SQLite Objects

Deleting tables and other SQLite objects is done in exactly the same was as creating them. Format the appropriate SQLite statements and execute them. For example, to drop our tables and triggers, we can execute three SQL statements:

```
mDatabase.execSQL("DROP TABLE tbl_books;");
mDatabase.execSQL("DROP TABLE tbl_authors;");
mDatabase.execSQL("DROP TRIGGER IF EXISTS fk_insert_book;");
```

Closing a SQLite Database

You should close your database when you are not using it. You can close the database using the `close()` method of your `SQLiteDatabase` instance, like this:

```
mDatabase.close();
```

Deleting a SQLite Database Instance Using the Application Context

The simplest way to delete a `SQLiteDatabase` is to use the `deleteDatabase()` method of your application `Context`. Databases are deleted by name and the deletion is permanent. All data and schema information is lost.

```
deleteDatabase("my_sqlite_database.db");
```

Designing Persistent Databases

Generally speaking, an application creates a database and uses it for the rest of the application's lifetime—by which we mean until the application is uninstalled from the phone. So far, we've talked about the basics of creating a database, using it, and then deleting it. Actually, that is exactly what the "FullDatabase" sample application provided on the CD and book Web site does.

In reality, most mobile applications do not create a database on-the-fly, use them, and then delete them. Instead, they create a database the first time they need it and then use it. The Android SDK provides a helper class called `SQLiteOpenHelper` to help you manage your application's database.

To create a SQLite database for your Android application using the `SQLiteOpenHelper`, you need to extend that class and then instantiate an instance of it as a member variable for use within your application. To illustrate how to do this, let's create a new Android project called PetTracker.

> **Tip**
>
> You can find the PetTracker project on the CD provided at the end of this book or online at the book Web site. This project creates and maintains a simple database of pet names and species. The user interface contains two screens: a form to input data and a screen to display the data. No complicated data-binding is performed in this version of the application. We build upon this example in future sections of this chapter.

Keeping Track of Database Field Names

You've probably realized by now that it is time to start organizing your database fields programmatically to avoid typos and such in your SQL queries. One easy way to do this is to make a class to encapsulate your database schema in a class, such as `PetDatabase`, shown here:

```
import android.provider.BaseColumns;

public final class PetDatabase {
```

```
    private PetDatabase() {}

    public static final class Pets implements BaseColumns {
        private Pets() {}
        public static final String PETS_TABLE_NAME="table_pets";
        public static final String PET_NAME="pet_name";
        public static final String PET_TYPE_ID="pet_type_id";
        public static final String DEFAULT_SORT_ORDER="pet_name ASC";
    }

    public static final class PetType implements BaseColumns {
        private PetType() {}
        public static final String PETTYPE_TABLE_NAME="table_pettypes";
        public static final String PET_TYPE_NAME="pet_type";
        public static final String DEFAULT_SORT_ORDER="pet_type ASC";
    }
}
```

By implementing the BaseColumns interface, we begin to set up the underpinnings for
using database-friendly user interface widgets in the future, which often require a specially named column called _id to function properly. We rely on this column as our primary key.

Extending the SQLiteOpenHelper Class

To extend the SQLiteOpenHelper class, we must implement several important methods,
which help manage the database versioning. The methods to override are onCreate(),
onUpgrade(), and onOpen(). We use our newly defined PetDatabase class to generate
appropriate SQL statements, as shown here:

```
import android.content.Context;
import android.database.sqlite.SQLiteDatabase;
import android.database.sqlite.SQLiteOpenHelper;

import com.androidbook.PetTracker.PetDatabase.PetType;
import com.androidbook.PetTracker.PetDatabase.Pets;

class PetTrackerDatabaseHelper extends SQLiteOpenHelper {

    private static final String DATABASE_NAME = "pet_tracker.db";
    private static final int DATABASE_VERSION = 1;

    PetTrackerDatabaseHelper(Context context) {
        super(context, DATABASE_NAME, null, DATABASE_VERSION);
    }

    @Override
    public void onCreate(SQLiteDatabase db) {
```

```
        db.execSQL("CREATE TABLE " +PetType.PETTYPE_TABLE_NAME+" ("
            + PetType._ID + " INTEGER PRIMARY KEY AUTOINCREMENT ,"
            + PetType.PET_TYPE_NAME + " TEXT"
            + ");");
        db.execSQL("CREATE TABLE " + Pets.PETS_TABLE_NAME + " ("
            + Pets._ID + " INTEGER PRIMARY KEY AUTOINCREMENT ,"
            + Pets.PET_NAME + " TEXT,"
            + Pets.PET_TYPE_ID + " INTEGER" // FK to pet type table
            + ");");
    }


    @Override
    public void onUpgrade(SQLiteDatabase db, int oldVersion,
        int newVersion){
        // Housekeeping here.
        // Implement how "move" your application data
        // during an upgrade of schema versions
        // Move or delete data as required. Your call.
    }


    @Override
    public void onOpen(SQLiteDatabase db) {
        super.onOpen(db);
    }
}
```

Now we can create a member variable for our database like this:

```
PetTrackerDatabaseHelper mDatabase = new
PetTrackerDatabaseHelper(this.getApplicationContext());
```

Now, whenever our application needs to interact with its database, we request a valid database object. We can request a read-only database or a database that we can also write to. We can also close the database. For example, here we get a database we can write data to:

```
SQLiteDatabase db = mDatabase.getWritableDatabase();
```

Binding Data to the Application User Interface

In many cases with application databases, you want to couple your user interface with the data in your database. You might want to fill drop-down lists with values from a database table, or fill out form values, or display only certain results. There are various ways to bind database data to your user interface. You, as the developer, can decide whether to use built-in data-binding functionality provided with certain user interface widgets, or you can build your own user interfaces from the ground up.

Working with Database Data Like Any Other Data

If you peruse the PetTracker application provided on the CD, you notice that its functionality includes no magical data-binding features, yet the application clearly uses the database as part of the user interface.

Specifically, the database is leveraged

- When you save new records using the Pet Entry Form (Figure 9.2, left).
- When you fill out the Pet Type field, the AutoComplete feature is seeded with pet types already in listed in the table_pettypes table (Figure 9.2, middle).
- When you display the Pet List screen, we query for all pets and use a Cursor to programmatically build a TableLayout on-the-fly (Figure 9.2, right).

This might work for small amounts of data; however, there are various drawbacks to this method. For example, all the work is done on the main thread, so the more records you add, the slower your application response time becomes. Second, there's quite a bit of custom code involved here to map the database results to the individual user interface components. If you decided you want to use a different widget to display your data, you would have quite a lot of rework to do. Third, we constantly requery the database for fresh results, and we might be requerying far more than necessary.

Figure 9.2   The PetTracker application: Entry Screen (left, middle) and
Pet Listing Screen (right).

Authors' Note

Yes, we really named our pet bunnies after data structures and computer terminology. We are that geeky. Null, for example, is a rambunctious little black bunny. Shane enjoys pointing at him and calling himself a Null Pointer.

Binding Data to Widgets Using Data Adapters

Ideally, you'd like to bind your data to user interface widgets and let them take care of the data display. For example, we can use a fancy `ListView` to display the pets instead of building a `TableLayout` from scratch. We can spin through our `Cursor` and generate `ListView` child items manually, or even better, we can simply create a data adapter to map the `Cursor` results to each `TextView` child within the `ListView`.

We included a project called "SuperPetTracker" on the CD accompanying this book (also available on the book Web site) that does this. It behaves much like the "PetTracker" sample application, except that it uses the `SimpleCursorAdapter` with `ListView` and an `ArrayAdapter` to handle `AutoCompleteTextView` features.

Binding Data Using SimpleCursorAdapter

Let's now look at how we can create a data adapter to mimic our Pet Listing screen, with each pet's name and species listed. We also want to continue to have the ability to delete records from the list.

As you remember from Chapter 7, "Designing Android User Interfaces with Layouts," the `ListView` container widget can contain children such as `TextView` objects. In this case, we want to display each Pet's name and type. We therefore create a layout file called `pet_item.xml` which becomes our `ListView` item template:

```xml
<?xml version="1.0" encoding="utf-8"?>
<RelativeLayout
    xmlns:android="http://schemas.android.com/apk/res/android"
    android:id="@+id/RelativeLayoutHeader"
    android:layout_height="wrap_content"
    android:layout_width="fill_parent">
    <TextView
        android:id="@+id/TextView_PetName"
        android:layout_width="wrap_content"
        android:layout_height="?android:attr/listPreferredItemHeight"
        android:layout_alignParentLeft="true" />
    <TextView
        android:id="@+id/TextView_PetType"
        android:layout_width="wrap_content"
        android:layout_height="?android:attr/listPreferredItemHeight"
        android:layout_alignParentRight="true" />
</RelativeLayout>
```

And in our main layout file for the Pet List, we place our `ListView` in the appropriate place on the overall screen. The `ListView` portion of the layout file might look something like this:

```
<ListView
    android:layout_width="wrap_content"
    android:layout_height="wrap_content"
    android:id="@+id/petList" android:divider="#000" />
```

Now to programmatically fill our `ListView`, we must take the following steps:

1. Perform our query and return a valid `Cursor` (a member variable).
2. Create a data adapter that maps the `Cursor` columns to the appropriate `TextView` widgets within our `pet_item.xml` layout template.
3. Attach the adapter to the `ListView`.

In the following code, we perform these steps.

```
SQLiteQueryBuilder queryBuilder = new SQLiteQueryBuilder();
queryBuilder.setTables(Pets.PETS_TABLE_NAME +", " +
    PetType.PETTYPE_TABLE_NAME);

queryBuilder.appendWhere(Pets.PETS_TABLE_NAME + "." +
    Pets.PET_TYPE_ID + "=" + PetType.PETTYPE_TABLE_NAME + "." +
    PetType._ID);

String asColumnsToReturn[] = { Pets.PETS_TABLE_NAME + "." +
    Pets.PET_NAME, Pets.PETS_TABLE_NAME +
    "." + Pets._ID, PetType.PETTYPE_TABLE_NAME + "." +
    PetType.PET_TYPE_NAME };

mCursor = queryBuilder.query(mDB, asColumnsToReturn, null, null,
    null, null, Pets.DEFAULT_SORT_ORDER);

startManagingCursor(mCursor);

ListAdapter adapter = new SimpleCursorAdapter(this,
    R.layout.pet_item, mCursor,
    new String[]{Pets.PET_NAME, PetType.PET_TYPE_NAME},
    new int[]{R.id.TextView_PetName, R.id.TextView_PetType });

ListView av = (ListView)findViewById(R.id.petList);
av.setAdapter(adapter);
```

Notice that the _id column as well as the expected name and type columns appears in the query. This is required for the adapter and `ListView` to work properly.

Using a `ListView` (Figure 9.3, left) instead of a custom user interface allows us to take advantage of the `ListView` widget's built-in features, such as scrolling when the list becomes longer, and the ability to provide context menus as needed. The _id column is used as the unique identifier for each `ListView` child node. If we choose a specific item on the list, we can act on it using this identifier, for example, to delete the item.

Now we reimplement the Delete functionality by listening for onItemClick()
events and providing a Delete Confirmation dialog (Figure 9.3, right).

```
av.setOnItemClickListener(new AdapterView.OnItemClickListener() {
    public void onItemClick( AdapterView<?> parent, View view,
        int position, long id) {

        final long deletePetId =  id;

        new AlertDialog.Builder(SuperPetList.this).setMessage(
          "Delete Pet Record?").setPositiveButton(
          "Delete", new DialogInterface.OnClickListener() {

            @Override
            public void onClick(DialogInterface dialog,int which) {
                deletePet(deletePetId);
                mCursor.requery();
        }}).show();
    }
});
```

You can see what this would look like on the screen in Figure 9.3.

Figure 9.3   The SuperPetTracker application: Pet Listing Screen
ListView (left) with Delete feature (right).

Note that within the SuperPetTracker sample application, we also use an `ArrayAdapter` to bind the data in the `pet_types` table to the `AutoCompleteTextView` on the Pet Entry screen. Although our next example shows you how to do this in a preferred manner, we left this code in the PetTracker sample to show you that you can always intercept the data your `Cursor` provides and do what you want with it. In this case, we create a `String` Array for the AutoText options by hand. We use a built-in Android layout resource called `android.R.layout.simple_dropdown_item_1line` to specify what each individual item within the AutoText listing will look like. You can find the built-in layout resources provided within your Android SDK directory under the directory **tools\lib\res\default\layout**.

Storing Nonprimitive Types (like Images) in the Database

Because SQLite is a single file, it makes little sense to try to store binary data within the database. Instead store the *location* of data, as a file path or a URI in the database and access it appropriately. We show an example of storing image URIs in the database in the next section.

Sharing Data Between Applications with Content Providers

The PetTracker application is nice and all, but it could really use some pizzazz. Wouldn't it be lovely if we could include photos of our pets? Well, let's do it!

There's only one catch: We need to access pictures provided through another application on the Android system—the Media Store application. To do this, we need to know a little bit more about content providers: the mechanism Android provides for applications to share information.

We included a sample application called "MediaPetTracker" on the CD at the end of this book and on the book Web site. In Figure 9.4, you can see the results of extending our previous Pet Tracking projects by adding graphics.

Leveraging a Content Provider to Access Images on the Device

Now that you can visualize what adding photos would look like, let's break down the steps needed to achieve this. The MediaPetTracker application has the same basic structure as our previous PetTracking and SuperPetTracker projects, with several key differences:

- On the Pet Entry screen, you can choose a photo from a `Gallery` widget, which displays all the images available on the SD card, or simulated SD card on the emulator, by accessing the `MediaStore` Content Provider (Figure 9.4, left).

- On the Pet Listing screen, each picture is displayed in the `ListView` (Figure 9.4, right), again using the `MediaStore` Content Provider to access specific images.

- On the Pet Listing screen each item in the `ListView` (Figure 9.4, right) is a custom layout. The sample application shows two methods of doing this: once by inflating a custom layout XML file, and the other by generating the layout programmatically.

- Internally, we extend `BaseAdapter` on two different occasions to successfully bind data to the `ListView` and `Gallery` with our own custom requirements.

- Finally, we provide custom implementations of the methods for `SimpleCursorAdapter.CursorToStringConverter` and `FilterQueryProvider` to allow the `AutoCompleteTextView` to bind directly to the internal SQLite database table called `pet_types` (Figure 9.4, middle), and change the `AutoCompleteTextView` behavior to match all substrings, not only the beginning of the word. Although we won't go into detail about this in the subsequent text, check out the sample code for more information on the specific details of implementation.

First, we need to decide where we are going to get our photos. We can take pictures with the built-in camera and access those, but for simplicity sake with the emulator (which can only take "fake pictures"), it will be easier if we download those cute, fuzzy pictures from the browser onto the SD card and access them that way.

Figure 9.4   The MediaPetTracker application: Entry Screen (left, middle) and Pet Listing Screen (right).

> **Tip**
>
> For the MediaPetTracker sample application to work, you need to configure your emulator to use a virtual SD card and then update your project's Debug Configuration to load it on launch. To keep the code simple and readable, we do not provide error handling for when this is not set up or where there are no images, nor do we check the content type of the media.
>
> You can find step-by-step details on how to configure an SD card disk image in Appendix A, "The Android Emulator Quick-Start Guide." You'll know you've set things up correctly when you can launch the browser on the emulator, browse to a website, and download some pictures. You can see these pictures in the Pictures application or through the Camera interface (which has a shortcut to the Pictures application in its Context Menu).
>
> To download an image through the browser, select an image to download by choosing it (pressing with mouse works), and then select the Download option. Go ahead and download your own pet (or kid or whatever) images from whatever Web site you like onto the SD card. If you don't have pets (or kids or whatever), you can borrow our personal bunny pictures, which we use in our example, from www.perlgurl.org/archives/2004/03/rabbits_rabbits.html.

Locating Content on the Android System Using URIs

Most access to content providers comes in the form of queries: a list of contacts, a list of bookmarks, a list of calls, a list of pictures, and a list of audio files. Applications make these requests much as they would access a database, and they get the same type of structured results. The results of a query are often iterated through using a cursor. However, instead of crafting queries, we use URIs.

You can think of a URI as an "address" to the location where content exists. URI addresses are hierarchical. Most content providers, such as the Contacts and the MediaStore, have predefined URI addresses defined. For example, to access the External Media Device (a.k.a the SD card), we use the following URI:

```
Uri mMedia = Media.EXTERNAL_CONTENT_URI;
```

Using the `managedQuery()` Method to Retrieve Data from a Content Provider

We can query the Media Store content provider using the URI much like we would query a database. We now use the managedQuery() method to return a managed Cursor containing all media available on the SD card.

```
String[] projection = new String[] { Media._ID, Media.TITLE };

Uri mMedia = Media.EXTERNAL_CONTENT_URI;

Cursor mCursorImages = managedQuery(mMedia, projection, null, null,
    Media.DATE_TAKEN + " ASC"); // Order-by clause.
```

Now we have retrieved the records for each piece of media available on the SD card.

Now we have this Cursor, but we still have some legwork to get our Gallery widget to display the individual images.

Data-Binding to the Gallery Widget

We need to extend the `BaseAdapter` class for a new type of data adapter called `ImageUriAdapter` to map the URI data we retrieved to the `Gallery` widget. Our custom `ImageUriAdapter` maps the `Cursor` results to an array of `GalleryRecord` objects, which correspond to the child items within the `Gallery` widget. Although the code for the `ImageUriAdapter` is too long to show here, we go over some of the methods you must implement for the adapter to work properly.

- The `ImageUriAdapter()` constructor is responsible for mapping the `Cursor` to an array of `GalleryRecord` objects, which encapsulate the base URI and the individual image's `id`, which is tacked on to the end of the URI, resulting in a fully qualified URI for the individual image.

- The `getItem()` and `getItemId()` methods return the unique identifier for the specific image. This is the value we require when the user clicks on a specific image within the `Gallery`. We save this information in our database so that we know which image corresponds to which pet.

- The `getView()` method returns the custom `View` widget that corresponds to each child `View` within the `Gallery`. In this case, we return an `ImageView` with the corresponding image. We set each view's `Tag` property to the associated `GalleryRecord` object, which includes all our `Cursor` information we mapped for that record. This is a nifty trick for storing extra information with widgets for later use.

After all this magic has been implemented, we can set our newly defined custom adapter to the adapter used by the `Gallery` with our new `Cursor`.

```
ImageUriAdapter iAdapter = new ImageUriAdapter(this,
    mCursorImages, mMedia);

final Gallery pictureGal = (Gallery) findViewById(R.id.GalleryOfPics);
    pictureGal.setAdapter(iAdapter);
```

Retrieving the Chosen Gallery Image and Saving It to the Database

Notice that we added two new columns to our SQLite database: the base URI for the image and the individual image `id`, which is the unique identifier tacked to the end of the URI. We do not save the image itself in the database, only the URI information to retrieve it.

When the user presses the Save button on the Pet Entry screen, we examine the `Gallery` item selected and extract the information we require from the `Tag` property of the selected `View`, like this:

```
final Gallery gall = (Gallery) findViewById(R.id.GalleryOfPics);

ImageView selectedImageView = (ImageView) gall.getSelectedView();
```

```
GalleryRecord galleryItem;

if (selectedImageView != null) {
    galleryItem = (GalleryRecord)selectedImageView.getTag();
    long imageId = galleryItem.getImageId();
    String strImageUriPathString = galleryItem.getImageUriPath();
}
```

We can then save our Pet Record as we have before.

Displaying Images Retrieved from the SD Card Using URIs

Now that our Pet Entry form is saved properly, we must turn our attention to the Pet
Listing screen. Our ListView is getting more complicated; each item needs to contain
an ImageView and two TextView widgets for the pet name and species. We begin by
defining a custom layout template for each ListView item called pet_item.xml. This
should be familiar; it contains an ImageView and two TextView objects.

We want to make sure this implementation is scalable, in case we want to add new
features to individual ListView items in the future. So instead of taking shortcuts and
using standard adapters and built-in Android layout templates, we implement another
custom adapter called PetListAdapter.

The PetListAdapter is similar to the ImageUriAdapter we previously implemented for the Gallery widget. Only this time, instead of Gallery child items, we work
with the ListView child records, which correspond to each pet. Again, the constructor
maps the Cursor data to an array of PetRecord objects.

The getView() method of the PetListAdapter is where the magic occurs. Here
we use a LayoutInflater to inflate our custom layout file called pet_item.xml for
each ListView item. Again we use the Tag property of the view to store any information about the record that we might use later. It is here that we use the URI information we stored in our database to rebuild the fully qualified image URI using the
Uri.parse() and ContentUris.withAppendedId() utility methods and assign this
URI to the ImageView widget using the setImageURI() method.

Now that we've set everything up, we then assign the PetListAdapter to our
ListView:

```
String asColumnsToReturn[] = {
    Pets.PETS_TABLE_NAME + "." + Pets.PET_NAME,
    Pets.PETS_TABLE_NAME + "." + Pets.PET_IMAGE_URI,
    Pets.PETS_TABLE_NAME + "." + Pets._ID,
    Pets.PETS_TABLE_NAME + "." + Pets.PET_IMAGE_ID,
    PetType.PETTYPE_TABLE_NAME + "." + PetType.PET_TYPE_NAME };

mCursor = queryBuilder.query(mDB, asColumnsToReturn, null, null,
    null, null, Pets.DEFAULT_SORT_ORDER);
startManagingCursor(mCursor);
```

```
SetListAdapter adapter = new PetListAdapter(this, mCursor);
ListView av = (ListView) findViewById(R.id.petList);
av.setAdapter(adapter);
```

That's about it. Note that you can also create the `ListView` item layout programmatically (see the `PetListItemView` class and the `PetListAdapter.getView()` method comments for more information).

Now you've seen how to leverage a content provider to make your application more robust, but this example has scratched only the surface of how powerful Content Providers can be. Let's look at some of the other Content Providers available on the Android platform and what you can do with them.

Exploring Some of Android's Built-In Content Providers

Android devices ship with a number of built-in applications, many of which expose their data as Content Providers. Your application can access Content Provider data from the contact application, media found on their phone such as that from the camera, and access the call log on the phone, among other things.

The Content Providers included with Android can be found in the package `android.provider`. Some useful Content Providers in this package are shown in Table 9.5.

Table 9.5   **Useful Built-In Content Providers**

Provider	Purpose
MediaStore	Audio-visual data on the phone and external storage
CallLog	Sent and received calls
Browser	Browser history and bookmarks
Contacts	Phone contact database or phonebook
UserDictionary	A dictionary of user-defined words for use with predictive text input (available in Android 1.5)

Now let's look at the individual content providers in more detail.

Using the `MediaStore` Content Provider

Let's start with the `MediaStore` Content Provider because we've already begun to explore it in the preceding MediaPetTracker sample application. You can use the `MediaStore` Content Provider to access media on the phone and on external storage devices. The primary types of media that can be accessed are audio, images, and video. These different types of media can be accessed through their respective Content Provider classes under `android.provider.MediaStore`.

Most of the `MediaStore` classes allow full interaction with the data. You can retrieve, add, and delete media files from the device. There are also a handful of helper classes that define the most common data columns that can be requested.

Some commonly used classes are found under `android.provider.MediaStore`, as shown in Table 9.6.

Table 9.6   **Common MediaStore Classes**

Class	Purpose
`Video.Media`	Manages video files on the device
`Images.Media`	Manages image files on the device
`Images.ThumbNails`	Retrieves thumbnails for the images
`Audio.Media`	Manages audio files on the device
`Audio.Albums`	Manages audio files organized by the album they are a part of
`Audio.Artists`	Manages audio files by the artist who created them
`Audio.Genres`	Manages audio files belonging to a particular genre
`Audio.Playlists`	Manages audio files that are part of a particular playlist

The following code demonstrates how to request data from a content provider. A query is made to the `MediaStore` to retrieve the titles of all the audio files on the SD card of the handset and their respective durations. This code requires that you load some audio files onto the virtual SD card in the emulator, much as we added image files in the MediaPetTracker sample application.

```
String[] requestedColumns = {
    MediaStore.Audio.Media.TITLE,
    MediaStore.Audio.Media.DURATION
};

Cursor cur = managedQuery(
    MediaStore.Audio.Media.EXTERNAL_CONTENT_URI,
    requestedColumns, null, null, null);

Log.d(debugTag, "Audio files: " + cur.getCount());
Log.d(debugTag, "Columns: " + cur.getColumnCount());

String[] columns = cur.getColumnNames();

int name = cur.getColumnIndex(MediaStore.Audio.Media.TITLE);
int size = cur.getColumnIndex(MediaStore.Audio.Media.DURATION);

cur.moveToFirst();
while (!cur.isAfterLast()) {
    Log.d(debugTag, "Title" + cur.getString(name));
    Log.d(debugTag, "Length: " +
        cur.getInt(size) / 1000 + " seconds");
    cur.moveToNext();
}
```

The `MediaStore.Audio.Media` class has predefined strings for every data field (or column) exposed by the content provider. You can limit the audio file data fields requested as part of the query by defining a string array with the column names required. In this case, we limit the results to only the track title and the duration of each audio file.

We then use a `managedQuery()` method call. The first parameter is the predefined `URI` of the content provider you want to query (in this case, the SD card). The second parameter is the list of columns to return (audio file titles and durations). The third and fourth parameters control any selection filtering arguments, and the fifth parameter provides a sort method for the results. We leave these null, as we want all audio files at this location. By using the `managedQuery()` method, we get a managed `Cursor` as a result. We then examine our `Cursor` for the results.

Using the `CallLog` Content Provider

Android provides a Content Provider to access the call log on the handset via the class `android.provider.CallLog`. At first glance, the `CallLog` might not seem to be a useful provider for developers, but it has some nifty features. You can use the `CallLog` to filter recently dialed calls, received, and missed calls. The date and duration of each call is logged and tied back to the Contact application for caller identification purposes.

The `CallLog` is a useful Content Provider for customer relationship management (CRM) applications. The user can also tag specific phone numbers with custom labels within the Contact application.

To demonstrate how the `CallLog` Content Provider works, let's look at a hypothetical situation where we want to generate a report of all calls to a number with the custom labeled `HourlyClient123`. Android allows for custom labels on these numbers, which we leverage for this example:

```
String[] requestedColumns = {
    CallLog.Calls.CACHED_NUMBER_LABEL,
    CallLog.Calls.DURATION
};

Cursor calls = managedQuery(
    CallLog.Calls.CONTENT_URI, requestedColumns,
    CallLog.Calls.CACHED_NUMBER_LABEL
    + " = ?", new String[] { "HourlyClient123" } , null);

Log.d(debugTag, "Call count: " + calls.getCount());

int durIdx = calls.getColumnIndex(CallLog.Calls.DURATION);
int totalDuration;

calls.moveToFirst();
while (!calls.isAfterLast()) {
    Log.d(debugTag, "Duration: " + calls.getInt(durIdx));
    totalDuration += calls.getInt(durIdx);
```

```
        calls.moveToNext();
}

Log.d(debugTag, "HourlyClient123 Total Call Duration: " + totalDuration);
```

This code is similar to the code shown for the MediaStore audio files. Again, we start
with listing our requested columns: the call label and the duration of the call. This time,
however, we don't want to get every call in the log, only those with a label of
HourlyClient123. To filter the results of the query to this specific label, it is necessary
to specify the third and fourth parameters of the managedQuery() call. Together, these
two parameters are equivalent to a database WHERE clause. The third parameter specifies
the format of the WHERE clause with the column name with selection parameters
(shown as ?s) for each selection argument value. The fourth parameter, the String array,
provides the values to substitute for each of the selection arguments (?s) in order as you
would do for a simple SQLite database query.

   As before, the Activity manages the Cursor object lifecycle. We use the same
method to iterate the records of the Cursor and add up all the call durations.

Some Content Providers Require Permissions

Your application needs a special permission to access the information provided by the
CallLog content provider. You can declare the uses-permission tag using the Eclipse
Wizard or by adding the following to your AndroidManifest.xml file:

```
<uses-permission
    xmlns:android="http://schemas.android.com/apk/res/android"
    android:name="android.permission.READ_CONTACTS">
</uses-permission>
```

Although it's a tad confusing, there is no CallLog permission. Instead, applications that
access the CallLog use the READ_CONTACTS permission. Although the values are cached
within this Content Provider, the data is similar to what you might find in the contacts
provider.

Tip
You can find all available permissions in the class android.Manifest.permission.

Using the Browser Content Provider

Another useful, built-in content provider is the Browser. The Browser Content
Provider exposes the user's browser site history and their bookmarked Web sites. This
Content Provider is accessed via the android.provider.Browser class. As with the
CallLog class, the information provided by the Browser Content Provider can be used
to generate statistics and to provide cross-application functionality. You might use the
Browser Content Provider to add a bookmark for your application support Web site.

In this example, we query the `Browser` Content Provider to find the top five most frequently visited bookmarked sites.

```
String[] requestedColumns = {
    Browser.BookmarkColumns.TITLE,
    Browser.BookmarkColumns.VISITS
};

Cursor faves = managedQuery(Browser.BOOKMARKS_URI, requestedColumns,
    Browser.BookmarkColumns.BOOKMARK + "=1", null,
    Browser.BookmarkColumns.VISITS + " DESC limit 5");

Log.d(debugTag, "Bookmarks count: " + faves.getCount());

int titleIdx = faves.getColumnIndex(Browser.BookmarkColumns.TITLE);
int visitsIdx = faves.getColumnIndex(Browser.BookmarkColumns.VISITS);
int bmIdx = faves.getColumnIndex(Browser.BookmarkColumns.BOOKMARK);

faves.moveToFirst();

while (!faves.isAfterLast()) {
    Log.d(debugTag, faves.getString(titleIdx) + " visited " +
        faves.getInt(visitsIdx) + " times");
    faves.getInt(bmIdx)!=0 ? "true" : "false") + " : " +
        faves.getInt(bmIdx));
    faves.moveToNext();
}
```

Again, the requested columns are defined, the query is made, and the cursor iterates through the results.

Note that the `managedQuery()` call has become substantially more complex. Let's take a look at the parameters to this method in more detail. The first parameter, `Browser.BOOKMARKS_URI`, is a URI for all browser history, not only the Bookmarked items. The second parameter is still the requested columns for the query results. The third parameter specifies the bookmark property must be true. This is a column needed to filter on it in the query. Now the results will only be browser history entries that have been bookmarked. The fourth parameter, selection arguments, is used only when replacement values are used, which is not used in this case, so the value is set to `null`. Lastly, the fifth parameter specifies an order to the results (most visited in descending order).

> **Tip**
>
> Notice that we also tacked on a LIMIT statement to the fifth parameter of `managedQuery()`. Although not specifically documented, we've found limiting the query results in this way works well and might even improve application performance in some situations where the query results are lengthy.

Using the Contacts Content Provider

The Contacts database is one of the most commonly used applications on the mobile phone. People always want phone numbers handy for calling friends, family, coworkers, and clients. Additionally, most phones show the identity of the caller based on the contacts application, including nicknames, photos, or icons.

Android provides a built-in Contact application, and the contact data is exposed to other Android applications using the Content Provider interface. As an application developer, this means you can leverage the user's contact data within your application for a more robust user experience.

The Contacts Content Provider Requires Permission to Access Private User Data

Your application needs special permission to access the private user information provided by the `Contacts` Content Provider. You must declare a `uses-permission` tag using the permission `READ_CONTACTS` to read this information.

The code to start reading contact data from the Contacts application should look familiar.

```
Cursor oneContact = managedQuery( People.CONTENT_URI, null, null, null,
    "name desc LIMIT 1");


Log.d(debugTag, "Count: " + oneContact.getCount());
```

This short example simply shows querying for a single contact. We used LIMIT to retrieve one contact record. If you actually look at the returned columns of data, you find that there is little more than the contact name and some indexes. The data fields are not explicitly returned. Instead, the results include the values needed to build specific URIs to those pieces of data. We need to request the data for the contact using these indexes.

Specifically, we retrieve the primary email and primary phone number for this contact.

```
int nameIdx = oneContact.getColumnIndex(Contacts.People.NAME);
int emailIDIdx = oneContact
    .getColumnIndex(Contacts.People.PRIMARY_EMAIL_ID);


int phoneIDIdx = oneContact
    .getColumnIndex(Contacts.People.PRIMARY_PHONE_ID);


oneContact.moveToFirst();
int emailID = oneContact.getInt(emailIDIdx);
int phoneID = oneContact.getInt(phoneIDIdx);
```

Now that we have the column index values for the contact's name, primary email address, and primary phone number, we need to build the `Uri` objects associated with those pieces of information and query for the primary email and primary phone number.

```
Uri emailUri = ContentUris.withAppendedId(
    Contacts.ContactMethods.CONTENT_URI,
    emailID);

Uri phoneUri = ContentUris.withAppendedId(
    Contacts.Phones.CONTENT_URI, phoneID);

Cursor primaryEmail = managedQuery(emailUri,
    new String[] {
        Contacts.ContactMethods.DATA
    },
    null, null, null);

Cursor primaryNumber = managedQuery(phoneUri,
    new String[] {
        Contacts.Phones.NUMBER
    },
    null, null, null);

startManagingCursor(primaryNumber);
```

After retrieving the appropriate column indexes for contact's specific email and phone number, we call `ContentUris.withAppendedId()` to create the new `Uri` objects from existing ones and the identifiers we now have. This allows direct selection of a particular row from the table when the index of that row is known. You can use a selection parameter to do this, as well. Lastly, we used the two new `Uri` objects to perform two calls to `managedQuery()`.

Now we take a shortcut with the requested columns `String` array because each query only has one column:

```
String name = oneContact.getString(nameIdx);
primaryEmail.moveToFirst();
String email = primaryEmail.getString(0);
primaryNumber.moveToFirst();
String number = primaryNumber.getString(0);
```

Finally, you notice that there is no error checking in this example. This has been left out to keep the listing short and focus on using the Content Provider. If an email or phone number doesn't exist, an `android.database.CursorIndexOutOfBoundsException` is thrown. This can be caught, or you can check to see that a result was actually returned in the `Cursor` first.

A More Efficient Way to Query for a Specific Contact

If that seemed like quite a lot of coding to get a phone number, you're not alone. For getting a quick piece of data, there is a faster way. This following block of code demonstrates how we can get the primary number and name for one contact. The primary number for a contact is designated as the default number within the contact manager on the handset. It might be useful to use the primary number field if you don't get any results back from the query.

```
String[] requestedColumns = {
    Contacts.Phones.NAME,
    Contacts.Phones.NUMBER,
};

Cursor contacts = managedQuery(
    Contacts.Phones.CONTENT_URI,
    requestedColumns,
    Contacts.Phones.ISPRIMARY + "<>0",
    null, "name desc limit 1");

Log.d(debugTag, "Contacts count: "
    + contacts.getCount());

int nameIdx = contacts
    .getColumnIndex(Contacts.Phones.NAME);
int phoneIdx = contacts
    .getColumnIndex(Contacts.Phones.NUMBER);

contacts.moveToFirst();
Log.d(debugTag, "Name: " + contacts.getString(nameIdx));
Log.d(debugTag, "Phone: " + contacts.getString(phoneIdx));
```

This block of code should look somewhat familiar, yet it is a much shorter and more straightforward method to query for phone numbers by Contact name. The Contacts.Phones.CONTENT_URI contains phone numbers but is also happens to have the contact name. This is similar to the CallLog Content Provider.

Using the UserDictionary Content Provider

Another useful Content Provider is the UserDictionary provider, which was introduced in Android 1.5. This Content Provider can be used for predictive text input on text fields and other user input mechanisms. Individual words stored in the dictionary are weighted by frequency and organized by locale. You can use the addWord() method within the UserDictionary.Words class to add words to the custom user dictionary.

Modifying Data in Content Providers

Content Providers are not only static sources of data. They can also be used to add, update, and delete data, if the Content Provider application has implemented this functionality. Your application must have the appropriate permissions (that is, WRITE_CONTACTS as opposed to READ_CONTACTS) to perform some of these actions.

Adding Records

Using the Contacts Content Provider, we can, for example, add a new record to the contacts database programmatically.

```
ContentValues values = new ContentValues();

values.put(Contacts.People.NAME, "Sample User");

Uri uri = getContentResolver().insert(
    Contacts.People.CONTENT_URI, values);

Uri phoneUri = Uri.withAppendedPath(uri,
    Contacts.People.Phones.CONTENT_DIRECTORY);

values.clear();

values.put(Contacts.Phones.NUMBER, "2125551212");
values.put(Contacts.Phones.TYPE, Contacts.Phones.TYPE_WORK);

getContentResolver().insert(phoneUri, values);

values.clear();

values.put(Contacts.Phones.NUMBER, "3135551212");
values.put(Contacts.Phones.TYPE, Contacts.Phones.TYPE_MOBILE);

getContentResolver().insert(phoneUri, values);
```

Just as we used the `ContentValues` class to insert records into an application's SQLite database, we use it again here. The first action we take is to provide a name for the `Contacts.People.Name` column. We need to create the contact with a name before we can assign information, such as phone numbers. Think of this as creating a row in a table that provides a one-to-many relationship to a phone number table.

Next, we insert the data in to the database found at the `Contacts.People.CONTENT_URI` path. We use a call to `getContentResolver()` to retrieve the `ContentResolver` associated with our `Activity`. The return value is the `Uri` of our new contact. We need to use it for adding phone numbers to our new contact. We then reuse the `ContentValues` instance by clearing it and adding a `Contacts.Phones.NUMBER` and the `Contacts.Phones.TYPE` for it. Using the `ContentResolver`, we insert this data into the new `Uri` created.

Tip

At this point, you might be wondering how the structure of the data can be determined. The best way is to thoroughly examine the documentation from the specific Content Provider you want to integrate your application with.

Updating Records

Inserting data isn't the only change you can make. One or more rows can be updated, as well. This following block of code shows how to update data within a Content Provider. In this case, we're updating a note field for a specific contact, using its unique identifier.

```
ContentValues values = new ContentValues();
values.put(People.NOTES, "This is my boss");
Uri updateUri = ContentUris.withAppendedId(People.CONTENT_URI, rowId);
int rows = getContentResolver().update(updateUri, values, null, null);
Log.d(debugTag, "Rows updated: " + rows);
```

Again, we use an instance of the `ContentValues` object to map the data field we want to update with the data value—in this case, the note field. This replaces any current note stored in the NOTES field currently stored with the contact. We then create the `Uri` for the specific contact we will update. A simple call to the `update()` method of the `ContentResolver` class completes our change. We can then confirm that only one row was updated.

> **Tip**
>
> The filter values can be used when updating rows. This allows you to make changes to values across many rows at the same time. The Content Provider must support this, though. We have found that the Contacts Provider blocks this on the People URI, preventing developers from making sweeping or global changes to contacts.

Deleting Records

Now that you cluttered up your contacts application with sample user data, you might want to delete some of it. Deleting data is fairly straightforward.

Deleting All Records

The following code deletes all rows at the given URI, although you'll want to execute operations like this with extreme care:

```
int rows = getContentResolver().delete(People.CONTENT_URI, null, null);
Log.d(debugTag, "Rows: "+ rows);
```

The `delete()` method deletes all rows at a given URI filtered by the selection parameters. In this case, that would include all rows at the `People.CONTENT_URI` location; in other words, all contact entries.

Deleting Specific Records

Often you want to select specific rows to delete by adding the unique identifier index to the end of the URI or remove rows matching a particular pattern.

For example, the following deletion matches all contact records with the name "Sample User," which we used when we created sample contacts previously in the chapter.

```
int rows = getContentResolver().delete(People.CONTENT_URI,
    People.NAME + "=?",
    new String[] {"Sample User"});
Log.d(debugTag, "Rows: "+ rows);
```

Extending Your Android Application with a Custom Content Provider

Do you have data in your application? Can another application do something interesting with that data? To share the information within your application with other applications, you need to become a Content Provider by providing the standardized Content Provider interface for other applications; then you must register your application as a Content Provider within the Android manifest file. The most straightforward way to become a Content Provider is to store the information you want to share in a SQLite database.

One example is a Content Provider for GPS track points. This Content Provider allows users of it to query for points and store points. The data for each point contains a time stamp, the latitude and longitude, and the elevation.

Inheriting from a Content Provider

Here is the skeleton code for the basic interface that an application needs to implement to become a Content Provider. In a following section, code for sample implementations of these five main methods will be given.

> **Tip**
>
> You can use Eclipse to easily create a new class and include the basic overrides that you need. To do this, right-click on the package you want to add the new class to, choose New, and then Class. Type the name of your Content Provider in the Name field, choose `android.content.ContentProvider` as your superclass, and check the box next to Inherited abstract methods.

```
public class TrackPointProvider extends ContentProvider {

    public int delete(Uri uri,
        String selection, String[] selectionArgs) {
        return 0;
    }

    public String getType(Uri uri) {
        return null;
    }

    public Uri insert(Uri uri, ContentValues values) {
        return null;
```

```
    }

    public boolean onCreate() {
        return false;
    }

    public Cursor query(Uri uri, String[] projection,
        String selection, String[] selectionArgs, String sortOrder) {
        return null;
    }

    public int update(Uri uri, ContentValues values,
        String selection, String[] selectionArgs) {
        return 0;
    }
}
```

Defining the Data URI

The provider application needs to define a base URI that other applications will use to
access this Content Provider. This must be in the form of a public static final
Uri named CONTENT_URI, and it must start with content://. The URI must be
unique. The best practice for this naming is to use the fully qualified class name of the
Content Provider. Here, we have created a URI name for our GPS track point provider
book example:

```
public static final Uri CONTENT_URI =
    Uri.parse("content://com.androidbook.TrackPointProvider");
```

Defining Data Columns

The user of the content provider needs to know what columns the Content Provider
has available to it. In this case, the columns used are timestamp, latitude and longitude,
and the elevation. We also include a column for the record number, which will be called
_id.

```
public final static String _ID = "_id";
public final static String TIMESTAMP = "timestamp";
public final static String LATITUDE = "latitude";
public final static String LONGITUDE = "longitude";
public final static String ELEVATION = "elevation";
```

Users of the Content Provider use these same strings. A Content Provider for data such
as this will often be storing the data within a SQLite database. If this is the case, matching these columns names to the database column names simplifies the code.

Implementing `query()`, `insert()`, `update()`, `delete()`, and `getType()`

This section shows example implementations of each of the methods that are used by the system to call this Content Provider when another application wants to use it. The system, in this case, is the `ContentResolver` interface that was used indirectly in the previous section when built-in Content Providers were used.

Some of these methods can make use of a helper class provided by the Android SDK, `UriMatcher`, which is used to match incoming `Uri` values to patterns that help speed up development. The use of `UriMatcher` is described and then used in the implementation of these methods.

Implementing `query()`

Let's start with a sample query implementation. Any query implementation needs to return a `Cursor` object. One convenient way to get a `Cursor` object is to return the `Cursor` from the underlying SQLite database that many Content Providers will use. In fact, the interface to `ContentProvider.query()` is compatible with the `SQLiteQueryBuild.query()` call. This example uses it to quickly build the query and return a `Cursor` object.

```
public Cursor query(Uri uri, String[] projection,
    String selection, String[] selectionArgs,
    String sortOrder) {

    SQLiteQueryBuilder qBuilder = new SQLiteQueryBuilder();

    qBuilder.setTables(TrackPointDatabase.TRACKPOINTS_TABLE);

    if ((sURIMatcher.match(uri)) == TRACKPOINT_ID) {
        qBuilder.appendWhere("_id=" + uri.getLastPathSegment());
    }

    Cursor resultCursor = qBuilder.query(mDB
        .getReadableDatabase(), projection,
        selection, selectionArgs, null, null,
        sortOrder, null);

    resultCursor.setNotificationUri(getContext()
        .getContentResolver(), uri);
    return resultCursor;
}
```

First, the code gets an instance of a `SQLiteQueryBuilder` object, which builds up a query with some method calls. Then, the `setTables()` method configures which table in the database will be used. The `UriMatcher` class checks to see which specific rows are requested. `UriMatcher` is discussed in greater detail later.

Next, the actual query is called. The Content Provider query has fewer specifications than the SQLite query, so the parameters are passed through and the rest is ignored. The instance of the SQLite database is read-only. Because this is only a query for data, it's acceptable.

Finally, the `Cursor` needs to know if the source data has changed. This is done by a call to the `setNotificationUri()` method telling it which URI to watch for data changes. The call to the application's `query()` method might be called from multiple threads, as it calls to `update()`, so it's possible the data can change after the `Cursor` is returned. Doing this keeps the data synchronized.

Exploring the `UriMatcher` Class

The `UriMatcher` class is a helper class for pattern matching on the URIs that are passed to this Content Provider. It is used frequently in the implementations of the Content Provider functions that must be implemented. Here is the `UriMatcher` used in these sample implementations:

```
public static final String AUTHORITY =
    "com.androidbook.TrackPointProvider"

private static final int TRACKPOINTS = 1;
private static final int TRACKPOINT_ID = 10;

private static final UriMatcher sURIMatcher =
    new UriMatcher(UriMatcher.NO_MATCH);
static {
    sURIMatcher.addURI(AUTHORITY, "points", TRACKPOINTS);
    sURIMatcher.addURI(AUTHORITY, "points/#", TRACKPOINT_ID);
}
```

First, arbitrary numeric values are defined to identify each different pattern. Next, a static `UriMatcher` instance is created for use. The code parameter that the constructor wants is merely the value to return when there is no match. A value for this is provided for use within the `UriMatcher` class itself.

Next, the URI values are added to the matcher with their corresponding identifiers. The URIs are broken up in to the authority portion, defined in `AUTHORITY`, and the path portion, which is passed in as a literal string. The path can contain patterns, such as the "#" symbol to indicate a number. The "*" symbol is used as a wildcard to match anything.

Implementing `insert()`

The `insert()` method is used for adding data to the Content Provider. Here is a sample implementation of the `insert()` method:

```
public Uri insert(Uri uri, ContentValues values) {

    int match = sURIMatcher.match(uri);
    if (match != TRACKPOINTS) {
```

```
        throw new IllegalArgumentException(
            "Unknown or Invalid URI " + uri);
    }

    SQLiteDatabase sqlDB = mDB.getWritableDatabase();

    long newID = sqlDB.
        insert(TrackPointDatabase.TRACKPOINTS_TABLE, null, values);

    if (newID > 0) {
        Uri newUri = ContentUris.withAppendedId(uri, newID);
        getContext()
            .getContentResolver().notifyChange(newUri, null);
        return newUri;
    }

    throw new SQLException("Failed to insert row into " + uri);
}
```

The Uri is first validated to make sure it's one where inserting makes sense. A Uri targeting a particular row would not, for instance. Next, a writeable database object instance is retrieved. Using this, the database insert() method is called on the table defined by the incoming Uri and with the values passed in. At this point, no error checking is performed on the values. Instead, the underlying database implementation throws exceptions that can be handled by the user of the Content Provider.

If the insert was successful, a Uri is created for notifying the system of a change to the underlying data via a call to the notifyChange() method of the ContentResolver. Otherwise, an exception is thrown.

Implementing update()

The update() method is used to modify an existing row of data. It has elements similar to the insert() and query() methods. The update is applied to a particular selection defined by the incoming Uri.

```
public int update(Uri uri, ContentValues values,
    String selection, String[] selectionArgs) {

    SQLiteDatabase sqlDB = mDB.getWritableDatabase();
    int match = sURIMatcher.match(uri);
    int rowsAffected;

    switch (match) {
        case TRACKPOINTS:
            rowsAffected = sqlDB.update(
                TrackPointDatabase.TRACKPOINTS_TABLE,
                values, selection, selectionArgs);
            break;
```

```
        case TRACKPOINT_ID:
            String id = uri.getLastPathSegment();
            if (TextUtils.isEmpty(selection)) {
                rowsAffected = sqlDB.update(
                    TrackPointDatabase.TRACKPOINTS_TABLE,
                    values, _ID + "=" + id, null);
            } else {
                rowsAffected = sqlDB.update(
                    TrackPointDatabase.TRACKPOINTS_TABLE,
                    values, selection + " and " + _ID + "="
                    + id, selectionArgs);
            }
            break;
        default:
            throw new IllegalArgumentException(
                "Unknown or Invalid URI " + uri);
    }

    getContext().getContentResolver().notifyChange(uri, null);
    return rowsAffected;
}
```

In this block of code, a writable SQLiteDatabase instance is retrieved and the Uri type the user passed in is determined with a call to the match() method of the UriMatcher. No checking of values or parameters is performed here. However, to block updates to a specific Uri, such as a Uri affecting multiple rows or a match on TRACKPOINT_ID, java.lang.UnsupportedOperationException can be thrown to indicate this. In this example, though, trust is placed in the user of this Content Provider.

After calling the appropriate update() method, the system is notified of the change to the URI with a call to the notifyChange() method. This tells any observers of the URI that data has possibly changed. Finally, the affected number of rows is returned, which is information conveniently returned from the call to the update() method.

Implementing delete()

Now it's time to clean up the database. The following is a sample implementation of the delete() method. It doesn't check to see if the user might be deleting more data than they should. You also notice that this is similar to the update() method.

```
public int delete(Uri uri, String selection, String[] selectionArgs) {
    int match = sURIMatcher.match(uri);

    SQLiteDatabase sqlDB = mDB.getWritableDatabase();
    int rowsAffected = 0;
    switch (match) {

        case TRACKPOINTS:
```

```
            rowsAffected = sqlDB.delete(
                TrackPointDatabase.TRACKPOINTS_TABLE,
                selection, selectionArgs);
            break;

      case TRACKPOINT_ID:
            String id = uri.getLastPathSegment();
            if (TextUtils.isEmpty(selection)) {
            rowsAffected =
                sqlDB.delete(TrackPointDatabase.TRACKPOINTS_TABLE,
                _ID+"="+id, null);
            } else {
                rowsAffected =
                    sqlDB.delete(TrackPointDatabase.TRACKPOINTS_TABLE,
                    selection + " and " +_ID+"="+id, selectionArgs);
            }
            break;
      default:
            throw new IllegalArgumentException(
                "Unknown or Invalid URI " + uri);
    }
    getContext().getContentResolver().notifyChange(uri, null);

    return rowsAffected;
}
```

Again, a writable database instance is retrieved and the `Uri` type is determined using the match method of `UriMatcher`. If the result is a directory `Uri`, the delete is called with the selection the user passed in. However, if the result is a specific row, the row index is used to further limit the delete, with or without the selection. Allowing this without a specific selection enables deletion of a specified identifier without having to also know exactly where it came from.

As before, the system is then notified of this change with a call to the `notifyChange()` method of `ContentResolver`. Also as before, the number of affect rows is returned, which we stored after the call to the `delete()` method.

Implementing `getType()`

The last method to implement is the `getType()` method. The purpose of this method is to return the MIME type for a particular `Uri` that is passed in. It does not need to return MIME types for specific columns of data.

```
public static final String CONTENT_ITEM_TYPE =
    ContentResolver.CURSOR_ITEM_BASE_TYPE +
    "/track-points";

public static final String CONTENT_TYPE =
```

```
        ContentResolver.CURSOR_DIR_BASE_TYPE +
        "/track-points";

public String getType(Uri uri) {
    int matchType = sURIMatcher.match(uri);
    switch (matchType) {

        case TRACKPOINTS:
            return CONTENT_TYPE;

        case TRACKPOINT_ID:
            return CONTENT_ITEM_TYPE;

        default:
            throw new
                IllegalArgumentException("Unknown or Invalid URI "
                + uri);
    }
}
```

First, a couple of MIME types are defined. The Android SDK provides some guideline values for single items and directories of items, which are used here. The corresponding string for each is vnd.android.cursor.item and vnd.android.cursor.dir, respectively. Finally, the match() method is used to determine the type of the provided Uri so that the appropriate MIME type can be returned.

Updating the Manifest File

Finally, you need to update your application's AndroidManifest.xml file so that it reflects that a Content Provider interface is exposed to the rest of the system. Here, the class name and the authorities, or what might considered the domain of the content:// URI, need to be set. For instance, content://com.androidbook. TrackPointProvider is the base URI used in this Content Provider example, which means the authority is com.androidbook.TrackPointProvider. The following XML shows an example of this:

```
<provider
    android:authorities="com.mamlambo.gpx.TrackPointProvider"
    android:multiprocess="true"
    android:name="com.mamlambo.gpx.TrackPointProvider"
</provider>
```

The value of multiprocess is set to true because the data does not need to be synchronized between multiple running versions of this Content Provider. It's possible that a Content Provider might be accessed by two or more applications at the same time, so proper synchronization might be necessary.

> **Tip**
>
> We frequently reference notifications that are sent to observers. In Chapter 16, "Working with Notifications," you learn about notifications that are sent to the device.

Working with Live Folders

Android 1.5 introduced the concept called a LiveFolder (`android.provider.LiveFolders`). A LiveFolder is a special folder with content generated by a Content Provider. For example, a user might want to create a `LiveFolder` with favorite contacts ("Fave Five"), most frequently viewed emails in a custom email application, or high-priority tasks in a task management application.

When the user chooses to create a `LiveFolder`, the Android system provides a list of all activities that respond to the `ACTION_CREATE_LIVE_FOLDER` Intent. If the user chooses your `Activity`, that `Activity` creates the `LiveFolder` and passes it back to the system using the `setResult()` method.

The `LiveFolder` consists of the following components:

- Folder name
- Folder icon
- Display mode (grid or list)
- Content Provider URI for the folder contents

The first task when enabling a Content Provider to serve up data to a `LiveFolder` is to provide an `<intent-filter>` for an `Activity` that handles enabling the `LiveFolder`. This is done within the `AndroidManifest.xml` file as follows:

```
<intent-filter>
    <action android:name=
        "android.intent.action.CREATE_LIVE_FOLDER" />
    <category
        android:name="android.intent.category.DEFAULT" />
</intent-filter>
```

Next, this action needs to be handled within the `OnCreate()` method of the `Activity` it has been defined for. Within the preceding provider example, the following code can be placed to handle this action:

```
super.onCreate(savedInstanceState);

final Intent intent = getIntent();
final String action = intent.getAction();
if (LiveFolders.ACTION_CREATE_LIVE_FOLDER.equals(action)) {

    final Intent resultIntent = new Intent();
```

```
resultIntent.setData(TrackPointProvider.LIVE_URI);
resultIntent.putExtra(LiveFolders.EXTRA_LIVE_FOLDER_NAME, "GPX Sample");
resultIntent.putExtra(LiveFolders.EXTRA_LIVE_FOLDER_ICON,
    Intent.ShortcutIconResource.fromContext(
    this, R.drawable.icon));
resultIntent.putExtra(LiveFolders.EXTRA_LIVE_FOLDER_DISPLAY_MODE,
    LiveFolders.DISPLAY_MODE_LIST);

setResult(RESULT_OK, resultIntent);
} // ... rest of onCreate()
```

This defines the core components of the `LiveFolder`: its name, icon, display mode, and `Uri`. The `Uri` is not the same as one that already existed because certain specific fields are needed for it to work properly. This leads directly to the next task: modifying the Content Provider to prepare it for serving up data to the `LiveFolder`.

First, a new `Uri` is defined. In this case, `"/live"` is added to the end of the existing `CONTENT_URI`. For example:

```
public static final Uri LIVE_URI = Uri.parse("content://"
    + AUTHORITY + "/" + TrackPointDatabase.TRACKPOINTS_TABLE
    + "/live");
```

This new `Uri` pattern is added to the `UriMatcher`. Next, the `query()` implementation is modified to recognize this new `Uri` and add a projection, which will be defined next:

```
switch (sURIMatcher.match(uri)) {
case TRACKPOINT_ID:
    qBuilder.appendWhere("_id=" + uri.getLastPathSegment());
    break;
case TRACKPOINTS_LIVE:
    qBuilder.setProjectionMap(
        TRACKPOINTS_LIVE_FOLDER_PROJECTION_MAP);
    break;
// ... other cases
}
Cursor c = qBuilder.query( // ...
```

The projection is critical for a working `LiveFolder` provider. There are two mandatory fields that must be in the resulting `Cursor`: `LiveFolder._ID` and `LiveFolder.NAME`. In addition to these, other fields, such as `LiveFolder.DESCRIPTION`, are available to modify the look and behavior of the view. In this example, the `TIMESTAMP` is used for the name, as shown here in the following projection implementation:

```
private static final HashMap<String,String>
    TRACKPOINTS_LIVE_FOLDER_PROJECTION_MAP;
static {
    TRACKPOINTS_LIVE_FOLDER_PROJECTION_MAP =
```

```
        new HashMap<String,String>();
    TRACKPOINTS_LIVE_FOLDER_PROJECTION_MAP.put(
        LiveFolders._ID, _ID + " as " + LiveFolders._ID);
    TRACKPOINTS_LIVE_FOLDER_PROJECTION_MAP.put(
        LiveFolders.NAME, TIMESTAMP + " as " + LiveFolders.NAME);
}
```

After this is done, the `LiveFolder` should be, well, live. In this example, only a list of dates show, as seen in Figure 9.5.

Figure 9.5   Sample `LiveFolder` list with dates.

Summary

There are a variety of different ways to store and manage application data on the Android platform. The method you use depends on what kind of data you need to store. With these skills you are well on your way to leveraging one of the more powerful and unique features of Android.

Your application can store data using the following mechanisms:

- Lightweight application preferences (Activity level and Application wide)
- Android file system file and directory support with XML file format support
- Application-specific SQLite databases for structured storage

You learned how to design persistent data-access mechanisms within your Android application, and you understand how to bind data from various sources to your user interface widgets, such as `ListView` and `Gallery` objects.

Your application can leverage the data available within other Android applications, if they expose that data as a Content Provider. The `MediaStore`, `Browser`, `CallLog`, and `Contacts` Content Providers are included with the Android and can be leveraged by other Android applications if they have the appropriate permissions. You can also share data with other applications by becoming a Content Provider. Becoming a Content Provider involves implementing a set of methods that manage how and what data you expose for use in other applications or even directly on the Home screen through the use of LiveFolders.

References and More Information

SQLite : www.sqlite.org/index.html
SQLzoo.net: http://sqlzoo.net/

10

Using Android Networking
APIs

Applications written with networking components are far more dynamic and content-rich than those that are not. Applications leverage the network for a variety of reasons: to deliver fresh and updated content, to enable social networking features of an otherwise standalone application, to offload heavy processing to high-powered servers, and to allow for data storage beyond what the user can achieve on the device.

Deciding how much networking support your application should contain is part of the application design process—something we talk more about in Chapter 18, "The Mobile Software Development Process."

Those accustomed to Java networking will find the `java.net` package familiar. There are also some helpful Android utility classes for various types of network operations and protocols. This chapter focuses on Hypertext Transfer Protocol (HTTP), the most common protocol for networked mobile applications.

Accessing the Internet (HTTP)

The most common way to transfer data to and from the network is to use HTTP. You can use HTTP to encapsulate almost any type of data and to secure the data with Secure Sockets Layer (SSL), which can be important when you transmit data that falls under privacy requirements. Also, most common ports used by HTTP are typically open from the phone networks.

> **Tip**
>
> Recall that as part of the Android Software Development Kit (SDK) License Agreement, developers agree to a number of best practices when it comes to network applications. If you plan to use network support in your application, you might want to review these points within the contract to ensure that your application complies with the agreement.

Reading Data from the Web

Reading data from the Web can be extremely simple. For example, if all you need to do is read some data from a Web site and you have the web address of that data, you can leverage the URL class (available as part of the `java.net` package) to read a fixed amount of text from a file on a web server, like this:

```
import java.io.InputStream;
import java.net.URL;

// …

try {
    URL text = new URL(
"http://api.flickr.com/services/feeds/photos_public.gne
➥?id=26648248@N04&amp;lang=en-us&amp;format=atom");

    InputStream isText = text.openStream();
    byte[] bText = new byte[250];
    int readSize = isText.read(bText);
    Log.i("Net", "readSize = " + readSize);
    Log.i("Net", "bText = "+ new String(bText));
    isText.close();
} catch (Exception e) {
    Log.e("Net", "Error in network call", e);
}
```

First, a new URL object is created with the URL to the data we want to read. A stream is then opened to the URL resource. From there, we read the data and close the InputStream. Reading data from a server can be that simple.

However, remember that because we work with a network resource, errors can be more common. Our phone might not have network coverage; the server might be down for maintenance or disappear entirely; the URL might be invalid; and network users might experience long waits and timeouts.

This method might work in some instances, for example if your application has lightweight, noncritical network features, but it's not particularly elegant. In many cases, you might want to know more about the data before reading from it from the URL. For instance, you might want to know how big it is.

Finally, for networking to work in any Android application, permission is required. Your application needs to have the following statement in its `AndroidManifest.xml` file:

```
<uses-permission
    android:name="android.permission.INTERNET"/>
```

Using `HttpURLConnection`

We can use the `HttpURLConnection` object to do a little reconnaissance on our URL before we transfer too much data. `HttpURLConnection` retrieves some information about the resource referenced by the URL object, including HTTP status and header information.

Some of the information you can retrieve from the `HttpURLConnection` includes the length of the content, content type, and date-time information so that you can check to see if the data changed since the last time you accessed the URL.

Here is a short example of how to use `HttpURLConnection` to query the same URL previously used:

```
import java.io.InputStream;
import java.net.HttpURLConnection;
import java.net.URL;

// …

URL text = new URL(
    "http://api.flickr.com/services/feeds/photos_public.gne
➥?id=26648248@N04&amp;lang=en-us&amp;format=atom");
HttpURLConnection http =
    (HttpURLConnection)text.openConnection();
Log.i("Net", "length = " + http.getContentLength());
Log.i("Net", "respCode = " + http.getResponseCode());
Log.i("Net", "contentType = "+ http.getContentType());
Log.i("Net", "content = "+http.getContent());
```

The log lines demonstrate a few useful methods with the `HttpURLConnection` class. If the URL content is deemed appropriate, you can then call `http.getInputStream()` to get the same `InputStream` object as before. From there, reading from the network resource is the same, but more will be known about the resource.

> **Note**
>
> Android ships with Apache Foundation's HTTPClient v4 (http://hc.apache.org/), which has substantial changes from previous versions. You can find more information about protocol interaction within the `org.apache.http` package.

Parsing XML from the Network

A large portion of data transmitted between network resources is stored in a structured fashion in Extensible Markup Language (XML). In particular, RSS feeds are provided in a standardized XML format and many web services provide data using these feeds.

Android SDK provides a variety of XML utilities. We dabbled with the XML Pull Parser in Chapter 5, "Managing Application Resources." We also covered the various SAX and DOM support available in Chapter 9, "Using Android Data and Storage APIs."

Parsing XML from the network is similar to parsing an XML resource file or a raw file on the file system. Android provides a fast and efficient XML Pull Parser, which is a parser of choice for networked applications.

The following code demonstrates how to use the XML Pull Parser to read an XML file from flickr.com and extract specific data from within it. A `TextView` called `status` is assigned before this block of code is executed and displays the status of the parsing operation.

```
import java.net.URL;

import org.xmlpull.v1.XmlPullParser;
import org.xmlpull.v1.XmlPullParserFactory;

// …

URL text = new URL(
    "http://api.flickr.com/services/feeds/photos_public.gne
➥?id=26648248@N04&amp;lang=en-us&amp;format=atom");

XmlPullParserFactory parserCreator =
    XmlPullParserFactory.newInstance();
XmlPullParser parser = parserCreator.newPullParser();

parser.setInput(text.openStream(), null);

status.setText("Parsing...");
int parserEvent = parser.getEventType();
while (parserEvent != XmlPullParser.END_DOCUMENT) {
    switch(parserEvent) {
        case XmlPullParser.START_TAG:
            String tag = parser.getName();

            if (tag.compareTo("link") == 0) {
                String relType =
                    parser.getAttributeValue(null, "rel");

                if (relType.compareTo("enclosure") == 0 ) {
                    String encType =
➥parser.getAttributeValue(null, "type");

                    if (encType.startsWith("image/")) {
                        String imageSrc =
➥parser.getAttributeValue(null, "href");            Log.i("Net",
                            "image source = " + imageSrc);
                    }
                }
```

```
        }
            break;
        }
    parserEvent = parser.next();
    }
}
status.setText("Done...");
```

After the URL is created, the next step is to retrieve an `XmlPullParser` instance from the `XmlPullParserFactory`. A Pull Parser has a main method that returns the next event. The events returned by a Pull Parser are similar to methods used in the implementation of a SAX parser handler class. Instead, though, the code is handled iteratively. This method is more efficient for mobile use.

In this example, the only event that we check for is the `START_TAG` event, signifying the beginning of an XML tag. Attribute values are queried and compared. This example looks specifically for image URLs within the XML from a flickr feed query. When found, a log entry is made.

You can check for the following XML Pull Parser events:

- `START_TAG`: Returned when a new tag is found (that is, `<tag>`)
- `TEXT`: Returned when text is found (that is, `<tag>text</tag>` where text has been found)
- `END_TAG`: Returned when the end of tag is found (that is, `</tag>`)
- `END_DOCUMENT`: Returned when the end of the XML file has been reached

Additionally, the parser can be set to validate the input. Typically, parsing without validation is used when under constrained memory environments, such as a mobile environment. Compliant, nonvalidating parsing is the default for this XML Pull Parser.

Using Threads for Network Calls

The style of networking presented so far causes the UI thread it runs on to block until the operation finishes. For small tasks, this might be acceptable. However, when timeouts or additional processing is added, such as parsing XML, you want to move these time-intensive operations away from the main UI thread by launching a worker new thread. This provides a smoother experience for the user.

The following code demonstrates how to launch a new thread that connects to a remote server, retrieves and parses some XML, and posts a response back to the UI thread to change a `TextView`:

```
import java.net.URL;

import org.xmlpull.v1.XmlPullParser;
import org.xmlpull.v1.XmlPullParserFactory;

// ...
```

```
new Thread() {
    public void run() {
        try {
            URL text = new URL(
➥"http://api.flickr.com/services/feeds/photos_public
➥.gne?id=26648248@N04&amp;lang=en-
➥us&amp;format=atom");

            XmlPullParserFactory parserCreator =
                XmlPullParserFactory.newInstance();
            XmlPullParser parser =
                parserCreator.newPullParser();

            parser.setInput(text.openStream(), null);

            mHandler.post(new Runnable() {
                public void run() {
                    status.setText("Parsing...");
                }
            });

            int parserEvent = parser.getEventType();
            while (parserEvent !=
                XmlPullParser.END_DOCUMENT) {

                // Parsing code here …

                parserEvent = parser.next();
            }

            mHandler.post(new Runnable() {
                public void run() {
                    status.setText("Done...");
                }
            });

        } catch (Exception e) {
            Log.e("Net", "Error in network call", e);
        }
    }
}.start();
```

For this example, an anonymous `Thread` object will do. We create it and call its `start()` method immediately. However, now that code runs on a separate thread, the user interface updates must be posted back to the main thread. This is done by using a `Handler` object on the main thread and creating `Runnable` objects that execute to call `setText()` on the `TextView` widget named `status`.

The rest of the code remains the same as in the previous examples. Executing both the parsing code and the networking code on a separate thread allows the user interface to continue to behave in a responsive fashion while the network and parsing operations are done behind the scenes, resulting in a smooth and friendly user experience. This also allows for handling of interim actions by the user, such as canceling the transfer. You can accomplish this by implementing the `Thread` to listen for certain events and check for certain flags.

What's New in Android 1.5

In Android 1.5, a new class called `AsyncTask` was introduced into the `android.os` package. `AsyncTask` is an abstract helper class for managing background operations that will eventually post back to the UI thread. Instead of creating threads for background processing and using messages and message handlers for updating the UI, developers can create a subclass of `AsyncTask` and implement the appropriate event methods. The `onPreExecute()` method runs on the UI thread before background processing begins. The `doInBackground()` method handles background processing, whereas `publishProgress()` informs the UI thread periodically about the background processing progress. When the background processing finishes, the `onPostExecute()` method runs on the UI thread to give a final update.

The following code demonstrates an example implementation of AsyncTask to perform the same functionality as the code for the Thread:

```
private class ImageLoader extends
➥AsyncTask<URL, String, String> {

@Override
protected String doInBackground(
    URL... params) {
    // just one param
    try {
        URL text = params[0];

        // … parsing code {

        publishProgress(
            "imgCount = " + curImageCount);

        // … end parsing code }

    }
    catch (Exception e ) {
        Log.e("Net",
            "Failed in parsing XML", e);
        return "Finished with failure.";
    }
```

continues

continued

```
    return "Done...";
}


protected void onCancelled() {
    Log.e("Net", "Async task Cancelled");
}

protected void onPostExecute(String result) {
    mStatus.setText(result);
}


protected void onPreExecute() {
    mStatus.setText("About to load URL");
}

protected void onProgressUpdate(
    String... values) {
    // just one value, please
    mStatus.setText(values[0]);
    super.onProgressUpdate(values);
}}
```

When launched with the `AsyncTask.execute()` method, `doInBackground()` runs in a background thread while the other methods run on the UI thread. There is no need to manage a `Handler` or post `Runnable` object to it. This simplifies coding and debugging.

Displaying Images from a Network Resource

Now that we covered how you can use a separate thread to parse XML, let's take our example a bit deeper and talk about working with nonprimitive data types.

Continuing with the previous example of parsing for image locations from a flickr feed, let's display some images from the feed. The following example reads the image data and displays it on the screen, demonstrating another way that network resources can be used:

```
import java.io.InputStream;
import java.net.URL;

import org.xmlpull.v1.XmlPullParser;
import org.xmlpull.v1.XmlPullParserFactory;
```

```
import android.os.Handler;

// …

final String imageSrc =
    parser.getAttributeValue(null, "href");

final String currentTitle = new String(title);
imageThread.queueEvent(new Runnable() {
    public void run() {
        InputStream bmis;
        try {
            bmis = new URL(imageSrc).openStream();
            final Drawable image = new BitmapDrawable(
                BitmapFactory.decodeStream(bmis));
            mHandler.post(new Runnable() {
                public void run() {
                    imageSwitcher.setImageDrawable(image);
                    info.setText(currentTitle);
                }
            });
        } catch (Exception e) {
            Log.e("Net", "Failed to grab image", e);
        }
    }
});
```

You can find this block of code within the parser thread, as previously described. After the image source and title of the image have been determined, a new `Runnable` object is queued for execution on a separate image handling thread. The thread is merely a queue that receives the anonymous `Runnable` object created here and executes it at least 10 seconds after the last one, resulting in a slideshow of the images from the feed.

Caution

Although the preceding code is sound for local resources and URLs, for sources over slow connections, it might not work properly. This is a known issue with the Android SDK caused by a buffering issue with loading large bitmaps over slow connections. There is a relatively straightforward workaround that is found in the code provided for this chapter.

As with the first networking example, a new `URL` object is created and an `InputStream` retrieved from it. A `Drawable` object is needed to assign to the `ImageSwitcher`. Then we use the `BitmapFactory.decodeStream()` method, which takes an `InputStream`.

Finally, from this `Runnable` object, which runs on a separate queuing thread, spacing out image drawing, another anonymous `Runnable` object posts back to the main thread to actually update the `ImageSwitcher` with the new image. Figure 10.1 shows what the screen might look like showing decoding status and displaying the current image.

Figure 10.1   Screen showing a flickr image and decoding status of feed.

Although all this continues to happen while the feed from flickr.com is decoded, certain operations are slower than others. For instance, while the image is decoded or drawn on the screen, a distinct hesitation is noticeable in the progress of the decoding. This is to be expected on current mobile devices because most have only a single thread of execution available for applications. Careful design is needed to provide a reasonably smooth and responsive experience to the user.

Retrieving Android Network Status

The Android SDK provides utilities for gathering information about the current state of the network. This is useful to determine if a network connection is even available before trying to use a network resource. The `ConnectivityManager` class provides a number of methods to do this. The following code determines if the mobile (cellular) network is available and connected. In addition, it determines the same for the WiFi network:

```
import android.net.ConnectivityManager;
import android.net.NetworkInfo;

// …

ConnectivityManager cm = (ConnectivityManager)
    getSystemService(Context.CONNECTIVITY_SERVICE);
NetworkInfo ni =
    cm.getNetworkInfo(ConnectivityManager.TYPE_WIFI);
boolean isWifiAvail = ni.isAvailable();
boolean isWifiConn = ni.isConnected();
ni = cm.getNetworkInfo(ConnectivityManager.TYPE_MOBILE);
boolean isMobileAvail = ni.isAvailable();
boolean isMobileConn = ni.isConnected();

status.setText("WiFi\nAvail = "+ isWifiAvail +
    "\nConn = " + isWifiConn +
    "\nMobile\nAvail = "+ isMobileAvail +
    "\nConn = " + isMobileConn);
```

First, an instance of the `ConnectivityManager` object is retrieved with a call to the `getSystemService()` method, available as part of your application `Context`. Then this instance retrieves `NetworkInfo` objects for both `TYPE_WIFI` and `TYPE_MOBILE` (for the cellular network). These objects are queried for their availability but can also be queried at a more detailed status level to learn exactly what state of connection (or disconnection) the network is in. Figure 10.2 shows the typical output for the emulator in which the mobile network is simulated but WiFi isn't available.

If the network is available, that does not necessarily mean the server that the network resource is on is available. However, a call to the `ConnectivityManager` method `requestRouteToHost()` can answer this question. This way, the application can give the user better feedback when there are network problems.

> **Tip**
>
> Use the emulator networking settings to simulate various types of cellular networks, from GSM to HSDPA data rates. Additionally, you can control the latency of the network to be similar to that of the cellular networks. Although this is useful for testing how your application behaves in good conditions for the chosen network type, it can't simulate the real behavior of the network out in the field when the user is in bad coverage, goes on an elevator, or is on a train rapidly losing and reacquiring network coverage. Only physical handset testing can truly reveal these results.

Figure 10.2   Typical network status of the Android SDK emulator.

For your application to read the status of the network, it needs explicit permission.
The following statement is required to be in its `AndroidManifest.xml` file:

```
<uses-permission
    android:name="android.permission.ACCESS_NETWORK_STATE"/>
```

Browsing the Web with `WebView`

Applications that get data from the Web often end up displaying that data on the screen.
Instead of customizing various screens with widgets, an application can just use the
`WebView` widget, which uses the `WebKit` rendering engine, to draw HTML data on the
screen. This data can be HTML pages on the Web, as with our example, or it can be
locally sourced.

Here is an example of how to use a `WebView` widget to draw HTML.

```
final WebView wv = (WebView) findViewById(R.id.web_holder);
wv.loadUrl("http://www.perlgurl.org/");
wv.setInitialScale(30);
```

The corresponding layout file section for this follows:

```
<WebView
    android:id="@+id/web_holder"
    android:layout_height="wrap_content"
    android:layout_width="fill_parent"
/>
```

You do not need additional code to load the referenced web page on the screen. The call to the `setInitialScale()` method scales the view to 30 percent of the original size. For pages that specify absolute sizes, scaling the view is necessary to see the entire page on the screen. Some text might become too small to read though, so testing and page design changes, if under your control, might be required for a good user experience.

The `WebView` widget allows the user to navigate within the page and click on links. Clicking on links, by default, loads the default web browser on the system. Two classes, in particular, can help modify the behavior of the viewer and gather useful information from it. One of them is the `WebViewClient` class, which allows the application to listen for certain `WebView` status events, such as when a page is loading, when a form is submitted, and when a new URL is about to be loaded. The following is an example of how to handle the `onPageFinished()` method to draw the title of the page on the screen:

```
WebViewClient webClient = new WebViewClient() {

    public void onPageFinished(WebView view, String url) {
        super.onPageFinished(view, url);
        String title = wv.getTitle();
        pageTitle.setText(title);
    }

};


wv.setWebViewClient(webClient);
```

When the page finishes loading, as indicated by the call to `onPageFinished()`, a call to the `getTitle()` method of the `WebView` allows the title to be retrieved for use. The result of this call is shown in Figure 10.3.

Second, you can use the `WebChromeClient` class in a similar way to the `WebViewClient`. However, `WebChromeClient` is specialized for the sorts of items that will be drawn outside the region in which the web content is drawn, typically known as *browser chrome*. It also includes some callbacks for certain JavaScript calls, such as `onJsBeforeUnload()`, to confirm navigation away from a page.

Figure 10.3   `WebView` used to draw a web page at 30 percent with title showing.

The following code demonstrates interactivity from the user. An `EditText` and `Button` widget are added below the `WebView` and the `Button` handler is implemented as follows:

```
Button go = (Button) findViewById(R.id.go_button);
go.setOnClickListener(new View.OnClickListener() {

    public void onClick(View v) {
        wv.loadUrl(et.getText().toString());
    }

});
```

Calling the `loadUrl()` method again, as shown, is all that is needed to cause the `WebView` widget to download another HTML page for display, as shown in Figure 10.4. From here, a generic web browser can be built in to any application, but often restrictions will be applied so that the user is restricted to browsing relevant HTML documents (such as the application's home server).

Figure 10.4   `WebView` with `EditText` allowing the user to enter an
arbitrary web URL.

Whether you use `WebView` to display the main user interface of your application or
use it sparingly to draw such things as help pages, there are circumstances where it might
be the ideal widget for the job to save coding time, especially when compared to a custom screen design. Leveraging the power of the open source engine, `WebKit`, `WebView`
can provide a powerful, standards-based HTML viewer for applications. Support for
`WebKit` is widespread because it is used in various desktop browsers, including Safari and
Google Chrome, and a variety of mobile browsers, including those on the Apple iPhone
and Nokia S60.

Summary

Networking on the Android platform is standardized, using a combination of powerful
yet familiar technologies and libraries such as `java.net` and `WebKit`. Although the
implementation of networking features within applications is generally straightforward,
mobile application developers need to plan for less stable connectivity than one might
expect in a home or office network setting—connectivity depends on the location of
the users and their device.

Integrating networking features into your mobile application needs to be considered at the design level. Users demand responsive applications, so time-intensive operations should not block from the main UI thread. Finally, don't forget to handle application lifecycle events smoothly with network activities.

References and More Information

Java.net package information: http://developer.android.com/reference/java/net/package-summary.html

Android.net package information: http://developer.android.com/reference/android/net/package-summary.html

Android XML Pull Parser: http://developer.android.com/reference/org/xmlpull/v1/XmlPullParser.html

More information on XML Pull Parsing: www.xmlpull.org/

WebKit Open Source Project: http://webkit.org/

## 11

Using Location-Based Services (LBS) APIs

Whether for safety or for convenience, location-based features on cell phones are mostly standard these days. As such, incorporating location information, navigation, and mapping features into your project can make your application much more robust.

In this chapter, you learn how to leverage location-based services available within the Android SDK. You learn how to determine the location of the handset using a particular device hardware provider, such as a built-in Global Positioning Systems (GPS) unit. You also learn how to translate raw location coordinates into descriptive location names— and how to do the reverse. Finally, we explore a couple of different methods for mapping and utilities that work with the maps.

Using Global Positioning Services (GPS)

The Android Software Development Kit (SDK) provides means for accessing location via a built-in GPS device, when such hardware is available. If a GPS device isn't available, the Application Programming Interfaces (API) also provides for alternate location providers. These other providers might have advantages and disadvantages in terms of power use, speed, and accuracy of reporting.

Finding Your Location

To determine device location, you need to perform a few steps and make some choices. The following list summarizes this process:

1. Retrieve an instance of the `LocationManager` using a call to the `getSystemService()` method using the `LOCATION_SERVICE`.

2. Add an appropriate permission to the `AndroidManifest.xml` file, depending on what type of location information the application needs.

3. Choose a provider using either the `getAllProviders()` method or the `getBestProvider()` method.

4. Implement a `LocationListener` class.

5. Call the `requestLocationUpdates()` method with the chosen provider and the `LocationListener` object to start receiving location information.

Specific permissions are not needed to retrieve an instance of the `LocationManager` object. Instead, the permissions determine the available providers. The following code retrieves an instance of the `LocationManager` object:

```
import android.location.*;
…
LocationManager location =
    (LocationManager)getSystemService(Context.LOCATION_SERVICE);
```

The following block of XML provides the application with both coarse and fine location permissions when added within the `AndroidManifest.xml` permissions file:

```
<uses-permission
    android:name="android.permission.ACCESS_FINE_LOCATION" />
<uses-permission
    android:name="android.permission.ACCESS_COARSE_LOCATION" />
```

Now that the application has permissions to use location information and the `LocationManager` object is valid, we must determine what provider to use for location information. The following code configures a `Criteria` object and requests the provider based on this information:

```
Criteria criteria = new Criteria();
criteria.setAccuracy(Criteria.NO_REQUIREMENT);
criteria.setPowerRequirement(Criteria.NO_REQUIREMENT);

String bestProvider = location.getBestProvider(criteria, true);
```

The `setAccuracy()` method can take values for `ACCURACY_COARSE` and `ACCURACY_FINE` that can be used (along with the appropriate permissions) to request a provider that the application has permissions to use. The `setPowerRequirement()` method can be used to find a provider that fits certain power use requirements, such as `POWER_HIGH` or `POWER_LOW`. The `Criteria` object also enables us to specify if the provider can incur a monetary cost to the user, whether altitude is needed, and some other details. If the application has specific requirements, this is where they can be set. However, setting these criteria doesn't imply that the provider will be available to the user. Some flexibility might be required to allow use on a broad range of devices. A `Boolean` parameter of the `getBestProvider()` method enables the application to ask for only enabled providers.

Using the provider returned by the `getBestProvider()` method, the application can request the location. Before doing so, however, the application needs to provide an implementation of `LocationListener`. The `LocationListener` object consists of four methods: two tell the application if the provider has been disabled or enabled; one gives the status about the provider (such as the number of satellites the GPS receiver can see); and the last tells the application location information. The following is a sample implementation for the last method, the `onLocationChanged()`method:

```
public void onLocationChanged(Location location) {
    String locInfo = String.
        format("Current loc = (%f, %f) @ (%f meters up)",
        location.getLatitude(), location.getLongitude(),
        location.getAltitude() );
    if (lastLocation != null) {
        float distance = location.distanceTo(lastLocation);
        locInfo += String.
            format("\n Distance from last = %f meters", distance);
    }
    lastLocation = location;
    status.setText(locInfo);
}
```

The `onLocationChanged()` method receives a `Location` object with the most recent location information from the chosen provider. In this example, the application merely prints out the location, including the altitude, which might or might not be returned by the provider. Then, it uses a utility method of the `Location` object, `distanceTo()`, to calculate how far the handset has moved since the last time `onLocationChanged()` was called.

It is up to the application to determine how to use this location information. The application might want to turn the location information into an address, display the location on an embedded map, or launch the built-in map application centered at the location.

Locating Your Emulator

The Android emulator can simulate location-based services, but as you would expect, it does not have any "underlying hardware" to get a real satellite fix. The Android SDK provides a means to simulate location data with the use of a single location point, GPX file, or KML file. This works only with the emulator, not the physical handset, but it can be useful for testing your location-based application.

For more information on this, see Appendix A, "The Android Emulator Quick-Start Guide."

Geocoding Locations

Determining the latitude and longitude is useful for precise location, tracking, and measurements; however, it's not usually descriptive to users. The Android SDK provides some helper methods to turn raw location data into addresses and descriptive place names. These methods can also work in reverse, turning place names or addresses into raw location coordinates.

The `Geocoder` object can be used without any special permissions. The following block of code demonstrates using the `Geocoder` object to get the location names of a `Location` object passed in to the `onLocationChanged()` method of a `LocationListener`:

```
Geocoder coder = new Geocoder(this);
try {
    Iterator<Address> addresses = coder
        .getFromLocation(location.getLatitude(),
        location.getLongitude(), 3).iterator();
    if (addresses != null) {
        while (addresses.hasNext()) {
            Address namedLoc = addresses.next();
            String placeName = namedLoc.getLocality();
            String featureName = namedLoc.getFeatureName();
            String country = namedLoc.getCountryName();
            String road = namedLoc.getThoroughfare();
            locInfo += String.format("\n[%s][%s][%s][%s]",
                placeName, featureName, road, country);
            int addIdx = namedLoc.getMaxAddressLineIndex();
            while (addIdx >= 0 ) {
                String addLine = namedLoc.getAddressLine(addIdx);
                locInfo += String.
                    format("\nLine %d: %s", addIdx, addLine);
                addIdx--;
            }
        }
    }
} catch (IOException e) {
    Log.e("GPS", "Failed to get address", e);
}
```

You can extract information from the results of the call to the `getFromLocation()` method in two ways, both of which are demonstrated. Note that a particular location might have multiple `Address` results in the form of a `List<Address>` object. Typically, the first `Address` is the most detailed, and the subsequent `Address` objects have less detail and describe a broader region.

The first method is to query for specific information, such as by using the `getFeatureName()` method or the `getLocality()` method. These methods are not guaranteed to return useful information for all locations. They are useful, though, when you know you need only a specific piece of general information, such as the country.

The second method for querying information is by "address lines." This is generally used for displaying the "address" of a location to the user. It might also be useful to use the location in directions and in other cases where a street address is desired. That said, the addresses returned might not be complete. Simply call the `getAddressLine()`

method and iterate through the values returned by `getMaxAddressLineIndex()`.
Figure 11.1 shows a sample location with three resulting addresses.

Figure 11.1   Image showing location geocoded to three "addresses."

The `Geocoder` object also supports using named locations or address lines to generate latitude and longitude information. The input is forgiving and returns reasonable
results in most cases. For instance, all the following returns valid and correct results,
"Eiffel Tower," "London, UK," "Iceland," "BOS," "Yellowstone," and "1600 Pennsylvania
Ave, DC."

The following code demonstrates a button handler for computing location data based
on user input of this kind:

```
public void onClick(View v) {
    String placeName = name.getText().toString();

    try {
        List<Address> geocodeResults =
            coder.getFromLocationName(placeName, 3);

        Iterator<Address> locations = geocodeResults.iterator();
```

```
    String locInfo = "Results:\n";

    while (locations.hasNext()) {
        Address loc = locations.next();
        locInfo += String.format("Location: %f, %f",
            loc.getLatitude(), loc.getLongitude());
    }

    results.setText(locInfo);
} catch (IOException e) {
    Log.e("GeoAddress", "Failed to get location info", e);
}
}
```

The result of the call to the `getFromLocationName()` method is a `List` of `Address` objects, much like the previous example. Figure 11.2 shows the results for entering "Eiffel Tower."

Figure 11.2   The results for geocoding the term Eiffel Tower.

We have never actually seen more than one result, even when entering ambiguous place names (such as "Dublin"). However, this behavior is not guaranteed. Providing a picker for the user to choose the best location would certainly enhance the application. Another good way to confirm with the user that they entered the correct location is to map it. We now discuss a couple of different methods for mapping locations using Google Maps.

Mapping Locations

The Android SDK provides two different methods to show a location with Google Maps. The first method is to use a location `Uri` to launch the built-in Google Maps application with the specified location. The second method is to use a `MapView` embedded within your application to display the map location.

Mapping Intents

In the previous section, we demonstrated how to determine the latitude and longitude for a place name. Now we map the location using the built-in maps application. The following block of code demonstrates how to perform this:

```
String geoURI = String.format("geo:%f,%f", lat, lon);
Uri geo = Uri.parse(geoURI);
Intent geoMap = new Intent(Intent.ACTION_VIEW, geo);
startActivity(geoMap);
```

The first task is to create a `String` that conforms to the URI handled by the mapping application. In this case, it's `"geo:"` followed by the latitude and longitude. This URI is then used to create a new `Uri` object for creating a new `ACTION_VIEW Intent`. Finally, we call the `startActivity()` method. If the latitude and longitude are valid, such as the location for the Parthenon entered in the previous example, the screen would look like Figure 11.3.

Using this method of mapping launches the user into a built-in mapping application, in this case Google Maps. If the application does not want to bother with the details of a full mapping application or does not need to provide any further control over the map, this is a fast-and-easy method to use. Users will typically be accustomed to the controls of the mapping application on their handset, too.

Figure 11.3   The resulting map for geocoding the term "Parthenon" and launching a geo URI.

Mapping Views

Sometimes, though, we want to have the map integrated into our application for a more seamless user experience. Let's add a small map to our geocoding example to show the location immediately to the users when they enter a place name.

The following block of XML shows the change needed within the layout file to include a widget called the MapView:

```
<com.google.android.maps.MapView
    android:id="@+id/map"
    android:apiKey="yourMapKey"
    android:layout_width="fill_parent"
    android:layout_height="wrap_content" />
```

As you might have already noticed, the MapView XML is a little different. First, the tag name is the fully qualified name. And second, an apiKey attribute is needed. We get to the key in a moment.

The `AndroidManifest.xml` file also needs to be modified to allow for using the `MapView` with Google Maps. Here are the two changes needed:

```
<application
...
    <uses-library
        android:name="com.google.android.maps" />
</application>
<uses-permission
    android:name="android.permission.INTERNET" />
```

Both of these permission lines are required. The `MapView` object specifically requires the `INTERNET` permission and its library must be reference explicitly. Otherwise, an error will occur.

Finally, a `MapView` can be used only within a `MapActivity`. Accessing a `MapView` from outside a `MapActivity` results in an error. The `MapActivity` is similar to a normal `Activity`, but it requires implementing the `isRouteDisplayed()` method. This method must return true if a route will be displayed. Otherwise, false must be returned. Here is the default implementation for when no route is displayed:

```
@Override
protected boolean isRouteDisplayed() {
    // we do not display routes
    return false;
}
```

Now the application can use the `MapView` to display locations to the user. The following block of code demonstrates retrieval of a `MapController` object, which is used to control the location that the `MapView` displays:

```
MapView map = (MapView) findViewById(R.id.map);
map.setSatellite(true);
final MapController mapControl = map.getController();
mapControl.setZoom(17);
```

These lines of code set the display to show the satellite view, which is visually interesting. The `MapController` object then sets the zoom level of the map. Larger values are zoomed in farther, with 1 zoomed all the way out. The given value, 17, usually shows a few city blocks, but there are some areas where even this is too close for the data available. In a moment we talk about how to easily give control of this to the user.

Building on the previous example, the following lines of code are added to the button handler for geocoding a place name:

```
GeoPoint newPoint = new
    GeoPoint((int)(lat * 1E6), (int)(lon * 1E6));
mapControl.animateTo(newPoint);
```

In this case, we create a new `GeoPoint` to use with the `animateTo()` method. A `GeoPoint` object uses microdegrees, so we must multiply the result of the geocoding by `1E6` (1,000,000 or one million). The `animateTo()` method smoothly animates the `MapView` to the new location. How much of the interim mapping data displays depends on the speed of the Internet connection and what mode the `MapView` is in. The `setCenter()` method can set the center of the map.

Finally, this is almost enough to test the results. However, there is one last thing that needs to be taken care of. You need to get a Google Maps API Key from Google to use its API and mapping services.

Getting Your Debug API Key

To use a `MapView` within your applications, you must obtain a Google Maps API Key from Google. The key is generated from an MD5 fingerprint of a certificate that you use to sign your applications.

For production distribution, you need to follow these steps, substituting your release distribution signing certificate. You can read more about this in Chapter 20, "Selling Your Android Application." For testing purposes, you can use the debug certificate that is created by the Android SDK for your use.

The following steps need to be performed to generate the appropriate API key:

1. Generate an MD5 fingerprint for your debug certificate.
2. Sign in to http://code.google.com/android/maps-api-signup.html with a Google Account.
3. Accept the Terms of Service.
4. Paste in the fingerprint from step 1.
5. Save the Android Maps API key presented on the next screen.

The first step is performed on your development machine. Locate the debug certificate used by the Android SDK. On all platforms, the filename is `debug.keystore` by default. If you use Eclipse, the location of the file is listed under the Android Build preferences. Using this file, you then need to execute the following command (make sure the Java tools are in your path):

```
keytool -list -keystore /path/to/debug.keystore
```

The result is the fingerprint that you must paste into the form on step 4. Read the terms of service carefully before proceeding. Although the terms allow many types of applications, you need to make sure your application will be allowed and that your anticipated usage will be acceptable to Google.

When you have successfully completed the steps to get your key, you can then reference your map key in the `Layout` file definition for the `MapView` you use. Now, when you execute the code, you should be presented with a screen that looks like Figure 11.4.

Figure 11.4   **MapView** results for geocoding the term "Sydney Opera House."

> **Tip**
>
> If you work on multiple development machines or work as part of a team, you need to have an API key for everyone's debug certificate. Alternating, the debug certificate from one machine can be copied to other machines so that the signing and check against the Android Maps API key is successful. This can save time by not having to modify the code or layout files for each developer on the team.

Panning the Map View

Sometimes the locations returned either do not show the exact location that the user wanted or the user might want to determine where in the world they are by exploring the map a bit. One way to do this is through panning the map. Luckily, this is as easy as enabling clicking from within the layout file:

```
<com.google.android.maps.MapView
    android:id="@+id/map"
    android:clickable="true"
```

```
android:apiKey="mapApiKey"
android:layout_width="fill_parent"
android:layout_height="wrap_content" />
```

Now, if users were to search for "The Great Pyramid," they could then pan south a tad and see the results, as shown in Figure 11.5.

Figure 11.5   Results for "The Great Pyramid" on the left, panned south by about a screen on the right.

Zooming the Map View

Other times, panning around won't help the users. They might want to zoom in or out from the same location. Our application does not have to reimplement the zoom controls, though. They are provided in the Android SDK 1.5 through a single call.

```
map.setBuiltInZoomControls(true);
```

When the user clicks on the map, the zoom controls fade in to view and are functional, as shown in Figure 11.6.

When the user clicks on the map, the zoom controls fade in to view and are functional, as shown in Figure 11.6

Figure 11.6   On the right, you see a bird's eye view of the town of Wilmington, but zoom in and you see The Long Man of Wilmington as shown on the left.

What's New in Android 1.5

The call to `setBuiltInZoomControls()` was added in Android 1.5. The deprecated call to `getZoomControls()` is longer supported and should not be used for compatibility and performance reasons.

Marking the Spot

Now that users can pan and zoom around, they might lose their position. Sure, they can just search again. Wouldn't it be more interesting, though, to mark the spot for them? The Android SDK provides a few different ways to do this. One way is to use the `MapView` as a container for an arbitrary `View` object that can be assigned using a `GeoPoint` instead of typical screen or `View` coordinates. Another way is to use `ItemizedOverlay`, which is especially useful if you have more than one place to mark.

Finally, you can manually draw items over the map using the `Overlay` and implement the `onDraw()` method.

For the place name finder example, we use the first method. Assuming you have a suitable map marker as a drawable resource, the following code demonstrates how to do this:

```
GeoPoint newPoint = new GeoPoint((int)(lat * 1E6), (int)(lon*1E6));


// add a view at this point
MapView.LayoutParams mapMarkerParams = new
    MapView.LayoutParams(LayoutParams.WRAP_CONTENT,
    LayoutParams.WRAP_CONTENT,
    newPoint, MapView.LayoutParams.TOP_LEFT );


ImageView mapMarker = new ImageView(getApplicationContext());
mapMarker.setImageResource(R.drawable.paw);
map.addView(mapMarker, mapMarkerParams);
```

The `MapView` layout parameters enable you to set a `GeoPoint`. Doing this allows the added `View` to stay put at a geographic location and pan with the map, as shown in Figure 11.7.

Figure 11.7   The Kremlin at the top left of the marker (paw print in a circle).

Keep in mind that the added `View` sticks around as long as the `MapView` does. If the application needs to present multiple locations to the user, though, there is a simpler way. Just use the `ItemizedOverlay` object.

In this example, a static `ItemizedOverlay` will be created to represent the chain of backpacker huts in the White Mountains along the Appalachian Trail:

```
private class HutsItemizedOverlay
    extends ItemizedOverlay<OverlayItem> {

    public HutsItemizedOverlay(Drawable defaultMarker) {}

    protected OverlayItem createItem(int i) {}
    public int size() {}
}
```

To do this, we provide implementations for each of the required methods of `ItemizedOverlay<OverlayItem>`. First, we define the constructor:

```
public HutsItemizedOverlay(Drawable defaultMarker) {
    super(defaultMarker);

    boundCenterBottom(defaultMarker);

    populate();
}
```

The `Drawable` passed in is one that we define later in the `onCreate()` method of `MapActivity`. The system does not provide a default marker. The call to the `boundCenterBottom()` method is made so that the shadow will be cast from the bottom of the marker, which is a more natural look. The default shadow is from the top. If, however, we'd rather turn off the shadow completely, the `draw()` method could be overridden, as follows:

```
@Override
public void draw(Canvas canvas, MapView mapView, boolean shadow) {
    super.draw(canvas, mapView, false);
}
```

Finally, within the constructor we call the `populate()` method. This should be done as soon as the location data is available. Because we have it statically compiled into the application, we call it before returning. The `populate()` method calls our implementation of the `createItem()` method for as many items as we defined in our implementation of the `size()` method. Here is the implementation of our `createItem()` method, along with a small array of hut locations, in no particular order:

```
public GeoPoint hutPoints[] = new GeoPoint[] {
    // Lakes of the Clouds
    new GeoPoint(44258793, -71318940),
```

```
    // Zealand Falls
    new GeoPoint(44195798, -71494402),
    // Greanleaf
    new GeoPoint(44160372, -71660385),
    // Galehead
    new GeoPoint(44187866, -71568734),
    // Carter Notch
    new GeoPoint(44259224, -71195633),
    // Mizpah Spring
    new GeoPoint(44219362, -71369473),
    // Lonesome Lake
    new GeoPoint(44138452, -71703064),
    // Madison Spring
    new GeoPoint(44327751, -71283283)
};

@Override
protected OverlayItem createItem(int i) {

    OverlayItem item = new OverlayItem(hutPoints[i], null, null);
    return item;
}
```

In the array, we've multiplied all the location values by one million so that they are in microdegrees, as required by the GeoPoint object. Within the createItem() method, the location array is indexed with the passed in value. Neither of the two text fields, Title and Snippet, are used at this time, so they are set to null. The maximum index value is determined by the size() method, which, in this case, merely has to return the length of the array:

```
@Override
public int size() {
    return hutPoints.length;
}
```

The necessary ItemizedOverlay<OverlayItem> class is now implemented. Next, the application needs to tell the MapView about it. The following code demonstrates how to do this in the onCreate() method of our MapActivity:

```
@Override
protected void onCreate(Bundle data) {
    super.onCreate(data);
    setContentView(R.layout.huts);

    Drawable marker = getResources().getDrawable(R.drawable.paw);
    marker.setBounds(0, 0,
        marker.getIntrinsicWidth(), marker.getIntrinsicHeight());

    HutsItemizedOverlay huts = new HutsItemizedOverlay(marker);
```

```
MapView map = (MapView)findViewById(R.id.map);
map.setSatellite(true);

List<Overlay> overlays = map.getOverlays();
overlays.add(huts);

FrameLayout zoomFrame = (FrameLayout)
    findViewById(R.id.map_zoom_holder);
zoomFrame.addView(map.getZoomControls());
}
```

First, the `Drawable` is retrieved from the resources. We call `setBounds()` on it to force it to draw correctly as part of an `ItemizedOverlay`. Without this, the markers will not draw. Next, we instantiate the `HutsItemizedOverlay` object. The `OverlayItems` in it need to be added to the ones that might already exist within the `MapView`. The `getOverlays()` method of `MapView` returns a list of the current `Overlay` objects. Calling the `add()` method on this list inserts our new ones for each hut. Finally, the zoom controls are added to the `MapView` so that the user can zoom in and out. After launching this application and zooming in on New Hampshire, the user should see a screen like Figure 11.8.

Figure 11.8   A map with markers at each of the Appalachian Mountain Huts of New Hampshire.

Forcing the user to pan and zoom to the location of the huts is not user-friendly. Two of the utility methods that the `ItemizedOverlay<OverlayItem>` class provides returns values for the span of the location of the items. Combining this functionality with an override to the default behavior of the `getCenter()` method, which normally returns the location of the first item, enables the map to start to draw at a convenient zoom level covering all the huts. This block of code can be added to the `onCreate()` method to do just that:

```
MapController mapControl = map.getController();

mapControl.setCenter(huts.getCenter());
mapControl.zoomToSpan(
    huts.getLatSpanE6(), huts.getLonSpanE6());
```

The `getCenter()` method computes the average latitude and the average longitude across all the given hut locations. A central point could be provided, or the first item could be placed near the center of all the points requiring no override of the `getCenter()` method.

Doing More with Location-Based Services

What's New in Android 1.5

Android 1.5 added three new classes to the `android.location` package that can provide more detailed information about the GPS satellites used by the GPS engine. These classes are `GpsStatus`, `GpsStatus.Listener`, and `GpsSatellite`. The `GpsStatus` and its `Listener` subclass monitors the GPS engine and gets a list of the satellites used. The `GpsSatellite` class represents the current state of an individual satellite used by the GPS engine with state information such as satellite elevation and whether the particular satellite was used in the most recent GPS fix.

You have been introduced to a number of different location tools provided on Android; however, you should be aware of several more.

The `LocationManager` supports Proximity Alerts, which are alerts that trigger a `PendingIntent` when the handset comes within some distance of a location. This can be useful for warning the user of an upcoming turn in directions, for scavenger hunts, or help in geocaching.

You saw how to do `ItemizedOverlays`. In general, you can assign your own `Overlays` to draw custom objects and `Views` on the given `Canvas`. This is useful for drawing pop-up information for locations, putting logos over the map that don't move with the map, or putting hints for scavenger hunts over the map. This functionality is similar to displaying photos at a given location, which are often provided on Google Maps at famous locations.

Summary

The Android SDK, with Google Maps support available to applications that register for a key, can be used to enhance Android applications with location-rich information. Some applications want to build in seamless map support, whereas others might just launch the built-in map application for the user to leverage. Developers can add to the information provided on the map by using various types of overlays to include even more information to the user. The opportunities for using location-based services to improve Android applications are only just beginning to be explored.

References and More Information

Google Maps API Key: http://code.google.com/android/add-ons/google-apis/mapkey.html

12

Using Android Multimedia APIs

Multimedia—whether it's images, videos, or sounds—has become a key driver of mobile device sales. Nowadays, a device must have, at minimum, a camera, and as the technology improves, more and more devices have sophisticated video abilities. Users commonly use handsets to take and display pictures, to record sounds, and even to watch video clips.

The Android Software Development Kit (SDK) provides a variety of methods for applications to incorporate audio and visual media, including support for many different media types and formats. Individual Android devices and developers can extend the list of supported media to other formats.

In this chapter, you learn how to capture still images using the camera, as well as record and playback audio and video files.

Working with Still Images

We illustrated how to display still images such as bitmaps by using the `ImageView` widget in Chapter 6, "Exploring User Interface Screen Elements." If the user's handset has built-in camera hardware, the user can also capture still images using the `Camera` object of the Android SDK. In addition, images can be assigned as wallpaper using some helpful methods accessed from within the `Context` object.

Capturing Still Images Using the Camera

The `Camera` object (`android.hardware.Camera`) controls the camera on handsets that have camera support enabled. The preview feature of the camera relies on the assignment of a `SurfaceHolder` of an appropriate type. This enables applications to control the placement and size of the preview area that the camera can use.

Follow these steps to add camera capture capability to an application without having to draw preview frames.

1. Create a new class extending `SurfaceView` and implement `SurfaceHolder.Callback`. For this example, we name this class `CameraSurfaceView`.

2. In the `surfaceCreated()` method, get an instance of the `Camera` object.

3. In the `surfaceChanged()` method, configure and apply the `Camera.Parameters`; then call the `startPreview()` method.

4. Add a method in `CameraSurfaceView` for capturing images.

5. Add the `CameraSurfaceView` to an appropriate layout.

6. Include some way, such as a button, for the user to trigger the capturing of images.

7. Implement a `PictureCallback` class to handle storing of the captured image.

8. Add the `android.permission.CAMERA` permission to the `AndroidManifest.xml` file.

9. Release the `Camera` object in the `surfaceDestroyed()` method.

Let's start by looking at the `CameraSurfaceView` class.

```
import android.hardware.Camera;
import android.view.SurfaceHolder;
import android.view.SurfaceView;

private class CameraSurfaceView extends SurfaceView
    implements SurfaceHolder.Callback {

    private SurfaceHolder mHolder;
    private Camera camera = null;

    public CameraSurfaceView(Context context) {
        super(context);
        mHolder = getHolder();
        mHolder.addCallback(this);
        mHolder.setType(
            SurfaceHolder.SURFACE_TYPE_PUSH_BUFFERS);
    }

    public void surfaceChanged(SurfaceHolder holder,
        int format, int width, int height) {
    }

    public void surfaceCreated(SurfaceHolder holder) {
    }

    public void surfaceDestroyed(SurfaceHolder holder) {
    }
```

```
public boolean capture(Camera.PictureCallback
    jpegHandler) {
    }
}
```

The constructor for the `CameraSurfaceView` configures the `SurfaceHolder`, including setting the `SurfaceHolder` type to `SURFACE_TYPE_PUSH_BUFFERS`, which is used by the camera internals. The constructor is appropriate for calling from an activity's `onCreate()` method. When the display is ready, the `surfaceCreated()` method will be called. Here we instantiate the `Camera` object:

```
public void surfaceCreated(SurfaceHolder holder) {
    camera = Camera.open();
    camera.setPreviewDisplay(mHolder);
}
```

The `Camera` object has a static method to retrieve a usable instance. Because the `Surface` is now available, the configured holder can now be assigned to it. Information about the `Surface` might not yet be available, but at the next call to the `surfaceChanged()` method, the camera parameters will be assigned and the preview will start, as shown here:

```
public void surfaceChanged(SurfaceHolder holder,
    int format, int width, int height) {
    Camera.Parameters params = camera.getParameters();
    params.setPreviewSize(width, height);
    camera.setParameters(params);
    camera.startPreview();
}
```

The `surfaceChanged()` method provides the application with the proper width and height for use with the camera preview. After assigning this to the `Camera` object, the preview starts. At this point, the users see whatever is in front of the camera on their device. If, however, you debug this within the emulator, you see a black-and-white checkerboard with an animated square on it, as shown in Figure 12.1. This is the simulated camera preview so camera testing can take place, to some extent, on the emulator.

Note

The format parameter passed in to the `surfaceChanged()` method is not related to the format parameter of the `setPreviewFormat()` method of the `Camera` object.

When the `Surface` is no longer displayed, the `surfaceDestroyed()` method will be called. Here is an implementation of the `surfaceDestroyed()` method suitable for this example:

```
public void surfaceDestroyed(SurfaceHolder holder) {
    camera.stopPreview();
    camera = null;
}
```

Figure 12.1   Emulator screen showing simulated camera view.

In the `surfaceDestroyed()` method, the application stops the preview and releases the
`Camera` object. If the `CameraSurfaceView` is used again, the `surfaceCreated()`
method will be called again, so this is the appropriate place to perform this operation.

The final step required to capture a still image is to add some way to call the
`takePicture()` method of the `Camera` object. `CameraSurfaceView` could provide
public access to the `Camera` object, but in this example we provide a method to perform
this within the `CameraSurfaceView` class:

```
public boolean capture(Camera.PictureCallback jpegHandler) {
    if (camera != null) {
        camera.takePicture(null, null, jpegHandler);
        return true;
    } else {
        return false;
    }
}
```

You can also use the `takePicture()` method to assign a callback suitable to play a
shutter sound, or any other action just before the image is collected from the sensor. In
addition, a `PictureCallback` can also be assigned to get raw data from the camera.

> **Note**
>
> The format of the raw camera data can vary from device to device.

The `CameraSurfaceView` object is now ready for use within an `Activity`. For this example, an `Activity` with a layout that contains a `FrameLayout` widget for positioning the preview is used. Here is a sample implementation of assigning the `cameraView` to the layout:

```
final CameraSurfaceView cameraView = new
    CameraSurfaceView(getApplicationContext());
FrameLayout frame = (FrameLayout) findViewById(R.id.frame);
frame.addView(cameraView);
```

Next, a button click handler calls the `capture()` method of the `CameraSurfaceView` object. A sample implementation is shown here:

```
public void onClick(View v) {
    cameraView.capture(new Camera.PictureCallback() {

        public void onPictureTaken(byte[] data,
            Camera camera) {
            FileOutputStream fos;

            try {
                String filename = "capture.jpg";
                fos = openFileOutput("capture.jpg",
                    MODE_WORLD_READABLE);

                fos.write(data);
                fos.close();

            } catch (Exception e) {
                Log.e("Still", "Error writing file", e);
            }
        }
    });
}
```

The data that comes back from the callback can be written out directly to a JPEG file within the application file directory. If written as shown, though, the captured image will be usable only by the application. In some cases, this might be suitable. However, the application might want to share the image with the rest of the handset, for example, by including it within the Pictures application, which uses the `MediaStore` content provider. This is done by using the `ContentResolver` object to place an entry for the image in the media library.

Note

> As of this writing, the camera permission is not validated on either the emulator or the T-Mobile G1. This means that the camera can be used without having the permission in the `AndroidManifest.xml` file. However, we recommend setting this permission explicitly so that users know the application uses the camera and so the application will continue to work if and when the permission is checked.

Sharing Images

Storing an image in the local application directory, as demonstrated, might work for some applications; however, other applications might find it useful if the image goes in the shared image library on the device. The `ContentResolver` can be used in conjunction with the `MediaStore` object to push the image into the shared image library. The following example demonstrates storing the still image taken by the camera as an image file within the `MediaStore` content provider, using the same camera image callback:

```
public void onPictureTaken(byte[] data, Camera camera) {
    Log.v("Still", "Image data received from camera");
    try {
        Bitmap bm = BitmapFactory.decodeByteArray(
            data, 0, data.length);
        String fileUrl = MediaStore.Images.Media.
            insertImage(getContentResolver(), bm,
            "Camera Still Image",
            "Camera Pic Sample App Took");

        if (fileUrl == null) {
            Log.d("Still", "Image Insert failed");
            return;
        } else {
            Uri picUri = Uri.parse(fileUrl);
            sendBroadcast(new Intent(
                Intent.ACTION_MEDIA_SCANNER_SCAN_FILE,
                picUri));
        }
    } catch (Exception e) {
        Log.e("Still", "Error writing file", e);
    }
}
```

The image is turned into a `Bitmap` object, which is passed into the `insertImage()` method. This method creates an entry in the shared image library. After the image is inserted, we use the returned URL to create a `Uri` object representing the new image's location, which we instruct the Media Scanner to pick up by broadcasting a specialized intent. Now the image will be available to all applications that use the `MediaStore` content provider, such as the Pictures application.

> **Caution**
>
> To use the `MediaStore` with the emulator, you must have a mounted SD card image.
>
> Additionally, although it's technically not necessary to force the media scanner to scan for new images, we've found that the Pictures application on the emulator and handset might crash if the `MediaStore` does not perform a scan before trying to access the image. It's a good idea to send the `Intent`.

Assigning Images as Wallpapers

Wallpapers are a great way for users to personalize their phones with interesting and fun images. Unlike other media tasks, setting a graphic as a wallpaper is handled directly through `Context` calls. The current wallpaper can be retrieved with a call to the `getWallpaper()` or `peekWallpaper()` methods. The methods `getWallpaper DesiredMinimumHeight()` and `getWallpaperDesiredMinimumWidth()` enable the application to programmatically determine the size that a wallpaper should be on the particular handset. Finally, wallpaper can be assigned through a call to the `setWallpaper()` method.

The following callback of the `Camera` object sets the wallpaper:

```
public void onPictureTaken(byte[] data, Camera camera) {
    ByteArrayInputStream bais = new
        ByteArrayInputStream(data);
    try {
        setWallpaper(bais);
    } catch (Exception e) {
        Log.e("Still", "Setting wallpaper failed.", e);
    }
}
```

The image will be copied locally for the wallpaper, so the original doesn't need to be kept, which is good in this case, because it was never written to disk. The wallpaper can be removed completely with a call to the `clearWallpaper()` method of the `Context`.

Finally, your application needs the `android.permission.SET_WALLPAPER` permission within is `AndroidManifest.xml` file.

Working with Video

In recent years, video has become commonplace on handsets. Most handsets on the market now can record and playback video, and this is no different with Android, although the specific video features might vary from handset to handset.

Recording Video

In Android 1.1, only video playback was available. However, Android 1.5 R1 introduced the capability to record video using the `MediaRecorder` object. Using `MediaRecorder` is a matter of following a few simple steps.

1. Instantiate a new `MediaRecorder` object.
2. Set the video source.
3. Set the video output format.
4. Set the video size to record (optional).
5. Set the video frame rate (optional).
6. Set the video encoder.
7. Set the file to record to. (The extension must match output format.)
8. Set the preview surface.
9. Prepare the object for recording.
10. Start the recording.
11. Stop and release the recording object when finished.

Using some standard button controls, an `Activity` can be created to record and play back video using the preceding steps. The `onClick()` method for a record button might look like this:

```
public void onClick(View v) {
    if (videoRecorder == null) {
        videoRecorder = new MediaRecorder();
    }
    String pathForAppFiles =
        getFilesDir().getAbsolutePath();
    pathForAppFiles += RECORDED_FILE;

    videoRecorder.setVideoSource(
        MediaRecorder.VideoSource.CAMERA);

    videoRecorder.setOutputFormat(
        MediaRecorder.OutputFormat.MPEG4 );

    videoRecorder.setVideoSize(640, 480);
    videoRecorder.setVideoFrameRate(30);
    videoRecorder.setVideoEncoder(
        MediaRecorder.VideoEncoder.H264);

    videoRecorder.setOutputFile(pathForAppFiles);
    videoRecorder.setPreviewDisplay(surface);
```

```
        videoRecorder.prepare();
        videoRecorder.start();

        // button handling and other behavior here
}
```

The `videoRecorder` object is instantiated and given some video configuration values for the recording source. There are several values for each video configuration setting, however, supported values can vary by device.

A stop button configured with an `onClick()` handler might look like this:

```
public void onClick(View v) {
    if (videoRecorder!= null) {
        videoRecorder.stop();
        videoRecorder.release();
        videoRecorder = null;
    }
    // button handling and other behavior here
}
```

Finally, applications wanting to record video require the explicit permission `android.permission.CAMERA` set within the `AndroidManifest.xml` file.

Now it is time to add the playback functionality, so we can watch the video we just recorded.

Playing Video

The simplest way to playback video with the Android SDK is to use the `VideoView` widget along with the `MediaController` widget to provide basic video controls. The following is an implementation of an `onCreate()` method within an `Activity` that demonstrates a workable video playback solution:

```
@Override
protected void onCreate(Bundle savedInstanceState) {
    super.onCreate(savedInstanceState);
    setContentView(R.layout.moving);

    VideoView vv = (VideoView) findViewById(R.id.video);
    MediaController mc = new MediaController(this);
    Uri video = Uri.parse(MOVIE_URL);

    vv.setMediaController(mc);
    vv.setVideoURI(video);
}
```

A simple layout file with these controls might look like Figure 12.2. The `MediaController` presents a nice `ProgressBar` that shows download completion and current location. The use of the `setAnchorView()` method of the `MediaController` is not needed when used with the `setMediaController()` method of `VideoView`—it's automatically set to the `VideoView`.

Figure 12.2   Screen showing video playback with default media controller displayed.

The call to the `setVideoURI()` method automatically starts playback. You can create a listener for when playback finishes using the `setOnCompletionListener()` method of the `ViewView`. The `VideoView` object has several other helpful methods, such as `getDuration()` and direct control over playback through methods such as `pause()`. For finer control over the media, or for an alternate way to playback media, the `MediaPlayer` object can be used. Use of it is similar to using the `Camera`—you need a `SurfaceHolder`.

Caution

The `MediaController` can't be retrieved from a layout file XML definition by a call to `findViewById()`. It must be instantiated programmatically and uses the `Activity Context`, not the `Application Context`.

Working with Audio

Much like video, the Android SDK provides methods for audio playback and recording. Audio files can be resources, local files, or Uri objects to shared or network resources. Audio recording takes place through the built-in microphone on the device, if one is present (typically a requirement for a phone because one speaks into it quite often).

Recording Audio

The MediaRecorder object of the Android SDK provides audio recording functionality. Using it is a matter of following a few simple steps you should now find familiar.

1. Instantiate a new MediaRecorder object.
2. Set the audio source.
3. Set the audio format to record with.
4. Set the file format to store the audio in.
5. Set the file to record to.
6. Prepare the object for recording.
7. Start the recording.
8. Stop and release the recording object when finished.

Using a couple simple buttons, a simple Activity can be created to record and play back audio using the preceding steps. The onClick() method for a record button might look like this:

```
public void onClick(View v) {
    if (audioRecorder == null) {
        audioRecorder = new MediaRecorder();
    }
    String pathForAppFiles =
        getFilesDir().getAbsolutePath();
    pathForAppFiles += RECORDED_FILE;

    audioRecorder.setAudioSource(
        MediaRecorder.AudioSource.MIC);
    audioRecorder.setOutputFormat(
        MediaRecorder.OutputFormat.DEFAULT);
    audioRecorder.setAudioEncoder(
        MediaRecorder.AudioEncoder.DEFAULT);

    audioRecorder.setOutputFile(pathForAppFiles);

    audioRecorder.prepare();
    audioRecorder.start();
```

```
    // button handling and other behavior here
}
```

The `audioRecorder` object is instantiated, if necessary. The default values for the recording source and output file work fine for our purposes. However, there is only one audio source (`MIC`) and audio encoder (`AMR_NB`) currently defined in the current Android SDK. This might change in a future Android SDK release. Of the three output formats available, `MPEG_4, RAW_AMR`, and `THREE_GPP`, the audio can reside in any, but defaults to an MPEG4 container.

> **Caution**
>
> If you find recording does not start, check the file extension used. For instance, when using the MPEG4 container, the Android SDK requires that the file extension is `.mp4`, otherwise the recording will not start.

A stop button is configured with an `onClick()` handler that looks like this:

```
public void onClick(View v) {
    if (audioRecorder!= null) {
        audioRecorder.stop();
        audioRecorder.release();
        audioRecorder= null;
    }
    // button handling and other behavior here
}
```

Finally, applications wanting to record audio require the explicit permission `android.permission.RECORD_AUDIO` set within the `AndroidManifest.xml` file.

Now it is time to add the playback functionality, so we can listen to the audio we just recorded.

Playing Audio

The `MediaPlayer` object can be used to play audio. The followings steps are required to prepare a file for playback:

1. Instantiate a new `MediaPlayer` object.
2. Set the path to the file using the `setDataSource` method.
3. Call the `prepare()` method of the `MediaPlayer` object.
4. Call the `start()` method to begin playback.
5. Playback can then be stopped with a call to the `stop()` method.

The `onClick()` handler for a button to play the recorded audio from the previous example might look like the following:

```
public void onClick(View v) {
    if (player == null) {
```

```
        player = new MediaPlayer ();
    }
    try {
        String audioFilePath =
            getFilesDir().getAbsolutePath();
        audioFilePath += RECORDED_FILE;

        player.setDataSource(audioFilePath);

        player.prepare();
        player.start();
    } catch (Exception e) {
        Log.e("Audio", "Playback failed.", e);
    }
}
```

The audio data source can be a local file path, valid file object, or valid `Uri` to an audio resource. The sound playback can be stopped programmatically by a call to the `stop()` method. A `MediaPlayer.OnCompletionListener` can be set to get a callback when the playback finishes. When done with the `MediaPlayer` object, a call to the `release()` method should be used to free up any resources it might be using, much like the releasing of the `MediaRecorder` object.

Sharing Audio

Audio can be shared with the rest of the system. The `ContentResolver` can send the file to the `MediaStore` content provider. The following code snippet shows how to configure an audio entry in the audio library on the device:

```
ContentValues values = new ContentValues(9);

values.put(MediaStore.MediaColumns.TITLE, "RecordedAudio");
values.put(MediaStore.Audio.Media.ALBUM,
    "Your Groundbreaking Album");
values.put(MediaStore.Audio.Media.ARTIST, "Your Name");
values.put(MediaStore.Audio.Media.DISPLAY_NAME,
    "The Audio File You Recorded In Media App");
values.put(MediaStore.Audio.Media.IS_RINGTONE, 1);
values.put(MediaStore.Audio.Media.IS_MUSIC, 1);
values.put(MediaStore.MediaColumns.DATE_ADDED,
    System.currentTimeMillis() / 1000);
values.put(MediaStore.MediaColumns.MIME_TYPE, "audio/mp4");
values.put(MediaStore.Audio.Media.DATA, pathForAppFiles);

Uri audioUri = getContentResolver().insert(
    MediaStore.Audio.Media.EXTERNAL_CONTENT_URI, values);
if (audioUri == null) {
```

```
    Log.d("Audio", "Content resolver failed");
    return;
}
```

Setting these values allows the recorded audio to be used by different audio-oriented applications on the handset. For example, setting the `IS_MUSIC` flag enables the audio file to appear in the various sections of the music player and can be sorted by its Album information. Setting the `IS_RINGTONE` flag enables the audio file to appear in the list of ringtones for the device.

Periodically, the handset scans for new media files. However, to speed up this process, a `BroadcastIntent` can be sent telling the system about new audio files. The following code demonstrates this for the audio added to the content library:

```
sendBroadcast(new Intent(
    Intent.ACTION_MEDIA_SCANNER_SCAN_FILE,audioUri));
```

After this broadcast `Intent` is handled, the audio file immediately appears in the designated applications.

Working with Ringtones

Much like wallpapers, ringtones are a popular way to personalize a handset. The Android SDK provides a variety of ways to manage ringtones through the `RingtoneManager` object. The recorded audio from the previous example can be assigned as the current ringtone with the following static method call:

```
RingtoneManager.setActualDefaultRingtoneUri(
    getApplicationContext(),
    RingtoneManager.TYPE_RINGTONE, audioUri);
```

The type can also be `TYPE_ALARM` or `TYPE_NOTIFICATION` to configure sounds of other system events that use audio tones. To successfully perform this operation, though, the application must have the `android.permission.WRITE_SETTINGS` permission set in the `AndroidManifest.xml` file. The default ringtone can also be queried with a call to the static `RingtoneManager.getActualDefaultRingtoneUri()` method. You can use the resulting `Uri` to play the ringtone, which might be useful within applications that want to alert the user.

Summary

Use of multimedia within many applications can dramatically increase their appeal, usefulness, and even usability. The Android SDK provides a variety of APIs for recording audio, video, and images using the camera and microphone hardware; it also provides the ability to play audio and video and display still images. Multimedia can be private to a specific application or shared among all applications using the `MediaStore` content provider.

13

Using Android Telephony APIs

Although the Android platform has been designed to run on almost any type of device, the Android devices available on the market are primarily phones. Applications can take advantage of this fact by integrating phone features into their feature set.

Generally speaking, developers should consider an Android device first and foremost as a phone. Although these devices might also run applications, phone operations generally take precedence. Your application should not interrupt a phone conversation, for example. To avoid this kind of behavior, your application should know something about what the user is doing, so that it can react differently. For instance, an application might query the state of the phone and determine that the user is talking on the phone and then choose to vibrate instead of play an alarm.

Phones typically support a Short Message Service (SMS), which is popular. Enabling the capability to leverage this feature from an application can enhance the appeal of the application and add features that can't be easily replicated on a desktop environment.

Finally, because it is a phone, applications that deal with phone numbers, such as a contacts database or yellow pages application, can directly access the phone dialer. This enables a more integrated user experience and enhances the overall value of the application to the users.

This chapter introduces you to various telephony-related APIs found within the Android SDK.

Working with Telephony Utilities

The Android SDK provides a number of useful utilities for applications to integrate phone features available on the device.

Among these are the ability to request the hook state of the phone, information of the phone service, and utilities for handling and verifying phone numbers. The `TelephonyManager` object within the `android.telephony` package is a great place to start.

Gaining Permission to Access Phone State Information

Many of the method calls in this section require explicit permission set with the Android application manifest file. The READ_PHONE_STATE permission is required to retrieve information such as the call state, handset phone number, and device identifiers or serial numbers. The ACCESS_COARSE_LOCATION permission is required for cellular location information. We talk more about Location-Based Services in Chapter 11, "Using Location-Based Services (LBS) APIs."

The following block of XML is typically needed in your application's AndroidManifest.xml file to access basic phone state information:

```
<uses-permission
    android:name="android.permission.READ_PHONE_STATE" />
```

Requesting Call State

You can use the TelephonyManager object to retrieve the state of the phone and some information about the phone service itself, such as the phone number of the handset.

An instance of TelephonyManager can be requested using the getSystemService() method.

```
TelephonyManager telManager = (TelephonyManager)
    getSystemService(Context.TELEPHONY_SERVICE);
```

With a valid TelephonyManager instance, an application can now make several queries. One important method is getCallState(). This method can determine the voice call status of the handset. The following block of code shows how to query for the call state and all the possible return values:

```
int callStatus = telManager.getCallState();
String callState = null;

switch (callStatus) {
        case TelephonyManager.CALL_STATE_IDLE:
            callState = "Phone is idle.";
            break;
        case TelephonyManager.CALL_STATE_OFFHOOK:
            callState = "Phone is in use.";
            break;
        case TelephonyManager.CALL_STATE_RINGING:
            callState = "Phone is ringing!";
            break;
        }
Log.i("telephony", callState);
```

The three call states can be simulated with the emulator through the Dalvik Debug Monitor Service (DDMS) tool, which is discussed in detail in Appendix B, "The Android DDMS Quick-Start Guide."

Querying for the call state can be useful in certain circumstances. However, listening for changes in the call state can allow an application to react appropriately to something the user might be doing. For instance, a game might automatically pause and save state information when the phone rings so that the users can safely answer it. An application can register to listen for changes in the call state by making a call to the `listen()` method of `TelephonyManager`.

```
telManager.listen(new PhoneStateListener() {
    public void onCallStateChanged(
        int state, String incomingNumber) {
            String newState = getCallStateString(state);
        if (state == TelephonyManager.CALL_STATE_RINGING) {
            Log.i("telephony", newState +
                " number = " + incomingNumber);
        } else {
            Log.i("telephony", newState);
        }
    }
}, PhoneStateListener.LISTEN_CALL_STATE);
```

The listener will be called, in this case, whenever the phone starts ringing, the user makes a call, the user answers a call, or a call is disconnected. The listener is also called right after it is assigned so an application can get the initial state.

Another useful state of the phone is determining the state of the service. This information can tell an application if the phone has coverage at all, if it can only make emergency calls, or if the radio for phone calls is turned off as it might be when in airplane mode. To do this, an application can add the `PhoneStateListener.LISTEN_SERVICE_STATE` flag to the listener above and implement the `onServiceStateChanged` method, which receives an instance of the `ServiceState` object. Alternatively, an application can check the state by constructing a `ServiceState` object and querying it directly, as shown here.

```
int serviceStatus = serviceState.getState();
String serviceStateString = null;
switch (serviceStatus) {

    case ServiceState.STATE_EMERGENCY_ONLY:
        serviceStateString = "Emergency calls only";
        break;

    case ServiceState.STATE_IN_SERVICE:
        serviceStateString = "Normal service";
        break;

    case ServiceState.STATE_OUT_OF_SERVICE:
        serviceStateString = "No service available";
        break;
```

```
        case ServiceState.STATE_POWER_OFF:
            serviceStateString = "Telephony radio is off";
            break;
    }
Log.i("telephony", serviceStateString);
```

In addition, status such as whether the handset is roaming can be determined by a call to the `getRoaming()` method. A friendly and frugal application can use this method to warn the user before performing any costly roaming operations such as data transfers within the application.

Requesting Service Information

In addition to call and service state information, other information about the device can be retrieved. This information is less useful for the typical application but can diagnose problems or provide specialized services available only when on certain provider networks. The following code retrieves several pieces of service information.

```
String opName = telManager.getNetworkOperatorName();
Log.i("telephony", "operator name = " + opName);

String phoneNumber = telManager.getLine1Number();
Log.i("telephony", "phone number = " + phoneNumber);

String providerName = telManager.getSimOperatorName();
Log.i("telephony", "provider name = " + providerName);
```

The network operator name is the descriptive name of the current provider that the handset connects to. This is typically the current tower operator. The SIM operator name is typically the name of the provider that the user is subscribed to for service. The phone number for this application programming interface (API) is defined as the MSIDN, typically the directory number of a GSM handset—the number someone would dial to reach it.

Working with Phone Numbers

Applications that deal with telephony, or even just contacts, frequently have to deal with the input, verification, and usage of phone numbers. The Android SDK includes a set of helpful utility functions that simplify handling of phone numbers strings. Applications can have phone numbers formatted based on the current locale setting. For example, the following code uses the `formatNumber()` method:

```
String formattedNumber =
    PhoneNumberUtils.formatNumber("9995551212");
Log.i("telephony", formattedNumber);
```

The resulting output to the log would be the string "999-555-1212" in my locale. Phone numbers can also be compared using a call to the `PhoneNumberUtils`.

compare() method. An application can also check to see if a given phone number is an emergency phone number by calling PhoneNumberUtils.isEmergencyNumber(). Checking this can be used to warn a user before they call an emergency number. This method is useful when the source of the phone number data might be questionable. In SDK Version 1.5, a new utility method called formatJapaneseNumber() was added for formatting numbers with special prefixes in the Japanese style.

The formatNumber() method can also take an Editable as a parameter to format a number in place. The useful feature here is that the PhoneNumberFormattingTextWatcher object can be assigned to watch a TextView (or EditText for user input) and format phone numbers as they are entered. The following code demonstrates the ease of config-uring an EditText to format phone numbers that are entered:

```
EditText numberEntry = (EditText) findViewById(R.id.number_entry);
    numberEntry.addTextChangedListener(
        new PhoneNumberFormattingTextWatcher());
```

While the user is typing in a valid phone number, the number will be formatted in a way suitable for the current locale. Just the numbers for "19995551212" were entered on the EditText shown in Figure 13.1.

Figure 13.1   Screen showing formatting results after entering only digits.

Using SMS

SMS usage has become ubiquitous in the last several years. Integrating messaging services, even if only outbound, to an application can provide familiar social functionality to
the user. SMS functionality is provided to applications through the `android.-`
`telephony.gsm` package.

> **Caution**
>
> The current version of the Android SDK uses the `android.telephony.gsm` package. If
> Android runs on a device that is something other than a GSM device, this package might
> not work.

Gaining Permission to Send and Receive SMS Messages

SMS functionality requires two different permissions, depending on if the application
sends or receives messages. The following XML, to be placed with
`AndroidManifest.xml`, shows the permissions needed for both actions:

```
<uses-permission
    android:name="android.permission.SEND_SMS" />
<uses-permission
    android:name="android.permission.RECEIVE_SMS" />
```

Sending an SMS

To send an SMS, an application first needs to get an instance of the `SmsManager`. Unlike
other system services, this is achieved by calling the static method `getDefault()` of
`SmsManager`:

```
final SmsManager sms = SmsManager.getDefault();
```

Now that the application has the `SmsManager`, sending SMS is as simple as a single call.

```
Sms.sendTextMessage(
    "9995551212", null, "Hello!", null, null);
```

The application will not know if the actual sending of the SMS was successful or not
without providing a `PendingIntent` to receive the broadcast of this information. The
following code demonstrates configuring a `PendingIntent` to listen for the status of the
SMS:

```
Intent msgSent = new Intent("ACTION_MSG_SENT");

final PendingIntent pendingMsgSent =
    PendingIntent.getBroadcast(this, 0, msgSent, 0);
registerReceiver(new BroadcastReceiver() {
    public void onReceive(Context context, Intent intent) {
```

```
        int result = getResultCode();
        if (result != Activity.RESULT_OK) {
            Log.e("telephony",
                "SMS send failed code = " + result);
            pendingMsgReceipt.cancel();
        } else {
            messageEntry.setText("");
        }


    }
}, new IntentFilter("ACTION_MSG_SENT"));
```

The `PendingIntent pendingMsgSent` can be used with the call to the `sendTextMessage()`. The code for the message-received receipt is similar but is called when the sending handset receives acknowledgment back from the network that the destination handset received the message.

If we put all this together with the preceding phone number formatting `EditText`, a new entry field for the message, and a button, we can create a simple form for sending an SMS message. The code for the button handling will look like the following:

```
Button sendSMS = (Button) findViewById(R.id.send_sms);
sendSMS.setOnClickListener(new View.OnClickListener() {
    public void onClick(View v) {
        String destination =
            numberEntry.getText().toString();

        String message =
            messageEntry.getText().toString();

        sms.sendTextMessage(destination, null, message,
            pendingMsgSent, pendingMsgReceipt);

        registerReceiver(…);
    }
}
```

After this code is hooked in, the result should look something like Figure 13.2. Within this application we used the emulator "phone number" trick (its port number). This is a great way to test sending SMS messages without using hardware or without incurring charges by the handset operator.

A great way to extend this would be to set the sent receiver to modify a graphic on the screen until the sent notification is received. Further, another graphic could be used to indicate when the recipient has received the message. Alternatively, `ProgressBar` widgets could be used to track the progress to the user.

Figure 13.2   Two emulators, one sending an SMS from an application
and one receiving an SMS.

Receiving an SMS

Applications can also receive SMS messages. To do so, your application must register a
`BroadcastReceiver` to listen for the `Intent` action associated with receiving an SMS.
An application listening to SMS in this way doesn't prevent the message from getting to
other applications.

Expanding on the previous example, the following code shows how any incoming
text message can be placed within a `TextView` on the screen.

```
final TextView receivedMessage = (TextView)findViewById(
    R.id.received_message);

rcvIncoming = new BroadcastReceiver() {

    public void onReceive(Context context, Intent intent) {
        Log.i("telephony", "SMS received");
        Bundle data = intent.getExtras();
        if (data != null) {
            Object pdus[] =
```

```
                    (Object[]) data.get("pdus");

                String message = "New message:\n";
                String sender = null;

                for (Object pdu : pdus) {
                    SmsMessage part = SmsMessage.
                        createFromPdu((byte[])pdu);

                    message += part.
                        getDisplayMessageBody();

                    if (sender == null) {
                        sender = part.
                            getDisplayOriginatingAddress();
                    }
                }
                receivedMessage.setText(
                    message + "\nFrom: "+sender);
                numberEntry.setText(sender);
            }
        }
};

registerReceiver(rcvIncoming, new IntentFilter(
    "android.provider.Telephony.SMS_RECEIVED"));
```

This block of code is placed within the onCreate() method of the Activity. First, the
message Bundle is retrieved. In it, an array of Objects holds several byte arrays that contain PDU data—the data format that is customarily used by wireless messaging protocols. Luckily, the Android SDK can decode these with a call to the static
SmsMessage.createFromPdu() utility method. From here, we can retrieve the body of
the SMS message by calling getDisplayMessageBody().

The message that comes in might be longer than the limitations for an SMS. If it is, it
will have been broken up in to a multipart message on the sending side. To handle this,
we loop through each of the received Object parts and take the corresponding body
from each while only taking the sender address from the first.

> **Tip**
>
> When dealing with multipart text messages, it's important to know that the user might be
> charged the full texting charge for each part of the message. This can add up quickly. Care
> should be taken to warn users that applications that use any text messaging, sending or
> receiving, might incur charges by their operator.
>
> An application can send a similar multipart message by taking advantage of the
> SmsManager.divideMessage() method. This method breaks up a String into parts
> no larger than the maximum size allowed by the SMS specification. The application could
> then use the method called sendMultipartTextMessage(), passing in the result of
> the call to divideMessage().

Next, the code updates the text string in the `TextView` to show the user the received message, as shown in Figure 13.3. The sender address is also updated so that the recipient can respond with less typing.

Figure 13.3   The application shows the message at the bottom and
places the sender number in the phone number field.

Finally, we register the `BroadcastReceiver` with the system. The `IntentFilter` used here, `android.provider.Telephony.SMS`, is a well-known, but undocumented, `IntentFilter` used for this. As such, we have to use the string literal for it.

Caution

We strongly recommend watching for updates to the Android SDK in relation to this functionality. Future versions of the SDK might either add this string officially or remove the feature entirely.

Making Phone Calls

It might come as a surprise to the younger generation, but phones are often still used for making phone calls. You've seen how to find out if the handset is ringing. Now you learn how your application can make a phone call.

Building on the previous example, which sent and received SMS messages, we now walk through similar functionality that adds a call button to the screen to call the phone number instead of messaging it.

The Android SDK enables phone numbers to be passed to the dialer in two different ways. The first way is to launch the dialer with a phone number already entered. The user then needs to press the Send button to actually initiate the call. This method does not require any specific permissions. The second way is to actually place the call. This method requires the `android.permission.CALL_PHONE` permission to be added to the application's `AndroidManifest.xml` file.

> ### Caution
>
> Although the `android.permission.CALL_PHONE` permission is required for immediately calling a number when using the T-Mobile G1 handset, this permission is not enforced on the emulator as of this writing. Remember to test on actual devices to verify correct behavior.

The following code demonstrates how to launch the dialer after the user presses the Call button. We extract the phone number the user entered in the `EditText` field (or the most recently received SMS when continuing with the previous example).

```
Button call = (Button) findViewById(R.id.call_button);
call.setOnClickListener(new View.OnClickListener() {
    public void onClick(View v) {
        Uri number = Uri.parse("tel:" +
            numberEntry.getText().toString());
        Intent dial = new Intent(
            Intent.ACTION_DIAL, number);
        startActivity(dial);
    }
});
```

First, the phone number is requested from the `EditText` and `"tel:"` is prepended to it, making it a valid `Uri` for the `Intent`. Then, a new `Intent` is created with `Intent.ACTION_DIAL` to launch in to the dialer with the number dialed in already. `Intent.ACTION_VIEW` can also be used and functions the same. Replacing it with `Intent.ACTION_CALL`, however, immediately calls the number entered. This is generally not recommended; otherwise, calls might be made by mistake. Finally, the `startActivity()` method is called to launch the dialer, as shown in Figure 13.4.

> ### Tip
>
> Two emulator instances can also be used to test calling to another handset. As with the SMS sending, the port number of the emulator is the phone number that can be called.

Figure 13.4   One emulator calling the other after pressing the Call button within the application.

Summary

The Android SDK provides many helpful telephony utilities to handle making and receiving phone calls and SMS messages (with appropriate permissions) and tools to help with formatting phone numbers entered by the user or from other sources.

These telephony utilities enable applications to work seamlessly with the device's core phone features. Developers might also integrate voice calls and messaging features into their own applications, resulting in compelling new features. Messaging is more popular than ever, so integrating text messaging into an application can add a familiar and exciting social feature that users will likely enjoy.

References and More Information

3GPP Specifications (SMS): /www.3gpp.org/specifications
Wikipedia on SMS: http://en.wikipedia.org/wiki/SMS

## 14

Using Android 3D Graphics with OpenGL ES

The world around us is not two-dimensional but rich with depth. Although the phone display is a flat surface, presenting games and applications with visual depth has long been a way to enhance and add realism to them. For this purpose, the Android Software Development Kit (SDK) provides an implementation of OpenGL ES.

OpenGL ES is a graphics application programming interface (API) for embedded systems based on the OpenGL desktop standard. It is popular on wireless platforms and is supported on all major mobile phone platforms, including Windows Mobile, Symbian, BREW, Apple iPhone, and now Android. In its current form, Android supports OpenGL ES 1.0. There is limited support for OpenGL ES 1.1 within Android, but it is not complete so we will not discuss it here.

This chapter discusses how to use OpenGL ES in the Android SDK. Familiarity with OpenGL concepts can be helpful. This chapter does not teach you OpenGL, but it shows you how to perform a variety of common tasks with OpenGL ES on Android devices. These include configuring EGL and GL, drawing objects, animating objects and scenes, lighting a scene, and texturing objects.

Defining OpenGL ES

Before 1992, Silicon Graphics (SGI) had a proprietary graphics standard called Integrated Raster Imaging System Graphics Library (IRIS GL) and known typically as just GL. In 1992, to clean up the code and make GL more maintainable, SGI created OpenGL and set up a consortium of companies to maintain the open standard form of GL. Today, this consortium is known as the nonprofit Khronos Group, with more than 100 member companies. OpenGL ES was developed in the early 2000s to extend this open library to embedded devices. OpenGL ES is a subset of OpenGL. EGL was developed shortly thereafter to provide a common interface layer to native platform graphics.

Within the interfaces, OpenGL is simply referred to as GL. This is true within OpenGL ES, as well. Within the text of this chapter, GL typically refers to the underlying objects and interfaces within OpenGL to be consistent with the naming conventions within the code. OpenGL ES typically refers to the Android implementation of the OpenGL ES subset of OpenGL. Finally, OpenGL is used in a more generic fashion to refer to the generic concept or library.

Using OpenGL ES for 3D Applications with Android

Using OpenGL ES on Android is a mix of using Android `View` object concepts and regular OpenGL ES concepts. As with many problems, there are multiple solutions. We present one method for getting OpenGL up and running on the Android SDK, but there are other methods available.

The following steps to initialize OpenGL ES enable you to start drawing on the screen via the OpenGL interface:

1. Initialize `SurfaceView` with a surface of type `SURFACE_TYPE_GPU`.
2. Start a thread for OpenGL; all OpenGL calls will be performed on this thread.
3. Initialize EGL.
4. Initialize GL.
5. Start drawing!

When OpenGL ES is initialized on a particular thread of your application, all subsequent calls must be on this same thread; otherwise, they will fail. Although you can use your application's main thread, the extra processing and loops can cause your application to become less responsive. This does introduce some thread synchronization consequences that must be handled. We discuss this later in the chapter.

> **Note**
>
> There are various examples of using OpenGL ES with Android provided on the CD and Web site, including code for drawing a triangle (`BasicGL.java`), drawing a cube (`BasicGLCube.java`), drawing a lit cube (`SimpleLitGLCube.java`), displaying performance (`SimpleFPSDisplay.java`), and texturing the cube (`TextureGL.java`). The main entry point is `OpenGLPlay.java`, which provides a menu to these items to see the results.

Creating Your `SurfaceView`

What's New in Android 1.5

Starting with Android 1.5, the Android SDK provides the `GLSurfaceView` and `GLSurfaceView.Renderer` classes. Essentially, the `GLSurfaceView` class handles the EGL initialization, threading, and calls in to a user-defined `Renderer` class. The `Renderer` class handles the drawing and GL initialization. Toward the end of this chapter, we give an example of how this works. Additionally, the code is provided in the `AndroidOpenGL.java` file included with the OpenGL project for this book.

We have also provided a custom implementation of leveraging OpenGL without using `GLSurfaceView` for users who need to develop for Android versions previous to Android 1.5 or who have a need for tighter control of the rendering pipeline and initialization. The concepts for either method don't change, though, making this discussion useful even if you choose to use only the included `GLSurfaceView` method.

The first step to drawing fancy 3D graphics on the screen is to create your `SurfaceView`. This involves extending `SurfaceView` and implementing callbacks for `SurfaceHolder.Callback`. The following is an empty implementation that we complete shortly:

```
private class BasicGLSurfaceView
    extends SurfaceView
    implements SurfaceHolder.Callback {

    SurfaceHolder mAndroidHolder;

    BasicGLSurfaceView(Context context) {
        super(context);
        mAndroidHolder = getHolder();
        mAndroidHolder.addCallback(this);
        mAndroidHolder.setType(
            SurfaceHolder.SURFACE_TYPE_GPU);
    }

    public void surfaceChanged(SurfaceHolder holder,
        int format, int width, int height) {}

    public void surfaceCreated(SurfaceHolder holder) {}

    public void surfaceDestroyed(SurfaceHolder holder) {}
}
```

First, within the constructor, `getHolder()` is called to get and store the `SurfaceHolder`. Because the `SurfaceView` implements the `SurfaceHolder.Callback` interface, this `SurfaceView` is assigned for receiving callbacks for those events. Finally, the surface type must be set to `SURFACE_TYPE_GPU` for OpenGL ES calls to work on it. This class is initialized and set as the content `View` for the activity as follows:

```
protected void onCreate(Bundle savedInstanceState) {
    super.onCreate(savedInstanceState);
    mAndroidSurface = new BasicGLSurfaceView(this);
    setContentView(mAndroidSurface);
}
```

Although setting the `SurfaceView` as the entire content `View` works fine, it isn't flexible if you want other functionality on the screen besides the 3D area. One way to place the `SurfaceView` on your screen and still have the benefits of using an XML layout file is to use one of the container widgets, such as `FrameLayout`, and add this `View` to it. For instance, consider this `FrameLayout` definition, which can exist anywhere within a layout:

```
<FrameLayout
    android:id="@+id/gl_container"
    android:layout_height="100px"
    android:layout_width="100px" />
```

This puts a 100×100 pixel square container somewhere on the screen, depending on the rest of the layout. Now, the following code uses the identifier for this `FrameLayout` to place the child `SurfaceView` within the `FrameLayout`.

```
mAndroidSurface = new TextureGLSurfaceView(this);
setContentView(R.layout.constrained);
FrameLayout v = (FrameLayout) findViewById(R.id.gl_container);
v.addView(mAndroidSurface);
```

In this example, `R.layout.constrained` is our layout resource, which contains the `FrameLayout` with the particular identifier we used. You see why this works regardless of what is drawn in the OpenGL surface as we continue through the initialization of OpenGL ES on Android.

Starting Your OpenGL ES Thread

Within Android you can update only the screen from the main thread of your application, sometimes referred to as the UI thread. The `SurfaceView` widget, however, is used so that we can offload graphics processing to a secondary thread, which can update this part of the screen. This will be our OpenGL thread. Like updating the screen from the UI thread, all OpenGL calls must be within the same thread.

Recall that the `SurfaceView` presented also implemented the `SurfaceHolder.Callback` interface. The underlying surface of the `SurfaceView` is accessible only after surfaceCreated() has been called and before surfaceDestroyed() is called. Between these two calls is the only time that we have a valid surface for our OpenGL instance to draw to.

As such, we won't bother creating the OpenGL thread until surfaceCreated() is called. The following is an example implementation of surfaceCreate(), which starts up the OpenGL thread:

```
public void surfaceCreated(SurfaceHolder holder) {
    mGLThread = new BasicGLThread(this);
    mGLThread.start();
}
```

As promised, little more than launching the thread takes place here. The SurfaceView is passed to the thread. This is done because the OpenGL calls need to know which SurfaceView to draw upon.

The BasicGLThread class is an implementation of a Thread that contains the code we run in the OpenGL thread described. The following code block shows which functionality is placed where. The BasicGLThread is placed as a private member of the Activity class.

```
private class BasicGLThread extends Thread {
    SurfaceView sv;
    BasicGLThread(SurfaceView view) {
        sv = view;
    }

    private boolean mDone = false;
    public void run() {
        initEGL();
        initGL();
        while (!mDone) {
            // drawing code
        }
    }

    public void requestStop() {
        mDone = true;
        try {
            join();
        } catch (InterruptedException e) {
            Log.e("GL", "failed to stop gl thread", e);
        }
        cleanupGL();
    }

    public void cleanupGL() {}
```

```
    public void initGL() {}
    public void initEGL() {}

    // main OpenGL variables
}
```

During creation, the `SurfaceView` is saved for later use. In the `run()` method, EGL and GL are initialized, which we describe later in this chapter. Then, the drawing code is executed either once or, as shown here, in a loop. Finally, the thread can safely be stopped from outside the thread with a call to the `requestStop()` method. This also cleans up the OpenGL resources. More on this is found in the section "Cleaning Up OpenGL ES" later in this chapter.

Initializing EGL

Up to this point, the application has a `SurfaceView` with a valid `Surface` and an OpenGL thread that has just been launched. The first step with most OpenGL implementations is to initialize EGL, or the native hardware. This is done in basically the same way each time and is a good block of code to write once and reuse. The following steps must be performed to initialize EGL on Android:

1. Get the EGL object.
2. Initialize the display.
3. Get a configuration.
4. Link the `EGLSurface` to an Android `SurfaceView`.
5. Create the EGL context.
6. Tell EGL which display, surface, and context to use.
7. Get our GL object for use in rendering.

The Android SDK provides some utility classes for use with OpenGL ES. The first of these is the `GLDebugHelper` class. OpenGL calls don't directly return errors. Instead, they set an error internally that can be queried. You can use the `GLDebugHelper` class to wrap all EGL and GL calls and have the wrapper check for errors and throw an exception. The first call for getting the EGL object uses this wrapper, as shown here:

```
mEGL = (EGL10) GLDebugHelper.wrap(
    EGLContext.getEGL(),
    GLDebugHelper.CONFIG_CHECK_GL_ERROR |
    GLDebugHelper.CONFIG_CHECK_THREAD,
    null);
```

Here, the `EGL10` object is retrieved and wrapped. Turning on the `CONFIG_CHECK_GL_ERROR` flag checks for all GL Errors. In addition, the wrapper makes sure all our GL and EGL calls will be made from the correct thread since `CONFIG_CHECK_THREAD` is enabled.

Now we can proceed with initializing the display, as shown here:

```
mGLDisplay = mEGL.eglGetDisplay(EGL10.EGL_DEFAULT_DISPLAY);
```

The default display, `EGL10.EGL_DEFAULT_DISPLAY`, is configured by the internals of the Android implementation of OpenGL ES. Now that we have the display, we can initialize EGL and get the version of the implementation:

```
int[] curGLVersion = new int[2];
mEGL.eglInitialize(mGLDisplay, curGLVersion);
```

For now, the version is typically 1.0. This is true on both the emulator and the current hardware of the T-Mobile G1. With the display initialized, we can request which configuration is closest to the one we require.

```
int[] mConfigSpec = { EGL10.EGL_RED_SIZE, 5,
                      EGL10.EGL_GREEN_SIZE, 6,
                      EGL10.EGL_BLUE_SIZE, 5,
                      EGL10.EGL_DEPTH_SIZE, 16,
                      EGL10.EGL_NONE };
EGLConfig[] configs = new EGLConfig[1];
int[] num_config = new int[1];
mEGL.eglChooseConfig(mGLDisplay, mConfigSpec,
                     configs, 1, num_config);
mGLConfig = configs[0];
```

The preceding configuration works on the emulator and the current hardware. If you are unsure that the configuration you've chosen will for work with your application's target platforms, this is a good way to check the resulting list of configurations.

Now we can create the EGL surface based on this configuration:

```
mGLSurface = mEGL.eglCreateWindowSurface
    (mGLDisplay, mGLConfig, sv.getHolder(), null);
```

Recall that we stored our `SurfaceView` for use later. Here, we use it to pass the native Android surface to EGL so they can be linked up correctly. We still need to get the EGL context before we can finalize and get our instance of the GL object.

```
mGLContext = mEGL.eglCreateContext(
    mGLDisplay, mGLConfig,EGL10.EGL_NO_CONTEXT, null);
```

Now that we have our display, surface, and context, we can get our GL object.

```
mEGL.eglMakeCurrent(mGLDisplay, mGLSurface,
    mGLSurface, mGLContext);
mGL = (GL10) GLDebugHelper.wrap(
    mGLContext.getGL(),
    GLDebugHelper.CONFIG_CHECK_GL_ERROR |
    GLDebugHelper.CONFIG_CHECK_THREAD, null);
```

Once again, we use `GLDebugHelper` to wrap the GL object so that it checks errors and confirms the thread for us. This completes the initialize of EGL on Android. Next, we can initialize GL to set up our projection and other rendering options.

Initializing GL

Now the fun begins. We have EGL fully initialized, and we have a valid GL object, so now we can initialize our drawing space. For this example, we won't be drawing anything complex. We leave most options at their default values.

Typically, one of the first calls made to initialize GL is to set the viewport. Here is an example of how to set the viewport to the same dimensions as our `SurfaceView`:

```
int width = sv.getWidth();
int height = sv.getHeight();
mGL.glViewport(0, 0, width, height);
```

The location of the surface on the screen is determined internally by EGL. We will also use the following width and height of the `SurfaceView` to determine the aspect ratio for GL to render in. In the following code, we complete the configuration of a basic GL projection setup.

```
mGL.glMatrixMode(GL10.GL_PROJECTION);
mGL.glLoadIdentity();
float aspect = (float) width/height;
GLU.gluPerspective(mGL, 45.0f, aspect, 1.0f, 30.0f);
mGL.glClearColor(0.5f,0.5f,0.5f,1);
```

The Android SDK provides a few helpers similar to those found in GLUT (OpenGL Utility Toolkit). Here, we use one of them to define a perspective in terms of the vertical angle of view, aspect ratio, and near and far clipping planes. The `gluPerspective()` method is useful for configuring the projection matrix, which transforms the 3D scene into a flat surface. Finally, we clear the screen to gray.

Drawing

Now that EGL and GL are initialized, objects can be drawn to the screen. For this example, to demonstrate that we've set everything up to actually draw, we put a simple three-vertex flat surface (in layman's terms, a triangle) on the screen. Here is some sample code to do this:

```
mGL.glMatrixMode(GL10.GL_MODELVIEW);
mGL.glLoadIdentity();
GLU.gluLookAt(mGL, 0, 0, 10f, 0, 0, 0, 0, 1, 0f);
mGL.glColor4f(1f, 0f, 0f, 1f);
while (!mDone) {
    mGL.glClear(GL10.GL_COLOR_BUFFER_BIT |
        GL10.GL_DEPTH_BUFFER_BIT);
```

```
mGL.glRotatef(1f, 0, 0, 1f);

triangle.draw(mGL);

mEGL.eglSwapBuffers(mGLDisplay, mGLSurface);
}
```

If it looks like something is missing, you are correct. This code doesn't actually show the draw command for the triangle. However, it does use an Android SDK utility method to transform the model view matrix with the intuitive `gluLookAt()` method. Here, it sets the eye point 10 units away from the origin and looks toward the origin. The up value is, as usual, set to the positive y-axis. Within the loop, notice that the identity matrix is not assigned. This gives the `glRotatef()` method a compounding effect, causing the triangle to rotate in a counter-clockwise direction. In the next section, "Drawing 3D Objects," we discuss the details of drawing with OpenGL ES in Android.

When launched, a screen similar to that in Figure 14.1 should display.

Figure 14.1   A red triangle rendered using OpenGL ES on the Android
emulator.

You now have a working OpenGL ES environment within the Android SDK. We continue from this point to talk more about drawing within the environment.

Drawing 3D Objects

Now that you have the OpenGL ES environment working within Android, it's time to do some actual drawing. This section leads you through a number of examples, each building upon the previous. In doing so, these examples introduce new Android-specific concepts with OpenGL ES.

Drawing Your Vertices

OpenGL ES supports two primary drawing calls, `glDrawArrays()` and `glDrawElements()`. Both of these methods require the use of a vertex buffer assigned through a call to `glVertexPointer`. Because Android runs on top of Java, though, an arbitrary array cannot just be passed in as the array contents might move around in memory. Instead, we have to use a `ByteBuffer`, `FloatBuffer`, or `IntBuffer` so the data stays at the same location in memory. Converting various arrays to buffers is common, so we have implemented some helper methods. Here is one for converting a float array into a `FloatBuffer`:

```
FloatBuffer getFloatBufferFromFloatArray(float array[]) {
    ByteBuffer tempBuffer =
        ByteBuffer.allocateDirect(array.length * 4);
    tempBuffer.order(ByteOrder.nativeOrder());
    FloatBuffer buffer = tempBuffer.asFloatBuffer();
    buffer.put(array);
    buffer.position(0);
    return buffer;
}
```

This creates a buffer of 32-bit float values with a stride of 0. The resulting `FloatBuffer` can then be stored and assigned to OpenGL calls. Here is an example of doing this, using the triangle we showed previously in this chapter:

```
float[] vertices = {
    -0.559016994f, 0, 0,
    0.25f, 0.5f, 0f,
    0.25f, -0.5f, 0f
};
mVertexBuffer = getFloatBufferFromFloatArray(vertices);
```

With the buffer assigned, we can now draw the triangle, as shown here:

```
void drawTriangle(GL10 gl) {
    gl.glEnableClientState(GL10.GL_VERTEX_ARRAY);
    gl.glVertexPointer(3, GL10.GL_FLOAT, 0, mVertexBuffer);
    gl.glDrawArrays(GL10.GL_TRIANGLES, 0, 3);
}
```

We have to enable the GL_VERTEX_ARRAY state, though this could be done in GL configuration, as it is required to draw anything with OpenGL ES. We then assign the vertex buffer through a call to glVertexPointer(), also telling GL that we're using float values. Fixed point values, through GL_FIXED, can also be used and might be faster with some Android implementations. Finally, a call to glDrawArrays() is made to draw the triangles using three vertices from the first one. The result of this can be seen in Figure 14.1.

Coloring Your Vertices

In OpenGL ES, you can use an array of colors to individually assign colors to each vertex that will be drawn. This is accomplished by calling the glColorPointer() method with a buffer of colors. The following code sets up a small buffer of colors for three vertices:

```
float[] colors = {
    1f, 0, 0, 1f,
    0, 1f, 0, 1f,
    0, 0, 1f, 1f
    };
mColorBuffer = getFloatBufferFromFloatArray(colors);
```

With the buffer available, we can now use it to color our triangle, as shown in the following code:

```
void drawColorful(GL10 gl) {
    gl.glEnableClientState(GL10.GL_COLOR_ARRAY);
    gl.glColorPointer(4,GL10.GL_FLOAT, 0, mColorBuffer);
    draw(gl);
    gl.glDisableClientState(GL10.GL_COLOR_ARRAY);
}
```

First, the client state for GL_COLOR_ARRAY is enabled. Then, calling the glColorPointer method sets the preceding color buffer created. The call to draw() draws the triangle like the colorful one seen in Figure 14.2.

Figure 14.2   A triangle with red, green, and blue vertices smoothly blended.

Drawing More Complex Objects

A standard cube has eight vertices. However, in OpenGL ES, each of the six faces needs
to be drawn with two triangles. Each of these triangles needs three vertices. That's a total
of 36 vertices to draw an object with just 8 of its own vertices. There must be a better
way.

OpenGL ES supports index arrays. An index array is a list of vertex indexes from the
current vertex array. The index array must be a buffer, and in this example we use a
`ByteBuffer` because we don't have many vertices to indicate. The index array lists the
order that the vertices should be drawn when used with `glDrawElements()`. Note that
the color arrays (and normal arrays that we get to shortly) are still relative to the vertex
array and not the index array. Here is some code that draws an OpenGL cube using just
eight defined vertices:

```
float vertices[] = {
    -1,1,1, 1,1,1, 1,-1,1, -1,-1,1,
    1,1,-1, -1,1,-1, -1,-1,-1, 1,-1,-1
};
byte indices[] = {
```

```
    0,1,2, 2,3,0,  1,4,7, 7,2,1,  0,3,6, 6,5,0,
    3,2,7, 7,6,3,  0,1,4, 4,5,0,  5,6,7, 7,4,5
};
FloatBuffer vertexBuffer =
    getFloatBufferFromFloatArray(vertices);
ByteBuffer indexBuffer =
    getByteBufferFromByteArray(indices);
gl.glVertexPointer(3, GL10.GL_FLOAT, 0, vertexBuffer);
gl.glDrawElements(GL10.GL_TRIANGLES, indices.length,
    GL10.GL_UNSIGNED_BYTE, indexBuffer);
```

The vertices define the typical shape for a cube. Then, however, we use the index array
to define in what order the vertices will be drawn to create the cube out of the 12 triangles that we need (recalling that OpenGL ES does not support quads). Now you have
a red shape on your screen that looks like Figure 14.3 (a). It doesn't actually look much
like a cube, though, does it? Without some shading, it looks too much like a random
polygon. If, however, the `glDrawElements()` is switched to `GL_LINE_LOOP` instead of
`GL_TRIANGLES`, you see a line-drawing version of the shape, like Figure 14.3 (b). Now
you can see that it really is a cube. The vertices buffer can be reused with different index
buffers, too. This is useful if you can define multiple shapes using the same set of vertices
and then draw them in their own locations with transformations.

Figure 14.3   (a) A solid cube with no shading and (b) the same cube
with only lines.

Lighting Your Scene

The last 3D object that we drew was a cube that looked like some strange polygon on your flat, 2D screen. The colors of each face could be made different by applying coloring between each call to draw a face. However, that will still produce a fairly flat looking cube. Instead, why not shine some light on the scene and let the lighting give the cube some additional depth?

Before you can provide lighting on a scene, each vertex of each surface needs a vector applied to it to define how the light will reflect and, thus, how it will be rendered. Although this vector can be anything, most often it is perpendicular to the surface defined by the vertices; this is called the normal of a surface. Recalling our cube from the preceding example, we see now that a cube can't actually be created out of eight vertices as each vertex can carry only one normal array, and we would need three per vertex because each vertex belongs to three faces. Instead, we have to use a cube that does, in fact, contain the entire lot of 24 vertices. (Technically, you could define a bunch of index arrays and change the normal array between calls to each face, but it's more commonly done with a large list of vertices and a single list of normal vectors.)

Like the color array, the normal array is applied to each vertex in the vertex array in order. Lighting is a fairly complex topic and if it's unfamiliar, you need to check out the Reference section at the end of this chapter where you can learn more. For now, we just give an example of how to use the lighting features of Open GL ES within Android.

Here is some code for enabling simple lighting:

```
mGL.glEnable(GL10.GL_LIGHTING);
mGL.glEnable(GL10.GL_LIGHT0);
mGL.glLightfv(GL10.GL_LIGHT0, GL10.GL_AMBIENT,
    new float[] {0.1f, 0.1f, 0.1f, 1f}, 0);
mGL.glLightfv(GL10.GL_LIGHT0, GL10.GL_DIFFUSE,
    new float[] {1f, 1f, 1f, 1f}, 0);
mGL.glLightfv(GL10.GL_LIGHT0, GL10.GL_POSITION,
    new float[] {10f, 0f, 10f, 1f}, 0);
mGL.glEnable(GL10.GL_COLOR_MATERIAL);
mGL.glShadeModel(GL10.GL_SMOOTH);
```

This code enables lighting, enables GL_LIGHT0, and then sets the color and brightness of the light. Finally, the light is positioned in 3D space. In addition, we enable GL_COLOR_MATERIAL so the color set for drawing the objects is used with the lighting. The smooth shading model is also enabled, which helps remove the visual transition between triangles on the same face. Color material definitions can also be used for fancier lighting and more realistic-looking surfaces, but that is beyond the scope of this book.

Here is the drawing code for our cube, assuming we now have a full vertex array of all 24 points and an index array defining the order they will be drawn in:

```
gl.glEnableClientState(GL10.GL_NORMAL_ARRAY);
gl.glVertexPointer(3, GL10.GL_FLOAT, 0, mVertexBuffer);
gl.glNormalPointer(GL10.GL_FLOAT, 0, mNormalBuffer);
gl.glDrawElements(GL10.GL_TRIANGLES, indices.length,
GL10.GL_UNSIGNED_BYTE, mIndexBuffer);
```

Notice that the normal array and normal mode are now turned on. Without this, the lighting won't look right. As with the other arrays, this has to be assigned through a fixed buffer in Java, as this code demonstrates:

```
float normals[] = {
    // front
    0, 0, 1, 0, 0, 1, 0, 0, 1, 0, 0, 1,
    // back
    0, 0, -1, 0, 0, -1, 0, 0, -1, 0, 0, -1,
    // top
    0, 1, 0, 0, 1, 0, 0, 1, 0, 0, 1, 0,
    // bottom
    0, -1, 0, 0, -1, 0, 0, -1, 0, 0, -1, 0,
    // right
    1, 0, 0, 1, 0, 0, 1, 0, 0, 1, 0, 0,
    // left
    -1, 0, 0, -1, 0, 0, -1, 0, 0, -1, 0, 0 };
mNormalBuffer = getFloatBufferFromFloatArray(normals);
```

The above code uses one of the helper methods we talked about previously to create a **FloatBuffer**. We use a floating point array for the normals. This also shows the normals and how each vertex must have one. (Recall that we now have 24 vertices for the cube.) You can create various lighting effects by make the normals not actually perpendicular to the surface, but for more accurate lighting it's usually better to just increase the polygon count of your objects or add textures. Figure 14.4 shows the solid cube, now shaded to show depth better.

Figure 14.4   A cube with a light shining from the right to shade it.

Texturing Your Objects

Texturing surfaces, or putting images on surfaces, is a rather lengthy and complex topic. It's enough for our purposes to focus on learning how to texture with Android, so we use the previously lit and colored cube and texture it.

First, texturing needs to be enabled, as shown in the following code:

```
mGL.glEnable(GL10.GL_TEXTURE_2D);
int[] textures = new int[1];
mGL.glGenTextures(1, textures, 0);
```

This code enables texturing and creates an internally named slot for one texture. We use this slot to tell OpenGL what texture we operate on in the next block of code.

```
gl.glBindTexture(GL10.GL_TEXTURE_2D, textures[0]);

Bitmap bitmap = BitmapFactory.decodeResource(
    c.getResources(), R.drawable.android);
```

```
Bitmap bitmap256 = Bitmap.createScaledBitmap(
    bitmap, 256, 256, false);

GLUtils.texImage2D(GL10.GL_TEXTURE_2D, 0, bitmap256, 0);

bitmap.recycle();
bitmap256.recycle();
```

You've probably begun to wonder what happened to Android-specific code. Well, it's back. OpenGL ES needs bitmaps to use as textures. Lucky for us, Android comes with a `Bitmap` class that can read in nearly any format of image, including PNG, GIF, and JPG files. You can do this straight from a `Drawable` resource identifier, too, as demonstrated in the preceding code. OpenGL requires that textures be square and have sides that are powers of two, such as 64×64 or 256×256. Because the source image might or might not be in one of these exact sizes, we scale it again with just a single Android method call. If the source image weren't square though, the original aspect ratio will not be kept. Sometimes it is easier to scale down with the original aspect ratio and add colored padding around the edges of the image instead of stretching it, but this is beyond the scope of this example.

Finally, `GLUtils.texImage2D()` assigns an Android `Bitmap` to an OpenGL texture. OpenGL keeps the image internally, so we can clean up the `Bitmap` objects with a call to the `recycle()` method.

Now that OpenGL ES knows about the texture, the next step is to tell it where to draw the texture. This can be accomplished through using a texture coordinate buffer. This is similar to all the other buffer arrays in that it must be assigned to a fixed Java buffer and enabled. Here is the code to do this with our cube example:

```
float texCoords[] = {
    1,0, 1,1, 0,1, 0,0,
    1,0, 1,1, 0,1, 0,0,
    1,0, 1,1, 0,1, 0,0,
    1,0, 1,1, 0,1, 0,0,
    1,0, 1,1, 0,1, 0,0,
    1,0, 1,1, 0,1, 0,0,
    };
mCoordBuffer = getFloatBufferFromFloatArray(texCoords);
gl.glEnableClientState(GL10.GL_TEXTURE_COORD_ARRAY);
gl.glTexCoordPointer(2, GL10.GL_FLOAT, 0, mCoordBuffer);

draw(gl);
```

As promised, this code creates a fixed buffer for the texture coordinates. We set the same ones on each face of the cube, so each vertex has a texture coordinate assigned to it. (0,0 is the lower-left portion of the texture and 1,1 is the upper–right.) Next, we enable the `GL_TEXTURE_COORD_ARRAY` state and then tell OpenGL which buffer to use. Finally, we draw the cube. Now, we left the code the same as before, which produces the output you see in Figure 14.5 (a). The coloring does still apply, even with textures. If coloring is not applied, the output will look like what you see in Figure 14.5 (b).

Figure 14.5   (a) A red colored cube with texture and (b) the same cube without red coloring.

Interacting with Android Views and Events

Now that you have gone through this introduction to OpenGL ES on Android, you have seen how to draw 3D objects on the screen. Actually, these 3D objects are drawn on a `SurfaceView`, which has all the typical Android attributes found on `View` widgets. We now use these attributes to interact with the rest of the application.

First, we show you how to send information from the OpenGL thread back to the main thread to monitor performance. Then, we give an example of how to forward key events from the main thread to the OpenGL thread to control the animation on the screen.

Enabling the OpenGL Thread to Talk to the Application Thread

The Android SDK provides a helper class for running code on another thread. The `Handler` class can allow a piece of code to run on a target thread—the thread that the `Handler` was instantiated in. For the purpose of this example, this is done within the `Activity` class.

```
public final Handler mHandler = new Handler();
```

This enables the OpenGL thread to execute code on the `Activity` thread by calling the `post()` method of the `Handler`. This allows us to act on other `View` objects on the screen that we can't act on from outside of the `Activity` thread on the OpenGL thread. For this example, the frame rate of the scene rendered will be calculated in the OpenGL thread and then posted back to the `Activity` thread. Here is a method that does just that:

```
public void calculateAndDisplayFPS() {
    if (showFPS) {
        long thisTime = System.currentTimeMillis();
        if (thisTime - mLastTime < mSkipTime) {
            mFrames++;
        } else {
            mFrames++;
            final long fps =
                mFrames / ((thisTime-mLastTime)/1000);
            mFrames = 0;
            mLastTime = thisTime;
            mHandler.post(new Runnable() {
                public void run() {
                    mFPSText.setText("FPS = " + fps);
                }
            });
        }
    }
}
```

The `calculateAndDisplayFPS()` method is called from within the animation loop of the OpenGL thread. The math is fairly straightforward: the number of frames divided by the duration for those frames in seconds. Then we take that and post it to the `Handler` for the `Activity` thread by creating a new `Runnable` object that applies a `String` to the `TextView` that holds the current frame rate.

However, doing this every iteration causes the performance to drop substantially. Instead, a counter tracks the number of frames drawn, and we do the calculation and display every time the duration of `mSkipTime` has gone by. A value of 5000ms has worked well to avoid influencing the performance too much by simply measuring the performance. Figure 14.6 shows the display with the frame rate.

Figure 14.6   A textured, lit, shaded cube with frame rate displayed.

Enabling the Application Thread to Talk to the OpenGL Thread

Now let's look at the reverse situation. We want the main application thread to communicate with the OpenGL thread. We could use a `Handler` to post code to the OpenGL thread for execution. However, if we are not going to execute any OpenGL code, we aren't required to run it within the OpenGL thread context. Instead, we can add a key event handler to the `SurfaceView` to either speed up or stop the animation within the OpenGL thread.

A `SurfaceView` needs to be the current focus before it receives key events. A couple of method calls configure this:

```
setFocusable(true);
setFocusableInTouchMode(true);
```

Setting focusable for both touch modes enables key events to come in regardless of the mode. Now, within the `SurfaceView`, key event handlers need to be implemented. First, a handler for toggling the frame rate on and off will be implemented. The following is a sample implementation of the `onKeyDown()` method override:

```
public boolean onKeyDown(int keyCode, KeyEvent event) {
    switch (keyCode) {
        case KeyEvent.KEYCODE_F:
            mGLThread.toggleFPSDisplay();
        return true;
    }
    return super.onKeyDown(keyCode, event);
}
```

When the user presses the F key, a call to the `toggleFPSDisplay()` method of the OpenGL ES thread is made. This merely changes the state of the `boolean` flag. The `onKeyDown()` method will be called multiple times if the key is held, xxx xxx toggle the display until the key is released. There are multiple methods to prevent this, such as just handling it within `onKeyUp()` or using different keys to enable and disable the state.

The next control we provide to the user is the ability to pause the animation while the P key is held down. The following case statement is added to `onKeyDown()`:

```
case KeyEvent.KEYCODE_P:
    mGLThread.setAnim(false);
    return true;
```

Here, the state is forced to `false` regardless of how many times `onKeyDown()` is called. Next, an implementation of `onKeyUp()` is needed to resume the animation when the user lifts their finger.

```
public boolean onKeyUp(int keyCode, KeyEvent event) {
    switch (keyCode) {
        case KeyEvent.KEYCODE_P:
            mGLThread.setAnim(true);
            return true;
    }
    return super.onKeyUp(keyCode, event);
}
```

Again, the value is forced and set to `true` so that when the users lifts their finger off the key the animation resumes regardless of the current state. An `if` statement around the inner part of the entire `while()` animation loop can pause the entire rendering in this example.

In these examples, the code does not actually run in the OpenGL thread to change the state of the flags. This is acceptable for the following reasons:

- The values are set in this way exclusively (no concurrency problems).
- The exact state of the flags is unimportant during the loop.
- No calls to OpenGL are made.

The first two reasons mean that we don't have to perform thread synchronization for the functionality to work acceptably and safely. The last reason means that we don't need to create a `Handler` on the OpenGL thread to execute OpenGL calls in the proper thread. There are many circumstances where these aren't met. Discussing thread synchronization is not within the scope of this chapter, however. Standard Java methods are available for doing this, though.

Cleaning Up OpenGL ES

It is necessary for your application to clean up OpenGL when your application is done using it. This happens when the application is quitting or the `Activity` has changed in some way. The recommended process for gracefully shutting down OpenGL is to reset as the surface and context, destroy the surface and context you configured, and then terminate the EGL instance. This can be done with the following code:

```
private void cleanupGL() {
    mEGL.eglMakeCurrent(mGLDisplay, EGL10.EGL_NO_SURFACE,
        EGL10.EGL_NO_SURFACE, EGL10.EGL_NO_CONTEXT);
    mEGL.eglDestroySurface(mGLDisplay, mGLSurface);
    mEGL.eglDestroyContext(mGLDisplay, mGLContext);
    mEGL.eglTerminate(mGLDisplay);
}
```

First, `eglMakeCurrent()` removes the surface and context that were used. Next, `eglDestroySurface()` and `eglDestroyContext()` release any resources held by OpenGL for the surface and the context. Finally, OpenGL is terminated through a call to `eglTerminate()`. If OpenGL runs in a separate thread, the thread can now be terminated as well.

It is up to the application to clean up OpenGL properly. There are no helper methods available for managing all of it automatically within the Android lifecycle as there are with `Cursor` objects and the like.

Using the `GLSurfaceView` Class

The Android 1.5 SDK introduced a helper class for OpenGL ES usage called `GLSurfaceView`. To use `GLSurfaceView`, you can either extend it or instantiate it directly. Either way, it then needs to be provided with a `GLSurfaceView.Renderer` implementation that contains callback methods for drawing and GL initialization. The `Activity` must pass `onPause()` and `onResume()` events on to the `GLSurfaceView`. The EGL initialization is handled by the `GLSurfaceView` object and threading is used to offload the processing away from the main thread. This effectively means less code to write so that you can focus more on the actual GL portions of the drawing.

The following code demonstrates an entire `Activity` that duplicates the colorful triangle we drew earlier in this chapter, as shown in Figure 14.2:

```
public class AndroidOpenGL extends Activity {
CustomSurfaceView mAndroidSurface = null;
```

```
protected void onPause() {
    super.onPause();
    mAndroidSurface.onPause();
}

protected void onResume() {
    super.onResume();
    mAndroidSurface.onResume();
}

protected void onCreate(Bundle savedInstanceState) {
    super.onCreate(savedInstanceState);

    mAndroidSurface = new CustomSurfaceView(this);
    setContentView(mAndroidSurface);
}

private class CustomSurfaceView extends GLSurfaceView {
    final CustomRenderer mRenderer = new CustomRenderer();

    public CustomSurfaceView(Context context) {
        super(context);
        setFocusable(true);
        setFocusableInTouchMode(true);
        setRenderer(mRenderer);
    }

    public boolean onKeyDown(int keyCode, KeyEvent event) {
        switch (keyCode) {
        case KeyEvent.KEYCODE_P:
            queueEvent(new Runnable() {
                public void run() {
                    mRenderer.togglePause();
                }
            });
            return true;
        }
        return super.onKeyDown(keyCode, event);
    }
}

private class CustomRenderer implements
    GLSurfaceView.Renderer {
    TriangleSmallGLUT mTriangle = new TriangleSmallGLUT(3);
    boolean fAnimPaused = false;
```

```java
public void onDrawFrame(GL10 gl) {
    if (!fAnimPaused) {
        gl.glClear(GL10.GL_COLOR_BUFFER_BIT |
            GL10.GL_DEPTH_BUFFER_BIT);
        gl.glRotatef(1f, 0, 0, 1f);

        if (mTriangle != null) {
            mTriangle.drawColorful(gl);
        }
    }
}

public void togglePause() {
    if (fAnimPaused == true) {
        fAnimPaused = false;
    } else {
        fAnimPaused = true;
    }
}

public void onSurfaceChanged(GL10 gl, int width,
    int height) {
    gl.glViewport(0, 0, width, height);

    // configure projection to screen
    gl.glMatrixMode(GL10.GL_PROJECTION);
    gl.glLoadIdentity();
    gl.glClearColor(0.5f, 0.5f, 0.5f, 1);
    float aspect = (float) width / height;
    GLU.gluPerspective(gl, 45.0f, aspect, 1.0f, 30.0f);
}

public void onSurfaceCreated(GL10 gl,
    EGLConfig config) {
    gl.glEnableClientState(GL10.GL_VERTEX_ARRAY);

    // configure model space
    gl.glMatrixMode(GL10.GL_MODELVIEW);
    gl.glLoadIdentity();
    GLU.gluLookAt(gl, 0, 0, 10f, 0, 0, 0, 0, 1, 0f);
    gl.glColor4f(1f, 0f, 0f, 1f);
}
}}
```

As you can see, this code demonstrates creating a new GLSurfaceView and a new
GLSurfaceView.Renderer. The end result, with proper implementation of the triangle

drawing class (included with the book code and discussed earlier in this chapter), is a spinning triangle that can be paused with the press of the P key. The GLSurfaceView implementation contains its own renderer, which is less generic than assigning it externally, but with the key handling we implemented. The two classes must work closely together.

The GLSurfaceView implements key handling by overriding the onKeyDown() method of the regular View class. The action is passed on to the Renderer through a helper method called queueEvent(). The queueEvent() method passes the Runnable object on to the Renderer thread held by the GLSurfaceView.

Next, the Renderer implementation provides the drawing in the onDrawFrame() method. This is either called continuously or on demand, depending on the render mode set via a call to the GLSurfaceView.setRenderMode() method. The implementation of onSurfaceChanged() is now where we set up the screen projection—an appropriate place because this method is called on orientation or size changes of the surface. Then, in onSurfaceCreated(), the basic GL configuration is performed, including setting client states and static data, such as the model view.

All the EGL configuration is now performed internally to GLSurfaceView, so the application need not worry about it. If, however, the application needs to perform custom configuration of the EGL, this is passed in to the onSurfaceCreated() method.

If you choose to use this method to bring up a GL surface on Android, the implementation of the rendering code doesn't need to change at all.

Summary

In this chapter, you learned the basics for using OpenGL ES from within an Android application. You first learned how to initialize OpenGL ES within its own thread. Then you learned how to draw, color, and light objects using a variety of OpenGL and Android helper methods. You then learned how your application thread and the OpenGL thread can interact with each other. Finally, you learned how to clean up OpenGL.

Creating fully functional 3D applications and games is a vast topic, more than enough to fill entire books. You have learned enough to get started drawing in three dimensions on Android and can use the knowledge to apply general OpenGL concepts to Android. The reference following section contains some links to more OpenGL ES information to help you deepen your OpenGL ES knowledge.

References and More Information

OpenGL ES 1.0 API Documentation: www.khronos.org/opengles/sdk/1.1/docs/man/
OpenGL ES Information: www.khronos.org/opengles/
OpenGL Information: www.opengl.org/

## 15

Using Android's Optional Hardware APIs

The Android Software Development Kit (SDK) provides a variety of application programming interfaces (APIs) for accessing low-level hardware features on the handset. Device sensors available on Android devices include the magnetic and orientation sensors, WiFi sensor, and battery indicator. The magnetic sensor can be used as a compass, and the accelerometer sensor can detect motion. The WiFi sensor can read network status and determine nearby wireless access points. You can also monitor the state of the battery and power management state information. Other hardware, such as the camera and location-based services, we talked about in Chapter 12, "Using Android Multimedia APIs," and Chapter 11, "Using Location-Based Services (LBS) APIs," respectively.

Using the Device Sensor

The Android SDK provides access to raw data from sensors on the device. The `SensorManager` object listens for data from the sensors. It is a system service, and an instance can be retrieved with the `getSystemService()` method, as shown here:

```
SensorManager sensors =
    (SensorManager) getSystemService(Context.SENSOR_SERVICE);
```

The `SensorManager` object defines a number of identifiers for the various sensors that might be found on a device. Not all sensors are available on each device. The most interesting sensors are listed here:

- `SENSOR_ACCELEROMETER`: Measures acceleration in three directions
- `SENSOR_LIGHT`: Measures light brightness
- `SENSOR_MAGNETIC_FIELD`: Measures magnetism in three directions; the compass
- `SENSOR_ORIENTATION`: Combines other measurements to determine the device's orientation
- `SENSOR_TEMPERATURE`: Measures the temperature

- `SENSOR_PROXIMITY`: Measures the distance to an object
- `SENSOR_ALL`: Includes all sensors

In addition to these identifiers, the `SensorManager` object also has a number of constants that can be useful with certain sensors. For instances, the `STANDARD_GRAVITY` constant can be used with the accelerometer and the `LIGHT_SUNLIGHT` constant can be used with the light sensor.

> **Note**
>
> The `SensorManager` seems to contain far more Easter eggs (undocumented and hidden feature, or jokes) than any other class in the Android SDK. For example, the `SensorManager` class includes constants for `GRAVITY_DEATH_STAR_I` (Star Wars), `GRAVITY_THE_ISLAND` (Lost), and a `SENSOR_TRICORDER` (Star Trek). Keep this in mind when looking through the values. They might be more useful in games than for real-world use.

Sensor values are sent back to an application using a `SensorListener` object that the application must implement. There are two required methods: `onAccuracyChanged()` and `onSensorChanged()`. Here is a sample implementation of `onSensorChanged()`:

```
public void onSensorChanged(int sensor, float[] values) {
    TextView status = (TextView) findViewById(R.id.status);
    String allSensor = "Sensor = \n";
    switch (sensor) {
    case SensorManager.SENSOR_ACCELEROMETER:
        for (float value : values) {
            allSensor += "accel val = " + value + "\n";
        }
        break;

    case SensorManager.SENSOR_MAGNETIC_FIELD:
        for (float value : values) {
            allSensor += "magnetic val = " + value + "\n";
        }
        break;

    case SensorManager.SENSOR_TEMPERATURE:
        for (float value : values) {
            allSensor += "temp val = " + value + "\n";
        }
        break;

    case SensorManager.SENSOR_ORIENTATION:
        for (float value : values) {
            allSensor += "orientation val = " + value + "\n";
```

```
        }
        break;
    }

    status.setText(allSensor);
}
```

To receive method calls with the updated sensor data, the `SensorListener` must be registered with the `SensorManager` like so:

```
boolean isAvailable =
    sensors.registerListener(Sensors.this,
        SensorManager.SENSOR_ACCELEROMETER,
        SensorManager.SENSOR_DELAY_NORMAL);
```

In this case, the accelerometer sensor will be watched. The `onSensorChanged()` method will be called at particular intervals defined by the delay value in `registerListener()`, which is the default value in this case. The `onSensorChanged()` method is called with the sensor that provides data if more than one has been registered. Additionally, the values from the sensor are provided in an array. The `SensorManager` object has constants defining which indices are which values. The accelerometer provides six values, and they might look like those shown in Figure 15.1.

Figure 15.1   Sensor sample application showing accelerometer values.

What's New in Android 1.5

Android 1.5 includes a redesigned `SensorManager` and introduced a new class called `GeomagneticField` to the `android.hardware` package. The `GeomagneticField` class uses the World Magnetic Model (http://www.ngdc.noaa.gov/geomag/WMM/DoDWMM.shtml) to estimate the magnetic field anywhere on the planet, which is typically used to determine magnetic variation between compass north and true north. This model, developed by the United States National Geospatial-Intelligence Agency (NGA), is updated every 5 years for precision. This model expires in December 2009, although results will be accurate enough for most purposes for some time after that date, at which point the Android `GeomagneticField` class will likely be updated to the latest model.

The sensor values won't be useful to the application until they are calibrated. One way to calibrate would be to ask the user to click a button to calibrate the sensor. The application can then store the current values. Then new values can be compared against the original values to see how they have changed from their original values (delta). Although the phone sensors have a specific orientation, this would allow the user to use them in either portrait or landscape mode and held up in front of them or down below them.

When registering a sensor, the `registerListener()` method returns `true` if the sensor is available and can be activated. It returns `false` if the sensor isn't available or cannot be activated.

Tip

Not all these sensors are available on shipping handsets. For instances, the T-Mobile G1 has the accelerometer, magnetic sensor (compass), and orientation sensor but does not have temperature, light, or proximity sensors.

Unfortunately, the emulator does not provide any sensor data. All sensor testing must be done on a physical device. Alternatively, OpenIntents.org also provides a handy Sensor Simulator (www.openintents.org/en/node/23). This tool simulates accelerometer, compass, orientation sensors, and a temperature sensor, and transmits data to the emulator.

The sensor values are typically quite sensitive. For most uses, an application will probably want to provide some smoothing of the values to reduce the effects of any noise or shaking. How this is done depends on the purpose of the application. For instance, a simulated bubble level might need less smoothing than a game where too much sensitivity can be frustrating.

The orientation values might be appropriate in cases where only the handset's orientation is needed but not the rate at which it is changed (accelerometer) or specific direction it's pointing (compass).

Working with WiFi

The Android SDK provides a set of APIs for retrieving information about the WiFi networks available to the device and WiFi network connection details. This information can be used for tracking signal strength, finding access points of interest, or performing actions when connected to specific access points. This section describes how to get WiFi information. However, if you are looking for information on networking, that is more thoroughly discussed as part of Chapter 10, "Using Android Networking APIs."

The following samples require two explicit permissions in the `AndroidManifest.xml` file. The `CHANGE_WIFI_STATE` permission is needed when an application is accessing information about WiFi networks that can turn on the WiFi radio, thus changing its state. The `ACCESS_WIFI_STATE` permission is needed, as well, to request any information from the WiFi device. These can be added to the `AndroidManifest.xml` file as follows:

```
<uses-permission
    android:name="android.permission.CHANGE_WIFI_STATE" />
<uses-permission
    android:name="android.permission.ACCESS_WIFI_STATE" />
```

The next thing the application needs is an instance of the `WifiManager` object. It is a system service, so the `getSystemService()` method works.

```
WifiManager wifi =
    (WifiManager) getSystemService(Context.WIFI_SERVICE);
```

Now that the `WifiManager` object is available, the application can do something interesting or useful with it. First, the application performs a WiFi scan to see what access points are available in the local area. To perform a scan, a few steps need to be performed:

1. Start the scan with the `startScan()` method of the `WifiManager` object.
2. Register a `BroadcastReceiver` for the `SCAN_RESULTS_AVAILABLE` Intent.
3. Call `getScanResults()` to get a list of `ScanResult` objects.
4. Iterate over the results and do something with them.

The first two steps can be performed with the following code:

```
wifi.startScan();

registerReceiver(rcvWifiScan,
    new IntentFilter(WifiManager.SCAN_RESULTS_AVAILABLE_ACTION));
```

The sample `BroadcastReceiver` object, shown here, performs the last two steps. It will be called regularly until the `stopScan()` method is called on the `WifiManager` object.

```
rcvWifiScan = new BroadcastReceiver() {

    public void onReceive(Context context, Intent intent) {
```

```
        List<ScanResult> resultList = wifi.getScanResults();
        int foundCount = resultList.size();

        Toast.makeText(WiFi.this,
            "Scan done, " + foundCount + " found",
            Toast.LENGTH_SHORT).show();
        ListIterator<ScanResult> results = resultList.listIterator();
        String fullInfo = "Scan Results : \n";
        while (results.hasNext()) {
            ScanResult info = results.next();
            String wifiInfo = "Name: " + info.SSID +
                "; capabilities = " + info.capabilities +
                "; sig str = " + info.level + "dBm";

            Log.v("WiFi", wifiInfo);

            fullInfo += wifiInfo + "\n";
        }

        status.setText(fullInfo);
    }
};
```

The `ScanResult` object contains a few more fields than demonstrated here. However, the `SSID`, or name, property is probably the most recognizable to users. The `capabilities` property lists such things as what security model can be used (such as "WEP"). The signal strength (`level`), as given, isn't all that descriptive for most users.

However, the `WifiManager` object provides a couple of helper methods for dealing with signal levels. The first is the `calculateSignalLevel()` that effectively turns the number into a particular number of "bars" of strength. The second, `compareSignalLevel()`, can be used to compare the relative signal strengths of two results.

> **Note**
>
> The emulator does not provide WiFi emulation but the `WifiManager` APIs do work. However, there will not be any results when using them. Perform testing of WiFi APIs on actual hardware that has a functional WiFi radio.

The `WifiManager` object can be used to list known access points. These are typically access points that the user has configured or connected to in the past. The following code demonstrates the use of the `getConfiguredNetworks()` method:

```
ListIterator<WifiConfiguration> configs =
    wifi.getConfiguredNetworks().listIterator();
```

```
String allConfigs = "Configs: \n";
while (configs.hasNext()) {
    WifiConfiguration config = configs.next();
    String configInfo = "Name: " + config.SSID +
        "; priority = " + config.priority;

    Log.v("WiFi", configInfo);

    allConfigs += configInfo + "\n";
}

status.setText(allConfigs);
```

The returned `WifiConfiguration` object does not include all the fields that it could. For instance, it does not fill any network key fields. It does, however, fill in similar fields to those found in the `ScanResults` object. This could be used, for instance, to notify the users when they are in range of known WiFi networks if their device is set to not automatically connect.

The `WifiManager` object can be used to configure WiFi networks, get the state of the WiFi radio, and more. See the `android.net.wifi` package for more information.

Monitoring the Battery

Mobile devices operate with the use of the battery. Although many applications do not need to know the state of the battery, some types of applications might want to change their behavior based on the battery level or charging state. For instance, a monitoring application can reduce the monitoring frequency when the battery is low and can increase it if the handset is powered by an external power source. The battery levels could also monitor the efficiency of an application and find areas where behavior can be modified to improve battery life. Doing so will be appreciated by users.

To monitor the battery, the application must have the `BATTERY_STATS` permission. The following XML added to the `AndroidManifest.xml` file will suffice:

```
<uses-permission
    android:name="android.permission.BATTERY_STATS" />
```

Then the application needs to register for a particular `BroadcastIntent`. In this case, it must be `Intent.ACTION_BATTERY_CHANGED`. The following code demonstrates this:

```
registerReceiver(batteryRcv,
    new IntentFilter(Intent.ACTION_BATTERY_CHANGED));
```

Next, the application needs to provide an implementation of the `BroadcastReceiver`. The following is an example of a `BroadcastReceiver`:

```
batteryRcv = new BroadcastReceiver() {
```

```
public void onReceive(Context context, Intent intent) {
    int level = intent.getIntExtra("level", -1);
    int maxValue = intent.getIntExtra("scale", -1);
    int batteryStatus = intent.getIntExtra("status", -1);
    int batteryHealth = intent.getIntExtra("health", -1);
    int batteryPlugged = intent.getIntExtra("plugged", -1);
    String batteryTech = intent.getStringExtra("technology");
    int batteryIcon = intent.getIntExtra("icon-small", -1);
    float batteryVoltage = (float)intent.
        getIntExtra("voltage", -1)/1000;
    boolean battery = intent.getBooleanExtra("present", false);
    float batteryTemp = (float)intent.
        getIntExtra("temperature", -1)/10;

    int chargedPct = (level * 100)/maxValue ;

    String batteryInfo = "Battery Info:\nHealth=" +
        (String)healthValueMap.get(batteryHealth)+"\n" +
        "Status="+(String)statusValueMap.get(batteryStatus)+"\n" +
        "Charged % = "+chargedPct+"%\n"+
        "Plugged = " + pluggedValueMap.get(batteryPlugged) + "\n" +
        "Type = " + batteryTech + "\n"        +
        "Voltage = " + batteryVoltage + " volts\n" +
        "Temperature = " + batteryTemp + "°C\n"+
        "Battery present = " + battery + "\n";

    status.setText(batteryInfo);
    icon.setImageResource(batteryIcon);

    Toast.makeText(Battery.this, "Battery state changed",
        Toast.LENGTH_LONG).show();
}

};
```

There are a couple of interesting items here. First, notice that the battery level isn't used directly. Instead, it's used with the scale, or maximum value, to find the percentage charged. The raw value wouldn't have much meaning to the user. The next property is the status. The values and what they mean are defined in the `android.os.BatteryManager` object. This is typically the charging state of the battery. Next, the health of the battery, also defined in the `android.os.BatteryManager` object, is an indication of how worn out the battery is. It can also indicate other issues, such as overheating. Additionally, the plugged value indicates if the device is plugged in and, if it is, whether it is using AC or USB power.

Caution

On specific devices, not all this information might be available or accurate. For instance, even though we see good data for most fields, we have noted in several instances that devices are returning false for the `"present"` field. Proper device testing might be required before relying on these fields.

Some other information is returned as well, including an icon identifier that can visually display the state of the battery and some technical details, such as the type of battery, current voltage, and temperature. All displayed, this information looks something like that in Figure 15.2.

Figure 15.2   Screen capture showing values from the battery monitor from a physical handset.

Tip

Testing of the battery information can be partially done with the emulator. See Appendix A, "The Android Emulator Quick-Start Guide," for more information on the power controls.

Summary

Unlike many other mobile platforms, Android allows useful access to the underlying hardware on the device, including the capability to read raw device sensor data, use built-in WiFi support, and monitor battery usage. It is important to remember that different devices have different underlying hardware. For example, not all Android devices are guaranteed to have WiFi or a built-in camera support. Always verify the functionality available on each target phone platforms during the planning stage of your Android project.

V

More Android Application Design Principles

## 16

Working with Notifications

Applications frequently need to alert the user to actions even when the application isn't actively running in the foreground. An email application might notify users when new messages arrive. A news reader application might notify users when there are new articles to read. A weather application might notify users of special weather alerts. A stock market application might notify the user when certain stock price targets are met.

This chapter teaches you how to build these notifications into your applications. You can alert the users with text, vibration, colorful lights, and even audio. Users appreciate these notifications because they help drive application workflow, reminding the users when they need to launch the application. These notifications must be appropriate to the application and event, too, so the users aren't interrupted without cause.

Notifying with the Status Bar

The standard notification area at the top of the screen shows an icon and optional ticker text. Additionally, the status bar, in which the notifications, time, and other pieces of information are shown, can be dragged down to show expanded notification information and to clear old notifications. In this section, you learn how to create a basic notification.

All notifications are created with the help of the `NotificationManager`. The `NotificationManager` (within the `android.app` package) is a system service that must be requested. The following code demonstrates how to create this object:

```
NotificationManager notifier = (NotificationManager)
    getSystemService(Context.NOTIFICATION_SERVICE);
```

The `NotificationManager` is not useful without having a valid `Notification` object to use with the `notify()` method. The `Notification` object defines what information displays to the user when the `Notification` is triggered. This includes text that displays on the status bar, a couple of lines of text that display on the expanded status bar, an icon displayed in both places, a count of the number of times this `Notification` has been triggered, and a time for when the last event that caused this `Notification` took place.

The icon and ticker text, both of which display on the status bar, can be set through the constructor for the `Notification` object. Additionally, both can be set through public member variable assignment. Both methods are shown here:

```
Notification notify = new Notification(
    R.drawable.android_32, "Hello!", System.currentTimeMillis());

// ... or these can be assigned directly

notify.icon = R.drawable.android_32;
notify.tickerText = "Hello!";
notify.when = System.currentTimeMillis();
```

A couple more pieces of information need to be set before the call to the `notify()` method takes place. We need to make a call to the `setLastEventInfo()` method, which configures a `View` that displays in the expanded status bar. Here is an example:

```
Intent toLaunch = new Intent(Notifications.this, Notifications.class);
PendingIntent intentBack =
    PendingIntent.getActivity(Notifications.this, 0, toLaunch, 0);

notify.setLatestEventInfo(Notifications.this,
    "Hi there!", "This is even more text.", intentBack);
```

The `notify()` method takes an `Intent` and a couple of text fields. When the status bar is expanded, both text fields are shown, along with the icon, and the time of the notification. The `Intent` will be initiated when the user clicks on the notification in the expanded status bar. In this case, we're using our own `Activity` so that when the user clicks on the notification our `Activity` launches again.

> **Note**
>
> When the expanded status bar is pulled down, the current `Activity` lifecycle is still treated as if it were the top (displayed) `Activity`. Triggering system notifications while running in the foreground, though, isn't particularly useful. An application that is in the foreground would be better suited using a `Dialog` or `Toast` to notify the user, not by using notifications.

Now the application is ready to actually notify the user of the event. All that is needed is a call to the `notify()` method of the `NotificationManager` with an identifier and the `Notification` we configured. This is demonstrated with the following code:

```
private static final int NOTIFY_1 = 0x1001;
// ...
notifier.notify(NOTIFY_1, notify);
```

The identifier matches up a `Notification` with previous `Notification` instances of that type. When the identifiers match, the old `Notification` is updated instead of creating a new one. You might have a `Notification` that some file is being downloaded. You could update the `Notification` when the download is complete, instead of filling the `Notification` queue with a separate `Notification,` which quickly becomes obsolete. This `Notification` identifier only needs to be unique within your application.

The notification displays as an icon and ticker text showing up on the status bar. This is shown at the top of Figure 16.1.

Figure 16.1   Status bar notification showing icon and ticker text.

Shortly after the ticker text displays, the status bar returns to normal with each notification icon shown. If the users expand the status bar, they see something like what is shown in Figure 16.2.

When the identifiers match, the old notification is updated. When a notification with matching identifier is posted, the ticker text does not draw a second time. To show the user that something has changed, a counter can be used. The value of the `number` member variable of the `Notification` object tracks and displays this. For instance, we can set it to the number 4, as shown here:

```
notify.number = 4;
```

Figure 16.2   Expanded status bar showing the icon, both text fields, and
the time of the notification.

This would be displayed to the user as a small number over the icon. This is only displayed in the status bar and not in the expanded status bar, although an application could update the text to also display this information. Figure 16.3 shows what this might look like in the status bar.

When a user clicks on the notification, the `Intent` assigned will be triggered. At some point after this, the application might want to clear the notification from the system notifications queue. This is done through a call to the `cancel()` method of the `NotificationManager` object. For instance, the notification we created earlier could be canceled with the following call:

```
notifier.cancel(NOTIFY_1);
```

This cancels the notification that has the same identifier. However, if the application doesn't care what the user does after clicking on the notification, there is an easier way to cancel notifications. Simply set a flag to do so, as shown here:

```
notify.flags |= Notification.FLAG_AUTO_CANCEL;
```

Figure 16.3   Status bar notification with the count of "4" showing over
the icon.

Setting the `Notification.FLAG_AUTO_CANCEL` flag causes notifications to be canceled
when the user clicks on them. This is convenient and easy for the application when just
launching the `Intent` is good enough.

The `Notification` object is a little different from other Android objects you might
have encountered. Most of the interaction with it will be through direct access to its
public variables instead of through helper methods. This is useful for a background application or service, discussed in Chapter 17, "Working with Services." The `Notification`
object can be kept around and only the values that need to be changed can be modified.
After any change, the `Notification` needs to be posted again by calling the `notify()`
method.

Vibrating the Phone

Vibration is a great way to break through noisy environments or alert the user when visible and audible alerts are not appropriate. (Though a vibrating phone is often noisy on a
hard desktop surface.) Android notifications give a fine level of control over how vibration is performed. However, before the application can use vibration with a notification,

an explicit permission is needed. The following XML within your application's `AndroidManifest.xml` file is required to use vibration:

```
<uses-permission
    android:name="android.permission.VIBRATE" />
```

Caution

The vibrate feature must be tested on the handset. The emulator does not indicate vibration in any way.

Without this permission, the vibrate functionality will not work nor will there be any error. With this permission enabled, the application is free to vibrate the phone however it wants. This is accomplished by describing the `vibrate` member variable, which determines the vibration pattern. An array of `long` values describes the vibration duration. Thus, the following line of code enabled a simple vibration pattern that occurs whenever the notification is triggered:

```
notify.vibrate = new long[] {200, 200, 600, 600};
```

This vibration pattern vibrates for 200 milliseconds and then stops vibrating for 200 milliseconds. After that, it vibrates for 600 milliseconds and then stops for that long. To repeat the Notification alert, a notification flag can be set so it doesn't stop until the user clears the notification.

```
notify.flags |= Notification.FLAG_INSISTENT;
```

An application can use different patterns of vibrations to alert the user to different types of events or even present counts. For instance, think about a grandfather clock with which you can deduce the time based on the tones that are played.

Tip

Using short, unique patterns of vibration can be useful and users become accustomed to them.

Blinking the Lights

Blinking lights are a great way to pass information silently to the user when other forms of alert would fail or be rude. The Android SDK provides reasonable control over a multicolored indicator light. Users might recognize this light as a service indicator or battery level warning. An application can control it as well.

> **Caution**
>
> Although the light is present on existing hardware, there is no guarantee it will be available on all hardware. Additionally, certain notifications appear to take precedence over the light. For instance, we have found that the light on the T-Mobile G1 is always solid green when plugged in to USB, regardless of other activities. You must unplug the phone for the colors to change. Finally, the emulator does not display the light's state. This mandates testing on actual hardware.

To use the indicator light, a flag must be set on the `Notification` object. Then, the color of the light must be set and information about how it should blink. The following block of code configures the indicator light to shine green and blink at rate of 1 second on and 1 second off:

```
notify.flags |= Notification.FLAG_SHOW_LIGHTS;

notify.ledARGB = Color.GREEN;
notify.ledOnMS = 1000;
notify.ledOffMS = 1000;
```

Although arbitrary color values can be set, a typical physical implementation of the indicator light has three small LEDs in red, green, and blue. Although the colors blend reasonably well, they won't be as accurate as the colors on the screen. For instance, on the T-Mobile G1, the color white looks a tad pink.

An application can use different colors and different blinking rates to indicate different information to the user. For instance, the more times an event occurs, the more urgent the indicator light could be. The following block of code shows changing the light based on the number of notifications that have been triggered:

```
notify.number++;
notify.flags |= Notification.FLAG_SHOW_LIGHTS;

if (notify.number < 2) {
    notify.ledARGB = Color.GREEN;
    notify.ledOnMS = 1000;
    notify.ledOffMS = 1000;
} else if (notify.number < 4) {
    notify.ledARGB = Color.BLUE;
    notify.ledOnMS = 500;
    notify.ledOffMS = 500;
} else {
    notify.ledARGB = Color.RED;
    notify.ledOnMS = 50;
    notify.ledOffMS = 50;
}
```

The blinking light continues until the `Notification` is cleared by the user. The use of the `Notification.FLAG_INSTENT` flag does not affect this as it does vibration effects.

Color and blinking rates could also be used to indicate other information. For instance, temperature from a weather service could be indicated with red and blue plus blink rate. Use of such colors for passive data indication can be useful even when other forms would work. It is far less intrusive. For instance, a simple glance at the handset could tell the user some useful piece of information without the need to launch any applications or change what they are doing.

Making Noise

Sometimes, the handset has to make noise to get the user's attention. Luckily, the Android SDK provides a means for this using the `Notification` object. Simply assign a `Uri` object to the `sound` member variable and that sound plays when the notification is triggered. The following code demonstrates this:

```
notify.sound =
    Uri.parse("file:/system/media/audio/ringtones/VeryAlarmed.ogg");
```

The sound file used in this example is one that is available on both the emulator and the T-Mobile G1. Any valid sound file could be used, though. No specific permissions are needed for this form of notification.

By default, the audio file will be placed once. As with the vibration, the `Notification.FLAG_INSISTENT` flag can be used to repeat incessantly until the user clears the notification.

Customizing the Notification

The default notification display in the expanded status bar tray is sufficient for most purposes. However, developers can use the `RemoteViews` object to customize the look and feel of a notification.

The following code demonstrates creating a `RemoteViews` object and assigning custom text to it:

```
RemoteViews remote =
    new RemoteViews(getPackageName(), R.layout.remote);

remote.setTextViewText(R.id.text1, "Big text here!");
remote.setTextViewText(R.id.text2, "Red text down here!");
notify.contentView = remote;
```

To better understand this, here is the layout file `remote.xml` referenced by the preceding code:

```
<LinearLayout
    xmlns:android="http://schemas.android.com/apk/res/android"
```

```
        android:orientation="vertical"
        android:layout_width="fill_parent"
        android:layout_height="fill_parent">
    <TextView
        android:id="@+id/text1"
        android:layout_width="fill_parent"
        android:layout_height="wrap_content"
        android:textSize="14pt"
        android:textColor="#000" />
    <TextView
        android:id="@+id/text2"
        android:layout_width="fill_parent"
        android:layout_height="wrap_content"
        android:textSize="8pt"
        android:textColor="#f00" />
</LinearLayout>
```

This particular example is similar to the default notification but does not contain an icon. The `setLatestEventInfo()` method is normally used to assign the text to the default layout. In this example, we use our custom layout instead. The `Intent` still needs to be assigned, though, as follows:

```
Intent toLaunch = new Intent (Notifications.this, Notifications.class);
PendingIntent intentBack =
    PendingIntent.getActivity(Notifications.this, 0, toLaunch, 0);

// assign the Intent directly
notify.contentIntent = intentBack;
notifier.notify(NOTIFY_5, notify);
```

The end result looks something like Figure 16.4. Using a custom notification layout can provide better control over the information on the expanded status bar. Additionally, it can help differentiate your application's notifications from other applications by providing a themed or branded appearance.

Note

The size of the area that a layout can use on the expanded status bar is fixed for a given device. However, the exact details might change from device to device. Keep this in mind when designing a custom notification layout. Additionally, be sure to test the layout on all target devices in all modes of screen operation so that you can be sure the notification layout will draw properly.

The default layout includes two fields of text, an icon and a time field for when the notification was triggered. Users will be accustomed to this information. An application, where feasible and where it makes sense, should try to conform to at least this level of information when using custom notifications.

Figure 16.4   Custom notification showing with just two lines of text.

Summary

Applications can interact with their users outside the normal activity boundaries by using notifications. Notifications can be visual, auditory, or use the vibrate feature of the device. Various methods can customize these notifications to provide rich information to the user. Special care must be taken to provide the right amount of appropriate information to the user without the application becoming a nuisance or the application being installed and forgotten about.

## 17

Working with Services

A service within the Android Software Development Kit (SDK) can mean one of two things. First, it can mean a background process, performing some useful operations at regular intervals. Second, a service can be an interface for a remote object, called from within your application. In both cases, the service object extends the `Service` class from the Android SDK, and it can be a stand-alone or part of an application with a complete user interface.

In this chapter, you learn how to create and interact with an Android service. You also learn how to define a remote interface using the Android Interface Definition Language (AIDL). Finally, you learn how to pass objects through this interface by creating a class that implements a `Parcelable` object.

Creating a Service

Creating an Android service involves extending the `Service` class and adding a service block to the `AndroidManifest.xml` permissions file. The `Service` class overrides the `onCreate()`, `onStart()`, and `onDestroy()` methods to begin with. Defining the service name allows other applications to start the service that runs in the background and stop it.

For this example, we implement a simple service that generates a GPX track file, logging location information at regular intervals when the service runs. The following code gives a simple definition to the `Service` class called `GPXService`:

```
public class GPXService extends Service {
    public static final String GPX_SERVICE =
        "com.androidbook.GPXService.SERVICE";

    private LocationManager location = null;
    private NotificationManager notifier = null;

    @Override
    public void onCreate() {
        super.onCreate();
    }
```

```
    @Override
    public void onStart(Intent intent, int startId) {
        super.onStart(intent, startId);
    }

    @Override
    public void onDestroy() {
        super.onDestroy();
    }
}
```

You need to understand the lifecycle of a service because it's different from that of an activity. If a service will be started by the system with a call to the `Context.StartService()` method, the `onCreate()` method is called just before the `onStart()` method. However, if the service will be bound to with a call to the `Context.bindService()` method, the `onCreate()` method will be called just before the `onBind()` method. The `onStart()` method will not be called in this case. We talk more about binding to a service in a moment. Finally, when the service is finished—that is, it is stopped and no other process is bound to it, the `onDestroy()` method is called. Everything for the service must be cleaned up in this method.

With this in mind, here is the full implementation of the `onCreate()` method for the `GPXService` class previously introduced:

```
public void onCreate() {
    super.onCreate();

    location = (LocationManager)
        getSystemService(Context.LOCATION_SERVICE);
    notifier = (NotificationManager)
        getSystemService(Context.NOTIFICATION_SERVICE);
}
```

Because the object doesn't yet know if the next call will be to the `onStart()` method or the `onBind()` method, we make a couple of quick initialization calls, but no background processing is started. Even this might be too much if neither of these objects were used by the interface provided by the binder.

Next, let's look at the `onStart()` method in greater detail.

```
@Override
public void onStart(Intent intent, int startId) {
    super.onStart(intent, startId);
    updateRate = intent.getIntExtra(EXTRA_UPDATE_RATE, -1);
    if (updateRate == -1) {
        updateRate = 60000;
    }

    Criteria criteria = new Criteria();
```

```
criteria.setAccuracy(Criteria.NO_REQUIREMENT);
criteria.setPowerRequirement(Criteria.POWER_LOW);

location = (LocationManager)
    getSystemService(Context.LOCATION_SERVICE);

String best = location.getBestProvider(criteria, true);

location.requestLocationUpdates(best,
    updateRate, 0, trackListener);

// notify that we've started up
Notification notify = new
    Notification(android.R.drawable.stat_notify_more,
    "GPS Tracking", System.currentTimeMillis());
notify.flags |= Notification.FLAG_AUTO_CANCEL;

Intent toLaunch = new Intent(getApplicationContext(),
    ServiceControl.class);
PendingIntent intentBack =
    PendingIntent.getActivity(getApplicationContext(),
    0, toLaunch, 0);

notify.setLatestEventInfo(getApplicationContext(),
    "GPS Tracking", "Tracking start at " +
    updateRate+"ms intervals with [" + best +
    "] as the provider.", intentBack);
notifier.notify(GPS_NOTIFY, notify);
}
```

The onStart() method is where the background processing starts. In this example, though, the background processing is actually just registering for an update from another service. For more information about using Location-based services and the LocationManager, see Chapter 11, "Using Location-Based Services (LBS) APIs," and for more information on Notification calls, see Chapter 16, "Working with Notifications."

Tip

The use of a callback to receive updates is recommended over doing background processing to poll for updates. Most mobile devices have limited battery life. Continual running in the background, or even just polling, can use a substantial amount of battery power. In addition, implementing callbacks for the users of your service is also more efficient for the same reasons.

In this case, we turn on the GPS for the duration of the process, which might impact battery life even though we request a lower power method of location determination. Keep this in mind when developing services.

The `Intent` extras object retrieves data passed in by the process requesting the service. Here, we retrieve one value, `EXTRA_UPDATE_RATE`, for determining the length of time between updates. The string for this, `update-rate`, must be published externally, either in developer documentation or in a publicly available class file so that users of this service know about it.

The implementation details of the `LocationListener` object, `trackListener`, are not interesting to the discussion on services. However, processing should be kept to a minimum to avoid interrupting what the user is doing in the foreground. Some testing might be required to determine how much processing a particular phone can handle before the user notices performance issues.

There are two common methods to communicate data to the user. The first is to use `Notifications`. This is the least-intrusive method and can be used to drive users to the application for more information. It also means the users don't need to be actively using their phone at the time of the notification because it is queued. For instance, a weather application might use notifications to provide weather updates every hour.

The other method is to use `Toast` messages. From some services, this might work well, especially if the user expects frequent updates and those updates work well overlaid briefly on the screen, regardless of what the user is currently doing. For instance, a background music player could briefly overlay the current song title when the song changes.

The `onDestroy()` method is called when no clients are bound to the service and a request for the service to be stopped has been made via a call to the `Context.stopService()` method, or a call has been made to the `stopSelf()` method from within the service. At this point, everything should be gracefully cleaned up because the service ceases to exist.

Here is an example of the `onDestroy()` method:

```
@Override
public void onDestroy() {
    if (location != null) {
        location.removeUpdates(trackListener);
        location = null;
    }

    // notify that we've stopped
    Notification notify = new
        Notification(android.R.drawable.stat_notify_more,
        "GPS Tracking", System.currentTimeMillis());
    notify.flags |= Notification.FLAG_AUTO_CANCEL;

    Intent toLaunch = new Intent(getApplicationContext(),
        ServiceControl.class);
```

```
PendingIntent intentBack =
    PendingIntent.getActivity(getApplicationContext(),
    0, toLaunch, 0);
notify.setLatestEventInfo(getApplicationContext(),
    "GPS Tracking", "Tracking stopped", intentBack);

    notifier.notify(GPS_NOTIFY, notify);

    super.onDestroy();
}
```

Here, we stop updates to the LocationListener object. This stops all our background processing. Then, we notify the user that the service is terminating. Only a single call to the onDestroy() method happens, regardless of how many times the onStart() method is called.

The system will not know about a service unless it is defined within the AndroidManifest.xml permissions file using the service tag.

```
<service
    android:enabled="true"
    android:name="GPXService">
    <intent-filter>
        <action android:name=
            "com.androidbook.GPXService.SERVICE" />
    </intent-filter>
</service>
```

This block of XML defines the service name, GPXService, and that the service is enabled. Then, using an Intent filter, we use the same string that we defined within the class. This is the string that is used later on when controlling the service. With this block of XML inside the application section of the manifest, the system now knows that the service exists and it can be used by other applications.

Controlling a Service

At this point, the example code has a complete implementation of a Service. Now we write code to control the service we previously defined.

```
Intent service = new Intent("com.androidbook.GPXService.SERVICE");
service.putExtra("update-rate", 5000);
startService(service);
```

Starting a service is as straightforward as creating an Intent with the service name and calling the startService() method. In this example, we also set the update-rate Intent extra parameter to 5 seconds. That rate is quite frequent but works well for testing. For practical use, we'd probably want this set to 60 seconds or more. This code triggers a call to the onCreate() method, if the Service isn't bound to or running already. It also triggers a call to onStart() method, even if the service is already running.

Later, when we finish with the service, it needs to be stopped using the following code:

```
Intent service = new Intent("com.androidbook.GPXService.SERVICE");
stopService(service);
```

This code is essentially the same as starting the service but with a call to the `stopService()` method. This calls the `onDestroy()` method if there are no bindings to it. However, if there are bindings, `onDestroy()` will not be called until those are also terminated. This means background processing might continue despite a call to the `stopService()` method. If there is a need to control the background processing separate from these system calls, a remote interface will be required.

Implementing a Remote Interface

Sometimes it is useful to have more control over a service than just system calls to start and stop its activities. However, before a client application can bind to a service for making other method calls, the interface needs to be defined. The Android SDK includes a useful tool and file format for remote interfaces for this purpose.

To define a remote interface, you must declare the interface in an AIDL file, implement the interface, and then return an instance of the interface when the `onBind()` method is called.

Using the example `GPXService` service we already built in this chapter, we now create a remote interface for it. This remote interface will have a method, which can be called especially for returning the last location logged. Only primitive types and objects that implement the `Parcelable` protocol can be used with remote service calls. This is because these calls cross process boundaries where memory can't be shared. The AIDL compiler handles the details of crossing these boundaries when the rules are followed. The `Location` object implements the `Parcelable` interface so it can be used.

Here is the AIDL file for this interface, `IRemoteInterface`:

```
package com.androidbook.services;

interface IRemoteInterface {
    Location getLastLocation();
}
```

When using Eclipse, this AIDL file, `IRemoteInterface.aidl`, can be added to the project under the appropriate package and the Android SDK plug-in does the rest. Now we must implement the code for the interface. Here is an example implementation of this interface:

```
private final IRemoteInterface.Stub
    mRemoteInterfaceBinder = new IRemoteInterface.Stub() {
        public Location getLastLocation() {
            Log.v("interface", "getLastLocation() called");
```

```
            return lastLocation;
        }
    };
```

The service code already stored off the last location received as a member variable, so we can simply return that value. With the interface implemented, it needs to be returned from the `onBind()` method of the service:

```
@Override
public IBinder onBind(Intent intent) {
    // we only have one, so no need to check the intent
    return mRemoteInterfaceBinder;
}
```

If multiple interfaces are implemented, the `Intent` passed in can be checked within the `onBind()` method to determine what action is to be taken and which interface should be returned. In this example, though, we have only one interface and don't expect any other information within the `Intent`, so we simply return the interface.

We also add the class name of the binder interface to the list of actions supported by the intent filter for the service within the `AndroidManifest.xml` file. Doing this isn't required but is a useful convention to follow and allows the class name to be used. The following block is added to the service tag definition:

```
<action android:name =
    "com.androidbook.services.IRemoteInterface" />
```

The service can now be used through this interface. This is done by implementing a `ServiceConnection` object and calling the `bindService()` method. When finished, the `unbindService()` method must be called so the system know that the application is done using the service. The connection remains even if the reference to the interface is gone.

Here is an implementation of a `ServiceConnection` object's two main methods, `onServiceConnection()` and `onServiceDisconnected()`:

```
public void onServiceConnected(ComponentName name,
    IBinder service) {

    mRemoteInterface =
        IRemoteInterface.Stub.asInterface(service);
    Log.v("ServiceControl", "Interface bound.");
}

public void onServiceDisconnected(ComponentName name) {
    mRemoteInterface = null;
    Log.v("ServiceControl",
        "Remote interface no longer bound");
}
```

When the `onServiceConnected()` method is called, an `IRemoteInterface` instance is retrieved that can be used to make calls to the interface we previously defined. A call to the remote interface would look like any call to an interface now:

```
Location loc = mRemoteInterface.getLastLocation();
```

> **Tip**
>
> Remember that remote interface calls operate across process boundaries and are complet-ed synchronously. If a call takes a while to complete, it should be placed within a separate thread, as any lengthy call would be.

To use this interface from another application, the AIDL file should be placed within the project and appropriate package. The call to `onBind()` triggers a call to the `onServiceConnected()` after the call to the service's `onCreate()` method. Remember, the `onStart()` method is not called in this case.

```
bindService(new Intent(IRemoteInterface.class.getName()),
    this, Context.BIND_AUTO_CREATE);
```

In this case, the `Activity` we call from also implements the `ServiceConnection` inter-face. This code also demonstrates why it is a useful convention to use the class name as an intent filter. Because we have both intent filters and we don't check the action on the call to the `onBind()` method, we can also use the other intent filter, but the code here is clearer.

When done with the interface, a call to `unbindService()` disconnects the interface. However, a callback to the `onServiceDisconnected()` method does not mean that the service is no longer bound; the binding is still active at that point, just not the connec-tion.

Implementing a Parcelable Class

In the example so far, we have been lucky in that the `Location` class implements the `Parcelable` interface. What if a new object needs to be passed through a remote interface?

Let's take the following class, `GPXPoint`, as an example:

```
public final class GPXPoint {

    public int latitude;
    public int longitude;
    public Date timestamp;
    public double elevation;

    public GPXPoint() {
    }
}
```

The `GPXPoint` class defines a location point that is similar to a `GeoPoint` but also includes the time the location was recorded and the elevation. This data is commonly found in the popular GPX file format. On its own, this is not a basic format that the system recognizes to pass through a remote interface. However, if the class implements the `Parcelable` interface and we then create an AIDL file from it, the object can be used in a remote interface.

To fully support the `Parcelable` type, we need to implement a few methods and a `Parcelable.Creator<GPXPoint>`. The following is the same class now modified to be a `Parcelable` class:

```
public final class GPXPoint implements Parcelable {

    public int latitude;
    public int longitude;
    public Date timestamp;
    public double elevation;

    public static final Parcelable.Creator<GPXPoint>
        CREATOR = new Parcelable.Creator<GPXPoint>() {

        public GPXPoint createFromParcel(Parcel src) {
            return new GPXPoint(src);
        }

        public GPXPoint[] newArray(int size) {
            return new GPXPoint[size];
        }

    };

    public GPXPoint() {
    }

    private GPXPoint(Parcel src) {
        readFromParcel(src);
    }

    public void writeToParcel(Parcel dest, int flags) {
        dest.writeInt(latitude);
        dest.writeInt(longitude);
        dest.writeDouble(elevation);
        dest.writeLong(timestamp.getTime());
    }

    public void readFromParcel(Parcel src) {
        latitude = src.readInt();
```

```
        longitude = src.readInt();
        elevation = src.readDouble();
        timestamp = new Date(src.readLong());
    }

    public int describeContents() {
        return 0;
    }
}
```

The `writeToParcel()` method is required and flattens the object in a particular order using supported primitive types within a `Parcel`. When the class is created from a `Parcel`, the `Creator` is called, which, in turn, calls the private constructor. For readability, we also created a `readFromParcel()` method that reverses the flattening, reading the primitives in the same order that they were written and creating a new `Date` object.

Now the AIDL file for this class must be created. It should be placed next to the Java file and named `GPXPoint.aidl` to match. The contents should be made to look like the following:

```
package com.androidbook.services;

parcelable GPXPoint;
```

Now the `GPXPoint` class can be used in remote interfaces. This is done in the same way as any other native type or `Parcelable` object. The `IRemoteInterface.aidl` file can then be modified to look like the following:

```
package com.androidbook.services;

import com.androidbook.services.GPXPoint;

interface IRemoteInterface {
    Location getLastLocation();
    GPXPoint getGPXPoint();
}
```

Additionally, we can provide an implementation for this method within the interface, as follows:

```
public GPXPoint getGPXPoint() {
    if (lastLocation == null) {
        return null;
    } else {
        Log.v("interface", "getGPXPoint() called");
        GPXPoint point = new GPXPoint();

        point.elevation = lastLocation.getAltitude();
        point.latitude =
```

```
            (int) (lastLocation.getLatitude() * 1E6);
        point.longitude =
            (int) (lastLocation.getLongitude() * 1E6);
        point.timestamp =
            new Date(lastLocation.getTime());

        return point;
    }
}
```

As can be seen, nothing particularly special needs to happen. Just by making the object `Parcelable`, it can now be used for this purpose.

Summary

The Android SDK provides the `Service` mechanism that can be used to implement background tasks and to share functionality across multiple applications. By creating an interface through the use of AIDL, a `Service` can expose functionality to other applications without having to distribute libraries or packages. Creating objects with the `Parcelable` interface allows developers to extend the data that can be passed across process boundaries, as well.

Care should be taken when creating a background service. Poorly designed background services might have substantial negative impact on handset performance and battery life. In addition to standard testing, a `Service` implementation should be tested with respect to these issues.

Prudent creation of a `Service`, though, can dramatically enhance the appeal of an application or service you might provide. `Service` creation is a powerful tool provided by the Android SDK for designing applications simply not possible on other mobile platforms.

VI

Deploying Your Android Application to the World

18

The Mobile Software Development Process

The mobile development process is much like the traditional desktop software process with a couple of distinct differences. Understanding how differences affect your development team is critical to running a successful mobile development project. This information and insight into the mobile development process is invaluable to veterans and those new to mobile development, to those in management and planning and the developers and testers in the trenches. In this chapter, we take a look at each step in the mobile software development process and discuss some of the peculiarities of mobile development.

An Overview of the Mobile Development Process

Mobile development teams are often small in size and project schedules are short in length. The entire project lifecycle is often condensed, and whether you're a team of one or one hundred, understanding the mobile development considerations for each part of the development process can save you a lot of wasted time and effort.

Some hurdles a successful mobile development team must overcome include

- Choosing an appropriate software methodology for your mobile project
- Understanding how target handsets dictate the functionality of your application
- Performing thorough, accurate, and ongoing feasibility analyses
- Mitigating the risks associated with preproduction handsets
- Keeping track of handset functionality through configuration management
- Designing a responsive, stable application on a memory restrictive system
- Designing user interfaces for a variety of devices with different user experiences
- Testing the application thoroughly on the target handsets
- Incorporating third-party requirements that affect where you can sell your application
- Deploying and maintaining a mobile application

Choosing a Software Methodology

Developers can easily adapt most modern software methodologies to mobile development. Whether your team opts for traditional Rapid Application Development (RAD) principles or more modern variants of Agile Software Development like Scrum, mobile applications have some unique requirements.

Understanding the Dangers of Waterfall Approaches

The short development cycle might tempt some to use a Waterfall approach, as shown in Figure 18.1, but developers should beware of the inflexibility that comes with this choice. It is generally a bad idea to design and develop an entire mobile application without taking into account the many changes that tend to occur during the development cycle. Changes to target handsets (especially preproduction models), ongoing feasibility, and performance concerns, and the need for quality assurance to test early and often on the target devices (not just the emulator) make it difficult for strict waterfall approaches to succeed with mobile projects.

Figure 18.1   The Dangers of Waterfall Development. (Graphic courtesy of Amy Tam Badger).

Understanding the Value of Iteration

Because of the speed at which mobile projects tend to progress, iterative methods have been the most successful strategies adapted to mobile development. Rapid prototyping enables developers and quality assurance personnel ample opportunity to evaluate the feasibility and performance of the mobile application on the target handsets and adapt as needed to the change that inevitably occurs over the course of the project.

Gathering Application Requirements

Requirements analyses for mobile applications can be more complex than that of traditional desktop applications. Requirements must often be tailored to work across a number of handsets—handsets that might have vastly different user interfaces and input methods. This makes development assumptions tricky.

Determining Project Requirements

When multiple handsets are involved, there are generally two approaches to determining project requirements: the lowest common denominator method and the customization method. Each method has its benefits and its drawbacks.

With the lowest common denominator method, you design the application to run sufficiently well across a number of devices. In this case, the primary target handset is typically the device with the fewest features—basically, the most inferior handset. Only requirements that can be met by all devices are included in the specification to reach the broadest range of devices—requirements such as input methods, screen resolution, and the Software Development Kit (SDK) version.

> **Note**
>
> The lowest common denominator method is roughly equivalent to developing a desktop application with the following minimum system requirements: (1) Windows 2000 and (2) 128 megabytes of RAM, on the assumption that the application will be forward compatible with the latest version of Windows (and every other version in between). It's not ideal, but in some cases, the trade-offs are acceptable.

Some light customization, such as resources and the final compiled binary (and the version information) is usually feasible. The main benefit of this method is that there is only one major source code tree to work with; bugs are fixed in one place and apply across the board. You can also easily add other handsets without changing much code, provided they too meet the minimum hardware requirements. The drawbacks include the fact that the resulting generalized application does not maximize any phone-specific features. Also, if a device-specific problem arises or you misjudge the lowest common denominator and later find that an individual handset lacks the minimum requirements, the team might be forced to implement a workaround (hack) or branch the code at a later date, losing the early benefits of this method but keeping all the drawbacks.

What's New in Android 1.5

The tool suite introduced in Android 1.5 allows developers to write for multiple target Android SDK versions from a single Android SDK installation. Developers should take care to identify target platforms early in the design phase and not rely on backward compatibility when it comes to supporting individual devices.

Also, firmware updates have been a fairly regular occurrence, so the Android SDK version on a specific device might change after an over-the-air update in the field. The upgrade from Android SDK 1.1 to 1.5 compelled many Android developers to publish compatible updates to existing applications.

Using the customization method, the application is tailored for specific handsets. This method works well for projects targeting a small number of target handsets but does not scale well from a resource management perspective. There is generally a core application framework (classes or packages) shared across all versions of the application. All versions of a client-server application would likely share the same server and interact with it in the same way, but the client implementation is tailored to take advantage of specific phone features. That is the key benefit of this approach. Some drawbacks include source code fragmentation (many branches of the same code), increased testing requirements, and the fact that it can be more difficult to add new handsets in the future.

In truth, mobile development teams usually use a hybrid approach incorporating some of the aspects from both methods. It's pretty common to see sets of handsets grouped together based on functionality. For example, a game application might group handsets based on graphics performance, screen resolution, or input methods. A Location Based Service (LBS) application might group handsets based on the available internal sensors. Other applications might develop one version of an application for phones with built-in cameras and one version for those without cameras. These groupings are arbitrary and set by the developer to keep the code and testing manageable. They will, in large part, be driven by the details of a particular application and any support requirements.

Tip

A single, unified version of an application is cheaper to support than distinctly different versions. However, a game will probably sell better with custom versions that leverage the distinct advantages and features of a specific handset. A vertical business application would likely benefit more from a unified application design that works the same, is easier to train users across multiple handsets, and would thus have lower support costs for the business.

Developing Use Cases for Mobile Applications

Use cases should be first written in general terms for the application before adapted to specific handsets, which impose their own limitations. For example, a high-level use case for an application might be this: "Enter Form Data" but the individual handsets might use different methods to perform this on the specific phone hardware, whether the phone has a keyboard, and so on.

> **Tip**
>
> Developing an application for multiple handsets is much like developing an application for different operating systems and input devices (such as handling Mac keyboard shortcuts versus those on Windows)—subtle and not-so-subtle differences must be accounted for. These differences might be obvious, such as not having a keyboard for input, or not so obvious, such as handset-specific bugs or different conventions for right and left soft keys.

Incorporating Third-Party Requirements

In addition to the requirements imposed by your internal requirements analyses, your team needs to incorporate any requirements imposed by others. Third-party requirements can come from any number of sources, including

- Android License Agreement Requirements
- Google Maps API License Agreement Requirements (if applicable)
- Third-Party API Requirements (if applicable)
- Android Market Requirements
- Mobile Carrier/Operator Requirements
- Other Application Store Requirements (if applicable)
- Application Certification Requirements (if applicable)

Incorporating these requirements into your project plan early is essential not only for keeping your project on schedule but also so that these requirements are built into the application from the ground up, as opposed to applied as afterthoughts that can be risky.

Managing a Handset Database

As your mobile development team builds applications for a growing number of handsets, it becomes more and more important to keep track of the target handset information for revenue estimation and maintenance purposes. Creating a handset database is a great way to keep track of both marketing and device specification details for target handsets. When we say "database," we mean anything from a Microsoft Excel spreadsheet to a little local database. The point is that the information is shared across the team or company and kept up to date.

The phone database is best implemented early, when project requirements are just determined and target handsets are determined. Figure 18.2 illustrates how handset information can be tracked and used by different members of the application development team.

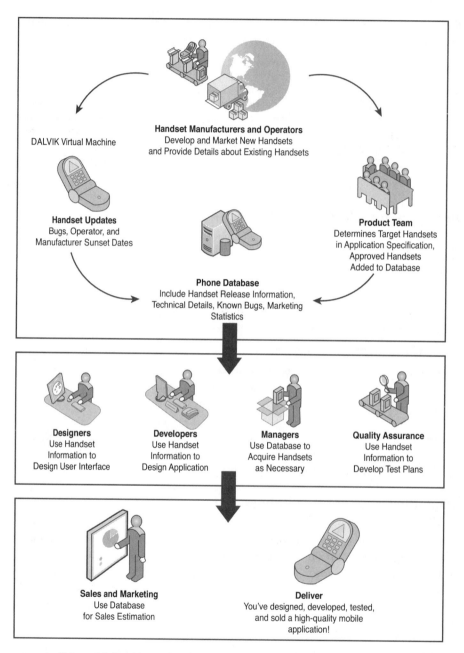

Figure 18.2   How a development team uses the handset database.

Determining Which Handsets to Track

Some companies track only the handsets they actively develop for, whereas others also track handsets they might want to include in the future, or lower priority handsets. Handsets can be included in the database during the Requirements phase of a project but also later as a change in project scope. They can also be added as subsequent porting projects long after the initial application has been released.

Storing Handset Data

The handset database should be designed to contain any information about a given handset that would be helpful for developing and selling applications. This might require that someone be tasked with keeping track of a continual stream of information from carrier and manufacturers. Still, this information can be useful for all mobile projects at a company. This data should include

- Important handset technical specification details (screen resolution, hardware details, supported media formats, input methods, localization)
- Any known issues with handsets (bugs and important limitations)
- Handset carrier information (any firmware customizations, release and sunset dates, expected user statistics, such as if a phone is highly anticipated and expected to sell a lot, or well received for vertical market applications, and so on)
- Firmware upgrade information (as it becomes available, changes might have no impact on the application or warrant an entirely separate handset entry)
- Actual testing handset information (which handsets have been purchased or loaned through manufacturer or carrier loaner programs, how many are available)

The handset carrier information can also be cross-referenced with sales figures from the carrier, application store, and internal metrics.

The actual testing handset information is often best implemented as a library check-out system. Team members can reserve handsets for testing and development purposes. When a loaner phone needs to be returned to the manufacturer, it's easy to track. This also facilitates sharing handsets across teams.

Using Handset Data

Remember that the database can be shared across multiple mobile development projects. Handset resources can be shared, and sales statistics can be compared to see on which handsets your applications perform best. Different team members can use the handset database in different ways.

- Product designers use the database to develop the most appropriate application user interface for the target phones.
- Media artists use the database to generate application assets such as graphics, videos, and audio in supported media file formats and resolutions appropriate for the target phones.

- Project managers use the database to determine the handsets that must be acquired for development and testing purposes on the project and development priorities.

- Software developers use the database to design and develop applications compatible with target handset device specifications.

- Quality assurance personnel use the database to design and develop test plans target handset device specifications and to test the application thoroughly.

- Marketing and sales professionals use the database to estimate sales figures for released applications. For example, it is important to be aware that application sales will drop as handset availability drops.

The information in the database can also help determine the most promising target handsets for future development and porting.

Using Third-Party Phone Databases

There are third-party databases for phone information including screen size and internal device details and carrier support details, but subscribing to such information can be costly for a small company. Many mobile developers instead choose to create a custom phone database with only the phones they are interested in and the specific data they need for each phone, which is often absent from open and free databases.

Assessing Project Risks

In addition to the normal risks any software project must identify, mobile projects need to be aware of the outside influences that can affect their project schedule and whether the project requirements can be met. Some of the risk factors include identifying and acquiring target handsets and continually reassessing application feasibility.

Identifying Target Handsets

Just as most sane software developers wouldn't write a desktop application without deciding what operating systems (and their versions) the application would run on first, mobile developers must consider the target handsets their application will run on. Each handset will have different capabilities, a different user interface, and unique device limitations.

Target handsets are generally determined in one of two ways:

- There's a popular "killer" phone you want to develop for.
- You want to develop an application for maximum coverage.

In the first instance, you have your initial target handset figured out; in the second instance, you want to look at the available (and soon to be available) phones on the market and adjust your application specification to cover as many as is reasonably feasible.

Understanding How Carriers Fit into the Equation

It's also important to note that we've seen popular phones, such as the Motorola RAZR, customized by a number of operators. An operator might ship its custom version of a handset, including big bundles of custom applications (taking up a bunch of space on the device) and disabling specific handset features (such as Bluetooth or WiFi), which effectively makes it impossible for your application to run. All these factors must be taken into account when considering your application requirements and abilities. Your application's running requirements must match the features shared across all target handsets and handle optional feature use appropriately in all cases.

Understanding How Handsets Move Through the Marketplace over Time

New handsets are developed and carriers and manufacturers retire (sunset) handsets all the time. Handsets also leave the market all the time. Note that different carriers might carry the same (or similar) phone but might sunset (retire) the phones at a different time.

> **Tip**
>
> Companies should set a policy, made clear to users, of how long an application will be supported after the carrier or manufacturer stops supporting a specific handset. This policy might need to be different for various carriers because carriers impose their own support requirements.

You need to determine how different kinds of phone models can move through the worldwide marketplace. Some phones are available (or become popular) only in certain geographic regions. Sometimes phones are released worldwide, but often they are released regionally. The T-Mobile G1, for example, was first released in the United States but is available now in other markets as the HTC Dream.

Historically, it's common for a phone to become available in market-driving Asia first and then show up in Europe, North America and Australia where phone users often upgrade every year or two and will pay premium rates for applications. Finally, these same phones become available in Central and South America, and China and India, where subscribers often don't have landlines nor do they have the same levels of income. Regions such as China and India must often be treated like entirely separate mobile marketplaces—with more affordable handsets requiring vastly different revenue models. Here applications sell for less, but revenue is instead derived from the huge and growing subscriber base.

Acquiring Target Handsets

The earlier you can get your hands on the target handsets, the better off you're going to be. Sometimes this is as easy as going to the store and grabbing a new phone.

It is quite common for an application developer to target upcoming phones—phones not yet shipping or available to consumers. There is a great competitive advantage to have your application ready to run the moment consumers have the handset in their hand for the first time. For preproduction handsets, you can join manufacturer and operator developer programs. These programs help you keep abreast of changes to the handset lines (upcoming models, discontinued models). Many of these programs also include preproduction phone loan programs, allowing developers to get their hands on the phone before consumers do.

> **Tip**
>
> Google has made available the Android Dev Phone 1, a phone compatible with Android 1.0 and 1.1, for registered Android developers.

There are risks for developers writing applications for specific preproduction handsets because handset shipment dates often slide. Handsets are delayed or canceled. Handset features (especially new and interesting ones) are not set in stone until the handset ships and the developer verifies that those features work as expected. Exciting new handsets are announced all the time—handsets you might want your application to support. Your project plan must be flexible enough to change and adapt with the market as necessary.

Determining Feasibility of Application Requirements

Mobile developers are at the mercy of the handset limitations, which vary in terms of memory and processing power. Mobile developers do not have the luxury traditional desktop application developers have of saying an application requires "more memory" or "more space." Handset limitations are fixed, and if a mobile application is to run, it runs within the handset's limitations, or not at all.

True feasibility assessment can be done only on the physical handset, not the software emulator. Your application might work beautifully in the emulator but falter on the actual device. Mobile developers most constantly revisit feasibility, application responsiveness, and performance throughout the development process.

Understanding Quality Assurance Risks

The quality assurance team has its work cut out because the testing environment is generally less than ideal.

Testing Early, Testing Often

Get those target handsets in-hand as early as possible. For preproduction handsets, it can take months to get the hardware in hand from the manufacturer. Cooperating with carrier handset loaner programs and buying handsets from retail locations is frustrating but sometimes necessary. Don't wait until the last minute to gather the test hardware.

Testing on the Handset

It cannot be said enough: *Testing on the emulator is helpful, but testing on the handset is essential*. In reality, it doesn't matter if the application works on the emulator—no one uses an emulator in the real world.

There is often no easy way to "wipe" a phone and return it to a clean starting state, so the quality assurance team needs to determine what a clean state on the phone is as a testing policy and stick to it. Testers might require the skills and capability to flash handsets with different firmware versions.

Mitigating the Risk of Limited Real-World Testing Opportunities

In some ways, every quality assurance tester works within a controlled environment. This is doubly true for mobile testers. They often work with phones not on real networks and preproduction phones that might not match those in the field. Add to this that because testing generally takes place in a lab, the location (including primary cell tower, satellite fixes and related phone signal strength, availability of data services, LBS information, locale information) is fixed. The quality assurance team needs to get creative to mitigate the risks of testing too narrow a range of these factors. For example, it is essential to test all applications when the phone has no signal (and in airplane mode, and such) to make sure they don't crash and burn under such conditions that we all experience at some point in time.

Testing Client-Server Applications

Make sure the quality assurance team understands its responsibilities. Mobile applications often have network components and server-side functionality. Make sure thorough server testing is part of the overall test plan—not just the phone client portion of the overall solution. This might require the development of desktop or web applications to exercise network portions of the overall solution.

Writing Essential Project Documentation

You might think that with its shorter schedules, smaller teams, and simpler functionality, mobile software project documentation would be less onerous. Unfortunately, this is not the case—quite the opposite. In addition to the traditional benefits any software project enjoys, good documentation serves a variety of purposes in mobile development.

Some documentation you should consider including in your project includes

- Requirements Analysis and Prioritization
- Risk Assessment and Management
- Application Architecture and Design
- Feasibility Studies including Performance Benchmarking
- Technical Specifications (Overall, Server, Handset-Specific Client)
- Detailed User-Interface Specifications (General, Handset-Specific)
- Test Plans, Test Scripts, Test Cases (General, Handset-Specific)
- Scope Change Documentation

Much of this documentation is common in your average software development project. But perhaps your team finds that skimping on certain aspects of the documentation process has been doable in the past. Before you think to cut corners in a mobile development project, consider some of these documentation requirements for a successful project. Some project documentation might be simpler than that of larger scale software projects, but other portions might need to be fleshed out in finer detail—especially user interface and feasibility studies.

Developing Test Plans for Quality Assurance Purposes

Quality assurance relies heavily on the functional specification documentation and the user interface documentation. Screen real estate is valuable on the small screens of mobile devices, and user experience is vital to the successful mobile project.

Understanding the Importance of User Interface Documentation for Testing

There's no such thing as a killer application with a poorly designed user interface. Thoughtful user interface design is one of the most important details to nail down during the design phase of any mobile software project. Application workflow (application state) must be thoroughly documented at the screen-by-screen level and can include detailed specifications for key usage patterns and how to gracefully fallback when certain keys or features are missing. Usage cases should be clearly defined in advance.

Leveraging Third-Party Testing Facilities

Some companies opt to have quality assurance done offsite by a third party; most quality assurance teams require detailed documentation including use case workflow diagrams to determine correct application behavior. If you do not provide adequate and detailed documentation to the testing facility, you will not get deep and detailed testing. By providing detailed documentation, you raise the bar from "it works" to "it works correctly." What might seem straightforward to some people might not be to others.

Providing Documentation Required by Third Parties

If you are required to submit your application to a software certification program or even, in some cases, to a mobile application store, part of your submission is likely to require some documentation about your application. Some stores require, for example, that your application include a Help feature or technical support contact information. Certification programs might require you to provide detailed documentation on application functionality, user interface workflow, and application state diagrams.

Providing Documentation for Maintenance and Porting Purposes

Mobile applications are often ported to additional handsets and other mobile platforms. This porting work is frequently done by a third party, making the existence of thorough functional and technical specifications even more crucial.

Implementing Configuration Management Systems for Mobile Applications

There are many wonderful source control systems out there for developers, and most that work well for traditional development will work fine for a mobile project. Versioning your application, on the other hand, is not necessarily as straightforward as you might think.

Choosing a Source Control System

Mobile development considerations impose no surprise requirements for source control systems. Some considerations for developers evaluating how they handle configuration management for a mobile project are

- Ability to keep track of source code (Java) and binaries (Android packages, and so on)
- Ability to keep track of application resources by handset configuration (Graphics, and so on)
- Integration with the developer's chosen development environment (Eclipse)

One consideration is integration between the development (IDE) (such as Eclipse) and the source control system. Common source control systems such as Perforce, Subversion, and CVS work well with Eclipse.

Implementing a Version System That Works

Developers should also decide early on a versioning scheme that takes into account the handset particulars and the software build. It is often not sufficient to version the software by build alone (that is, Version 1.0.1).

Mobile developers often combine the traditional versioning scheme with the target handset configuration (Version 1.0.1.HandsetModel). This helps quality assurance, technical support personnel, and end-users who might not know the model names of their handsets or only know them by marketing names developers are often unaware of. Be aware that handset configuration can include carrier-specific handset customizations, such as the T-Mobile G1.

If you use the hybrid model for grouping project requirements that we previously discussed in the chapter, you can add this information to the version as well. For example, the application developed with camera support might be versioned 1.0.1.C.HandsetName where C stands for "Camera Support," whereas the same application for a handset without camera support might have a version such as 1.0.1.NC.HandsetName, where NC stands for "No Camera Support" source branch. If you had two different maintenance engineers supporting the different source code trees, you would know just by the version name who to assign bugs to.

Just to make things a tad more confusing, you might need to plan for different versions of the firmware on a specific handset. For example, the T-Mobile G1 has received firmware upgrades. If an upgrade spawns a rebuild of your application, you might want to version it appropriately: Version 1.0.1.N.G1.Upg1.1, and such.

Yes, this can get out of control, so don't go overboard, but if you design your versioning system intelligently upfront, it can be useful later when you have different handset builds floating around internally and with users. It's not uncommon to field a support call for a particular handset identified by users only to find out based on a great version numbering scheme that they either don't have the handset they thought they had or have the wrong version on the handset.

Designing Mobile Applications

When designing an application for mobile, the developer must consider the constraints the handset imposes and decide what type of application framework is best for a given project.

Understanding Mobile Device Limitations

Applications are expected to be fast, responsive, and stable, but developers must work with limited resources. The memory and processing power constraints of all target handsets must be kept in mind when designing and developing mobile applications.

Exploring Common Mobile Application Architectures

Mobile applications have traditionally come in two basic models: stand-alone applications and network-driven applications.

Stand-alone applications are packaged with everything they require and rely on the handset to do all the heavy lifting. All processing work is done locally, in memory, and is subject to the limitations of the device. Stand-alone applications might use network functions, but they do not rely on them for core application functionality. An example of a reasonable stand-alone application is a Solitaire game.

Network-driven applications provide a lightweight handset client but rely on the network to provide a portion of its content and functionality. Network-driven applications are often used to offload intensive processing to the server, but they can also be used to add functionality long after the application has been installed. They also have the added benefit of allowing developers to build one smart server and a large number of handset clients across many different mobile operating systems to support a larger audience of users. Good examples of network-driven applications include

- Customizable content such as ringtone and wallpaper applications

- Applications with noncritical process and memory intensive operations that can be offloaded to a powerful server and the results delivered back to the client

- Any application that provides additional features at a later date without a full update to the binary

How much you rely on the network to assist in your application's functionality is up to you. You can use the network to provide only content updates (popular new ringtones), or you can use it to dictate how your application looks and behaves (for instance, adding new menu options or features on-the-fly).

Designing for Extensibility and Maintenance

Applications can be written with a fixed user interface and a fixed feature set, but they need not be. Network-driven applications can be more complex to design but offer flexibility for the long term—here's an example.

Let's say you want to write a wallpaper application. Your application can be a stand-alone version, partially network-driven or completely network-driven. Regardless, your application will have two required functions:

- Show a bunch of images and allow the user to choose one.
- Take the chosen image and register it as the wallpaper on the phone.

A super simple stand-alone wallpaper application might come with a set of wallpapers. If they're a generic size for all target handsets, you might need to reformat them for the specific handset. You could write this application, but it would waste space and processing. You can't update the wallpapers available, and it is generally just a bad design.

The partially network-driven wallpaper application might allow the user to browse a fixed menu of wallpaper categories, which show images from a generic image server. The application downloads a specific graphic and then formats the image for the handset. You can add new wallpapers to the server anytime, but you would need to build a new application every time you want to add a new handset configuration. If you want to change the menu, for example to add animated wallpapers at a later date, you would need to write a new version of your application. This application is feasible, but it isn't using its resources wisely either and isn't particularly extensible. However, you could use the single server to write clients for Android, BREW, J2ME, and Blackberry clients, so we are still in a better position than we were with the stand-alone wallpaper application.

The fully network-driven version of the wallpaper application does the bare minimum it needs to on the phone. It asks the server what menus to display and where they go. The user browses the image server just like the partially network-driven version does, but when the user chooses a wallpaper, the mobile application just sends a request to the server: "I want this image and I am this kind of handset." The server keeps track of what formatting requirements each handset has. The server reformats and resizes the image (process intensive operations) and sends the perfect tailored image down to the application, which the application then sets as the wallpaper. Adding support for more handsets is straightforward—deploy the lightweight client with any necessary changes and add support for that handset configuration to the server. Adding a new menu item for animated wallpapers is just a server change, resulting in all handsets (or whichever handsets the server dictates) getting that new category. The response time of this application depends upon network performance, but the application is the most extensible and dynamic.

Stand-alone applications are straightforward and great for one-shot, one-handset applications and those that are meant to be network-independent. Network-driven applications require a bit more forethought and are sometimes more complicated to develop but might save a lot of time in the long run.

Designing for Application Interoperability

Mobile application designers should consider how they will interface with other applications on the handset, including other applications written by the same developer. Some issues to address are

- Will your application rely on other content providers?
- Are these content providers guaranteed to be installed on the phone?
- Will your application act as a content provider? What data will it provide?
- Will your application have background features? Act as a service?
- Will your application rely on third-party services or optional components?
- Will your application expose its functionality through a remote interface (AIDL)?

Developing Mobile Applications

Mobile application implementation follows the same design principles as other platforms. The steps mobile developers take during implementation are fairly straightforward:

- Write and compile the code.
- Run the application in the software emulator.
- Test and debug the application in the software emulator.
- Package and deploy the application to the target handset.
- Test and debug the application on the target handset.
- Incorporate changes from team and repeat until application is complete.

We talk more about development strategies for building solid Android applications in Chapter 19, "Developing and Testing Bulletproof Android Applications."

Testing Mobile Applications

There is a mobile quality assurance mantra:

Test early, test often, test on the actual device.

It's unfortunate, but even now, most quality assurance (QA) testing is done manually on the handset. Testers face many challenges, including handset fragmentation (many handsets, each with different features), defining device states (what is a clean state?), and handling real-world events (phone calls, loss of coverage). Gathering the handsets needed for testing can be costly and difficult, so there is an active market for mobile testing houses.

The good news for mobile QA teams is that the Android SDK includes a number of useful tools for testing applications both on the emulator and the handset. There are many opportunities for leveraging white box testing. Automation of handset testing might not be an option (although there are companies working in this direction), but do seize the opportunities to use traditional QA automation software such as Borland SilkTest for performing emulator testing for build validation, smoke testing, and any early testing when handsets are not readily available.

Defect tracking systems must be modified to handle testing across handset configurations and carriers. For thorough testing, QA team members generally cannot be given the device and told to "try to break it." There are many shades of gray for testers, between black box and white box testing. Testers should know their way around the Android Emulator and the other utilities provided with the Android SDK.

> **Tip**
>
> In Chapter 7, "Designing Android User Interfaces with Layouts," we explain how to use the Hierarchy View utility to design and validate user interface design and take pixel-perfect screenshots on the handset. In Part VII, "Appendixes," of this book, you'll find Quick-Start Guides for the Android emulator (Appendix A), the DDMS utility (Appendix B), and Android Debug Bridge (Appendix C). These tools are valuable not just to developers, but allow testers much more control over the handset configuration.

Mobile quality assurance involves a lot of edge case testing and, again, a preproduction model of a handset might not be exactly the same as what eventually ships to consumers. We talk more about testing Android applications in Chapter 19.

Deploying Mobile Applications

Developers need to determine what methods they use to distribute applications. With Android, you have several options. You can market applications yourself and leverage third-party marketplaces like the Android Market. Consolidated mobile marketplaces, such as Handango, also have Android distribution channels you can take advantage of.

Determining Target Markets

Developers must take into account any requirements imposed by third parties offering application distribution mechanisms such as the Android Market and Handango.

Including Market Requirements in Application Requirements

Specific distributers might impose rules for what types of applications they distribute on your behalf. They might impose quality requirements such as testing certifications (although there are none specific to Android applications at the time this book went to print) and accompanying technical support, and documentation and adherence to common user interface workflow standards (that is, the Back button should behave like this) and performance metrics for responsive applications. Distributers might also impose content restrictions such as barring objectionable content.

We talk more about selling Android applications in Chapter 20, "Selling Your Android Application."

Supporting and Maintaining Mobile Applications

Generally speaking, mobile application support requirements are minimal if you come from a traditional software background, but they do exist. Carriers and operators generally serve as the front line of technical support to end users. As a developer, you aren't usually required to have 24/7 responsive technical support staff or toll-free phone numbers and such. In fact, the bulk of application maintenance can fall on the server side and be limited to content maintenance—such as posting new media such as ringtones, wallpapers, videos, or alerts.

That said, the hardware on the market changes quickly, and mobile development teams need to stay on top of the market. Here are some of the maintenance and support considerations unique to mobile application development.

Maintaining Adequate Application Documentation

Maintenance is often not done by the same engineers who developed the initial application. Here, keeping adequate development and testing documentation, including specifications and test scripts, is even more vital.

Managing Live Server Changes

Always treat any live server with the care it deserves. This means backups and upgrades need to be timed appropriately. Data needs to be safeguarded and user privacy maintained at all times. Rollouts should be managed carefully because live mobile application users might rely on its availability. Do not underestimate the server-side development or testing needs. Always test server rollouts in a safe testing environment before "going live."

Identifying Low-Risk Porting Opportunities

If you've implemented the handset database we previously talked about in the chapter, now is the ideal time to analyze handset similarities to identify easy porting projects. For example, you might discover the following: An application was originally developed for a specific handset, but now there are several popular handsets on the market with similar specifications. Porting an existing application to these new handsets sometimes is as straightforward as generating a new build (with appropriate versioning) and testing the application on the new handsets.

Summary

Mobile software development has evolved over time and differs in some important ways from traditional desktop software development. In this chapter, you gained some practical advice to adapting traditional software processes to mobile, from identifying target handsets to testing and deploying your application to the world. There's always room for improvement when it comes to software process. Hopefully some of these insights can help you avoid the pitfalls new mobile companies sometimes fall into or simply improve the processes of veteran teams.

References and More Information

Wikipedia on Software Process: http://en.wikipedia.org/wiki/Software_development_process
Wikipedia on Rapid Application Development (RAD):
http://en.wikipedia.org/wiki/Rapid_application_development
Wikipedia on Iterative Development: http://en.wikipedia.org/wiki/Iterative_and_incremental_development
Wikipedia on Waterfall Development Process: http://en.wikipedia.org/wiki/Waterfall_model
Extreme Programming: www.extremeprogramming.org/

19

Developing and Testing Bulletproof Android Applications

In this chapter, we cover tips and tricks from our years in the trenches of mobile software design, development, and testing. We also warn you—the project managers, software developers, and testers of mobile applications—of the various and sundry pitfalls to do your best to avoid.

Reading this chapter all at one time when you're new to mobile development might be a bit overwhelming. Instead, consider reading specific sections when planning the specific parts of the overall process. Not all our advice is appropriate for your specific project, and processes can always be improved, but hopefully this information about how mobile development projects succeed (or fail) can give you some insight into how you might improve the chances of success for your own mobile development projects.

Best Practices in Designing Bulletproof Mobile Applications

The "rules" of mobile application design are straightforward and apply across all mobile platforms. These rules were crafted to remind us that our applications play a secondary role on the device, which is, at the end of the day, a phone. They also make it clear that we do operate, to some extent, because of the infrastructure managed by the carriers and handset manufacturers. These rules are echoed throughout the Android Software Development Kit (SDK) License Agreement and those of third-party application marketplace Terms and Conditions.

These "rules" are

- Don't interfere with handset voice and messaging service.
- Don't break the phone hardware, firmware, software, or OEM components.
- Don't abuse or cause problems on operator networks.
- Don't abuse the user's trust (no malware).

Now perhaps these rules sound like no-brainers, but even the most well-intentioned developer can accidentally fall into some of these categories on occasion if they aren't careful and don't test the application thoroughly before distribution. This is especially true for applications that leverage networking support and low-level hardware APIs on the device, and those that store private user data such as names, locations, and contact information.

Meeting Mobile Users' Demands

Mobile users also have their own set of demands for applications they install on their handsets. Applications are expected to.

- Be responsive, stable, and secure.
- Have straightforward user interfaces, easy to get up and running.
- Get the job done with minimal frustration to the user.
- Be available 24 hours a day, 7 days a week (that is, server uptime).
- Include a Help and/or About Screen for feedback and support contact information.

Designing User Interfaces for Mobile Devices

Designing effective user interfaces (UIs) for mobile devices, especially applications that run on a number of different devices, is something of a black art. We've all seen bad mobile application UIs and clunky UIs. A frustrating UI can turn a user off, and a good UIs can win a user's loyalty to your brand long term. It can also give your application an edge over the competition, even if your functionality is similar. A great UIs can win over users even when the functionality is behind the competition. Great UI is *that* important on mobile.

Here are some tips for great mobile UIs:

- Fill screens sparingly; too much information on one screen overwhelms the user.
- Be consistent with user interface workflows, menu types, and buttons. Consider the handset norms with this consistency, as well.
- Make Touch Mode "hit areas" large enough and spaced appropriately.
- Use big, readable fonts and large icons.
- Keep localization in mind when designing text-heavy user interfaces. Some languages are lengthier than others.
- Reduce keys or clicks needed as much as possible.
- Do not assume specific input mechanisms (such as specific buttons or the existence of a keyboard) will be available on all handsets.
- Try to design the default use case of each screen to require only the user's thumb. Special cases might require other buttons, input methods, but encourage "thumbing" by default.

- Size graphics appropriately for phone. Do not include oversized resources and assets because they use valuable device resources and load more slowly, even if they resize appropriately. Also consider stripping out unnecessary information, such as EXIF or IPTC metadata, using tools such as ImageMagick or PNGOptimizer. The Draw 9 Patch tool can also help optimize your Android graphics files. (Read more about this in Chapter 5, "Managing Application Resources.")

- In terms of "friendly" user interfaces, assume users do not read the application permissions when they approve them to install your application. If your application does anything that could cause the user to incur significant fees or shares private information, consider informing them again (as appropriate) when your application performs such actions.

Optimizing User Interfaces for Portrait and Landscape Modes

One way to design for different orientations is to try to keep a "working square" area where most of your application activity takes place. This area remains unchanged (or changes little) when the screen orientation changes. Only functionality displayed outside of the "working square" changes substantially when screen orientation changes (see Figure 19.1).

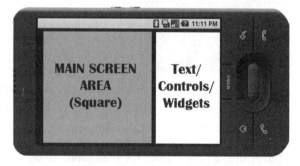

Figure 19.1   The "working square" principle.

An example of a "working square" is the Desktop area of the T-Mobile G1 and the emulator (see Figure 19.2). In Portrait mode (see Figure 19.2, left), the pull-out Application tray is on the bottom of the screen; in Landscape mode (see Figure 19.2, right), the pull-out Application tray moves to the right side, but the bulk of the Desktop changes little (spreads or shrinks only slightly in different orientations).

Figure 19.2   The "working square" principle in use with the emulator Desktop.

Designing Stable and Responsive Mobile Applications

Mobile device hardware has come a long way in the past few years, but developers must still work with limited resources. Users do not have the luxury of upgrading the RAM in their phones as they might their laptops. Removable storage devices such as SD cards provide some "extra" space for media storage but cannot be relied upon on all devices.

Mobile developers find that spending some time upfront to design a stable and responsive application results in gains for the long term. The following are some tips for designing robust and responsive mobile applications:

- Use efficient data structures and algorithms; these choices manifest themselves in app responsiveness and happy users.
- Use recursion with care; these functional areas should be code reviewed and performance tested.

- Keep application state at all times. Android activity stack makes this work well, but you should take extra care to go above and beyond.

- Save your state and assume your application will be suspended or stopped at any moment. If your application is suspended or closed, you cannot expect a user to verify anything (click a button, and so on). If your application resumes gracefully, your users will be grateful.

- Start up fast and resume fast. You cannot afford to have the user twiddling thumbs waiting for your application to start. Instead, you need to strike a delicate balance between preloading and on-demand data because your application may be suspended (or closed) with no notice.

- Inform users during long operations by using progress bars. Consider offloading heavy processing to a server instead of performing these operations on the handset because these operations might drain battery life beyond the limits users might accept.

- Ensure long operations are likely to succeed before embarking upon them. For example, if your application downloads large files, check for network connectivity, file size, and available space before attempting the download.

- Verify that your application resource consumption model matches your target audience. Gamers might anticipate shorter battery life on graphics-intensive games, but productivity applications should not drain the battery unnecessarily and be lightweight for people "on the go" who do not always have their phone charging.

We also talk about some of the different design strategies for mobile applications, such as the benefits and drawbacks of networked applications versus stand-alone applications, in Chapter 18, "The Mobile Software Development Process."

> **Tip**
>
> The Android Developers blog (http://android-developers.blogspot.com/) is another fantastic resource for Android developers. Run by the Google Android team, this Web site provides detailed insight into the Android platform that goes beyond the typical documentation. Here you can find tips, tricks, best practices, and shortcuts on relevant Android development topics such as memory management (like Context management), view optimization (avoiding deep view hierarchies), and layout tricks to improve UI speed. Savvy Android developers visit this blog regularly and incorporate these practices and tips into their Android coding standards.

Designing Secure Mobile Applications

Many mobile applications integrate with existing handset features such as the phone and Contact database. Make sure you take all the proper precautions necessary to secure and protect private data such as names and contact information used by your application.

> **Tip**
>
> If your application accesses or uses private data, especially usernames, passwords, or contact information, it's a good idea to include an End User License Agreement (EULA) and a Privacy Policy with your application.

Handling Private Data on the Handset

To begin with, limit the private or sensitive data your application stores as much as possible. Don't store this information in plain text, and don't transmit it as such. Do not try to work around any security mechanisms imposed by the handset operating system or Android Framework. Consider using the `javax.crypto` package provided with the Android framework for your encyrption needs.

Transmitting Private Data over the Network

The same applies to any server-side data storage or transmission. Make sure any servers your application relies on are properly secured against identity theft and invasion of privacy. Treat any servers your application uses like any other part of the system—test them thoroughly. Any private data transmitted should be secured using typical security mechanisms such as SSL.

> **Caution**
>
> Watch out for server latency problems. A slow server can lead to a slow application. It's a good idea to thoroughly load test your server prior to application deployment.

Designing Mobile Applications for Maximum Profit

For billing and revenue generation, mobile applications generally fall into one of four categories:

- Free applications (including those who leverage advertising revenue)
- Single payment (pay once, often seen with games)
- Subscription payments (pay on a schedule, often seen with productivity and service applications)
- On-demand payment for content (pay for specific content, such as a ringtone)

Applications can use multiple types of billing, depending on which marketplaces and billing APIs they use. Not all methods might be available for all applications. With Android, the billing methods can be provided by third parties, so the sky is the limit.

When designing your mobile application, consider the functional areas where billing can come into play and factor this into your application design. Consider the transactional integrity of specific workflow areas of the application that can be charged for. For example, if your application has the capability to deliver data to the handset, make sure this process is transactional in nature so that if you decided to charge for this type of service, the billing features can be dropped in, and when the user pays, the delivery occurs, or the entire transaction is rolled back.

You learn more about the different methods currently available to market your application in Chapter 20, "Selling Your Android Application."

Leveraging Third-Party Standards for Android Application Design

There are currently no certification programs for Android applications. However, as more applications are developed, third-party standards might be developed to differentiate quality applications from the masses. For example, mobile marketplaces might impose quality requirements. Developers with an eye on financial applications would do well to consider conformance requirements.

> **Caution**
>
> With Android, the market is expected to manage itself. Do not make the mistake of interpreting that as "no rules" when it really means "few rules imposed by Android."

It can be highly beneficial to examine the certification programs available in other mobile platforms and adjust them for Android. You might also want to examine the certification programs for desktop and server applications (again, we're thinking of banking and financial applications, but this can apply to any vertical market application) and consider how the requirements can be applied within Android. For example, if a specific type of encryption is required, and it's available within Android, you can consider using it within your application. Planning for conformance in advance can result in a quality application now and make porting easier in the future.

Designing Mobile Applications for Ease of Maintenance and Upgrades

Generally speaking, it's best to make as few assumptions about the handset configurations as possible when developing a mobile application. You'll be rewarded later when you want to port your application or provide an easy upgrade. What assumptions you do make should be carefully considered.

Leveraging Network Diagnostics for Easy Application Maintenance

In addition to providing adequate documentation and easy-to-decipher code, you can leverage some tricks to help maintain and monitor mobile applications in the field. Most of these tricks apply only to mobile applications leveraging an application server, but you can sometimes gather information from third-party reports, such as application sales figures from mobile marketplaces.

For networked applications, it can be highly useful to build in some lightweight auditing, logging, and reporting on the application server side to keep your own statistics and not rely solely on third-party numbers. For example, you can easily keep track of

- How many users launch the application for the first time?
- How many users regularly use the application?
- What are the most popular usage patterns and trends?
- What are the least popular usage patterns and features?
- What handsets (determined by application versioning) are the most popular?

Often these figures can be translated into rough estimates of expected sales, which can later be compared with actual sales figures from third-party marketplaces. The most popular usage patterns can be streamlined and made more efficient. The least popular features can be reviewed. Sometimes you can even identify potential bugs, such as features that are not working at all, just by noting that a feature has never been used in the field. Finally, you can begin to determine which handsets are most appropriate for your specific application and user base.

> **Tip**
>
> Gathering anonymous diagnostics is fairly common in these sorts of situations, but avoid keeping any data that can be considered private. Make sure your sample sizes are large enough to obfuscate any personal user details, and make sure to factor out any live QA testing data from your results (especially when considering sales figures).

Designing for Easy Upgrades

Mobile application upgrades pose some challenges to developers. It's best to consider how you will drive users from one version of your application to the next early in the development process. This might be as simple as providing a method to inform users that a new application is available, or as complicated as walking them through the entire upgrade process including migrating their data. There are generally two types of upgrade situations for mobile applications:

- A minor upgrade of content, provided by the application itself from a server
- A major upgrade of the application software, generally purchased through an application store

Minor upgrades are actually built into the application functionality as a feature. This includes the capability to deploy fresh content or features to the handset, and the process is entirely controlled by the developer. Building this sort of functionality into your application can keep your users happy longer, and content is less likely to become dated.

Until recently, major upgrades on mobile applications were unusual. Generally speaking, the software developer was not responsible for helping users migrate data to a new version of the software. However, this is changing. Users now expect that their data, which can be difficult to input into a phone, should follow them when they upgrade.

If your application stores important user data on a server, upgrades can be quite straightforward. However, if application data is available only on the handset, you want to consider how it might be accessed at a future time for upgrade purposes. Perhaps consider an "export data" feature or implement a Content Provider interface for an upgraded application that can be leveraged to extract data from the old version.

What's New in Android 1.5

A new broadcast Intent, `ACTION_PACKAGE_REPLACED`, was introduced in Android 1.5. This Intent notifies interested parties when an application package has been replaced and the application has completed a successful upgrade.

Designing for Easy Porting and Localization

Almost inevitably, a developer must adjust to handset changes in the field. Perhaps you develop for a handset that is retired ("sun setting") soon after you deploy your application, but a new version of that handset is available with minor changes. It helps to design your application with these sorts of potential future problems in mind.

Leveraging Android Tools for Android Application Design

The Android SDK and developer community provide a number of useful tools and resources for application design. You might want to leverage the following tools during this phase of your development project:

- The Android emulator is a good place to start for rapid proof of concept, before you have specific handsets. Remember to test on real handsets for true feasibility analysis.
- The Hierarchy Viewer in Pixel Perfect View allows for accurate user interface design.
- The Draw Nine Patch tool can create stretchable graphics for mobile use.
- Physical handsets, when available.
- Technical specifications for handsets, available from manufacturers and carriers.

Avoiding Silly Mistakes in Android Application Design

Last but not least, here is a list of some of the silly mistakes Android designers should generally do their best to steer clear of.

- Designing or developing for months without performing feasibility testing on the handset

- Designing for a single phone, in a single language, for a single carrier
- Designing as if your device has a large amount of storage and processing power and is always plugged in to a power source
- Developing for the wrong version of the Android SDK (verify handset SDK version)
- Trying to adapt applications to smaller screens after the fact by having the phone "scale"
- Deploying oversized graphics and media assets with an application instead of sizing them appropriately

Best Practices in Developing Bulletproof Mobile Applications

As we previously discussed, developing applications for mobile is not that different from traditional desktop development. However, developers might find developing mobile applications more restrictive, especially resource constrained. Again, let's start with some best practices or "rules" for mobile application development.

- Test assumptions regarding feasibility early and often on the target handsets.
- Keep application size as small and efficient as possible.
- Choose efficient data structures and algorithms appropriate to mobile.
- Exercise prudent memory management.
- Assume handsets are running primarily on battery power.

Designing a Development Process That Works for Mobile Development

A successful project's backbone is a good software process. It ensures standards, good communication, and reduces risks. We talked about the overall mobile development process in Chapter 18. Again, here are a few general tips of successful mobile development processes:

- Use an iterative development process.
- Use a regular, reproducible build process with adequate versioning.
- Communicate scope changes to all parties—changes often affect testing most of all.

Testing the Feasibility of Your Application Early and Often

It cannot be said enough: You must test developer assumptions on the handset. There is nothing worse than designing and developing an application for a few months only to find it needs serious redesign to work on the handset. Just because your application works on the emulator does not, in any way, guarantee that it will work on the handset. Some functional areas to examine carefully for feasibility include

- Functionality that interacts with peripherals and device hardware
- Network speed and latency
- Memory footprint and usage
- Algorithm efficiency
- User interface suitability for small screens
- Device input restrictions when compared to required input methods
- File size and storage usage

We know, we sound like a broken record but, truly, we've seen this mistake happen over and over again. Projects are especially vulnerable to this when target handsets aren't yet available. What happens is that engineers are forced closer to the waterfall method of software development with a big, bad surprise after weeks or months of development on the emulator.

We don't need to explain why waterfall approaches are dangerous again, do we? You can never be too cautious about this stuff. Think of it as the preflight airline safety speech of mobile software development.

Using Coding Standards, Reviews, and Unit Tests to Improve Code Quality

Developers who spend the time and effort necessary to develop efficient mobile application will be rewarded by their users. The following is a representative list of some of the efforts that can be taken:

- Centralizing core features in shared Java packages
- Developing to the specific version of the Android SDK compatible with target handsets
- Using built-in controls and widgets appropriate to the application, customizing only where needed to keep code size small

Use system settings to derive default data, such as language (built-into Android) and local time, and so on. If you change system settings in your app, change them back when your app exits/pauses, as necessarily.

Defining Coding Standards

Developing a set of well-communicated coding standards for the development team can help drive home some of the important requirements of mobile applications. Some standards might include

- Implementing robust error handling and handle exceptions gracefully.
- Moving lengthy or process-intensive operations off the main UI thread.

- Releasing objects and resources you aren't actively using.

- Practicing prudent memory management. Memory leaks can render your application useless.

- Using resources appropriately for future localization. Don't hardcode strings and other assets in code or layout files.

- Avoiding obfuscation; comments are worthwhile.

- Considering using standard document generation tools, such as Javadoc.

- Instituting and enforce naming conventions—in code and in database schema design.

Performing Code Reviews

Performing code inspections can improve the quality of project code, help enforce coding standards, and identify problems before QA gets their hands on a build and spends time and resources testing it.

It can also be helpful to pair developers with the individual QA personnel who test specific functional areas to build a closer relationship between the teams. If testers understand (even less-technical personnel) how the system functions internally, they can test it more thoroughly. This might or might not be done as a formal code review process. For example, a tester can identify defects related to type-safety just by noting the type of input expected (but not validated) on a form input field of a layout or by reviewing Submit or Save button handling function with the developer.

Developing Code Diagnostics

The Android SDK provides a number of packages related to code diagnostics. By building a framework for logging, unit testing, and exercising your application to gather important diagnostic information, such as the frequency of method calls and performance of algorithms, can help you develop a solid, efficient, and effective mobile application.

It should be noted that these diagnostic utilities are generally not used in production, after the application is distributed, because they might impose significant performance reductions and greatly reduce application responsiveness.

Using Application Logging

In Chapter 3, "Writing Your First Android Application," we discuss how to leverage the built-in logging class `android.util.Log` to implement many levels of diagnostic logging, which can be monitored via a number of Android tools, such as the LogCat utility (available within DDMS, ADB, and Android Plug-in for Eclipse [ADT]).

Developing Unit Tests

Unit testing can help developers move one step closer to the elusive 100 percent of code coverage testing. The Android SDK includes basic unit testing classes and a more robust package for Android-specific testing mechanisms.

Using Basic JUnit Support

Basic JUnit support is provided through the `junit.framework` and `junit.runner` packages. Here you find the familiar framework for running basic unit tests with helper classes for individual test cases. These test cases can be combined into test suites. There are utility classes for your standard assertions and test result logic.

> **What's New in Android 1.5**
>
> Android Plug-in for Eclipse (ADT) was updated for Android 1.5, including improved Android unit testing support in the `android.test` package.

Using the Android Testing Framework

The Android SDK also includes the `android.test` package, which includes an extensive array of testing tools designed specifically for Android applications. This package builds upon the JUnit framework and adds many interesting features, such as the following:

- Simplified Hooking of Test Instrumentation (`android.app.Instrumentation`) with `android.test.InstrumentationTestRunner`, which can be run via ADB shell commands
- Performance Testing (`android.test.PerformanceTestCase`)
- Single Activity (or Context) Testing (`android.test.ActivityUnitTestCase`)
- Full Application Testing (`android.test.ApplicationTestCase`)
- Services Testing (`android.test.ServiceTestCase`)
- Utilities for generating events such as Touch events (`android.test.TouchUtils`)
- Many more specialized assertions (`android.test.MoreAsserts`)
- `View` validation (`android.test.ViewAsserts`)

Handling Defects Occurring on a Single Handset

Occasionally, you have a situation in which you need to provide code for a specific handset. Handling bugs that occur only on a single handset can be tricky. You don't want to branch code unnecessarily, so here are some of your choices:

- If possible, keep the client generic, and use the server to serve up handset-specific items.
- If the conditions can be determined programmatically on the client, try to craft a generic solution that allows developers to continue to develop under one source code tree, without branching.

- If the handset is not a high-priority target, consider dropping it from your requirements if the cost-benefit ratio suggests that a workaround is not cost effective.
- If required, branch the code.

Leveraging Android Tools for Android Application Development

The Android SDK and developer community provide a number of useful tools and resources for application development. You might want to leverage the following tools during this phase of your development project:

- The Eclipse development environment with the ADT
- The Android emulator and physical handsets for unit testing and bug reproduction
- The Android Dalvik Debug Monitor Service (DDMS) tool for debugging and interaction with the emulator or handset
- The Android Debug Bridge (ADB) tool for logging, debugging, and shell access tools
- The `sqlite3` command-line tool for application database access (available via ADB shell)
- The Hierarchy Viewer for user interface debugging of views
- The Traceview tool for graphical logging functionality
- The dx tool for generating .dex files and Android bytecode from class files

Avoiding Silly Mistakes in Android Application Development

Here are some of the frustrating and silly mistakes Android developers should try to avoid:

- Forgetting to add new application Activities and necessarily permissions to the `AndroidManifest.xml` file
- Forgetting to display `Toasts` using the `show()` method
- Hard-coding information like network information, test user information, and other data into the application
- Forgetting to disable diagnostic logging before release
- Distributing live applications with debug mode enabled

Best Practices in Testing Mobile Applications

Like all QA processes, mobile development projects benefit from a well-designed defect tracking system, regularly scheduled builds, and planned, systematic testing. There are also plentiful opportunities for white box (or gray box) testing and some limited opportunities for automation.

Designing a Mobile Application Defect Tracking System

Most defect tracking systems can be customized to work for the testing of mobile applications. The defect tracking system must encompass tracking of issues for specific handset defects and problems related to any centralized application servers (if applicable).

Logging Important Defect Information

A good mobile defect tracking system includes the following information about a typical handset defect:

- Build version information, language, and so on.
- Handset configuration and state information including handset type, firmware version, screen orientation, network state, and carrier information.
- Steps to reproduce the problem using specific details about exactly which input methods were used (touch versus click).
- Device screenshots that can be taken using the Hierarchy Viewer tool provided with the Android SDK.

Tip
It can be helpful to develop a simple glossary of standardized terms for certain actions on the handsets, such as touch mode "swipes" and pressing the Call or Send button. This helps make the steps to reproduce more reproducible.

Redefining the Term Defect for Mobile Applications

It's also important to consider the larger definition of the term *defect*. Defects can occur on all handsets, on only some handsets, and on the application server (for client/server applications). Some types of defects typical on mobile applications include

- Application crashes and unexpected terminations.
- Features that do not function properly.
- Application uses too much disk space/memory on the handset.
- Inadequate input validation (typically, button mashing).
- Application state management problems (startup, shutdown, suspend, resume, power off).
- Application responsiveness issues (slow startup, shutdown, suspend, resume).
- Usability issues related to input methods, font sizes, and cluttered screen real estate.
- Pausing or "freezing" on the main UI thread (failure to implement asynchronous threading).

- Application indicators missing (failure to indicate progress).
- Application integration with other applications on the handset causing problems.
- Application "not playing nicely" on the handset (draining battery, disabling power-saving mode, overusing networking resources, incurring extensive user charges, obnoxious notifications).
- Application not conforming to third-party agreements, such as Android SDK License Agreement, Google Maps API terms, marketplace terms, or any other terms that apply to the application.
- Application client or server not handling protected/private data securely. This includes ensuring that the application server has adequate uptime and has adequate security measures taken to ensure it won't be hacked, and so on.

Managing the Testing Environment

Testing mobile applications poses a unique challenge to the QA team, especially in terms of configuration management. The difficulty of such testing is often underestimated. Don't make the mistake of thinking that mobile applications are easier to test because they have fewer features than desktop applications and are, therefore, simpler to validate.

Caution

Ensure that all changes in project scope are reviewed by the quality assurance team. Adding new handsets sometimes have little impact on the development schedule but can have significant consequences in terms of testing schedules.

Managing Handset Configurations

Handset fragmentation is perhaps the biggest challenge the mobile developer faces. Handsets come in various form-factors different resolution screens and different underlying hardware. They come with a variety of input methods such as buttons and touch screens. They come with optional features, such as cameras, WiFi, enhanced graphics, and different location-based service mechanisms. Keeping track of all the handsets, their functional abilities, and so on is a big job and much of the work falls on the test team.

QA personnel must have a detailed understanding of the functionality available of each target handset, including familiarity with what features are available and any handset-specific idiosyncrasies that exist. They must test each handset as it will be used in the field, which might not be the handset's default configuration or language. This means changing input modes, screen orientation, and locale settings.

> **Tip**
>
> Be aware of how carrier-related firmware can affect how your application works on the handset. For example, let's assume you've gotten your hands on an unbranded version of a target handset and testing has gone well. However, if certain carriers take that same handset, remove some default applications and load up others, this is valuable information to the developer. Just because your application runs flawlessly on the "vanilla" handset doesn't mean that this is how most users' devices will be configured by default. Do your best to get test handsets that closely resemble the ones in the field.

One hundred percent testing coverage is impossible, so QA must develop priorities thoughtfully. As we discuss in Chapter 18, developing a handset database can greatly reduce the confusion of mobile configuration management, help determine testing priorities, and keep track of physical hardware available for testing.

> **Tip**
>
> If you have trouble configuring handsets for real-life situations, you might want to look into the handset "labs" available through some carriers. Instead of loaner programs, the developer visits the carrier's onsite lab where they can rent time on specific handsets. Here, the developer installs their application and tests it—not ideal for recurring testing but much better than no testing, and some labs are staffed with experts to help out with handset specific issues.

Determining Clean Starting State on a Device

There is currently no way to "image" a handset so that you can return to the same starting state again and again. The QA test team needs to define what a "clean" handset is for the purposes of test cases. This can involve a specific uninstall process and some manual clean-up.

> **Tip**
>
> Using the Android SDK tools such as DDMS and ADB enables developers and testers access to the Android file system, including application SQLite databases. These tools can be used to monitor and manipulate data on the handset and the emulator. For example, testers might use the `sqlite3` command-line interface to "wipe" an application database or fill it with test data for specific test scenarios.

Mimicking Real-World Activities

It is nearly impossible (and certainly not cost-effective) to set up a complete isolated environment for mobile application testing. Although it's fairly common for networked applications to be tested against test (mock) application servers and then go "live" on a separate server with a similar configuration. However, in terms of handset configuration, mobile software testers must use real handsets with real service to test mobile applications properly. They need to properly make and receive phone calls, send and receive text messages, and do anything a phone would normally do.

Testing an application involves more than just making sure the application works properly. In the real world, your application does not exist in a vacuum but is one of many installed on the handset. Testing a mobile application involves ensuring that the software integrates well with other handset functions and applications. For example, let's say you were developing a game. Testers must verify that calls received while playing the game caused the game to automatically pause (keep state) and allow calls to be answered or ignored without issue.

Sometimes testers need to be creative when it comes to reproducing certain types of events. For example, testers must ensure that their application behaves appropriately during events such as losing phone service.

> **Tip**
>
> To test loss of signal, you could go out and test your application under a highway overpass, or you could just place the handset in the refrigerator. Don't leave it in the cold too long, though, or it will drain the battery. Tin cans work great, too, especially those that have cookies in them: First, eat the cookies; then place the phone in the can to seal off the signal.

Maximizing Testing Coverage

All test teams strive for 100 percent testing coverage, but most also realize such a goal is not reasonable or cost-effective. Testers must do their best to cover a wide range of scenarios, the depth and breadth of which can be daunting—especially for those new to mobile. Let's look at several specific types of testing and how QA teams have found ways—some tried-and-true and others new and innovative—to maximize coverage.

Validating Builds and Designing Smoke Tests

In addition to a regular build process, it can be helpful to institute a build acceptance test policy (also sometimes called build validation, smoke testing, sanity testing). Build acceptance tests are short and targeted at key functionality to determine if the build is good enough for more through testing to be completed. This is also an opportunity to quickly verify bug fixes expected to be in the build before a complete retesting cycle occurs.

Automating Functional Testing for Build Acceptance

Mobile build acceptance testing is typically done manually on the highest priority target handset; however, this is also an ideal situation for an automated "sanity" test. By creating a bare-bones functional test for the emulator which, as desktop software, can be used with typical QA automation platforms such as Borland SilkTest (www.borland.com/us/products/silk/silktest/index.html), the team can increase its level of confidence that a build is worth further testing, and the number of bad builds delivered to QA can be minimized.

Testing on the Emulator Versus the Handset

There is a well-established quality assurance mantra within the mobile development community.

Test early, test often, test on the device.

When you can get your hands on the actual handset your users will have, focus your testing there. Handsets and the service contracts that generally come with them are expensive. Your test team cannot be expected to set up test environments on every carrier or every country where your users will use your application. There are times when the Android emulator can reduce costs and improve testing coverage. Some of the benefits of using the emulator include

- Ability to simulate handsets when they are not available or in short supply
- Ability to test difficult test scenarios not feasible on live handsets
- Ability to be automated like any other desktop software

Testing Before Handsets Are Available Using the Emulator

Developers often target up-and-coming handsets not available to the general public. These handsets are often highly anticipated and developers who are ready with applications for these handsets on Day 1 of release often experience a sales bump because fewer applications are available to these users—less competition, more sales.

Often, developers can gain access to preproduction phones through carrier and manufacturer developer programs. However, developers and testers should be aware of the dangers of testing on preproduction phones: These phones are beta-quality. The final technical specifications and firmware can change without notice. These phone release dates can slip, and the phone might never reach production.

When preproduction phones cannot be acquired, testers can do some functional testing using emulator configurations that attempt to closely match the target platform, lessening the risks for a compact testing cycle when these handsets go live, allowing developers to release applications faster.

Taking Advantage of Automated Testing Opportunities Using the Emulator

How we wish we had better news, but we know of few automated device testing methods available to the mobile community.

> **Tip**
>
> There are some third-party solutions such as Mobile Complete's DeviceAnywhere (www.deviceanywhere.com/), which enable developers remote access to physical handsets, but the number of Android devices on the market at the time of this writing makes this kind of solution less enticing.

It's certainly possible to rig up automated testing software to exercise the software emulator. we can certainly *imagine* someone coming up with a solution—in our minds, the device looks a lot like the automated signature machine U.S. presidents use to sign pictures and Christmas cards. The catch is that every handset looks and acts differently, so any animatronic hand would need to be recalibrated for each device. The other problem is how to determine when the application has failed or succeeded. Again, there are no easy methods to determine this programmatically. If anyone is developing mobile software automated testing tools, it's likely a mobile software testing consultancy company. For the typical mobile software developer, the costs are likely prohibitive.

Understanding the Dangers of Relying on the Emulator

Unfortunately, the emulator is more of a "generic" Android device that pretends at many of the device internals. It does not represent the specific implementation of the Android platform that is unique to a given handset. It does not use the same hardware internals to determine signal, networking, or location information. The emulator can pretend to make and receive calls and messages, but this is a simulation and requires some setup (making virtual SD Cards, using multiple emulator instances, and so on). At the end of the day, it doesn't matter if the application works on the emulator if it doesn't work on the actual device.

Testing Strategies: White Box Testing

The Android tools provide ample tools for black box and white box testing.

Black box testers might require only testing handsets and test documentation. For black box testing, it is even more important that the testers have a working knowledge of the specific handsets, so providing handset manuals and technical specifications will also aid in more thorough testing.

White box testing has never been easier on mobile. White box testers can leverage the many affordable tools including the Eclipse development environment, which is free, and the many debugging tools available as part of the Android SDK. White box testers want to use the Android Emulator, DDMS, and ADB especially. For this, testers require a computer set up with a development environment, much like the developer's. The Android tools generally do not impose any substantial burden on the resources of your average laptop.

Testing the Mobile Application Server

Although testers often focus on the client portion of the application, they sometimes neglect to thoroughly test the server portion. Many mobile applications rely on networking and leverage an application server. If your application depends on a server to operate, testing the server side of your application is vital.

> **Caution**
>
> In the past, certain carriers tried to impose fees on mobile developers whose application servers go down or don't respond. We haven't seen this with Android applications, but you should understand that users expect applications to be available any time, day or night, 24/7. Minimize server down times and make sure the application notifies the users appropriately (and doesn't crash and burn) if the server is unavailable.

Versioning Server Builds

Server rollouts should be managed like any other part of the build process. The server should be versioned and rolled out in a reproducible way.

Employing Test Servers

Often, QA tests against a mock server in a controlled environment. This is especially true if the live server is already operational with real users.

Testing the Server

Most server testing should focus on the primary method the server will access—generally through the handset client. It's also important to test the server in other ways, such as

- Testing the server under load, including stress testing (many users, simulated clients)
- Testing the server security (hacking, SQL injection, and such)
- Testing server upgrades and rollbacks

These types of testing offer yet another opportunity for automated testing to be employed.

Testing Application Visual Appeal and Usability

Testing a mobile application is not only about finding dysfunctional features, but also about evaluating the usability of the application. Report areas of the application that lack visual appeal or are difficult to navigate or use.

We like to use the walking-and-chewing-gum analogy when it comes to mobile user interfaces. Mobile users frequently do not give the application their full attention. Instead, they walk or do something else while they use it. Applications should be as easy for the user as chewing gum.

Tip

Consider conducting usability studies to collect feedback from people who are not familiar with the application. Relying solely on the product team members, who see the application regularly, can blind the team to application flaws.

Leveraging Third-Party Standards for Android Testing

Make a habit to try to adapt traditional software testing principles to mobile. For example, veteran testers such as Vijay at Software Testing Help (www.softwaretestinghelp.com) have provided helpful online testing tips that can be easily applied to mobile software projects. Encourage quality assurance personnel to develop and share these practices within your company.

Again, no certification programs are specifically designed for Android applications at this time; however, nothing is stopping the mobile marketplaces from developing them. Consider looking over the certification programs available in other mobile platforms, such as the extensive testing scripts used for TRUE BREW testing and adjusting them for your Android applications. Whether you plan to apply for a specific certification, making an attempt to conform to well-recognized quality guidelines can improve your application's quality.

Handling Specialized Test Scenarios

In addition to functional testing, there are a few other specialized testing scenarios that any QA team should consider.

Testing Application Integration Points

It's necessary to test how the application behaves with other parts of the Android operating system. For example:

- Proper handling of interruptions from the operating system (incoming messages, calls and powering off)
- Validating Content Provider data exposed by your application
- Validating functionality triggered in other applications via an `Intent`
- Validating any known functionality triggered in your application via an `Intent`
- Validating any secondary entry points to your application as defined in the `AndroidManifest.xml`, such as application shortcuts
- Validating service-related features, if applicable

Testing Upgrades

When possible, perform upgrade tests of both the client and the server. If upgrade support is planned, have development create a mock upgraded Android application so that QA can validate that data migration occurs properly, even if the upgraded application does nothing with the data.

Testing Product Internationalization

It's a good idea to test internationalization support early in the development process—both the client and the server. You're likely to run into some problems in this area related to screen real-estate problems and issues with strings, dates, and times.

> **Tip**
>
> If your application will be localized for multiple languages, test in a foreign language—especially on a verbose one. The application might look flawless in English but be unreadable in German where words are generally longer.

Testing for Conformance

Make sure to review any policies, agreements, and terms that your application must conform to and make sure your application complies. For example, Android applications must by default conform to the Android Developer Agreement and the Google Maps terms of service (if applicable).

Installation Testing

Generally speaking, installation of Android applications is straightforward; however, you need to test installations on handsets with low resources and low memory and test installation from the specific marketplaces when your application "goes live."

Performance Testing

Application performance matters in the mobile world. The Android SDK has support for calculating performance benchmarks within an application and monitoring memory and resource usage. Familiarize the QA team with these utilities and use them often to help identify performance bottlenecks and dangerous memory leaks and misused resources.

Testing Application Billing

Billing is too important to leave to guesswork. Test it. You'll notice a lot of test applications on the Android marketplace—we wouldn't be surprised to see a sandbox test market area for this soon. As the Android platform acceptance grows, you might find carriers that have sandbox networks you can use for testing. If not, do what you can and always test the deployed application as soon as possible.

Testing for the Unexpected

Regardless of the workflow you design, understand that users will do random, unexpected things—on purposes and by accident. Some users are "button mashers," whereas others forget to set the keypad lock before putting the phone in their pocket, resulting in a weird set of key presses. A phone call or text message will inevitably come in during the farthest, most-remote edge cases. Your application must be robust enough to handle this. The Exerciser Monkey command-line tool is a good way to test for this type of event.

Testing to Increase Your Chances of Being a "Killer App"

Every mobile developer wants to develop a "killer app"—those applications that go viral, rocket to the top of the charts, make millions a month. Most people think that if they just find the right idea, they'll have a killer app on their hands. Developers are always scouring the top-ten lists, trying to figure out how to develop the next big thing.

But let us tell you a little secret: If there's one thing that all "killer apps" share, it's a higher-than-average quality standard. No clunky, slow, obnoxious, or difficult-to-use application ever makes it to the big leagues. Testing and enforcing quality standards can mean the difference between a mediocre application and a killer app.

If you spend any time examining the mobile marketplace, you notice a number of larger mobile development companies publish a variety of high-quality applications with a shared look and feel. These companies leverage user interface consistency, shared, and above-average quality standards to build brand loyalty and increases market share, while hedging their bets that perhaps just one of their many applications will have that magical combination of great idea and quality design. Other, smaller companies often have the great ideas but struggle with the quality aspects of mobile software development. The inevitable result is that the mobile marketplace is full of fantastic application ideas badly executed with poor user interfaces and crippling defects.

Leveraging Android Tools for Android Application Testing

The Android SDK and developer community provide a number of useful tools and resources for application testing and quality assurance. You might want to leverage these tools during this phase of your development project.

- The physical handsets for testing and bug reproduction
- The Android emulator for automated testing and testing of builds when handsets are not available
- The Android DDMS tool for debugging and interaction with the emulator or handset
- The ADB tool for logging, debugging, and shell access tools
- The Exerciser Monkey command-line tool for stress testing of input (available via ADB shell)
- The `sqlite3` command-line tool for application database access (available via ADB shell)
- The Hierarchy Viewer for user interface navigation and verification and for screenshots of the handset
- The Eclipse development environment with the ADT and related logging and debugging tools for white box testing

It should be noted that although we have used the Android tools such as the Android emulator and DDMS debugging tools with Eclipse, these are stand-alone tools that can be used by quality assurance personnel without the need for source code or a development environment.

Avoiding Silly Mistakes in Android Application Testing

Here are some of the frustrating and silly mistakes Android testers should try to avoid:

- Not testing the server side of an application as thoroughly as the client side.
- Not testing with the appropriate version of the Android SDK (handset versus development build versions).
- Not testing enough on the handset and assuming the emulator is acceptable.
- Not testing the live application (billing, installation, and such).
- Neglecting to test all entry points to the application.
- Neglecting to test using battery power only. Don't always have the device plugged in.

Outsourcing Testing Responsibilities

Mobile quality assurance can be outsourced. Remember, though, that the success of outsourcing your QA responsibilities depends on the quality and detail of the documentation you can provide. Outsourcing makes it more difficult to form the close relationships between QA and developers that help ensure thorough and comprehensive testing.

Summary

In this chapter, we armed you—the software designers, developers, and testers—with real-world knowledge and experience from veteran mobile developers. Feel free to pick and choose which information works well for your specific project, and keep in mind that software process, especially the mobile software process, is always open to improvement.

References and More Information

Software Testing Help: www.softwaretestinghelp.com
Wikipedia on Software Testing: http://en.wikipedia.org/wiki/Software_testing

## 20

Selling Your Android Application

After you've developed an Android application, the next logical step is to publish it so other people can enjoy it. You might even make some money. There are multiple revenue opportunities for Android applications. These include submitting the application to mobile marketplaces such as the Android Market and making your application available for download from your own server or Web site. Which methods you choose to employ depends on your sales goals and target user audience. Are you trying to reach the broadest audience, or have you developed a vertical market application?

Packaging Your Application for Publication

There are several steps developers must take when preparing an Android application for publication and distribution. Your application must also meet several important requirements imposed by the marketplaces.

The following steps are required for publishing an application:

1. Set the application icon and label attributes in the `ApplicationManifest.xml`.
2. Version the application appropriately.
3. Confirm that the manifest setting for `uses-sdk` is correct (1.1 is "2" and 1.5 is "3").
4. Digitally sign the application with a key that expires at a later date.

The preceding steps are required but not sufficient to guarantee a successful deployment. Developers should also:

1. Thoroughly test the application on all target handsets.
2. Turn off debugging, including Log statements and any other logging.
3. Verify permissions, making sure to add ones for services used and remove any that aren't used, regardless of whether they are enforced by the handsets.
4. Test the final, signed version with all debugging and logging turned off.

Now, let's explore each of these steps in more detail, in the order they might be performed.

Preparing Your Code to Package

An application that has undergone a thorough testing cycle might need changes made to it before it is ready for a production release. These changes will convert it from a debuggable, preproduction application in to a release-ready application.

Setting the Application Name and Icon

An Android application will have default settings for the icon and label. The icon appears in the application Launcher and can appear in various other locations, including download sites. As such, an application is required to have an icon. Preferably, this icon should be a custom icon suitable for the application. A typical icon will be a square 48-pixel PNG file. The label, or application name, is also displayed in similar locations and defaults to the package name. A user-friendly name should be chosen.

Versioning the Application

Next, proper versioning is required, especially if updates could occur in the future. The version name is up to the developer. The version code, though, is used internally by the Android system to determine if an application is an update. The version code should be incremented for each new update of an application. The exact value doesn't matter, but it must be greater than the previous version code. Versioning is discussed in detail in Chapter 4, "Understanding the Anatomy of an Android Application" and Chapter 18, "The Mobile Software Development Process."

Disabling Debugging and Logging

Next, debugging and logging should be turned off. Disabling debugging involves removing the `android:debuggable` attribute from the `<application>` tag of the `AndroidManifest.xml` file or setting it to `false`. Turning off the logging code within Java can be accomplished in a variety of different ways, from just commenting it out to using a build system that can do this automatically.

> **Tip**
>
> A common method for conditionally compiling debug code is to use a class interface with a single, public, static, final Boolean set to true or false. When used with an `if` statement and set to false, because it's immutable, the compiler should not include the unreachable code, and it certainly won't be executed. We recommend using some method other than just commenting out the Log lines and other debug code, even if you don't.

Verifying Application Permissions

Finally, the permissions used by the application should be audited. As of this writing, the Android emulator and handsets do not validate or enforce all permissions that might be required for certain functionality. Additionally, no check is made to see that a given permission is actually used by the application. Include all permissions that the application will need assuming permissions are enforced. Do not include any permission that the application does not currently use. Users will appreciate this.

Preparing Your Package

Now that the application is ready for publication, the file package—the `.apk` file—needs to be prepared for release. The package manager of an Android device will not install a package that has not been digitally signed. Throughout the development process, the Android tools have accomplished this through signing with a debug key. The debug key cannot be used for publishing an application to the wider world. Instead, a true key needs to be used to digitally sign the application.

Self-signing is typical of Android applications, and a certificate authority is not required. Creating a suitable key and securing it properly, though, is critical. The `keytool` and `jarsigner` applications that come with the JDK can be used for creating a suitable key, which can then be used to sign the release package files of your application.

The digital signature for Android applications can impact certain functionality. The expiry of the signature is verified at installation time, but once installed, an application will continue to function even if the signature has expired. An upgrade or update for an application must be signed with the same key or the installation will not be allowed.

Tip

This might impact activities such as installing the application over a version signed with the debug key. Before installing a release version of the application on a handset or emulator that has the debug version installed, the old debug version should be completely uninstalled. If the application appears to have been removed, but the error "Application install unsuccessful" appears, the version with the previous signature needs to be installed so it can be fully uninstalled before the newly signed version is installed. Updates do not remove data, but the data is tied to the original signature used. Only uninstalling the application can remedy this, and that option is available only when the application is fully installed.

Generating a suitable key can be done with the `keytool` application. The following command-line block shows the `keytool` commands and expected responses:

```
MBP:~ android$ keytool -genkey -v -keystore androidbook.keystore -alias
↪androidbook -keyalg RSA -validity 10000
Enter keystore password:  password
What is your first and last name?
  [Unknown]:  Android Book
What is the name of your organizational unit?
  [Unknown]:  AndroidBook
What is the name of your organization?
  [Unknown]:  AndroidBookOrg
```

```
What is the name of your City or Locality?
  [Unknown]:  Android City
What is the name of your State or Province?
  [Unknown]:  AC
What is the two-letter country code for this unit?
  [Unknown]:  US
Is CN=Android Book, OU=AndroidBook, O=AndroidBookOrg, L=Android City,
➥ST=AC, C=US correct?
  [no]:  yes
Generating 1,024 bit RSA key pair and self-signed certificate (MD5WithRSA)
    for: CN=Android Book, OU=AndroidBook, O=AndroidBookOrg, L=Android
➥City, ST=AC, C=US
Enter key password for <androidbook>
    (RETURN if same as keystore password):
[Storing androidbook.keystore]
MBP:~ android$
```

> **Note**
>
> The Google Android Market has specific requirements for application signing, which we dis-
> cuss in the "Preparing Your Application Package for the Android Market" section later in
> this chapter.

Now that a key is available within the `androidbook.keystore` file, this can be used to
sign an unsigned Android package file.

To create an Android application package in Eclipse, right-click on the project; then
choose Android Tools, Export Unsigned Application Package; and choose where to save
the .apk file. Unlike the regular debug process, exporting the package in this way creates
a package file that is not signed.

Now this package needs to be signed with a true key. To sign this file with the key
previously created, the following command can be executed:

```
MBP:keys android$ jarsigner -verbose -keystore androidbook.keystore
➥android_app.apk androidbook
Enter Passphrase for keystore: password
   adding: META-INF/MANIFEST.MF
   adding: META-INF/ANDROIDB.SF
   adding: META-INF/ANDROIDB.RSA
  signing: res/drawable/icon.png
  signing: res/layout/main.xml
  signing: AndroidManifest.xml
  signing: resources.arsc
  signing: classes.dex
MBP:keys android$
```

A package can also be checked to see if it's already signed using the following command:

```
MBP:keys android$ jarsigner -verbose -certs -verify android_app.apk

        409 Fri Mar 06 17:21:58 EST 2009 META-INF/MANIFEST.MF
        530 Fri Mar 06 17:21:58 EST 2009 META-INF/ANDROIDB.SF
        971 Fri Mar 06 17:21:58 EST 2009 META-INF/ANDROIDB.RSA
sm     3366 Mon Jan 26 18:24:44 EST 2009 res/drawable/icon.png


      X.509, CN=Android Book, OU=AndroidBook, O=AndroidBookOrg,
➥L=Android City, ST=AC, C=US
      [certificate is valid from 3/6/09 5:06 PM to 7/22/36 6:06 PM]


sm     1640 Fri Mar 06 17:15:00 EST 2009 res/layout/main.xml
<… and so on …>
```

The application package is ready for publication.

Testing the Release Version of Your Application Package

Now that you have configured your application for production, you should perform a full final testing cycle paying special attention to subtle changes to the installation process. An important part of this process is to verify that all debugging features have been disabled and logging has no negative impact on the functionality and performance of the application.

Certifying Your Android Application

If you're familiar with other mobile platforms, you might be familiar with the many strict certification programs found on platforms, such as the TRUE BREW or Symbian Signed programs. These programs exist to enforce a lower bound on the quality of an application.

As of this writing, Android does not have any certification or testing requirements. It is an open market with only a few content guidelines and rules to follow. This does not mean, however, that certification won't be required at some point or that certain distribution means won't require certification.

Typically, certification programs require rigorous and thorough testing, certain usability conventions must be met, and various other constraints that might be good common practice or operator-specific rules are enforced. The best way to prepare for any certification program is to incorporate its requirements into the design of your specific project. Following best practices for Android development and developing efficient, usable, dynamic, and robust applications will always pay off in the end—whether your application requires certification.

> **Tip**
>
> Because there is no specific certification program yet, we obviously can't go into any details. Chapter 19, "Developing and Testing Bulletproof Android Applications," provides a variety of tips and techniques to prepare robust applications, and much of it will also prepare your applications for certification programs, if they crop up.

Making Money

Now that you've prepared your application for publication, it's time to get your application out to users—for fun and profit. Unlike other mobile platforms, most Android distribution mechanisms support free applications and price plans.

Selling Your Application on the Android Market

The Android Market is the primary mechanism for distributing Android applications at this time. This is where your typical user will purchase and download applications from. As of this writing, it's available on every Android handset. As such, we show you how to check your package for preparedness, sign up for a developer account, and submit your application for sale on the Android Market.

Preparing Your Application Package for the Android Market

The Android Market has strict requirements on packages that are uploaded. The Market uses the `android:versionName` attribute of the `<manifest>` tag within the Android Manifest file to display version information to users. It also uses the `android:versionCode` attribute internally to handle application upgrades. The `android:icon` and `android:label` attributes must also be present because both are used by the Android Market to display the application name to the user with a visual icon.

> **Caution**
>
> The Android SDK allows the `android:versionName` attribute to reference a string resource. The Android Market, however, does not. An error will be generated if a string resource is used.

Finally, the digital signature validity period must end after October 22, 2033. This date might seem like a long way off and, for mobile, it certainly is. However, because an application must use the same key for upgrading and applications that want to work closely together with special privileges and trust relationships must also be signed with the same key, the key could be chained forward through many applications. Thus, Google is mandating that the key be valid for the foreseeable future so application updates and upgrades will be performed smoothly for users.

Note

Finding a third-party certificate authority that will issue a key valid for such a long duration can be a challenge, so self-signing is the most straightforward signing solution. Within the Android Market, there is no benefit to using a third-party certificate authority.

Signing Up for a Developer Account on the Android Market

To publish applications through the Android Market, you must register as a developer. This accomplishes two things. It verifies who you are to Google and signs you up for a Google Checkout account, which is used for billing of Android applications. To sign up for Android Market, you need to

1. Browse to http://market.android.com/publish/signup, as shown in Figure 20.1.

Figure 20.1   Web screen showing the Android Market publisher sign-up page.

2. Sign in with the Google Account you want to use. (This can't be changed yet, but contact email addresses can be changed.)
3. Enter developer information such as developer name, email, and Web site, as shown in Figure 20.2.

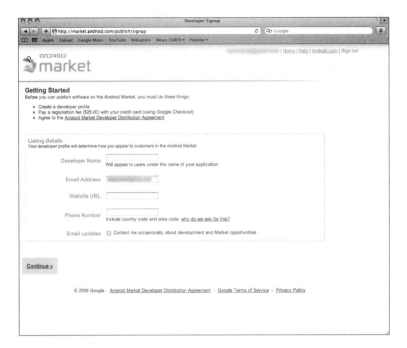

Figure 20.2   Web screen showing the Android Market publisher profile
page.

4. Confirm registration payment (as of this writing, $25 USD). For registration payment processing, Google Checkout will be used.

5. Signing up and paying to be an Android Developer also creates a mandatory Google Checkout Merchant account with which you'll also need to provide information for.

6. Agree to link your credit card and account registration to the Android Market Developer Distribution Agreement, as shown in Figure 20.3.

7. When successfully completed, you will be presented with the home screen of the Android Market that also confirms the Google Checkout merchant account was created, as shown in Figure 20.4.

Figure 20.3   Web screen showing the Android Market Developer
Distribution Agreement page.

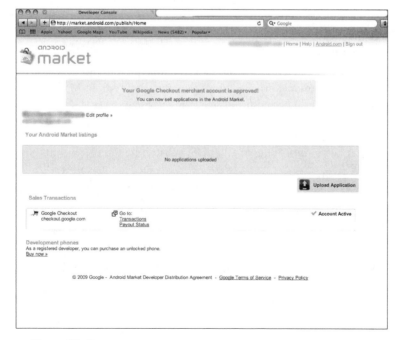

Figure 20.4   Browser screen showing Android Market Listings page.

Uploading Your Application to Android Market

Now that you have a developer account for publishing applications through Android
Market and a signed application package, you are ready to upload it. From the main page
of Android Market, sign in and press the button for uploading applications, as shown in
Figure 20.4.

A form is presented for uploading the package. Some of the information you must
enter includes

- The application title and description in several languages.

  The Android Market currently supports English (en_US), German (de_DE),
  French (fr_FR), Italian (it_IT), Spanish (es_ES), Dutch (nl_NL), Polish (pl_PL),
  and Czech (cs_CZ).

- The countries (Locations) where the application will be published.

  These locations are subject to export compliance laws, so choose your Locations
  carefully. New locations are added to the Android Market as devices become available throughout the world (with Canada, Portugal, Switzerland, and Ireland next in
  the queue). Developers can choose to make their applications available in specific
  Locations or "All Current and Future Locations." Not all locations support priced
  applications yet; some might not even have shipping Android devices yet.
  Generally, free applications are enabled for new countries first, with billing capabilities becoming enabled soon thereafter.

- The application type and category.

  Spend the time to set these fields appropriately, as defined by the Marketplace so
  that your application reaches its intended audience. Wrongly categorized applications do not sell well.

- The application price.

  The Android Market currently supports only one pricing model: single payment.
  No subscription model pricing exists yet within the Android Market. The developer must find other mechanisms for recurring payment pricing. Note that the
  Android Market currently imposes a 30 percent transaction fee for hosting applications within its marketplace. Prices can be set in USD, GBP, and EUR. Dollar
  prices can range from $0.99 to $200 USD. British pound prices from 0.50 GBP to
  100 GBP.

- Copy protection information.

  Make sure to register all the appropriate copyright and trademark information
  with the appropriate authorities.

- Support contact information.

  Defaults to the information you provided for the developer account.

The application package will be uploaded and verified while you fill out the form. Before publication you must show that the application meets Android Content Guidelines and United States export laws, regardless of your nationality.

> **Tip**
>
> After the application package has been successfully uploaded, the preceding information can be saved as a draft, which is great for verification before final publishing. Also, the application icon, name, version, localization information, and required permissions are shown so that you can verify you have configured the Android Manifest file properly.

Publishing Your Application on the Android Market

Finally, you are ready to press the Publish button. Your application will appear in the Android Market almost immediately. After publication, statistics including ratings, reviews, downloads, and active installs can be seen in the "Your Android Market Listings" section of the main page on your developer account. These statistics aren't updated as frequently as the publish action is, and you can't see review details directly from the listing. Clicking on the application listing allows you to edit the various fields. Although some details can be edited, pricing information can't be changed. (That is, if it started as a free application, it will remain that way.)

> **Note**
>
> As of this writing, the Android Market has a 24-hour refund policy. That is, applications can be returned within 24 hours and the user will receive a full refund. The Android Market has another 24 hours to complete the return transaction. As a developer, this means that sales aren't final until after the first 48 hours. However, this user return policy only applies to the first download and first return. If a particular user has already returned your application and wants to "try it again" he will be making a final purchase—he can't return it a second time. Although this limits abuse, you should still be aware that if your application has limited reuse appeal or all of it's value can come from just a few hours (or less) of use, you might find that you have a return rate that's too high to be worthwhile.

Removing Your Application from the Android Market

You can also use the unpublish action to remove the application from the Market from the developer account. The unpublish action is also immediate, but the application entry on the Market application might be cached on handsets that have viewed or downloaded the application.

Using Other Developer Account Benefits

In addition to managing your applications on the Android Market, an additional benefit to have a registered Android developer account is the ability to purchase development versions of Android handsets. These handsets are useful for general development and testing but might not be suitable for final testing on actual target handsets because some functionality might be limited, and the firmware version might be different than that found on consumer handsets.

Selling Your Application on Your Own Server

You can distribute Android applications directly from a Web site or server. This method is most appropriate for vertical market applications, content companies developing mobile marketplaces, and big brand Web sites wanting to drive users to their branded Android applications. It can also be a good way to get beta feedback from end users.

Although self-distribution is perhaps the easiest method of application distribution, it might also be the hardest to market, protect, and make money. The only requirement for self-distribution is to have a place to host the application package file.

The downside of self-distribution is that end users must configure their device to allow packages from unknown sources. This setting is found under the Applications section of the device Settings application, as shown in Figure 20.5.

Figure 20.5   Settings application showing required check box for downloading from unknown sources.

After that, the final step the user must make is to enter the URL of the application package in to the web browser on the handset and download the file (or click on a link to it). When downloaded, the standard Android install process occurs, asking the user to confirm the permissions and, optionally, confirm an update or replacement of an existing application if a version is already installed.

Selling Your Application Using Other Alternatives

The Android Market is not the only consolidated market available for selling Android applications. Android is an open platform, which means there is nothing preventing a handset manufacturer or an operator (or even you) from running an Android market Web site or building another Android application that serves as a market. Many of the mobile-focused stores, such as Handango, have been adding Android applications to their offerings.

Here are a few alternate marketplaces where you might consider distributing your Android applications:

- **Handango** distributes mobile applications across a wide range of devices with various billing models (www.handango.com).
- **SlideME** is an Android-specific distribution community for free and commercial applications using an on-device store (http://slideme.org).
- **AndAppStore** is an Android-specific distribution for free applications using an on-device store (www.andappstore.com).
- **MobiHand** distributes mobile applications for a wide range of devices for free and commercial applications (www.mobihand.com).

This list is not complete, nor do we endorse of any of these markets. That said, we feel it is important to demonstrate that there are a number of alternate distribution mechanisms available to developers. Application requirements vary by store. Third-party application stores are free to enforce whatever rules they want on the applications they accept, so read the fine print carefully. They might enforce content guidelines, require additional technical support, and enforce digital signing requirements. Only you and your team can determine which are suitable for your specific needs.

Protecting Your Intellectual Property

You've spent time, money, and effort to build a valuable Android application. Now you want to distribute it but perhaps you are concerned about reverse engineering of trade secrets and software piracy. As technology rapidly advances, it's impossible to perfectly protect against both.

If you're accustomed to developing Java applications, you might be familiar with code obfuscation tools. These are designed to strip easy-to-read information from compiled Java byte codes making the decompiled application more difficult to understand. For Android, though, applications are compiled for the Dalvik virtual machine. As such, existing Java tools might not work directly and might need to be updated. Some tools, such as ProGuard (http://proguard.sourceforge.net), do support Android applications because it can run after the `jar` file is created and before it's converted to the final package file used with Android.

Android Market supports a form of copy protection via a check box when you publish your application. The method that this uses isn't well documented currently. However, you can also use your own copy protection methods or those available through other markets if this is a huge concern for you or your company.

Billing the User

Unlike some other mobile platforms you might have used, Android does not currently provide built-in billing APIs that work directly from within applications or charge directly to the users' cell phone bill. Instead, Android Market uses Google checkout for processing payments. When an application is purchased, the user owns it. (Although they currently have 24 hours to return it for a full refund.)

Billing Recurring Fees or Content-Specific Fees

If your application requires a service fee and sells other goods within the application (that is, ringtones, music, e-books, and more), the application developer must develop a custom billing mechanism. Most Android devices can leverage the Internet, so using online billing services and APIs—Paypal, Google, Amazon to name a few—are likely be the common choice. Check with your preferred billing service to make sure it specifically allows mobile use.

Leveraging Ad Revenue

Another method to make money from users is to have an ad-supported mobile business model. This is a relatively new model for use within applications because many older application distribution methods specifically disallowed it. However, Android has no specific rules against using advertisements within applications. This shouldn't come as too much of a surprise, considering the popularity of Google's AdSense.

Summary

You've now learned how to design, develop, test, and deploy professional-grade Android applications. In this final chapter, you learned how to prepare your application package for publication using a variety of revenue-models. Whether you publish through your own Web site, the Android Market, or use one of the many alternative methods available (or use a combination), you can now build a robust application from the ground up and distribute it for profit or fame.

So now it's time to go out there, fire up Eclipse, and build some amazing applications. We want to encourage you to think outside of the box. The Android platform leaves the developer with a lot more freedom and flexibility. Take what works and reinvent what doesn't. You might just find yourself with a killer app.

Finally, if you're so inclined, we'd love to know about all the exciting applications you're building. You'll find our contact information and book blog at the beginning of this book.

Best of luck!

References and More Information:

Android Market: http://market.android.com/
Handango: http://handango.com
SlideME: http://slideme.org
AndAppStore: www.andappstore.com
MobiHand: www.mobihand.com

VII

Appendixes

A

The Android Emulator Quick-Start Guide

The most useful tool provided with the Android Software Development Kit (SDK) is the emulator. Developers use the emulator to quickly develop Android applications to develop powerful applications for a variety of hardware. This Quick-Start Guide is not a complete documentation of the emulator commands. Instead, it is designed to get you up and running with common tasks. Please see the emulator documentation provided with the Android SDK for a complete list of features, start-up commands, and functionality.

The Android emulator (shown in Figure A.1) is integrated with Eclipse using the Android Development Tools Plug-in for the Eclipse integrated development environment (IDE). The emulator is also available within the /Tools directory of the Android SDK and can be launched as a separate process.

> **Caution**
>
> The Android emulator is a powerful tool but no substitute for testing on the true target device.

Figure A.1   The Android emulator home screen with the default skin
(HVGA-P).

Getting Up to Speed Using the Default Emulator

Here are some tips for using the emulator effectively from the start:

- You can use keyboard commands to easily interact with the emulator.
- Mouse clicking works and mouse scrolling and dragging works. So do the keyboard arrow buttons.
- If you have an Internet connection, so does your emulator. The browser works.
- The gray tab with the triangle is the application tray. You can click it or pull it out to see installed applications.
- The Dev Tools application can be useful for setting development options.
- Don't forget the side buttons, such as the volume control. These work, too.
- To switch between portrait and landscape modes of the emulator (or other orientations that the current skin uses), use the 7 key and 9 key on the numeric keypad of the host machine (or F11 and F12 keys).

- Networking can be toggled using the F8 key.

- The Menu button is a context menu for the given screen, replacing traditional tabs along the button of the screen for functions such as Add, Edit, and Delete item.

- Application lifecycle-wise: To pause an application just press Home. To resume, launch the application again. It should begin where you left off, if the phone hasn't run low on memory and exited your application behind the scenes.

- You can access the Settings application on the application tray or by pressing the Menu button on the Home screen. You can use the Settings application to config- ure the Wireless controls, Call Settings, Sound & Display (ringtones, brightness, and so on), Data synchronization settings, Security & Location, Manage Applications, SD Card and phone storage, Date & Time, Text Input settings, and About Phone (phone status/software version, and such).

- Notifications such as incoming SMS messages appear in the white Notification bar at the top of the Home screen, along with battery life, and so on. You can pull down this status bar to see the messages, as shown in Figure A.2.

Figure A.2   An incoming SMS Message shown in the Notification
status bar.

Managing Emulator Configuration with Android Virtual Devices (AVDs)

The Android emulator is a not a real device, but a generic Android system simulator for testing purposes. Prior to Android 1.5, the Android emulator had some basic settings and little more. However, with the Android 1.5 SDK, developers can now model specific Android devices by creating Android Virtual Devices (AVDs). To use the Android emulator provided with the Android 1.5 R1 SDK, you must provide a valid AVD profile.

An AVD can contain the following information describing a specific Android device:

- The friendly, descriptive name of the AVD for use by the developer
- The target Android operating system, generally Android SDK 1.1 or 1.5 (with or without add-ons)
- Hardware device support details and features, including RAM, input methods, and optional hardware such as cameras and location sensors
- Various emulator settings, such as the emulator skin

To create and manage AVDs, you use the `android` command line tool provided with the Android SDK Tools directory. The basic `android` tool command line is

```
android <command>
```

Now let's walk through some of the commands you might use to create and manage AVDs in the course of typical Android development projects.

Listing Android Target Operating Systems

To create an AVD, you need to specify the target Android operating system that the Android emulator should simulate. To list available targets, use the `android` command line tool with the `list targets` command:

```
android list targets
```

This command will likely yield the following three targets:

```
Available Android targets:
id: 1
     Name: Android 1.1
     Type: Platform
     API level: 2
     Skins: HVGA (default), HVGA-L, HVGA-P, QVGA-L, QVGA-P
id: 2
     Name: Android 1.5
     Type: Platform
     API level: 3
     Skins: HVGA (default), HVGA-L, HVGA-P, QVGA-L, QVGA-P
```

```
id: 3
    Name: Google APIs
    Type: Add-On
    Vendor: Google Inc.
    Description: Android + Google APIs
    Based on Android 1.5 (API level 3)
    Libraries:
     * com.google.android.maps (maps.jar)
         API for Google Maps
    Skins: QVGA-P, HVGA-L, HVGA (default), QVGA-L, HVGA-P
```

The first target (`id: 1`) is a vanilla 1.1 installation with API Level 2. The second target (`id: 2`) is a vanilla 1.5 installation, and the third target (`id: 3`) is an Android 1.5 installation with the Google API add-ons included—both require API Level 3.

Creating AVDs

To create a new AVD, you use the `android` command line tool with the `create avd` command.

> **Tip**
>
> In recent versions of the Eclipse Plug-In, you can also click the little button on the toolbar that resembles a black cell phone to create and manage AVDs through the development environment.

Creating Simple AVDs

The typical `android` tool command line for creating AVDs is

```
android create avd -n <name> -t <target id>
```

To create an Android 1.5 AVD with all the defaults, use the following command:

```
android create avd -n vanilla1.5 -t 2
```

You will be asked if you want to create a custom hardware profile. For this installation with default settings, answer no. You have created a simple AVD called `vanilla1.5`. Now, within your Eclipse project, you can create a Debug Configuration and on the Target tab, specify the `vanilla1.5` AVD as the preferred AVD. When you launch your Debug configuration, the settings within the AVD will be used. Figure A.3 illustrates a debug configuration that specifies an AVD.

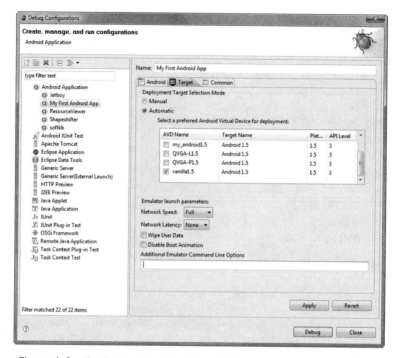

Figure A.3   Setting the Emulator Target Option with the Preferred AVD in
Eclipse.

Creating AVDs with Different Skins

If you develop Android applications that rely on screen orientation, you need to know
how to change the emulator look and feel, especially the orientation and screen size. The
Android SDK currently has three supported skins in addition to the HVGA portrait
mode skin used by default. These skins are described in detail in Table A.1 and shown in
Figure A.4.

Table A.1   **Emulator Skin Options**

Skin Name	Skin Description
HVGA-P	320×480 Screen
	Portrait mode
	Default skin in emulator
HVGA-L	480×320 Screen
	Landscape mode
	Same "phone" as Default Skin

Table A.1   **Continued**

Skin Name	Skin Description
QVGA-L	320×240 Screen
	Landscape mode
	Phone with full QWERTY keyboard
QVGA-P	240×320 Screen
	Portrait mode
	Input much like the HVGA skins

Figure A.4   Other emulator skins available (clockwise from top: HVGA-L, QVGA-P, and QVGA-L).

Notice that each target in the Android operating system target listing has a set of valid skins. As more Android devices are developed, new skins will become available for specific targets (most likely Android 1.5 and beyond). If you want to use a different skin with your AVD, such as the landscape QVGA mode, you can specify it using the –s command line option as follows:

```
android create avd -n QVGA-L1.5 -t 2 -s QVGA-L
```

Creating AVDs with SD Card Images

Some of your applications require data, such as images, to be stored on the emulator. The emulator allows only you to download images from the browser (using long click) if you have an SD Card disk image to save them on, for example. If you want to configure a 2GB SD Card image to use with an AVD, you can create it as part of the AVD using the –c command line option as follows:

```
android create avd -n vanilla1.5w2GigSD -t 2 -c 2048M
```

You can also use the –c command line option to specify the path to an existing SD card image created with the mksdcard command line tool.

Creating SD Card Disk Images with mksdcard

To create an SD Card disk image for use with an AVD and emulator, you can use the mksdcard tool provided with the Android SDK Tools directory. The mksdcard tool command line is

```
mksdcard [-l label] <size>[K|M] <file>
```

The volume label (-l) is optional, and you can create images in kilobytes or megabytes. For example, to create a simple 2GB SD Card Image called **mysdcard.iso,** use the following command:

```
mksdcard 2048M mysdcard.iso
```

Using the SD Card Disk Image with Eclipse

After you include an SD Card image with your AVD, you can test your SD card setup by launching the emulator with your AVD instance and navigating to the browser. Browse to your favorite Web site and "borrow" an image with a long-press on the image. The image will be downloaded, stored in the phone picture gallery (accessible through the Camera and Picture applications). You can access these images from your Android application using a built-in content provider, as discussed in Chapter 9, "Using Android Data and Storage APIs."

Creating AVDs with Custom Hardware Settings

If you want to set some hardware settings, simply modify the property as part of the AVD creation process. The hardware options available are shown in Table A.2.

Table A.2   **Hardware Profile Options**

Hardware Option	Description
hw.ramSize	Physical RAM on the device in megabytes. Default value: 96
hw.touchScreen	Touch screen exists on the device. Default value: yes
hw.trackBall	Trackball exists on the device. Default value: yes
hw.keyboard	QWERTY keyboard exists on the device. Default value: yes
hw.dPad	Directional Pad exists on the device. Default value: yes
hw.gsmModem	GSM modem exists in the device. Default value: yes
hw.camera	Camera exists on the device. Default value: no
hw.camera.maxHorizontalPixels	Maximum horizontal camera pixels. Default value: 640
hw.camera.maxVerticalPixels	Maximum vertical camera pixels. Default value: 480
hw.gps	GPS exists on the device. Default value: yes
hw.battery	Device can run on a battery. Default value: yes
hw.accelerometer	Accelerometer exists on the device. Default value: yes
hw.audioInput	Device can record audio. Default value: yes
hw.audioOutput	Device can play audio. Default value: yes
hw.sdCard	Device supports removable SD cards. Default value: yes
disk.cachePartition	Device supports/ache partition on the device. Default value: yes
disk.cachePartition.size	Device cache partition size. Default value: 66MB

For example, to create an AVD for Android 1.5 with camera support, but no GPS support, you can do the following:

```
android create avd -n camNoGPS1.5 -t 2
```

Then set the following hardware options when prompted:
```
Android 1.5 is a basic Android platform.
Do you wish to create a custom hardware profile [no]y

Device ram size: The amount of physical RAM on the device, in megabytes.
hw.ramSize [96]:
```

Touch-screen support: Whether there is a touch screen or not on the device.
hw.touchScreen [yes]:

Track-ball support: Whether there is a trackball on the device.
hw.trackBall [yes]:

Keyboard support: Whether the device has a QWERTY keyboard.
hw.keyboard [yes]:

DPad support: Whether the device has DPad keys
hw.dPad [yes]:

GSM modem support: Whether there is a GSM modem in the device.
hw.gsmModem [yes]:

Camera support: Whether the device has a camera.
hw.camera [no]:yes

Maximum horizontal camera pixels
hw.camera.maxHorizontalPixels [640]:

Maximum vertical camera pixels
hw.camera.maxVerticalPixels [480]:

GPS support: Whether there is a GPS in the device.
hw.gps [yes]:no

Battery support: Whether the device can run on a battery.
hw.battery [yes]:

Accelerometer: Whether there is an accelerometer in the device.
hw.accelerometer [yes]:

Audio recording support: Whether the device can record audio
hw.audioInput [yes]:

Audio playback support: Whether the device can play audio
hw.audioOutput [yes]:

SD Card support: Whether the device supports insertion/removal of virtual SD Cards
hw.sdCard [yes]:

Cache partition support: Whether we use a /cache partition on the device.
disk.cachePartition [yes]:

```
Cache partition size
disk.cachePartition.size [66MB]:
```

```
Created AVD 'camNoGPS1.5' based on Android 1.5
```

Listing All Known AVDs

The typical `android` tool command line for listing currently configured AVDs is

```
android list avds
```

The resulting list of AVDs might look like this:

```
Available Android Virtual Devices:
    Name: camNoGPS1.5
    Path: C:\Users\Me\.android\avd\camNoGPS1.5.avd
  Target: Android 1.5 (API level 3)
    Skin: HVGA
---------
    Name: QVGA-L1.5
    Path: C:\Users\Me\.android\avd\QVGA-L1.5.avd
  Target: Android 1.5 (API level 3)
    Skin: QVGA-L
---------
    Name: vanilla1.5
    Path: C:\Users\Me\.android\avd\vanilla1.5.avd
  Target: Android 1.5 (API level 3)
    Skin: HVGA
```

If you navigate to the default `.android` directory where AVDs are stored by default, you can read the configuration settings in the `config.ini` file within each AVD sub-directory.

Deleting AVDs

The `android` tool command line for deleting AVDs by name is

```
android delete avd -n <name>
```

So, to delete the AVD we created earlier, you could use the following command:

```
android delete avd -n vanilla1.5
```

Using Other AVD Commands

There are a variety of other features available for managing AVDs. You can change the default path for where to store the AVD configuration files. You can also move, update, and rename existing AVDs. For a complete list of the `android` command line tool features, just type

```
android
```

Controlling Emulator Behavior Using Startup Options

The Android emulator has a number of configuration options above and beyond those set in the AVD profile. Some of these settings include network speed and latency, the ability to disable boot animation upon startup and numerous other system settings. The emulator can be started as part of a Debug Configuration or Run Configuration from within Eclipse or from the command line. Some of the most common emulator startup options are shown in Table A.3.

Table A.3   **Useful and Common Emulator Startup Options**

Startup Option	Description
-wipe-data	Resets contents to user-data image.
-initdata <path>	Copies contents to new user-data image.
-wipe-data	Resets contents to user-data image.
-noaudio	Disable audio for emulator instance.
-dns-server <server list>	Comma delimited list of up to four DNS server names or IP addresses.
-http-proxy <proxy>	All TCP connections through proxy, which can be of the forms: http://<server>:<port> http://<username>:<password>@<server>:<port>
-netdelay <delay>	Network latency values: gprs, edge, umts, none, or an exact number of milliseconds.
-netspeed <speed>	Network speed values: gsm, hscsd, gprs, edge, umts, hsdpa, full, or an exact rate or set of rates.
-cpu-delay <delay>	Emulate CPU delay. Values: 0 to 1000.
-timezone <timezone>	Time zone of emulator in zone info format, for example, America/New_York. For a complete list of zones, see http://en.wikipedia.org/wiki/List_of_zoneinfo_time_zones.
-no-boot-anim	Speed startup of emulator by skipping the boot animation sequence.

The emulator is available within the /Tools directory of the Android SDK and can be launched as a separate process from the command line.

This list of emulator startup options is by no means complete. There are a number of other options for networking, debugging, and other settings. For a complete list of emulator startup options, consult the Android emulator documentation or simply type

```
emulator -help
```

Configuring Emulator Startup Options from the Command Line

The command line for starting the Android emulator requires that you designate a unique AVD:

```
emulator -avd <name>
```

You can also set specific emulator startup options, as follows:

```
emulator -avd <name> [other startup options]
```

For example, to start an emulator instance with the Android 1.5 AVD we created earlier, with options to disable audio and limit network speed to GSM (14.4kbps up and down), we would use the following command line:

```
emulator -avd vanilla1.5 —noaudio -netspeed gsm
```

Configuring Emulator Startup Options Using Eclipse

To set emulator startup options in Eclipse, you must edit the specific Run or Debug Configuration for your project.

You can change the Emulator Launch parameters on the Target tab. Some common startup options such as Network Speed are shown specifically and can be altered using the drop-down lists and check boxes, whereas others must be designated using the Additional Emulator Command Line options, much like you would with the command line. Figure A.5 shows a debug configuration with a designated AVD and startup options for setting network speed and disabling audio for the specific emulator instance.

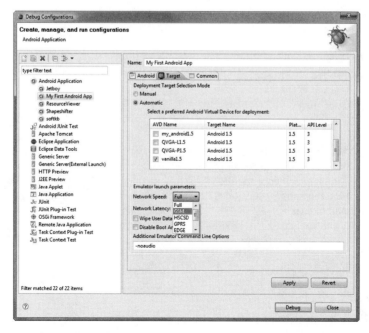

Figure A.5   Setting emulator startup options using Eclipse.

Configuring the Location Information of the Emulator

To work with Google Maps support in conjunction with location-based services, you need to begin by creating an AVD with target 3, which corresponds to Android SDK 1.5 plus Google add-ins. For example:

```
android create avd -n map1.5 -t 3 -c 2048M
```

The emulator does not have location sensors, so the first thing you need to do is seed your emulator with GPS coordinates. To do this, launch your emulator in debug mode and follow these steps:

In the emulator:

1. Launch the emulator. If you're running an application, press the Home button.

2. Choose Maps.

3. Click the Menu button.

4. Choose the My Location menu item. (It looks like a target.)

Then in Eclipse:

5. Click the Dalvik Debug Monitor Service (DDMS) perspective in the top right corner.

6. You see an Emulator Control pane on the left side of the screen. Scroll down to the Location Control.

7. Manually enter the longitude and latitude of your location. (Note they are in reverse order.)

8. Click Send.

Back in the emulator, you notice that the Google Map now shows the location you seeded. Your screen should now display your location as Yosemite, as shown in Figure A.6.

Your emulator now has a simulated location.

> **Tip**
>
> To find a specific set of GPS coordinates, you can go to http://maps.google.com. Navigate to the location you want and center the map on the location by right-clicking the map. Choose link to map and copy the URL. Take a closer look at the URL and weed out the "ll" variable, which represents the latitude/longitude of the location. For example, Yosemite Valley link has the value ll=37.746761,-119.588542, which stands for Latitude: 37.746761 and Longitude: -119.588542.

Figure A.6   Setting the location of the emulator to Yosemite Valley.

Calling Between Two Emulator Instances

You can have two emulator instances call each other using the Dialer application provided on the emulator, as shown in Figure A.7 and Figure A.8. The emulator's "phone number" is its port number, which can be found in the title bar of the emulator window. Figure A.7 shows a Landscape emulator (on the right) with port 5554 using the Dialer application to call the emulator on port 5556.

To simulate a phone call between two emulators, you must perform the following steps:

1. Launch two instances of the emulator. (The command line method is the simplest.)
2. Note the port number of the emulator you want to receive the call.
3. In the emulator that makes the call, launch the Dialer application.
4. Type the port number you noted as the number to call. Press Enter (or Send).
5. You see (and hear) an incoming call on the receiving emulator instance.

Appendix A The Android Emulator Quick-Start Guide

6. Answer the call by pressing Send.

7. Pretend to chat for a bit.

8. You can end either emulator call at any time by pressing the End key.

Figure A.7 The emulator on the left receiving a call from the emulator on the right.

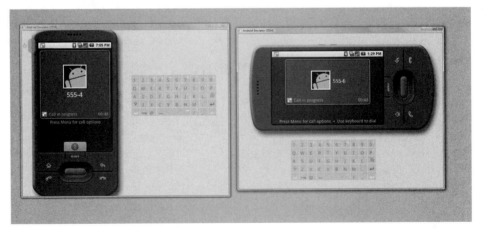

Figure A.8 Two emulators with a phone call in progress.

Messaging Between Two Emulator Instances

You can send SMS messages between two emulators exactly as previously described for simulating calls using the emulator port numbers as SMS addresses. In the emulator, launch the messaging application, press F11 (and F12, or using the numeric keypad, press 7 or 9) on the host computer keyboard to switch to landscape mode and trigger the slide out keyboard allowing text to be entered. Type the text message and press Send. You can also use DDMS or the console to send SMS messages to emulator instances.

Interacting with the Emulator Through the Console

You can interact with instances of the emulator by connecting to the Emulator console via telnet. For example, to connect to the Emulator console of the emulator using port 5554, you would do the following:

```
telnet localhost 5554
```

You can use the Emulator console to issue commands to the emulator. To end the session, just type `quit` or `exit`. You can shut this instance of the emulator using the `kill` command.

Using the Console to Simulate Incoming Calls

You can simulate incoming calls to the emulator from specified numbers. The command for issuing an incoming call is

```
gsm call <number>
```

For example, to simulate an incoming call from the number 555-1212, you would issue the following command:

```
gsm call 5551212
```

The result of this command in the emulator is shown in Figure A.9.

> **Tip**
>
> You can control inbound and outbound phone calls, busy signals, and such using other `gsm` subcommands. Gsm subcommands include `list`, `call`, `busy`, `hold`, `accept`, `cancel`, `data`, `voice`, and `status`.

Figure A.9   Incoming call from 555-1212, prompted via the Emulator console.

Using the Console to Simulate SMS Messages

You can simulate SMS messages to the emulator from specified numbers. The command for issuing an incoming SMS is

```
sms send <number> <message>
```

For example, to simulate an incoming SMS from the number 555–1212 asking "How are you?" in SMS slang, you would issue the following command:

```
sms send 5551212 HRU?
```

In the emulator, you get a notification on the white status bar informing you of a new message. It even displays the contents on the bar for a moment, and then rolls away, showing the Message icon. You can pull down the notification bar to see the new message or launch the Messaging application.

The result of the preceding command in the emulator is shown in Figure A.10.

Figure A.10   Incoming SMS from 555-1212, prompted via the emulator console.

Caution

The sms send command does not work as expected on all the platforms we tested. For example, if you include multiple words in your SMS message, you might want to enclose them in quotes to avoid the message displaying in the wrong encoding on the emulator. Unfortunately, the quotes might display in the message.

Using the Console to Send GPS Coordinates

You can use the Emulator console to issue commands to the emulator. The command for a simple GPS fix is

```
geo fix <longitude> <latitude> [<altitude>]
```

For instance, to set the fix for the emulator to the top of Mount Everest, launch the Maps application in the emulator by selecting Menu, My Location. Then, within the Emulator console, issue the following command to set the device's coordinates appropriately:

```
geo fix 86.929837 27.99003 8850
```

Using the Console to Monitor Network Status

You can monitor network status of the emulator and change the network speed and latency on-the-fly. The command for displaying network status is

```
network status
```

Typical results from this request look something like this:

```
network status
Current network status:
  download speed:        0 bits/s (0.0 KB/s)
  upload speed:          0 bits/s (0.0 KB/s)
  minimum latency:   0 ms
  maximum latency:   0 ms
OK
```

Using the Console to Manipulate Power Settings

You can manage "fake" power settings on the emulator using the power commands. You can turn the battery capacity to 99 percent charged as follows:

```
power capacity 99
```

You can turn the AC charging state off (or on) as follows:

```
power ac off
```

You can turn the Battery status to the following options: unknown, charging, discharging, not-charging, or full as follows:

```
power status full
```

You can turn the Battery Present state true (or false) as follows:

```
power present true
```

You can turn the Battery health state to the following options: unknown, good, overheat, dead, overvoltage, or failure as follows:

```
power health good
```

You can show the current power settings by issuing the following command:

```
power display
```

Typical results from this request look something like this:

```
power display
AC: offline
status: Full
health: Good
present: true
capacity: 99
OK
```

Using Other Console Commands

There are also commands for simulating hardware events, port redirection, checking, starting, and stopping the virtual machine.

Quality assurance personnel will want to check out the event subcommands, which can be used to simulate key events for automation purposes. It's likely this is the same interface used by the ADB Exerciser Monkey, which presses random keys and tries to crash your application.

Enjoying the Emulator

Here are a few more tips for using the emulator, just for fun:

- On the Home screen, press and hold the desktop to change the wallpaper and add applications, shortcuts, and widgets to the desktop.
- If you press and hold an icon (usually an application icon) in the application tray, you can place a shortcut to it on your Home desktop for easy access.
- If you press and hold an icon on your Home desktop, you can move it around or dump it into the trash to get it off the desktop.
- Press and fling the phone's Home desktop to the left and right for more space. The right side has a Google search, and the left is empty space where you can place other desktop items.
- Another way to change your wallpaper and add applications to your desktop is to press Menu on the desktop screen; then choose Add. Here you can also add shortcuts and picture frames widgets around your family photo, and so on, as shown in Figure A.11.

Figure A.11   Customizing the emulator's Home desktop screen with application shortcuts and widgets.

Understanding Emulator Limitations

The emulator is powerful, but it has several important limitations.

- It is not a device, so it does not reflect actual behavior, only simulated behavior.
- Simulation of phone calls, but you cannot place or receive true calls.
- Limited ability to determine device state (network state, battery charge).
- Limited ability to simulate peripherals (camera capture, headphones, SD Card insertion, location-based services).
- No USB or Bluetooth support.

B

The Android DDMS
Quick-Start Guide

The Dalvik Debug Monitor Service (DDMS) is a debugging tool provided with Android Software Development Kit (SDK). Developers use DDMS to provide a window into the emulator or the actual phone for debugging and file and process management. It's a blend of several tools: a Task Manager, a File Explorer, an Emulator console, and a Logging console. This Quick-Start Guide is not a complete documentation of the DDMS functionality. Instead, it is designed to get you up and running with common tasks. See the DDMS documentation provided with Android SDK for a complete list of features.

Using DDMS with Eclipse and as a Stand-Alone Application

If you use the Android Development Tools Plug-In for Eclipse integrated development environment (IDE), the DDMS tool is tightly integrated with your development environment. By using the DDMS Perspective (shown in Figure B.1, using the File Explorer to browse files on the emulator instance), you can explore any emulator instances running on the development machine and any Android devices connected via USB.

If you're not using Eclipse, the DDMS tool is also available within the /Tools directory of Android SDK and can be launched as a separate process, in which case it runs in its own process, as shown in Figure B.2 (sending an SMS message to the emulator).

> **Tip**
>
> There should be only one instance of the DDMS tool running at a given time. Other DDMS launches will be ignored. We have found the DDMS Eclipse Perspective to be far more stable than the stand-alone tool (which we are adept at crashing).

Figure B.1   The Eclipse DDMS Perspective with one emulator and one Android device connected.

Figure B.2   The DDMS tool with one emulator and one Android device connected.

Getting Up to Speed Using Key Features of DDMS

Whether you use DDMS from Eclipse or as a stand-alone tool, be aware of a few key features.

- In the top-left corner, you see find a list of running emulators and connected devices.
- The File Explorer enables you to browse files on the emulator or device (including application files, directories and databases) and pull and push files to the Android system.
- The `LogCat` window enables you to monitor the Android Logging console (`LogCat`). This is where calls to `Log.i()`, `Log.e()` and other `Log` messages display.
- Individual processes can be inspected (heap and thread updates). Individual threads can be inspected. Processes can be killed. You can prompt garbage collection on a process and then view the Heap for that application.
- You can take remote screenshots of the emulator or the device using the Screen Capture button.
- You have some helpful Emulator console functionality at your fingertips, such as the ability to send GPS information and to simulate incoming calls and SMS messages.

Some functionality applies only to the Eclipse DDMS Perspective; you can click on an individual process in an emulator or device and click the little green bug to attach a debugger to that process and debug using Eclipse, provided you have the source code open in the workspace.

Working with Processes

One of the most useful features of DDMS is the ability to interact with processes. As you might remember, each Android application runs in its own VM with its own user `id` on the operating system.

Using the left pane of DDMS, you can browse all instances of the VM running on a device, each identified by its package name.

You can

- Attach and debug applications in Eclipse
- Monitor threads
- Monitor the heap
- Stop processes
- Force Garbage Collection (GC)

For example, in Figure B.3, there is a package named `com.androidbook.`
`SuperDuperPetTracker` running on the emulator.

Figure B.3   The DDMS tool with debugger attached to Application package `com.androidbook.SuperDuperPetTracker`, displaying threading information.

Attaching a Debugger to an Android Application

Although you'll most likely use the Eclipse debug configurations to launch and debug your applications most of the time, you can also use DDMS to choose which application to debug and attach directly.

To attach a debugger to a process, you need to have the package source code open in your Eclipse workspace. Now perform the following steps to debug:

1. On the emulator or device, verify the application you want to debug is running.

2. In DDMS, find that application's package name and highlight it.

3. Choose the little green bug icon to debug that application.

4. Switch to the Debug Perspective of Eclipse as necessary; debug as you would normally.

Monitoring Thread Activity of an Android Application

You can use DDMS to monitor thread activity of an individual Android application. For an example of DDMS monitoring the threading activity of an application, see Figure B.3.

Follow these steps:

1. On the emulator or device, verify the application you want to monitor is running.

2. In DDMS, find that application's package name and highlight it.

3. Choose the three black arrows icon to display the threads of that application. They appear in the right portion of the Threads tab. This data updates every 4 seconds by default.

4. On the Threads tab, you can choose a specific thread and press the Refresh button to drill down within that thread. The resulting Classes in use display below.

Prompting Garbage Collection (GC) on an Android Application

You can use DDMS to force the Garbage Collector (GC) to run by following these steps:

1. On the emulator or device, verify the application you want to GC is running.

2. In DDMS, find that application's package name and highlight it.

3. Pull down the drop-down menu (upside-down triangle) and choose Cause GC. You can also do this from the Heap tab, as detailed next.

Monitoring Heap Activity of an Android Application

You can use DDMS to monitor heap statistics of an individual Android application. The heap statistics are updated after every GC. For an example of DDMS monitoring the heap status of an application, see Figure B.4.

Follow these steps:

1. On the emulator or device, verify the application you want to monitor is running.

2. In DDMS, find that application's package name and highlight it.

3. Choose the green cylinder icon to display the heap information for that application. The statistics appear in the right portion of the Heap tab. This data updates after every GC. You can also cause GC operations from the Heap tab using the button Cause GC.

4. On the Heap tab, you can choose a specific type of object. The resulting graph in use displays at the bottom of the Heap tab, as shown in Figure B.4.

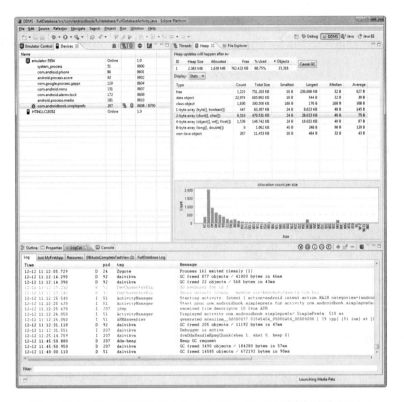

Figure B.4   The DDMS tool with debugger attached to the Application
package com.androidbook.SuperDuperPetTracker, displaying
heap information.

Stopping an Android Process

You can use DDMS to kill an Android application by following these steps:

1. On the emulator or device, verify the application you want to stop is running.
2. In DDMS, find that application's package name and highlight it.
3. Choose the red stop sign icon to stop that process.

Working with the File Explorer

You can use DDMS to browse and interact with the Android file system on an emulator
or device. Table B.1 shows some important areas of the Android file system.

Table B.1   **Important Directories in the Android File System**

Directory	Purpose
/data/data/<package name>/	Application top-level directory
	For example: **/data/data/com.androidbook.pettracker/**
/data/data/<package name>/shared_prefs/	Application shared preferences directory
	Named preferences stored as XML files
/data/data/<package name>/files/	Application file directory
/data/data/<package name>/cache/	Application cache directory
/data/data/<package name>/databases/	Application database directory
	For example: **/data/data/com.androidbook.pettracker/databases/test.db**
/sdcard/download/	Where browser images for the emulator are saved
/data/app/	Where third-party Android application APK files are stored

To browse the Android file system, follow these steps:

1. In DDMS, choose the emulator or device you want to browse.
2. Switch to the File Explorer tab. You see a directory hierarchy.
3. Browse to a directory or file location.

Copying Files from the Emulator or Device

You can use File Explorer to copy files or directories from an emulator or a device file system to your computer by following these steps:

1. Using File Explorer, browse to the file or directory to copy and highlight it.
2. From the top-right corner of the File Explorer, choose the Disk icon to pull the file from the device. Alternatively, you can pull down the drop-down menu next to the icons and choose Pull File.
3. Type in the path where you want to save the file or directory on your computer and press Save.

Copying Files to the Emulator or Device

You can use File Explorer to copy files to an emulator or a device file system from your computer by following these steps:

1. Using File Explorer, browse to the file or directory to copy and highlight it.

2. From the top-right corner of the File Explorer, choose the Phone icon to push a file to the device. Alternatively, you can pull down the drop-down menu next to the icons and choose Push File.

3. Select the file or directory on your computer and press Open.

Tip

The File Explorer also supports some drag-and-drop operations. This is the only way to push directories to the Android file system; however, copying directories to the Android file system is not recommended because there's no delete option for them. You need to delete directories programmatically if you have the permissions to do so. That said, you can drag a file or directory from your computer to the File Explorer and drop it in the location you want.

Deleting Files on the Emulator or Device

You can use File Explorer to delete files (but not directories) on the emulator or device file system. Follow these steps:

1. Using File Explorer, browse to the file you want to delete and highlight it.

2. In the top-right corner of the File Explorer, choose the red minus button to delete the file.

Caution

Be careful. There is no confirmation. The file is deleted immediately and is not recoverable.

Working with the Emulator Control

You can use DDMS to interact with instances of the emulator using the Emulator Control tab. The emulator you want to interact with must be selected for the Emulator Control tab to work. You can use the Emulator Control tab to

- Change telephony status
- Simulate incoming voice calls
- Simulate incoming SMS messages
- Send a location fix

Simulating Incoming Voice Calls

To simulate an incoming voice call using the Emulator Control tab, use the following steps:

1. In DDMS, choose the emulator you want to call.
2. Switch to the Emulator tab. You work with the Telephony Actions.
3. Input the Incoming phone number. This might include only numbers, +, and #.
4. Select the Voice radio button.
5. Press the Call button.
6. Over in the emulator, your phone is ringing. Answer the call.
7. The emulator can end the call as normal, or you can end the call in DDMS using the Hang Up button.

Simulating Incoming SMS Messages

DDMS provides the most stable method to send incoming SMS messages to the emulator. You send an SMS much as you initiated the voice call. To simulate an incoming SMS message using the Emulator Control tab, use the following steps:

1. In DDMS, choose the emulator you want to send a message to.
2. Switch to the Emulator tab. You work with the Telephony Actions.
3. Input the Incoming phone number. This might include only numbers, +, and #.
4. Select the SMS radio button.
5. Type in your SMS message, as shown in Figure B.5.
6. Press the Send button.
7. Over in the emulator, you receive an SMS notification.

Sending a Location Fix

The steps for sending GPS coordinates to the emulator are covered in Appendix A, "The Android Emulator Quick-Start Guide." Simply input the GPS information into the Emulator Control tab, press Send, and use the Maps application on the emulator to get the current position.

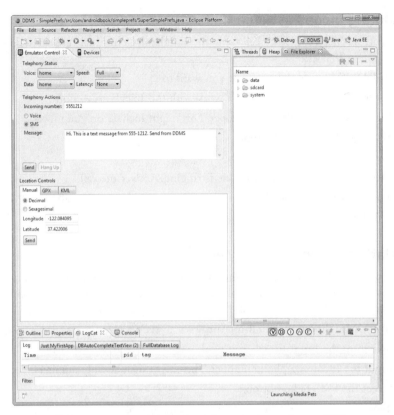

Figure B.5   The DDMS tool Emulator Control tab sending an SMS message to the emulator.

Working with Application Logging

The LogCat tool is integrated into DDMS. It is provided as a tab along the bottom of the DDMS user interface. You can control how much information displays by clicking on the little round circles with letters in them. The V stands for verbose (show everything) and is the default. The other options correspond to Debug (D), Information (I), Warning (W), and Error (E).

You can also create Filter tabs to display only the LogCat information associated with a Debug Tag. You can use the Plus (+) button to add a Filter tab and show only log entries matching a specific tag. It is helpful to create a unique debug tag string for your application logging. Then you can filter LogCat to show only your application logging activities. For example, if your application does this,

```
public static final String DEBUG_TAG = "MyFirstAppLogging";
Log.i(DEBUG_TAG, "This is info about MyFirstAndroidApp.");
```

then you can create a `LogCat` filter using the plus sign. Name the filter "Logging My App" and set the tag to "MyAppLog." That's it. Now you have a `LogCat` tab called Logging My App, which displays only logging information with the tag unique to your application, as shown in Figure B.6.

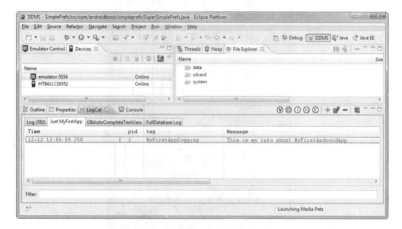

Figure B.6   The DDMS tool with a `LogCat` custom filter.

Taking Screen Captures of Emulator and Device Screens

You can take screen captures of the emulator and the device from DDMS. The device captures are most useful for debugging, and this makes the DDMS tool appropriate for quality assurance personnel and developers.

To take a screen capture, follow the following steps:

1. In DDMS, choose the emulator or device you want to take a capture of.

2. On the device or emulator, make sure you have the screen you want to take the screenshot of.

3. Choose the multicolored square picture icon to take a screen capture. A capture window launches, as shown in Figure B.7.

4. Within the capture window, choose Save to save the screen capture.

Figure B.7   The DDMS tool taking a screen capture.

C

The Android Debug Bridge Quick-Start Guide

The Android Debug Bridge (ADB) is a client-server tool that interacts directly with Android devices and emulators using a command-line interface. You can use this tool, provided as part of the Android Sorftware Development Kit (SDK), to manage and interact with emulator and device instances connected to a development machine and view logging and debugging information. ADB also provides the underpinnings for other tools, such as the Android Plug-In for Eclipse (ADT) and Dalvik Debug Monitor Service (DDMS). This Quick-Start Guide is not a complete documentation of the ADB functionality. Instead, it is designed to get you up and running with common tasks. See the ADB documentation provided with the Android SDK for a complete list of features.

Much of the functionality provided by the ADB (such as the `LogCat` Android logging utility or pushing and pulling files using the File Explorer) is closely integrated into the development environment through DDMS and ADT.

Developers might prefer to use these friendly methods to interact with devices and emulators; however, you can use ADB for automation and scripting purposes. You can also use ADB to customize functionality, instead of relying on the defaults exposed through secondary tools.

Listing Devices and Emulators Connected to a Machine

You can use ADB to list all Android devices and emulator instances connected to a development machine. To do this, simply use the `devices` command of the `adb` command line. For example:

```
adb devices
```

This command lists the emulators and devices attached to this machine by their serial number and state (`offline` or `device`). For emulator instances, the serial number is based on their unique port number. For example, in this case, we have one emulator instance (Port 5554) and one Android phone (a T-Mobile G1 connected via USB):

```
C:\>adb devices
List of devices attached
emulator-5554    device
HT841LC1977      device
```

Directing ADB Commands to Specific Devices

When you know the serial number of the device you want to connect to, you can issue commands as follows:

```
adb —s <serial number> <command>
```

For example, to get the state of a specific device, type

```
adb -s emulator-5554 get-state
```

Instead of using the —s flag with a unique serial number, you can also use the —d flag to direct a command to the *only* device instance connected or the —e flag to direct a command to the *only* emulator instance, provided you have only one of each type connected.

For example, if we have only one Android phone connected, we can query its serial number as follows:

```
adb -d get-serialno
```

Starting and Stopping the ADB Server Process

Sometimes you might need to manually restart the ADB Server process. We have, for example, needed to do this when we've had an emulator instance running for a long time and have repeatedly connected and disconnected the debugger, eventually resulting in a loss of LogCat logging. In this case, you might want to kill and restart the ADB server (and perhaps Eclipse).

Stopping the ADB Server Process

To terminate the ADB server process, use the kill-server command. For example, to kill the server for a specific emulator instance, type

```
adb -s emulator-5554 kill-server
```

Starting and Checking the ADB Server Process

You can start the ADB server using the start-server command.

```
adb -s emulator-5554 start-server
```

You can also use the start-server command to check whether the server is running.

Copying Files to and from Android Applications Using ADB

You can use the ADB command line to copy files to and from your hard drive to an Android device. You need to know the full path information to the file you want to copy. File operations are subject to your user permissions (locally and remotely).

Sending Files to a Device

You can copy files to the device using the `push` command, as follows:

```
adb push <local file path> <remote file path on device>
```

For example, to copy the file `Pic.jpg` from the local hard drive to T-Mobile G1's SD Card download directory, use the following command:

```
adb -s HT841LC1977 push c:\Pic.jpg /sdcard/download/Pic.jpg
```

Retrieving Files from a Device

You can copy files from the device using the `pull` command, as follows:

```
adb pull <remote file path on device> <local file path>
```

For example, to copy the file `Lion.jpg` to the local hard drive from T-Mobile G1's SD Card download directory, use the following command:

```
adb -s HT841LC1977 pull /sdcard/download/Lion.jpg C:\Lion.jpg
```

> **Tip**
>
> If you put picture files onto your SD Card—virtual or otherwise—using this method, you need to force the Android operating system to refresh using the Media Scanner (available in the Dev Tools application on the Emulator). If you use an older version of the Android SDK or use a device, such as the T-Mobile G1, which does not have this feature, you might need to restart the phone or eject the SD Card and reinsert it to get the files to refresh within the Picture application. For a programmatic method, try sending the `MEDIA_MOUNT-ED` broadcast `Intent`.

Installing and Uninstalling Android Applications Using ADB

You can use ADB to install and uninstall packages on a given Android device or emulator. Although the ADT does this for developers automatically, this functionality is useful for developers not using the Eclipse development environment and for those developers and testers who want to create automated build procedures and testing environments.

Applications are installed as packages created with the Android Asset Packaging Tool (aapt).

Installing Applications Using ADB

To install applications, first create an Android package (.apk) file, and then use the install command:

```
adb install <apk file path>
```

For example, to install the sample application `Snake` on the emulator, you could use the following command:

```
adb -e install C:\android-sdk\samples\Snake\bin\Snake.apk
198 KB/s (17512 bytes in 0.086s)
        pkg: /data/local/tmp/Snake.apk
Success
```

Reinstalling Applications Using ADB

You can use the −r to reinstall the application package without overwriting its data. For example, you can now reinstall the `Snake` application without losing your data by using the following command:

```
adb -e install -r C:\Snake.apk
```

Uninstalling Applications Using ADB

To uninstall an Android application, you need to know the name of its package—

```
adb uninstall <package>
```

For example, to uninstall the `Franglais` application from the emulator, you can use the following command:

```
adb -e uninstall com.androidbook.franglais
```

> **Tip**
>
> You might use this command often if you switch between computers and, thus, switch signatures frequently. You can read more about signing applications in Chapter 20, "Selling Your Android Application."

Working with `LogCat` **Logging**

Android logging information is accessible through the `LogCat` utility. This utility is integrated into DDMS and ADT, but you can also access it directly through ADB using the following command:

```
adb logcat <option> <filter>
```

Displaying All Log Information

To display all `LogCat` logging information from the emulator instance, type

```
adb -e logcat
```

By default, the logging mode is set to `brief`. For example, the following is an Informational (`I`) log message (`brief` mode) from the tag *AppLog* from process ID 20054:

```
I/AppLog(20054): An Informational Log message.
```

Changing Logging Modes to Include the Date and Time

Another useful mode is the `time` mode, which includes the date and time the log message was invoked. To change the logging mode, use the –v flag and specify the format. For example, to change to `time` mode, use the following command:

```
logcat -v time
```

The resulting log messages are formatted with the date and time, followed by the event severity, tag, process ID, and log message:

```
01-05 21:52:22.465 I/AppLog(20054): Another Log Message.
```

Filtering Log Information

All the log information available through the `LogCat` tool can be overwhelmingly verbose. Most of the time a filter or two is required to sift out only the messages you want to view.

Filters are formatted tags and event priority pairs. The format for each filter is

```
<Tag Name>:<Lowest Event Priority to Print>
```

For example, a filter to display Informational log messages (and higher priority messages including Warnings, Errors and Fatal messages) from log messages tagged with the string `AppLog` would look like this:

```
AppLog:I
```

You can also use the asterisk (*), which means "all." So if you use an asterisk on the Tag side of the filter, it means "All tags." If you put it on the Event Priority side, it's much like using the V priority—the lowest priority, so all messages display.

Filtering by Event Severity

You can create filters to display only log events of a certain severity. The severity types (from lowest priority or most verbose to highest priority or least verbose) follow:

- Verbose (V)
- Debug (D)
- Info (I)
- Warning (W)
- Error (E)
- Fatal (F)
- Silent (S)

For example, the following command displays all Errors and Fatal errors but suppresses warnings, informational messages, debug messages, and verbose messages:

```
logcat *:E
```

Filtering by Tag

You can use multiple filters, ending with a catch-all. Perhaps you want to see all messages from a specific application (a specific tag) and no others. In this case, you want to create a filter to show all messages for a given tag and another filter to suppress all other tags. We also change into time mode, so we get the date and time of the logged events messages.

The following command displays all **AppLog**-tagged logging information and suppresses all other tags:

```
logcat -v time AppLog:V *:S
```

This filter is roughly equivalent to this other command line:

```
logcat -v time AppLog:* *:S
```

The resulting log messages would be formatted with the date and time, followed by the event severity, tag, process ID, and message:

```
01-05 21:52:22.465 I/AppLog(20054): Another Log Message.
```

Clearing the Log

You can clear the log using the -c flag:

```
adb -e logcat -c
```

Redirecting Log Output to a File

You can redirect log output to a file on the device using the −f flag. For example, to direct all informational logging messages (and those of higher priority) from the emulator to the file `mylog.txt` in the `sdcard` directory, you can use the following command:

```
logcat -f /sdcard/mylog.txt *:I
```

Accessing the Secondary Logs

Android has several different logs. By default, you look at the main log. However, an events log and a radio log also exist. You can connect to the other log buffers using the −b flag. For example, to connect to the event log to review events, type:

```
logcat -b events
```

The radio log is similarly accessed as follows:

```
logcat −b radio
```

Generating Bug Reports

You can create a rather verbose bug report to attach to application defects using the `bugreport` command. For example, to print the debug information for the sole emulator instance running on your development machine, use

```
adb -e bugreport
```

To print the debug information for the sole phone connected via USB, you would issue this command instead:

```
adb −d bugreport
```

Issuing Shell Commands

ADB includes a shell interface (ash) where you can interact directly with the device and issue commands and run binaries. You can use the shell interface to run built-in command-line programs such as `sqlite3` (to examine SQLite application databases) and `monkey` (a stress testing application). You can also install custom binaries on the emulator or device.

The ash shell has your typical file access commands like `pwd` and `ls`. For more information on the ash shell, check out the Linux Blog Man page for ash: http://www.thelinuxblog.com/linux-man-pages/1/ash.

Issuing a Single Shell Command

You can issue a single shell command without starting a shell session using the following command:

```
adb shell <command>
```

For example, to list all the files in the /sdcard/download directory on the emulator, type

```
adb -e shell ls /sdcard/download
```

Starting and Using a Shell Session

Often you might want to issue more than one command. In this case, you might want to start a shell session. To do so, simply type

```
adb shell
```

For example, to connect to a specific device instance by serial number and start a shell session, type

```
adb -s emulator-5554 shell
# <type commands here>
# exit
```

You can then issue commands. Ending your session is as easy as typing exit.

Using the ADB Shell to Start and Stop the Emulator

Stopping the emulator makes it stop responding, although it still displays on your development machine. To stop the emulator, you can issue the stop command within the ADB shell.

```
adb -s emulator-5554 shell stop
```

You can then restart the emulator using the start command:

```
adb -s emulator-5554 shell start
```

You could also perform these commands from within a shell session, like this:

```
adb -s emulator-5554 shell
# stop
# start
```

Using the ADB Shell to Inspect SQLite Databases

You can use the standard sqlite3 database tool from within the ADB shell. This tool allows you to inspect and interact directly with a SQLite database. For a thorough explanation of the sqlite3 tool, see Appendix D, "The SQLite Quick-Start Guide."

Using the ADB Shell to Stress Test Applications Using Monkey

You can use the Exerciser/Monkey tool from within the ADB shell to send random user events to a specific application. Think of it as handing your phone (or emulator) to a monkey (or a baby, or a baby monkey) and letting them push random keys, causing random events on the phone—events that can crash your application if it doesn't handle them correctly. If your application crashes, the `Monkey` application stops and reports the error, making this a useful tool for quality assurance.

Letting the Monkey Loose on Your Application

To launch the `Monkey` tool, use the following command line:

```
adb shell monkey -p <package> <options> <event count>
```

For example, to have the monkey generate five random events within the `GroceryList` application within the emulator, you would do the following:

```
adb -s emulator-5554 shell
# monkey -p com.androidbook.grocerylist 5
```

Listening to Your Monkey

You can watch each event generated by using the verbose flag –v. For example, to see which events you send to the preceding `GroceryList` application, you would use this command:

```
adb -s emulator-5554 shell
# monkey -p com.androidbook.grocerylist -v 5
```

Here is the important output from this command:

```
:SendKey: 21     // KEYCODE_DPAD_LEFT
:Sending Trackball ACTION_MOVE x=-4.0 y=2.0
:Sending Trackball ACTION_UP x=0.0 y=0.0
:SendKey: 82     // KEYCODE_MENU
:SendKey: 22     // KEYCODE_DPAD_RIGHT
:SendKey: 23     // KEYCODE_DPAD_CENTER
:Dropped: keys=0 pointers=0 trackballs=0
// Monkey finished
```

You can tell from the verbose logging that the `Monkey` application sent five events to the `GroceryList` application: a navigation event (left), two trackball events, the Menu button, and then two more navigation events (right, center).

Direct your Monkey's Actions

You can specify the types of events generated by the `Monkey` application. You basically give weights (percentages) to the different types of events. The event types available are shown in Table C.1.

Table C.1 **Monkey Event Types**

Event Type	Description	Default Percentage	Command Line Flag	Event ID as Shown in Verbose Mode
Touch	Down/up event on a single screen location	15%	`--pct-touch`	0
Motion	Down event on a single location, followed by some movement; then an Up event in a different screen location	10%	`--pct-motion`	1
Trackball	Trackball Events, sometimes followed by a Click	15%	`--pct-trackball`	2
Basic Navigation	Up, Down, Left, Right	25%	`--pct-nav`	3
Major Navigation	Menu, Back, Center of DPAD, and such	15%	`--pct-majornav`	4
System Key	Home, Volume, Send, End, and such	2%	`--pct-syskeys`	5
Activity Switch	Randomly switch to other activities within the packages	2%	`--pct-appswitch`	6
Other Events	Key presses; other buttons	16%	`--pct-anyevent`	7

To use a different mix of events, you need to include the event type's command line flag as listed in Table C.1, followed by the desired percentage.

```
monkey [<command line flag> <percentage>…] <event count>
```

For example, to tell the Monkey to use only touch events, use the following command:

```
monkey -p com.androidbook.grocerylist --pct-touch 100 -v 5
```

Or let's say you want just Basic and Major navigation events (50%/50%):

```
monkey -p com.androidbook.grocerylist --pct-nav 50 --pct-majornav 50 -v 5
```

You get the picture.

Training Your Monkey to Repeat His Tricks

For random yet reproducible results, you can use the seed option. The seed feature allows you to modify the events that are produced as part of the event sequence, yet you can rerun sequence in the future (and verify bug fixes, for example).

To set a seed, use the —s flag.

```
monkey –p <package> -s <seed> –v <event count>
```

For example in our command we used previously, we can change the five events by setting a different starting seed. In this case, we set a seed of 555:

```
monkey -p com.androidbook.grocerylist -s 555 -v 5
```

Changing the seed changes the event sequence sent by the `Monkey`, so as part of a stress test, you might want to consider generating random seeds and sending them to the `Monkey` and logging the results. When the application fails on a given seed, keep that seed (and any other command line options like event type percentages) when you log the bug and rerun the test later to verify the bug fix.

Keeping the Monkey on a Leash

By default, the `Monkey` generates events as rapidly as possible. However, you can slow this behavior down using the throttle option as follows:

```
monkey --throttle <milliseconds> <event count>
```

For example, to pause for 1 second (1000 milliseconds) between each of the five events issued to the `GroceryList` application, use the following command:

```
monkey -p com.androidbook.grocerylist -v --throttle 1000 5
```

Learning More About Your Monkey

For more information about the `Monkey` application and other `Monkey` commands, see the Android SDK Reference Web site: http://developer.android.com/guide/developing/tools/monkey.html. You can also get a list of commands by typing monkey without any command options, like this:

```
adb -e shell monkey
```

Installing and Using Custom Binaries via the Shell

You can also install custom binaries on the emulator or device. For example, if you spend a lot of time working in the shell, you might want to install `BusyBox`, which is a free and useful set of command-line tools available under the GNU General Public License and has been called "The Swiss Army Knife of Embedded Linux" (thanks, Wikipedia for that little fact). `BusyBox` provides a number of helpful and familiar UNIX utilities, all packaged in a single binary. Utilities like find and more. BusyBox provides many useful functions (although some of which might not apply or be permissible) on Android, such as the following:

```
[, [[, addgroup, adduser, adjtimex, ar, arp, arping, ash,
awk, basename, bunzip2, bzcat, bzip2, cal, cat, catv,
chattr, chgrp, chmod, chown, chpasswd, chpst, chroot,
chrt, chvt, cksum, clear, cmp, comm, cp, cpio, crond,
crontab, cryptpw, cut, date, dc, dd, deallocvt, delgroup,
deluser, df, dhcprelay, diff, dirname, dmesg, dnsd, dos2unix, du, dumpkmap,
dumpleases, echo, ed, egrep, eject, env, envdir, envuidgid, ether-wake, expand,
expr, fakeidentd, false, fbset, fdflush, fdformat, fdisk, fgrep, find, fold,
free, freeramdisk, fsck, fsck.minix, ftpget, ftpput, fuser, getopt, getty, grep,
gunzip, gzip, halt, hdparm, head, hexdump, hostid, hostname, httpd, hwclock, id,
ifconfig, ifdown, ifup, inetd, init, insmod, install, ip, ipaddr, ipcalc, ipcrm,
ipcs, iplink, iproute, iprule, iptunnel, kbd_mode, kill, killall, killall5,
klogd, last, length, less, linux32, linux64, linuxrc, ln, loadfont, loadkmap,
logger, login, logname, logread, losetup, ls, lsattr, lsmod, lzmacat, makedevs,
md5sum, mdev, mesg, microcom, mkdir, mkfifo, mkfs.minix, mknod, mkswap, mktemp,
modprobe, more, mount, mountpoint, mt, mv, nameif, nc, netstat, nice, nmeter,
nohup, nslookup, od, openvt, passwd, patch, pgrep, pidof, ping, ping6,
pipe_progress, pivot_root, pkill, poweroff, printenv, printf, ps, pscan, pwd,
raidautorun, rdate, readlink, readprofile, realpath, reboot, renice, reset,
resize, rm, rmdir, rmmod, route, rpm, rpm2cpio, run-parts, runlevel, runsv,
runsvdir, rx, sed, seq, setarch, setconsole, setkeycodes, setlogcons, setsid,
setuidgid, sh, sha1sum, slattach, sleep, softlimit, sort, split,
start-stop-daemon, stat, strings, stty, su, sulogin, sum, sv, svlogd, swapoff,
swapon, switch_root, sync, sysctl, syslogd, tail, tar, taskset, tcpsvd, tee,
telnet, telnetd, test, tftp, time, top, touch, tr, traceroute, true, tty,
ttysize, udhcpc, udhcpd, udpsvd, umount, uname, uncompress, unexpand, uniq,
unix2dos, unlzma, unzip, uptime, usleep, uudecode, uuencode, vconfig, vi, vlock,
watch, watchdog, wc, wget, which, who, whoami, xargs, yes, zcat, zcip
```

All you need to do is install the binary (which is available online) using the following steps:

1. Download the BusyBox binary (at your own risk, or compile it for yourself). You can find the binary online at http://benno.id.au/blog/2007/11/14/android-busy-box, where Benno has kindly hosted it for you. (Thanks, Benno!)

2. Make a directory called /data/local/busybox/ on your emulator using the ADB shell, for example, adb —e shell mkdir /data/local/busybox/.

3. Copy the BusyBox binary to the directory you created, for example, adb —e push C:\busybox /data/local/busybox/busybox.

4. Launch the adb shell, for example, adb —e shell.

5. Navigate to the BusyBox directory, for example, #cd /data/local/busybox.

6. Change the permissions on the `BusyBox` file, for example, `#chmod 777 busy-box.`

7. Install `BusyBox`, for example, `# ./busybox —install.`

8. Export the path for ease of use. Note: You need to reset the PATH for each session, for example, `# export PATH=/data/busybox:$PATH.`

You can find out more about `BusyBox` at http://www.busybox.net.

Exploring Other ADB Commands

There are also handy ADB networking commands for configuring port forwarding and running PPP over USB, among other things. You can use port forwarding to connect the Java debugger to a specific JDWP process by ID. To get a list of all ADB commands, type

`adb help`

D

The SQLite
Quick-Start Guide

The Android System allows individual applications to have private SQLite databases in which to store their application data. This Quick-Start Guide is not a complete documentation of the SQLite commands. Instead, it is designed to get you up and running with common tasks. The first part of this appendix introduces the features of the `sqlite3` command-line tool. We then provide an in-depth database example using many common SQLite commands. See the online SQLite documentation (www.sqlite.org) for a complete list of features, functionality, and limitations of SQLite.

Exploring Common Tasks with SQLite

SQLite is a lightweight and compact, yet powerful, embedded relational database engine available as public domain. It is fast and has a small footprint, making it perfect for phone system use. Instead of the heavyweight server-based databases such as Oracle and Microsoft SQL Server, each SQLite database is contained within a self-contained single file on disk.

Android applications store their private databases (SQLite or otherwise) under a special application directory:

```
/data/data/<application package name>/databases/<databasename>
```

For example, the database for the `PetTracker` application provided in this book is found at

```
/data/data/com.androidbook.PetTracker/databases/pet_tracker.db
```

The database file format is standard and can be moved across platforms. You can use the Dalvik Debug Monitor Service (DDMS) File Explorer to pull the database file and inspect it with third-party tools, if you like.

Application-specific SQLite databases are private and accessible only from within that application. To expose application data to other applications, the application must become a content provider. Content providers are covered in Chapter 9, "Using Android Data and Storage APIs."

Using the `sqlite3` Command-Line Interface

In addition to programmatic access to create and use SQLite databases from within your applications, which we discuss in Chapter 9, you can also interact with the database using the familiar command-line `sqlite3` tool, which is accessible via the Android Debug Bridge (ADB) remote shell.

The command-line interface for SQLite, called `sqlite3`, is exposed using the ADB tool, which we covered in Appendix C, "The Android Debug Bridge Quick-Start Guide."

Launching the `sqlite3` Command-Line Interface and Connecting to a Database

You must launch ADB shell interface on the specific emulator or device to use the `sqlite3` commands.

Launching the ADB Shell

If only one Android device (or emulator) is running, you can connect by simply typing

```
c:\>adb shell
```

If you want to connect to a specific instance of the emulator, you can connect by typing

```
adb —s <serialNumber> shell
```

For example, to connect to the emulator at port 5554, you would use the following command:

```
adb —s emulator-5554 shell
```

For more information on how to determine the serial number of an emulator or device instance, please see Appendix C.

Connecting to the Database

Now you can connect to the Android application database of your choice by name. For example, to connect to the database we created with the Pet Tracker application, we would connect like this:

```
c:\>adb shell
# sqlite3 /data/data/com.androidbook.PetTracker/databases/pet_tracker.db
SQLite version 3.5.9
Enter ".help" for instructions
sqlite>
```

Now we have the `sqlite3` command prompt, where we can issue commands. You can exit the interface at any time by typing

```
sqlite>.quit
```

or

```
sqlite>.exit
```

Exploring Your Database

You can use the `sqlite3` commands to explore what your database looks like and inter-act with it. You can

- List available databases
- List available tables
- View all the indices on a given table
- Show the database schema

Listing Available Databases

You can list the names and file locations attached to this database instance. Generally, you have your main database and a temp database, which contains temp tables. You can list this information by typing

```
sqlite> .databases
seq  name file
---  ---- -------------------------------------------------
0    main /data/data/com.androidbook.PetTracker/databases/…
1    temp
sqlite>
```

Listing Available Tables

You can list the tables in the database you connect to by typing

```
sqlite> .tables
android_metadata  table_pets          table_pettypes
sqlite>
```

Listing Indices of a Table

You can list the indices of a given table by typing

```
sqlite>.indices table_pets
```

Listing the Database Schema of a Table

You can list the schema of a given table by typing

```
sqlite>.schema table_pets
CREATE TABLE table_pets (_id INTEGER PRIMARY KEY
AUTOINCREMENT,pet_name TEXT,pet_type_id INTEGER);
sqlite>
```

Listing the Database Schema of a Database

You can list the schemas for the entire database by typing

```
sqlite>.schema
CREATE TABLE android_metadata (locale TEXT);
CREATE TABLE table_pets (_id INTEGER PRIMARY KEY
AUTOINCREMENT,pet_name TEXT,pet_type_id INTEGER);
CREATE TABLE table_pettypes (_id INTEGER PRIMARY KEY
AUTOINCREMENT,pet_type TEXT);
sqlite>
```

Importing and Exporting the Database and Its Data

You can use the `sqlite3` commands to import and export database data and the schema and interact with it. You can

- Send command output to a file instead of to STDOUT (the screen).
- Dump the database contents as a SQL script (so you can re-create it later).
- Execute SQL scripts from files.
- Import data into the database from a file.

> **Note**
>
> The file paths are on the Android device, not your computer. You need to find a directory on the Android device in which you have permission to read-and-write files. For example, `/data/local/tmp/` is a shared directory.

Sending Output to a File

Often, you want the `sqlite3` command results to pipe to a file instead of to the screen. To do this, you can just type the `output` command followed by the file path to write to on the Android system. For example:

```
sqlite>.output /data/local/tmp/dump.sql
```

Dumping Database Contents

You can create a SQL script to create tables and their values by using the `dump` command. The `dump` command creates a transaction, which includes calls to CREATE TABLE and INSERT to populate the database with data. This command can take an optional table name or dump the whole database.

> **Tip**
>
> The `dump` command is a great way to do a full archival backup of your database.

For example, the following commands pipe the dump output for the `table_pets` table to a file and then sets the output mode back to the console.

```
sqlite>.output /data/local/tmp/dump.sql
sqlite>.dump table_pets
sqlite>.output stdout
```

You can then use DDMS and the File Explorer to pull the SQL file off the Android file system. The resulting `dump.sql` file looks like this:

```
BEGIN TRANSACTION;
CREATE TABLE table_pets (
_id INTEGER PRIMARY KEY AUTOINCREMENT,
pet_name TEXT,
pet_type_id INTEGER);

INSERT INTO "table_pets" VALUES(1,'Rover',9);
INSERT INTO "table_pets" VALUES(2,'Garfield',8);
COMMIT;
```

Executing SQL Scripts From Files

You can create SQL script files and run them through the console. These scripts must be on the Android file system. For example, let's put a SQL script called `myselect.sql` in the `/data/local/tmp/` directory of the Android file system.

The file has two lines

```
SELECT * FROM table_pettypes;
SELECT * FROM table_pets;
```

We can then run this SQL script by typing

```
sqlite>.read /data/local/tmp/myselect.sql
```

You see the query results on the command line.

Importing Data

You can import formatted data using the import and separator commands. Files like CSV use commas for delimiters, but other data formats might be spaces or tabs. You specify the delimiter using the separator command. You specify the file to import using the import command.

For example, put a CSV script called **some_data.csv** in the **/data/local/tmp/** directory of the Android file system.

The file has four lines. It is a comma-delimited file of pet type ids and pet type names:

```
18,frog
19,turkey
20,piglet
```

```
21,great white shark
```

You can then import this data into the `table_pettypes` table, which has two columns:
an `_id` column and a pet type name. To import this data, type the following command:

```
sqlite>.separator ,
sqlite>.import /data/local/tmp/some_data.csv table_pettypes
```

Now, if you query the table, you see it has four new rows.

Executing SQL Commands on the Command Line

You can also execute raw SQL commands on the command line. Simply type the SQL
command, making sure it ends with a semicolon (;).

If you use queries, you might want to change the output mode to column so that
query results are easier to read (in columns) and the headers (column names) are printed.

For example:

```
sqlite> .mode column
sqlite> .header on
sqlite> select * from table_pettypes WHERE _id < 11;
_id         pet_type
----------  ----------
8           bunny
9           fish
10          dog
sqlite>
```

You're not limited to queries, either. You can execute any SQL command you see in a
SQL script on the command line if you like.

> **Tip**
>
> We've found it helpful to use the `sqlite3` command line to test SQL queries if our
> Android SQL queries with `QueryBuilder` are not behaving. This is especially true of more
> complicated queries.

You can also control the width of each column (so text fields don't truncate) using the
`width` command. For example, the following command prints query results with the
first column 5 characters wide (often an ID column), followed by a second column 50
characters wide (text column).

```
sqlite> .width 5 50
```

Poking Around Within SQLite Internals

SQLite keeps the database schema in a special table called `sqlite_master`. You should
consider this table read-only. SQLite stores temporary tables in a special table called
`sqlite_temp_master`, which is also a temporary table.

Using Other `sqlite3` Commands

A complete list of `sqlite3` commands is available by typing

```
sqlite> .help
```

Understanding SQLite Limitations

SQLite is powerful, but it has several important limitations compared to traditional SQL Server implementations, such as the following:

- SQLite is not a substitute for a high-powered, server-driven database.
- Being file-based, the database is meant to be accessed in a serial, not a concurrent manner. Think "single user"—the Android application. It has some concurrency features, but they are limited.
- Access control is maintained by file permissions, not database user permissions.
- Referential integrity is not maintained. For example, FOREIGN KEY constraints are parsed (for example, in CREATE TABLE) but not enforced automatically. However, using TRIGGER functions can enforce them.
- ALTER TABLE support is limited. You can use only RENAME TABLE and ADD COLUMN. You may not drop or alter columns or perform any other such operations. This can make database upgrades a bit tricky.
- TRIGGER support is limited. You cannot use: `FOR EACH STATEMENT` or `INSTEAD OF`. You cannot create recursive triggers.
- You cannot nest TRANSACTION operations.
- VIEWs are read-only.
- No RIGHT OUTER JOINs or FULL OUTER JOINs.
- SQLite does not support STORED PROCEDUREs or auditing.
- The built-in FUNCTIONs of the SQL language are limited.
- For limitations on the maximum database size, table size, and row size, see the SQLite documentation, including the helpful Omitted SQL page www.sqlite.org/omitted.html and the Unsupported SQL Wiki page www.sqlite.org/cvstrac/wiki?p=UnsupportedSql.

Understanding SQLite By Example: Student Grade Database

Let's work through a Teacher "Grades" example database to show standard SQL commands to create and work with a database. Although you can create this database using the `sqlite3` command line, we suggest using the Android application to create the empty Grades database, so that it is created in a standard "Android" way.

The setup: The purpose of the Student grade database is to keep track of each student's test results for the class. Each student's grade is calculated from the performance on four quizzes, one Midterm and one Final. All tests are graded on a scale of 0–100.

Designing the Student Grade Database Schema

The Teacher "Grades" database has three tables: Students, Tests, and TestResults.

The Student table contains student information. The Tests table contains information about each test and how much it counts toward the student's overall grade. Finally, all students' test results are stored in the TestResults table.

Setting Column Datatypes

SQLite3 has support for the following common datatypes for columns:

- INTEGER (signed integers)
- REAL (floating point values)
- TEXT (UTF-8 or UTF-16 string; encoded using database encoding)
- BLOB (data chunk)

> **Tip**
>
> Do not store files like images in the database. Instead, store them as files in the application file directory and store the filename or URI path in the database.

Creating Simple Tables with AUTOINCREMENT

First, let's create the Students table. We want a student id to reference each student. We can make this the primary key and have it autoincrement. We also want the first and last name of each student, and we require these fields (no nulls). Here's our SQL statement:

```
CREATE TABLE Students (
id INTEGER PRIMARY KEY AUTOINCREMENT,
fname TEXT NOT NULL,
lname TEXT NOT NULL );
```

For the Tests table, we want a test id to reference each test or quiz, much like the Students table. We also want a friendly name for each test and a weight value for how much each test counts for the student's final grade (as a percentage). Here's our SQL statement:

```
CREATE TABLE Tests (
id INTEGER PRIMARY KEY AUTOINCREMENT,
testname TEXT,
weight REAL DEFAULT .10 CHECK (weight<=1));
```

Inserting Data into Tables

Before we move on, let's add some data to these tables. To add a record to the Students table, you need to specify the column names and the values in order. For example:

```
INSERT into Students
(fname, lname)
VALUES
('Harry', 'Potter');
```

Now, we're going to add a few more records to this table for Ron and Hermione. At the same time, we need to add a bunch of records to the Tests table. First we add the Midterm, which counts for 25 percent of the grade (and also a Final for 35 percent):

```
INSERT into Tests
(testname, weight)
VALUES
('Midterm', .25);
```

Then we add a couple quizzes, which use the default weight of 10 percent:

```
INSERT into Tests (testname) VALUES ('Quiz 1');
```

Finally, we add a final worth 35 percent of the total grade.

Querying Tables for Results with SELECT

How do we know the data we've added is in the table? Well, that's easy. We simply query for all rows in a table using a SELECT:

```
SELECT * FROM Tests;
```

This returns all records in the Tests table:

id	testname	weight
1	Midterm	0.25
2	Quiz 1	0.1
3	Quiz 2	0.1
4	Quiz 3	0.1
5	Quiz 4	0.1
6	Final	0.35

Now, ideally, we want the weights to add up to 1.0. Let's check using the SUM aggregate function to sum all the weight values in the table:

```
SELECT SUM(weight) FROM Tests;
```

This returns the sum of all weight values in the Tests table:

```
SUM(weight)
-----------
1.0
```

We can also create our own columns and alias them. For example, we can create a column alias called `fullname` that is a calculated column: It's the student's first and last names concatenated using the || concatenation.

```
SELECT fname||' '|| lname AS fullname, id FROM Students;
```

This gives us the following results:

```
fullname          id
-----------       --
Harry Potter      1
Ron Weasley       2
Hermione Granger  3
```

Creating Tables with Foreign Keys and Composite Primary Keys

Now that we have our students and tests all set up, let's create the TestResults table. This is a more complicated table. It's a list of student-test pairings, along with the score.

The TestResults table pairs up Student ids from the Student table with Test ids from the Tests table. Columns, which link to other tables in this way, are often called foreign keys. We want unique student-test pairings, so then we create a composite primary key from the student and test foreign keys. Lastly, we enforce that the scores are whole numbers between 0 and 100. No extra credit or retaking tests in this class!

```
CREATE TABLE TestResults (
studentid INTEGER REFERENCES Students(id),
testid INTEGER REFERENCES Tests(id),
score INTEGER CHECK (score<=100 AND score>=0),
PRIMARY KEY (studentid, testid));
```

> **Tip**
>
> SQLite does not enforce foreign key constraints, but you can set them up anyway and enforce the constraints by creating triggers. For an example of using triggers to enforce foreign key constraints in SQL, check out the FullDatabase project provided on the CD for Chapter 9.

Now it's time to insert some data into this table. Let's say Harry Potter received an 82 percent on the Midterm:

```
INSERT into TestResults
(studentid, testid, score)
VALUES
(1,1,82);
```

Now let's input the rest of the student's scores. Harry is a good student. Ron is not a good student, and Hermione aces every test (of course). When they're all added, we can list them. We can do a SELECT ★ to get all columns, or we can specify the columns we want explicitly like this:

```
SELECT studentid, testid, score FROM TestResults;
```

Here are the results from this query:

studentid	testid	score
1	1	82
1	2	88
1	3	78
1	4	90
1	5	85
1	6	94
2	1	10
2	2	90
2	3	50
2	4	55
2	5	45
2	6	65
3	6	100
3	5	100
3	4	100
3	3	100
3	2	100
3	1	100

Altering and Updating Data in Tables

Ron's not a good student, and yet he received a 90 percent on Quiz #1. This is suspicious, so as the teacher, we check the actual paper test to see if we made a recording mistake. He actually earned 60 percent. Now we need to update the table to reflect the correct score:

```
UPDATE TestResults
SET score=60
WHERE studentid=2 AND testid=2;
```

You can delete rows from a table using the DELETE function. For example, to delete the record we just updated:

```
DELETE FROM TestResults WHERE studentid=2 AND testid=2;
```

You can delete all rows in a table by not specifying the WHERE clause:

```
DELETE FROM TestResults;
```

Querying for Information Stored in Multiple Tables Using JOIN

Now that we have all our data in our database, it is time to use it. The preceding listing was not easy for a human to read. It would be much nicer to see a listing with the names of the Students and Names of the tests instead of their ids.

Combining data is often handled by performing a JOIN with multiple table sources; there are different kinds of JOINS. When you work with multiple tables, you need to specify which table a column belongs to (especially with all these different id columns). You can refer to columns by their column name or by their table name, then a dot (.), and then the column name.

Let's relist the grades again, only this time, include the name of the test and the name of the student. Also, we limit our results only to the score for the Final (`test id 6`):

```
SELECT
Students.fname||' '|| Students.lname AS StudentName,
Tests.testname,
TestResults.score
FROM TestResults
JOIN Students
        ON (TestResults.studentid=Students.id)
JOIN Tests
        ON (TestResults.testid=Tests.id)
WHERE testid=6;
```

which gives us the following results (you could leave off the WHERE to get all tests):

```
StudentName          testname          score
------------------   --------------    -----
Harry Potter         Final             94
Ron Weasley          Final             65
Hermione Granger     Final             100
```

Using Calculated Columns

Hermoine always likes to know where she stands. When she comes to ask what her final grade is likely to be, we can perform a single query to show all her results and calculate the weighted scores of all her results:

```
SELECT
Students.fname||' '|| Students.lname AS StudentName,
Tests.testname,
Tests.weight,
TestResults.score,
(Tests.weight*TestResults.score) AS WeightedScore
FROM TestResults
JOIN Students
        ON (TestResults.studentid=Students.id)
```

```
JOIN Tests
        ON (TestResults.testid=Tests.id)
WHERE studentid=3;
```

This gives us predictable results:

```
StudentName        testname   weight   score   WeightedScore
----------------   --------   ------   -----   -------------
Hermione Granger   Midterm    0.25     100        25.0
Hermione Granger   Quiz 1     0.1      100        10.0
Hermione Granger   Quiz 2     0.1      100        10.0
Hermione Granger   Quiz 3     0.1      100        10.0
Hermione Granger   Quiz 4     0.1      100        10.0
Hermione Granger   Final      0.35     100        35.0
```

We can just add up the Weighed Scores and be done, but we can also do it via the query:

```
SELECT
Students.fname||' '|| Students.lname AS StudentName,
SUM((Tests.weight*TestResults.score)) AS TotalWeightedScore
FROM TestResults
JOIN Students
        ON (TestResults.studentid=Students.id)
JOIN Tests
        ON (TestResults.testid=Tests.id)
WHERE studentid=3;
```

Here we get a nice consolidated listing:

```
StudentName        TotalWeightedScore
----------------   ------------------
Hermione Granger   100.0
```

If we wanted to get all our students' grades, we need to use the GROUP BY clause. Also, let's order them so the best students are at the top of the list:

```
SELECT
Students.fname||' '|| Students.lname AS StudentName,
SUM((Tests.weight*TestResults.score)) AS TotalWeightedScore
FROM TestResults
JOIN Students
        ON (TestResults.studentid=Students.id)
JOIN Tests
        ON (TestResults.testid=Tests.id)
GROUP BY TestResults.studentid
ORDER BY TotalWeightedScore DESC;
```

This makes our job as teacher almost too easy, but at least we're saving trees by using a digital grade book.

```
StudentName                   TotalWeightedScore
------------------------      -----------------
Hermione Granger              100.0
Harry Potter                  87.5
Ron Weasley                   46.25
```

Using Subqueries for Calculated Columns

You can also include queries within other queries. For example, you can list each Student and a count of how many tests they "passed," in which passing is getting a score higher than 60, as in the following:

```
SELECT
Students.fname||' '|| Students.lname AS StudentName,
Students.id AS StudentID,
(SELECT COUNT(*)
FROM TestResults
WHERE TestResults.studentid=Students.id
AND TestResults.score>60)
AS TestsPassed
FROM Students;
```

Again, we see that Ron needs a tutor:

```
StudentName       StudentID  TestsPassed
-----------       ---------  -----------
Harry Potter      1          6
Ron Weasley       2          1
Hermione Granger  3          6
```

Deleting Tables

You can always delete tables using the DROP TABLE command. For example, to delete the TestResults table, use the following SQL command:

```
DROP TABLE TestResults;
```

Index

B

D

E

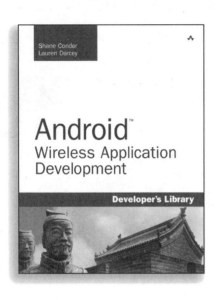

FREE Online Edition

Your purchase of **Android Wireless Application Development** includes access to a free online edition for 45 days through the Safari Books Online subscription service. Nearly every Addison-Wesley Professional book is available online through Safari Books Online, along with more than 5,000 other technical books and videos from publishers such as, Cisco Press, Exam Cram, IBM Press, O'Reilly, Prentice Hall, Que, and Sams.

SAFARI BOOKS ONLINE allows you to search for a specific answer, cut and paste code, download chapters, and stay current with emerging technologies.

Activate your FREE Online Edition at
www.informit.com/safarifree

> **STEP 1:** Enter the coupon code: JTNNJFH.

> **STEP 2:** New Safari users, complete the brief registration form.
> Safari subscribers, just log in.

If you have difficulty registering on Safari or accessing the online edition, please e-mail customer-service@safaribooksonline.com